MATERIALS FOR ARCHITECTURAL DESIGN

MATERIALS FOR ARCHITECTURAL DESIGN 2

VICTORIA BALLARD BELL

AND

PATRICK RAND

Laurence King Publishing

PUBLISHED IN 2014 BY LAURENCE KING PUBLISHING LTD
361-373 City Road
London EC1V 1LR
United Kingdom
Tel: +44 20 7841 6900
Fax: +44 20 7841 6910
e-mail: enquiries@laurenceking.com
www.laurenceking.com

A catalogue record for this book is available from the British Library

ISBN: 978 1 78067 089 8

Every reasonable attempt has been made to identify owners of copyright. Errors or omissions will be corrected in subsequent editions.

EDITOR Dan Simon
PHOTO EDITOR Meredith Baber
CONCEPT Paul Wagner
DESIGN Benjamin English

Front and back cover photographs:
Andreas Lechtape, NBK Keramik GmbH

SPECIAL THANKS TO Sara Bader, Janet Behning, Nicola Bednarek Brower, Megan Carey, Carina Cha, Andrea Chlad, Barbara Darko, Russell Fernandez, Will Foster, Jan Haux, Diane Levinson, Jennifer Lippert, Katharine Myers, Lauren Palmer, Margaret Rogalski, Jay Sacher, Rob Schaeffer, Elana Schlenker, Sara Stemen, Andrew Stepanian, and Joseph Weston of Princeton Architectural Press
—Kevin C. Lippert, publisher

Printed in China

Acknowledgments

Materials for Architectural Design 2 exists because of the favorable assessments made by readers and reviewers of the first volume of this title. Our thanks go to those readers, with hopes that this volume will build upon that positive foundation.

I treasured this chance to again collaborate with Victoria Ballard Bell. Equally important was the collaboration with the fine editors, designers, and production experts at Princeton Architectural Press. In particular, we wish to thank editor Dan Simon, who guided this edition with abundant talent and resourcefulness. Many thanks also go to Benjamin English, designer of this volume, who deftly set forth text and image in exquisite sequence, hierarchy, and beauty, in keeping with Paul Wagner's award-winning original concept.

I also acknowledge the talented architecture students who, after the publication of the first volume, called upon me to offer a Materials for Design graduate seminar at North Carolina State University. The class forced me to make explicit the analytical method I used to write the project narratives for the books, which these talented students then employed to prepare their own case studies. Helping them discover what made an excellent building really work catalyzed my own eagerness to do this again. Special thanks go to Laura Reed, one of those seminar students who later helped us compile files of the hundreds of worldwide projects that were identified as candidates for the sixty projects in the second volume.

I also thank my wife Christine Nalepa, whose patience, tolerance, and endless support were essential for the making of this volume.

Patrick Rand

Materials for Architectural Design 2 has been such a gift to write and a joy to produce.

I want to thank my amazingly supportive, encouraging and loving husband, Bryan Bell. His own work and passion are undeniably inspiring yet he never wavers in enthusiasm for anything I do. I also want to thank my two beautiful children who bring me daily joy: Lily Sky for her relentless bliss and great artistic talent and Cole for his focused and passioned interests. For better or worse at this young age they both want to be architects.

Thank you also to my mother and father, Valerie and Richard, who gave me so very much and always support anything I do. This book is dedicated to my dad, who always encouraged me to do what I believed in and whose love I will always feel. I feel his pride in me always.

Thank you to Pat for being the best coauthor and partner one could hope for. His great knowledge and sensitivity is evident throughout this book. Thank you to Jennifer Lippert at Princeton Architectural Press for reaching out to us and supporting the sequel, and to editor Dan Simon for his incredible expertise and hand-holding along the way; Meredith Baber's extraordinary organization was utterly fundamental to the project as well. Thank you to all of the students and architects who have helped give ideas for this book and to those who actually use the books in their classes and studios—it is our primary goal, and why we write.

Thank you lastly, but not least, to my extraordinary friends who always inspire me and fill my life with happiness.

Victoria Ballard Bell

Contents

8 **Introduction**

11 Glass

16 **Basque Health Department Headquarters**
Bilbao, Spain
Coll-Barreu Arquitectos

20 **Glass Townhouses**
Venice, California, USA
Sander Architects

24 **Factory Extension**
Murcia, Spain
Clavel Arquitectos

26 **Diana Center at Barnard College**
New York, New York, USA
Weiss/Manfredi Architecture/Landscape/Urbanism

30 **Spiral Gallery**
Shanghai, China
Atelier Deshaus

34 **The Crystal (Nykredit Bank)**
Copenhagen, Denmark
Schmidt Hammer Lassen Architects

38 **Cité du Design**
Saint-Étienne, France
LIN Architects

42 **Ernst Koller Pavilion**
Basel, Switzerland
Berrel Berrel Kräutler Architekten

46 **Apple Flagship Store**
Shanghai, China
Bohlin Cywinski Jackson

49 Concrete

56 **Hämeenlinna Provincial Archive**
Hämeenlinna, Finland
Heikkinen-Komonen Architects

58 **Casa Pentimento**
Quito, Ecuador
Jose Maria Sáez + David Barragán

60 **Design Indaba 10×10 Housing Project**
Cape Town, South Africa
Design Space Africa Architects (formerly MMA Architects)

64 **Hanil Visitors Center and Guesthouse**
Chungbuk, Korea
BCHO Architects with CAST (Center for Architectural Structures and Technology)

68 **Harmonia 57**
São Paulo, Brazil
Triptyque

70 **Hiroshi Senju Museum**
Karuizawa, Nagano, Japan
Ryue Nishizawa

72 **Italian Pavilion at World Expo 2010**
Shanghai, China
Iodice Architetti

76 **Nk'Mip Desert Cultural Centre**
Osoyoos, British Columbia, Canada
DIALOG (formerly Hoston Bakker Boniface Haden)

80 **RATP Bus Center**
Paris, France
ECDM

85 Wood

94 **Stork Nest Farm**
Dvůr Semtín, Olbramovice, Czech Republic
SGL Projekt

96 **Private Residence in Riedikon**
Uster, Switzerland
Gramazio & Kohler

100 **Viikki Church**
Helsinki, Finland
JKMM Architects

104 **Soe Ker Tie House**
Noh Bo, Thailand
TYIN Tegnestue Architects

108 **Harry Parker Community Boathouse**
Boston, Massachusetts, USA
Anmahian Winton Architects

112 **EcoWoodBox Kindergarten**
Hanover, Germany
Despang Architekten

116 **Nature Boardwalk at Lincoln Park Zoo**
Chicago, Illinois, USA
Studio Gang Architects

118 **Dairy House Annex**
Hadspen Estate, Somerset, England, UK
Skene Catling de la Peña

122 **Metropol Parasol**
Seville, Spain
J. Mayer H. Architects

126 **Skating Shelters**
Winnipeg, Manitoba, Canada
Patkau Architects

129 **Metals**

142 **Tampa Museum of Art**
Tampa, Florida, USA
Stanley Saitowitz | Natoma Architects

146 **St. Andrews Beach House**
Victoria, Australia
Sean Godsell Architects

150 **Prefabricated Nature**
Cedeira, Spain
MYCC Architects

152 **OMS Stage**
Winnipeg, Manitoba, Canada
5468796 Architecture

156 **Lady Bird Lake Hiking Trail Restrooms**
Austin, Texas, USA
Miró Rivera Architects

160 **Kunst-Depot, Henze & Ketterer Art Gallery**
Wichtrach, Switzerland
Gigon/Guyer Architekten

164 **Herstedlund Fælleshus Community Centre**
Albertslund, Denmark
Dorte Mandrup Arkitekter

168 **Halftecture O**
Chūō-ku, Osaka, Japan
Shuhei Endo

170 **Cantonal School Canteen**
Wettingen, Switzerland
:mlzd

172 **Artists' Studios in Aberystwyth**
Aberystwyth, Wales, UK
Heatherwick Studio

175 **Plastics**

182 **SelgasCano Architecture Office**
Madrid, Spain
SelgasCano Arquitectos

184 **El B Conference Hall and Auditorium**
Cartageña, Spain
SelgasCano Arquitectos

188 **Novartis Entrance Pavilion**
Basel, Switzerland
Architect Marco Serra

192 **UK Pavilion at World Expo 2010**
Shanghai, China
Heatherwick Studio

196 **Cellophane House**
New York, New York, USA
KieranTimberlake Architects

198 **Anansi Playground Building**
Utrecht, The Netherlands
Mulders vandenBerk Architecten

202 **Miroiterie Retail Building**
Lausanne, Switzerland
B+W Architecture

206 **International Committee of the Red Cross Logistics Complex**
Geneva, Switzerland
Group8

210 **Plastic House**
Gothenburg, Sweden
Unit Arkitektur

214 **MOOM Tensegrity Membrane Structure**
Chiba, Japan
Kazuhiro Kojima Laboratory / Tokyo University of Science

217 **Masonry**

224 **Secondary School**
Dano, Burkina Faso
Diébédo Francis Kéré

228 **Brandhorst Museum**
Munich, Germany
Sauerbruch Hutton

232 **Padre Pio Pilgrimage Church**
Foggia, Italy
Renzo Piano Building Workshop

236 **South Asian Human Rights Documentation Centre**
New Delhi, India
Anagram Architects

238 **NUWOG Headquarters and Housing**
Neu-Ulm, Germany
Fink+Jocher

240 **Pope John Paul II Hall**
Rijeka, Croatia
Randić-Turato Architects

244 **Chapel of St. Lawrence**
Vantaa, Finland
Avanto Architects

248 **Warehouse 8B Conversion**
Madrid, Spain
Arturo Franco Architecture Studio

252 **Butaro Doctor's Housing**
Burera District, Rwanda
Mass Design Group

256 **Silk Wall + J-Office**
Shanghai, China
Archi-Union Architects

258 **Center for Design Research**
Lawrence, Kansas, USA
Studio 804 / University of Kansas

262 **La Pallissa**
Catalonia, Spain
Cubus

266 **Index**

270 **Bibliography**

271 **Illustration Credits**

Introduction

Materials for Architectural Design 2 showcases projects that merge architects' design intention with a material palette, a synthesis called *materiality*. Materiality was first presented in the best-selling first volume, *Materials for Architectural Design*, and here sixty new case studies continue to document this comprehensive approach to design. As examples, they inspire and encourage the use of materials as an integral part of the design process.

Materials have been used to express architectural statements for years, but it is only recently in our history that *how* we use them has begun to advance and revolutionize architecture. Additionally, there is an ever-increasing palette of material options available to designers. Prior to the twentieth century, materiality spoke more to place, to locale, and in a way was more purely definitive as to what a building should look like. Architects tended to use materials that were available and plentiful in their location and thus uniquely representative of that place, such as the indigenous woods used for the saltboxes and meetinghouses of New England in the 1700s, or Thomas Jefferson's use of the red clay of Virginia to make the distinctive bricks that defined his buildings in the early 1800s. In the northeastern United States in the 1870s and '80s, Henry Hobson Richardson used stone to convey an idea of monumentality and permanence.

In Europe, bold statements of materiality were also made during the mid-nineteenth century. Henri Labrouste used iron, then a novel material in large public buildings, in his Bibliothèque Sainte-Geneviève in Paris (1850). Iron was a proclamation that this was a building of high technology. Joseph Paxton's Crystal Palace, built in London just one year later, was a modular cast-iron and glass exhibition hall. Paxton's large areas of glass and cast iron (a precursor to the glass curtain wall) were intentionally chosen to express Great Britain's industrial, technological, and economic superiority.

Throughout the modernized world, the twentieth century saw the rapidly increasing synergy between material and design intentions. The early purveyors of modernism used materiality to support and promote their aesthetic, especially when it came to concrete. A Frenchman, Auguste Perret, had begun using reinforced concrete throughout France in the early 1900s as a representation of a new architectural style, not just a new material to replace stone. He designed a garage for Renault in 1905 and the Théâtre des Champs-Élysées in 1913, both in Paris, as well as many other public and industrial buildings. Erik Gunnar Asplund's Stockholm Library (1918) also exemplified a new monolithic and clean-lined look of concrete. In the United States, Frank Lloyd Wright was using unprecedented amounts of poured-in-place concrete, first for the Unity Temple in Oak Park, Illinois (1906), and which also appears in the notorious Fallingwater in Mill Run, Pennsylvania (1934). The modern master of concrete (and former pupil of Perret) Le Corbusier used the material to achieve the monolithic and sculptural qualities he strove for. Through his villas and religious and civic buildings erected around the world, Corb reached a new level of sculptural architecture aided by the properties of a material, when no other would have achieved the desired effect.

Ludwig Mies van der Rohe was similarly able to push the use of steel with glass to provide a level of purity in construction and a minimalist quality in space. As modernism became more and more refined, materiality continued to support the design intentions of those willing to look at materials in innovative ways. One can think of Pierre Chareau's use of glass at Maison de Verre (1932), or more generally, of Alvar Aalto's love of wood and Eero Saarinen's obsession with concrete.

By the 1980s, postmodernists had begun to promote an alternative approach to materiality: they denied it as a part of architecture. Their use of faux veneers and imitation materials expressed a style that showed little regard for an ethic of truth to material. As these materials flooded the construction market, the distinction between true and false became harder than ever to identify. Architecture's approach to materiality had spun 180 degrees since that of the early modernists.

Today, materiality is an exciting and quickly expanding concept in the construction process. Global corporations like DuPont and Weyerhauser are continually generating new materials and new uses for existing materials. Industries that once serviced a small segment of products are now engaged in much more in-depth research and development of new materials that are more effective, more efficient, and more environmentally sensitive. Once merely a tool for architects and largely confined to the realm of engineering, materiality has now become an instrumental methodology for a clear and bold design statement.

The wealth of innovations in this realm has made materials an enormous field of study in itself. Practicing architects are challenged to keep pace with rapid advances in materials science, manufacturing methods, and installation practices. The use of plastics, for instance, has exploded with every technological advance, while traditional materials have stayed in demand as well. The wide range of colors and sizes of concrete block, for example, offers an exponential increase in selection. Green materials—those that are sustainable and sensitive to the environment—have also become more mainstream.

Materials have also entered into a new realm of distinction with this onset of advancement in engineering and technology. We are at a point in history when technology allows for the engineered design of materials to fit the unique needs of a building. Frank Gehry's signature metal panels are a great example; each is individually engineered for its precise position in the building. Such technological capacity has inducted a period of revelry in the glory of materials and their qualities. Materiality has become a mature philosophy in the field of architecture: How are materials expressed in a building—are they surface or structural, modern or vernacular? What kinds of materials are appropriate? How do the structural materials relate to those of the enclosure, or are they same? This book is organized to serve as a basic reference and examination of six materials that embody this philosophy—glass, concrete, wood, metal, plastic, and masonry. All of these materials have properties and characteristics that are still being discovered, harnessed, or used in new ways. Each chapter begins with a basic material primer, a brief history, design considerations, and a summary of the various types and/or production methods. The content has been selected to give the reader a basic understanding of the material.

These introductions are followed by case study projects offering examples of some of the best and most inspired uses made by architects from around the world in recent years. The case studies have been selected by a survey of contemporary practitioners for whom design intention and materials have been successfully joined. Projects range from small to moderate in scale, allowing a focus and clarity of expression to yield an understanding of the building in its entirety and provide a didactic prototype for the young designer. These architects love materials and are not concerned about deviating from the norm. There are examples of a material being pushed to new and experimental heights, such as the patented Apple Flagship Store resembling a glass lantern in Shanghai (Bohlin Cywinski Jackson) and the ridged concrete Hanil Visitors Center and Guesthouse in Chungbuk, Korea (BCHO Architects). There are examples of a conventional material being used in a new or unfamiliar way, such as the new South Asian Human Rights Documentation Centre in New Delhi (Anagram Architects), where red brick is laid in a twisted, complex pattern to achieve visual engagement, ventilation, and shelter. The Anansi Playground Building in Utrecht (Mulders vandenBerk Architecten) uses a hardy plastic that has been around for decades yet is rarely used in exterior architectural applications. There are also more modest projects where experimentation means creativity, and where doing the unconventional has yielded surprising success.

These projects make an expression not only with the types of materials used but also in how they are put together. The construction detail drawings for all of these projects have been highlighted because this is where we learn the most about the designers' ideas in putting their buildings together, as well as their unique philosophies regarding materials. This is where we begin to understand how a material is connected, how it needs to be treated, and how it relates to the other materials in the building. The different styles and formats of drawings and construction details are important to note, as these are learning tools themselves in representation and how critical specifics can be communicated in the design.

When a material is used in new and unexpected ways, or where its characteristics are presented in an unconventional condition, the level of design is raised. The Artists' Studios in Aberystwyth, Wales (Heatherwick Studio) employ a stainless-steel foil so thin it would never normally be considered for architectural purposes. The designers used creative ingenuity to not only meet their budgetary constraints but also to fabricate a compelling structure by using a material in a creative manner. Likewise, the use of wood veneer resin-core panels in the Harry Parker Community Boathouse in Boston (Anmahian Winton Architects) not only shows a new material cladding system but also holds a metaphorical reference to the building's function and meaning. In Lausanne, Switzerland, the Miroiterie Retail Building (B+W Architecture) was clad in translucent, air-inflated membrane cushions, presenting the advantages of new plastic fabric materials.

Most of the designers included here naturally think outside of the box, but it is when they mesh together the creative technicality of materiality with the function and meaning of the design that they produce truly successful projects. *Materials for Architectural Design 2* aims to inspire designers to think of materials as a palette from which to imagine how an idea or concept can be realized. This book is dedicated to all who love materials, and to all who love design. The two belong together.

Glass

THE BASICS

At its most simplified understanding, glass is a hard, brittle, usually transparent material composed of earthen elements that have been transformed by fire. The manufacturing process heats the raw materials until they are completely fused; they are then cooled quickly, becoming rigid without fully crystallizing. The resulting material contains properties of both a crystal (mechanical rigidity) and a liquid (random, disordered molecular arrangement) but actually is different from either state. Glass can be formed in many ways, some of the most common being cast, blown, rolled, extruded, and pressed. On a cellular level, glass fibers can be knit into a sort of wool, which can be used for acoustical and thermal insulation. Glass can also be used in electrical circuitry and highly specialized equipment components.

Because glass has the inherent qualities of transmitting and filtering light, it is often used for poetic metaphor and spiritual symbolism. Its ability to transform the appearance of light and intensify colors gives it an atmospheric value like no other material. Although glass is used in a vast array of industries and common objects, its presence in architecture is perhaps both profound and practical. It is an endlessly fascinating and versatile material, and is also desirable because it is 100 percent recyclable and has an unmatched resistance to deterioration.

Architectural glass can be defined as glazing in a building's openings and, in some situations, as its walls and roof. This glazing can be of many types, colors, and forms. Understanding the basic qualities and many different types of glass available to architects will allow a larger, more creative palette from which to design buildings.

Glass can be manipulated in a surprising number of ways. Molten glass can be blown, poured into a mold, or pressed into a form. Cold glass can be slowly heated to a pliable state, then manipulated to create other shapes, or it can be adhered to other pieces of glass or laminated with other materials through industrial adhesives.

The process of slowly cooling a molten material until it is solid is called *annealing*. The annealing of glass is very slow compared to molten steel or silver, but it is an integral step in the creation of glass as a material. If molten glass cools too quickly, it may be stressed at room temperature and break easily. This stress or strain can be critical for a large sheet of glass. Highly strained glass breaks easily if subjected to mechanical or thermal shock.

HISTORY

Glass is an ancient material, dating back more than 5,000 years. It is believed that the material originated around 3500–3000 BCE in Egypt and eastern Mesopotamia (present-day Iraq) with the creation of beadlike forms that were valued as highly as precious stones. Around 1700–1600 BCE, during Egypt's eighteenth dynasty, artisans developed the skill of creating translucent bottles, jars, and the first windowpanes for buildings. Their process used heat to transform sand, seaweed, brushwood, and lime into a range of forms and colors.

The earliest glass was most commonly cast in formwork, but a major breakthrough occurred some time between 27 BCE and 14 CE with the discovery of glassblowing, attributed to Phoenician craftsmen. The Romans began blowing glass inside molds in the last century BCE, allowing for a larger variety of hollow shapes. A bubble of molten glass was placed on a blowing iron and then manipulated by blowing it into a desired shape. Mouth-blown glass revolutionized the art form, allowing for a thinner, more translucent, light-transmitting material.

This revolutionary technique eventually led to the development in the sixth century of transparent glass windows, which replaced the thin, nearly opaque stonelike sheets of alabaster or marble used in buildings. The Romans, often credited with being the first to make glass large enough for windows, used colored glass sheets set in a frame of wood or bronze for a more translucent pane. In the Middle Ages, under the direction of the Catholic Church, glass began to be used not only as a means to create spiritual environments with vast arrays of colors and glistening light but also as a method of telling the story of the Christian faith in medieval and Gothic cathedrals. The explosion of stained glass in European architecture resulted in a proliferation of inspirational spaces decorated with colored reflections of light, producing structures like no others in the world.

Glass did not take on a significant structural capacity until many centuries later. In the mid-nineteenth century, the French artisan Gustave Falconnier mass-produced hand-blown glass bricks in oval and hexagonal forms, which became extremely popular—Le Corbusier and Auguste Perret enjoyed using them—despite their limited load-bearing capacity and problems due to condensation development. A French architect known as Joachim built the first structural dome of concrete and glass in 1904. In 1907 Friedrich Keppler, a German engineer, invented and patented interlocking solid glass blocks that could be placed into reinforced concrete structures, allowing for load-bearing capacity as well as light transmission. In the 1930s the Owens Illinois Glass Corporation produced the hollow glass block, which is commonly used today.

Laminated glass was invented in 1910 by Edouard Benedictus, a French scientist who patented the process of strengthening flat glass by inserting a celluloid material layer between two sheets of glass. It was marketed as a safety glass under the name Triplex.

In the 1950s, British inventor Alastair Pilkington completely transformed the way in which glass was used in architecture through his development of float glass—the process used to produce 90 percent of architectural glass today. In this process, molten glass floats on a bed of denser molten tin, mass-producing large sheets of flat, optically superior transparent glass at an affordable cost, thereby revolutionizing the way in which glass could be used in building design. Larger sheets of glass—and hence larger windows—were available with greater uniformity and fewer surface imperfections. Pilkington's invention, along with the developments of sealants, contributed to the onset of glazed office towers, as the glass curtain wall was quickly regarded as a status symbol for buildings representing progress and style. Ludwig Mies van der Rohe's use of glass and steel at the Illinois Institute of Technology (1940) in Chicago represents an early example, as does his Seagram Building (1958) in New York. Other landmarks of architectural glass include Skidmore, Owings & Merrill's Lever House (1952) in New York and Eero Saarinen's General Motors Technical Center (1955) in Detroit. In the 1960s and '70s, advances in reflective, tinted, coated, and insulating glass exploded, giving designers the ability to control the amount of heat and solar gain in curtain wall buildings. The ensuing decades of the twentieth century ushered further advancements of the glass industry into three distinct areas: environmental control, structural uses, and a vast array of surface and color treatments.

DESIGN CONSIDERATIONS

When selecting the type and use of glass in a project, one looks for an optimal balance between aesthetics and function. The wide variety of architectural glass commercially available coupled with the versatility and creativity one can explore with the material makes the design process exciting and challenging. Understanding the basic properties and terminology used in the vast glass industry will offer a designer a useful palette from which to design.

Glass is an inherently strong material and is weakened only by surface imperfections. *Tempered* or *heat-treated glass* is stronger and more resistant to thermal stress and impact than annealed glass. Glass also possesses a hard surface, resisting scratches and abrasions. When stressed, it will rebound to its original shape until it reaches its breaking point, which is again much higher if glass has been tempered. Glass is chemical- and corrosion-resistant, and is impervious to most industrial and food acids. It is also shock-resistant and can withstand intense heat or cold as well as sudden temperature changes.

Thermal conductivity is the measure of a material's ability to transmit heat through its body. Glass is thermally a poor insulator. When two or more sheets of glass are combined together with an airspace, however, heat loss can be reduced significantly. Two- and three-paned windows that have hermetically sealed airspaces between them are good insulating windows, especially for cold climates. Further, the thermal insulating qualities of glass can be improved by using a low-emissivity (*low-E*) coating on the glass.

The transparency and translucency of glass has historically given architecture an aesthetic quality like no other material. It gives a building the ability to change, to move, and to create certain environments. The way light pours through a piece of glass in a building can be a powerful design tool for an architect. How light changes throughout the day and how it appears within the space is a frequently overlooked factor. Designers often think about the quantitative considerations of light entering a building rather than the qualitative. The color or texture of a light beam or how it hits a surface can all be controlled and manipulated with specific intent. Glass can reflect, bend, transmit, and absorb light, all with great accuracy. When light hits a piece of glass, some is reflected from the surface, some passes through, and some is absorbed in the glass. The measurement of these three properties are called *reflectance* (R), *transmittance* (T), and *absorbency* (A). Each of these are expressed as a fraction of the total amount of light falling on a piece of glass, expressed by the formula $Light = R + T + A$. Most architectural glass is partially transparent with little reflectance and absorbency. This equation is important in understanding the wide range of types of glass from which a designer has to choose, as certain types may better fit a project than others. There are hundreds of glass compositions as well as different coatings, colors, thicknesses, and laminates, all of which affect the way light passes through the material.

When designing with glass, there are three types of forces to consider: *tensile* forces, which exert a pull on glass; *compressive* forces, which squeeze glass; and *shear* forces, the combination of tension and compression, which pull glass in two directions. Tensile forces are the most critical to understand, because glass is much weaker in tension than in compression. The strength of glass is highly dependent on the condition of its surface rather than its molecular composition. When it fails, it begins with a small fissure or crack that grows until breakage.

Glass can be strengthened through *prestressing*, *chemical coating*, or *lamination* in order to help it resist breakage. Prestressing is often done by a thermal tempering process in which glass is heated to the point of malleability and then is quickly cooled, creating a drastic clash in temperature between the cooler surface and the hotter interior of the glass. This differential eventually dissipates but forces the surface into a state of compression and the interior into a state of tension. Though it increases the strength of glass, when it does fail the stresses in the glass are released as it fractures favorably into many small pieces.

Glass can also be strengthened by a chemical process in which it is immersed in a molten salt bath, coating the surface with large ions of salt and displacing smaller ions. This coating produces compression on the surface, which strengthens the glass.

The lamination process simply sandwiches sheets of glass together with heat with a transparent vinyl interlayer between the glass. When this occurs, the inner sheets of glass shrink more when cooled, causing the outer sheets of glass to be put into compression. If laminated glass breaks, the vinyl interlayer holds the glass shards in place, making it a good glass for skylights or safety applications.

TYPES

There are six basic types of commercial glass made today, which are differentiated by composition and use:

Soda-lime glass

Soda-lime glass is the least expensive type of glass and, not surprisingly, is also the most common, accounting for 90 percent of all glass made, most typically seen in the production of bottles, jars, and common consumer items. Nearly all architectural glass is some type of soda-lime glass. It is usually composed of 60–75 percent silica, 12–18 percent soda, and 5–12 percent lime. It is not resistant to sudden temperature changes or high temperatures.

Lead glass

Lead glass is a relatively soft glass with a high percentage of lead oxide, used for electrical applications as well as some art glass. It is slightly more expensive than soda-lime glass and also does not withstand sudden changes in temperature or very high temperatures.

Borosilicate glass

Borosilicate glass is a silicate glass with at least 5 percent boron trioxide. It has a high resistance to temperature changes and chemical corrosions, properties that lend well to its use in products such as light bulbs, headlights, pipes, laboratory glassware, and bakeware.

Aluminosilicate glass

Aluminosilicate glass, commonly used for electronic circuitry, contains aluminum oxide and is similar to borosilicate glass but has a greater resistance to high temperatures and better chemical durability.

96 percent silica glass

96 percent silica glass is a borosilicate glass which has been melted to remove almost all of the non-silicate elements. It is very unyielding to heat, resisting heat shock up to 1,652°F (900°C). This glass contains 7–15 percent boron trioxide and has a low coefficient of thermal expansion. Since its thermal fatigue resistance is high, it is usually used where fire protection is needed.

Fused silica glass

Fused silica glass is a pure silicon dioxide in a non-crystalline (liquid-like) state. It is very rarely used, as it is a very expensive and difficult glass to fabricate. Its purposes are usually highly specialized, such as in specific components for medical and chemical equipment.

The technological evolution of architectural glass rapidly increased toward the end of the twentieth century with the development of new coatings and different laminates. The glass industry is vast and diverse, making it difficult to enumerate every type and variation of glass available. Additionally, there are a number of ways to manufacture glass. For architectural purposes, flat glass is the most common type produced, of which there are three basic varieties: plate, sheet, and float, all of which are still made today, though float glass is predominant.

Plate glass

Plate glass was the first large-scale production process for smooth, clear glass, devised in France in the late seventeenth century. Glass was cast on a flat surface and then rolled, ground, and polished for a relatively undistorted, clear transparency. Joseph Paxton's Crystal Palace in London in 1851 used mostly plate glass.

Sheet glass

Sheet glass, or *drawn glass*, was first developed in Belgium in the early twentieth century. Large sheets of transparent glass can be produced by drawing molten glass onto a flat surface, smoothing it out with a roller, then grinding and polishing it on both sides. Sheet glass has inherent distortions, which increase as the size of the sheet increases. This was a work-intensive process but was the only known way to produce sheets of glass until the invention of float glass a half-century later. Sheet glass is still used today in small window lites.

Float glass

Float glass truly revolutionized the way glass was used in architecture. It is created by floating molten glass on a surface of molten tin, then slowly annealing it to produce a flat, transparent sheet. It is often produced in continuous ribbons. Its surface is smooth and heat-polished and does not require any grinding or polishing as sheet and plate glass do. Different patterns, textures, thicknesses, and colors can also be produced this way.

Crown glass

Crown glass is created through a process in which molten glass is mouth-blown through a long, hollow iron stick, creating a large bubble that opens at one end in a bowlike shape. This is spun and reheated until it flares out to a flat disk. The molten glass is then cracked off and placed in a kiln, or lehr, to cool slowly to prevent cracking. Once cooled, sheets or panes are cut from the flat areas in the glass. The center of the sheet, where the iron was attached, is much thicker and more irregular than the outer edges. This is called the *bull-eye* or *bullion glass*, and in the seventeenth and eighteenth centuries was considered inferior, to be used as windowpanes in the homes of the lower class. Crown glass can be clear or artistically swirled with colors. It was perfected during the Middle Ages, when many artisans used crown glass for stained-glass windows. Today, only artists who specialize in the craft of historic glass still use this process.

Cast glass

Cast glass is made by pouring molten or liquid glass in a mold to form a particular shape before it is cooled and released. Cast glass is one of the oldest methods in glass history, with early vessels dating back to Egypt and Mesopotamia as early as the fifteenth century BCE. The method of casting glass is typically used today by artisans or for ornamental and design-specific purposes. Architecturally, cast glass is used in the forms of channel glass products, glass block, patterned (textured) glass, or in a custom-designed glass system. The thickness, shape, and surface texture can vary according to the mold that is made to hold the glass.

The following are additional types of glass that are made with different qualities to enhance their performance. These are more specialized forms of glass, each with highly developed capacities.

Tempered glass

Tempered glass, often called toughened glass, is considered a type of safety glass. It is four to five times stronger than normal annealed glass, and when shattered, it breaks into many small, cubed fragments rather than dangerous shards. It is float or plate glass that has been heated and rapidly cooled, increasing its inherent strength and ductility. It is used for windows that are exposed to high wind pressure or extreme heat or cold, as well as for windows and doors where there is a chance people could bump or fall into them. Almost all large sheets of architectural glass are tempered, thereby reducing the required thickness of the glass. It is more expensive than annealed glass and distortions can result from the tempering process.

Laminated glass

Laminated glass involves sandwiching a transparent sheet of polymer, such as polyvinyl butryal, between two or more layers of flat glass using an adhesive. This is a durable and versatile glass, and can be used in a variety of environments. Among other uses, laminated glass can be used to diffract sunlight in a skylight, insulate sound in a recording studio, or be used by security facilities in need of bulletproof or fire-retardant windows. It is useful in skylights or in storefronts because the product remains in place even if the surface glass is broken. Laminated glass can be used in structural conditions such as floors, stairs, and transparent curtain wall mullions. Triple-laminated, heat-strengthened glass is often used for structural and load-bearing areas in a building.

Glass blocks
Glass blocks are massive glass units that are available in a wide range of sizes, shapes, textures, and colors. Installed like unit masonry, these blocks are produced by melting glass and then casting it into shells; two shells are fused together to make one block, sometimes with a void in the center. Some glass-block walls can meet fire resistance codes.

Channel glass
Channel glass is a self-supporting, U-shaped glass system with a textured, translucent surface. It is produced by casting and is usually set vertically in an aluminum framing system. This glass system provides a wall that can support itself while also providing large areas of light transmission. It can be used for almost all applications, eliminating the need for vertical and horizontal frame members and only requiring a perimeter frame.

Insulating glass
Insulating glass is two or more sheets of glass separated by a hermetically sealed space for thermal insulation and condensation control. The airspace between the sheets of glass can be filled during the manufacturing process with either dry air or a low-conductivity gas, such as sulfur hexafluoride. This gas can enhance thermal efficiency approximately 12 to 18 percent and can also help with sound insulation. The thermal performance of double-glazed or triple-glazed windows can be further improved by the addition of a low-E coating on one or all of the layers of glass.

Wire glass
Wire glass involves steel wires rolled into sheets of glass. A wire mesh is inserted during the manufacturing of plate glass, allowing the glass to adhere together when cracked. It can qualify as safety glass for some applications and can be used as a fire-resistant glazing in doors and windows, although it is no stronger than glass without wire mesh.

Spandrel glass
Spandrel glass is used in curtain wall construction to hide or disguise the structural elements of the building. It is a glass that has been made opaque from the exterior to give an overall uniform appearance of glass. Spandrel glass often uses a ceramic frit process to coat a piece of vision glass. The ceramic coating is typically applied to the inner face of the outermost piece of glass, leaving the sheen and durability of the glass exterior surface unchanged.

Embossed glass
Embossed glass is where a coating (often a ceramic coating) is applied to the glass panel and baked to bond to the glass for a permanent adherence. Ceramic frit patterns can be screen printed onto the glass panels and baked in the same process as for spandrel glass. The frit patterns give designers a new way to control light, color, and pattern on glass walls.

Basque Health Department Headquarters

Bilbao, Spain — Coll-Barreu Arquitectos
Partially reflective glass, digital design and fabrication

DESIGN INTENTION

The Basque Health Department Headquarters is located on the last vacant site in the administrative and business district of Bilbao. The new facility unifies disparate staff from several buildings under one roof, gives the region's health department a recognizable identity, and improves the efficiency of this public service. The project represents an attempt to bring some of the aesthetic sensibilities of the nearby Guggenheim Museum to the inner city, but with a single fragmented structure that breathes with its fissures to interact with the surrounding city. The site is located at the intersection of two important streets of the city's Ensanche (designed in 1862) where restrictive preservation rules require that new construction mimic the shape of the neighboring walls, curve back in sections, and have chamfered corners.

The folded facade generates multiple visual directions from inside to the streets below, and from the highest floors to the landscape that surrounds the city. This is an effective means to incorporate urban vitality into the building. The project becomes a place to sit on the threshold, as if at the doorway of a house, looking down the road and then back into the home.

The program's seven floors of offices begin at sidewalk level, and have above them two floors for institutional use. The open office workspace benefits the permeable and livable volume of the building. The department's boardroom is in a double-height space on the top floor.

MATERIALITY

The double facade solves not only all the mentioned urban requirements but also those concerning energy, fire resistance, and acoustic insulation. Climatic improvement enabled the elimination of conventional air-conditioning installation as well as a false ceiling. As a result, the building produces less sound and avoids recirculating air in the workspace. The volume per floor is also reduced, saving resources consumed by the construction.

The facade incorporates the designers' research from previous projects, which understands the wrapper as a facade system and social vehicle as opposed to an internally driven building on one hand and a shaper of urban space on the other. The system was intended to provide a valid response to the multiple forces acting on the facade. The use of glass is appropriate for all of the functional qualities, but it also creates a faceted, sculptural presence in the city's landscape that can live and respond to Bilbao's urban reality. The angular glass pieces work well, directing views in a contextual response to the busy street. During the day, this glass building reflects and absorbs its surrounding city, creating a modern portrait of the surrounding city and sky.

TECHNICAL

The building concentrates services in a vertical spine attached to the long edge that abuts a neighboring building, leaving the two public facades free of solid masses that would otherwise weaken the connection between interiors and the urban space. Each reinforced concrete floor extends from the structural frame toward the streets, but leaves a residual space between the thermally enclosed envelope and the outer glass facade, which contains an undulating balcony.

Vertical stainless steel tubes at 47" (1,200 mm) on center serve as the structural frame for the sculpted glass facade. Stainless steel fittings make the connection between the 4" (110 mm) structural tubes and the anodized aluminum extrusions that hold the glass. The faceted mesh surface of the glass facade is composed of triangular and trapezoidal frames, each of which contains multiple uniquely shaped pieces of laminated glass. A pressure plate of aluminum holds these pieces in place at vertical seams, while silicone sealant and stainless steel clips are used at others. The result is a nighttime facade transparent to the interior, which during the day reflects numerous precisely framed reflections of the surrounding city or sky.

The laminated glass panels are partially reflective, both for visual effects and to reduce heat loads on the building interiors. Glass outer layers of these panels are 0.25" (6 mm) thick, with a layer of polyvinyl butyral laminated between them. The outer glass facade is a sunshade but is not insulated as part of the building's thermal envelope, which eased the fabrication of its pieces at sharply acute angles. In summer, natural convection ventilates the zone between the inner and outer glass facades for significant energy savings.

The frames bounding each facet are independent of their neighbors, leaving openings between them. The architects used precise digital tools for this design, locating each node in space using a three-axis coordinate system. Glass and aluminum fabricators used these same digital tools to prepare the material elements, as did builders to locate them accurately during construction.

01

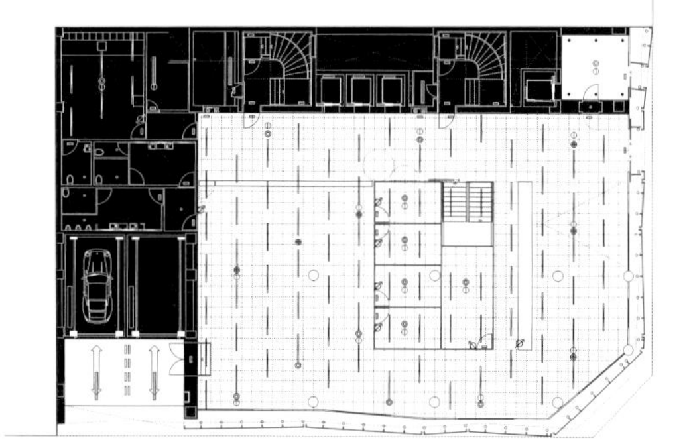

02

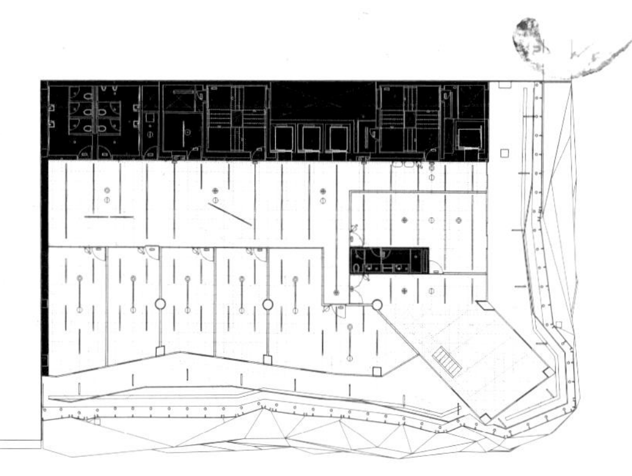

03

01 Exterior

02 Ground-floor plan

03 Seventh-floor plan

04

05

04 Balcony between building wall and glass facade

05 Meeting room interior

06 Glass facade details

07 Exterior wall section

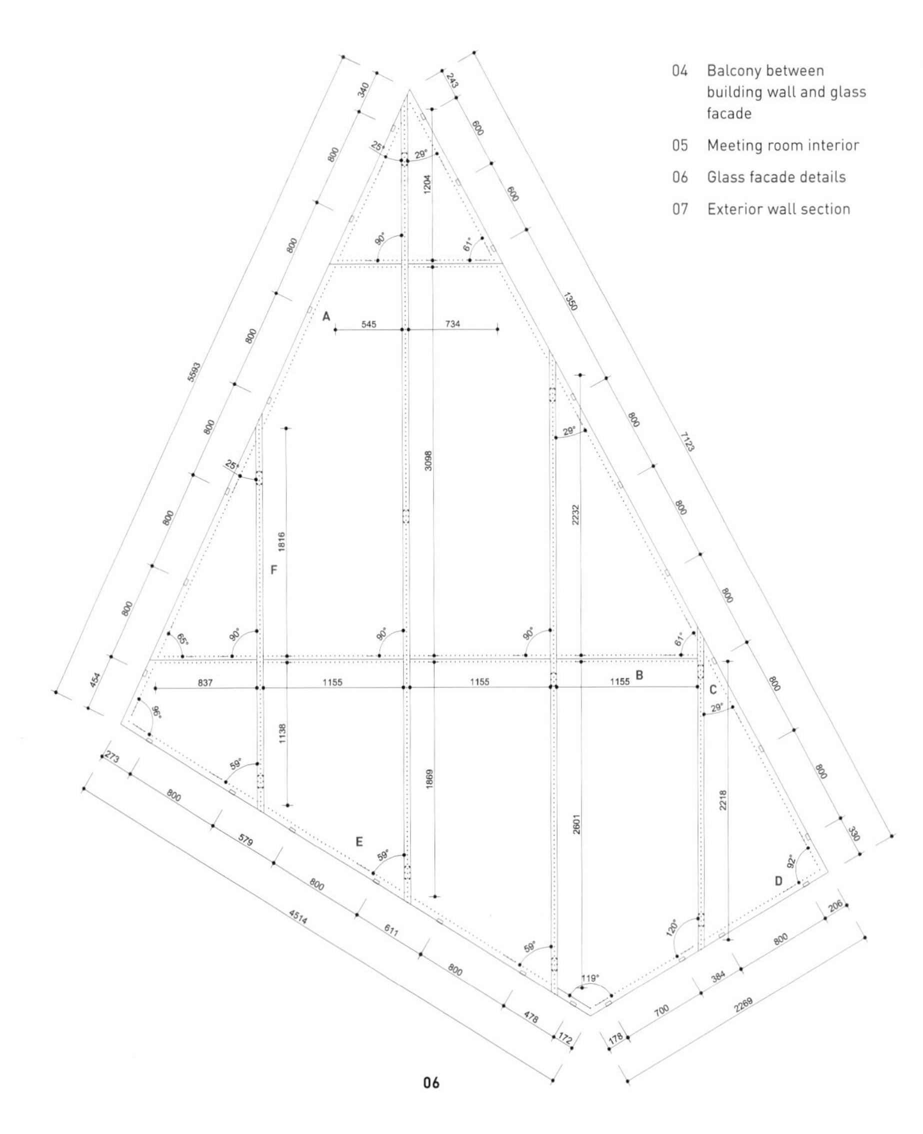

06

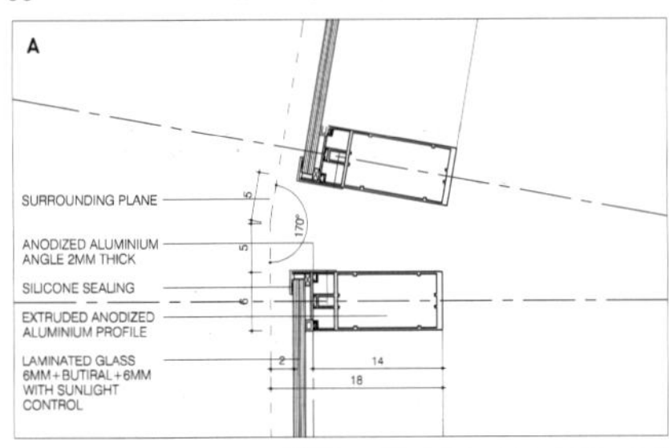

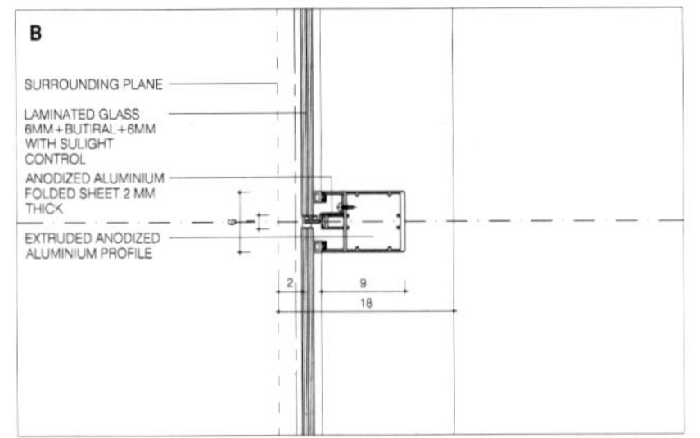

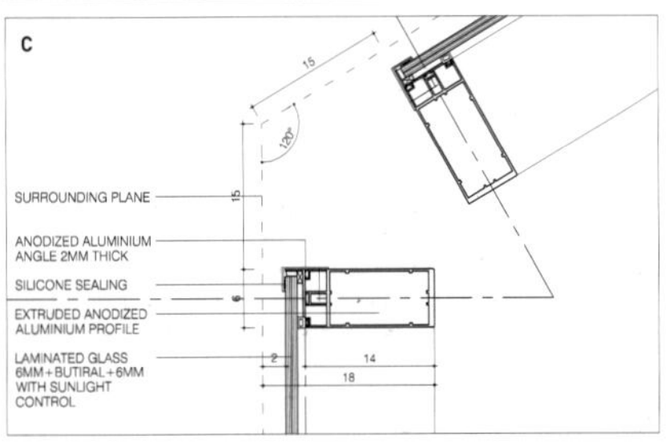

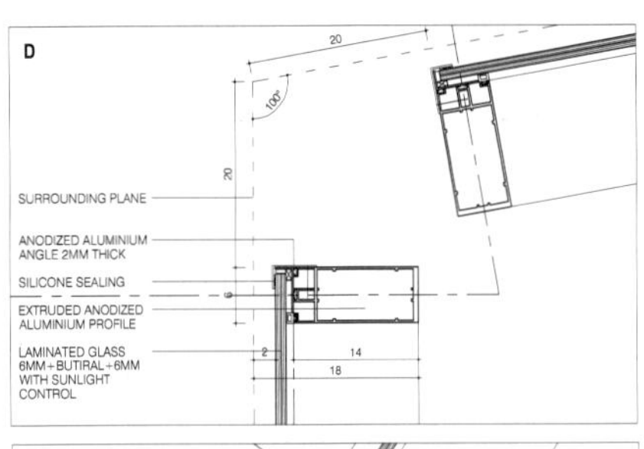

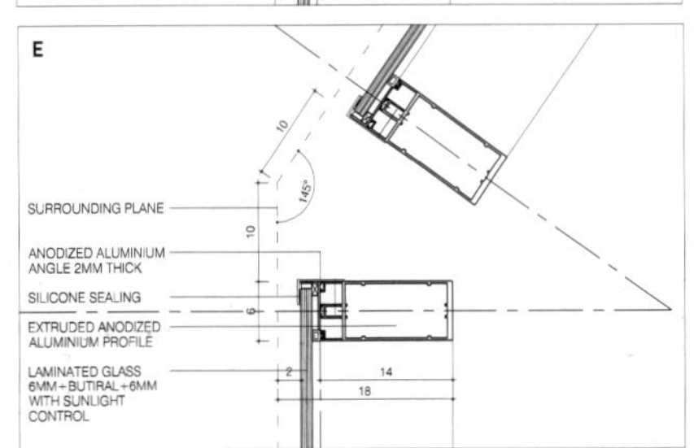

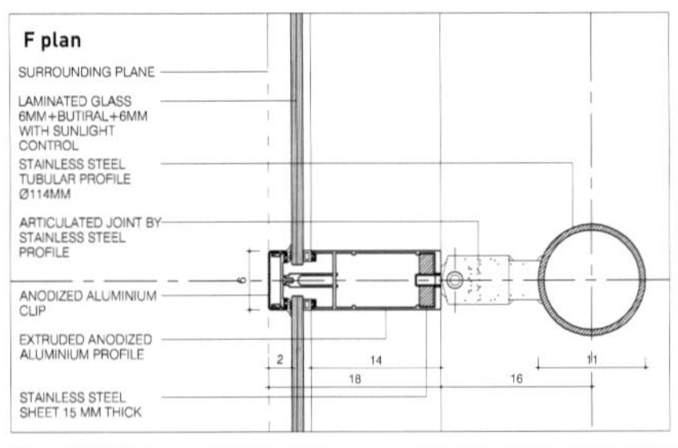

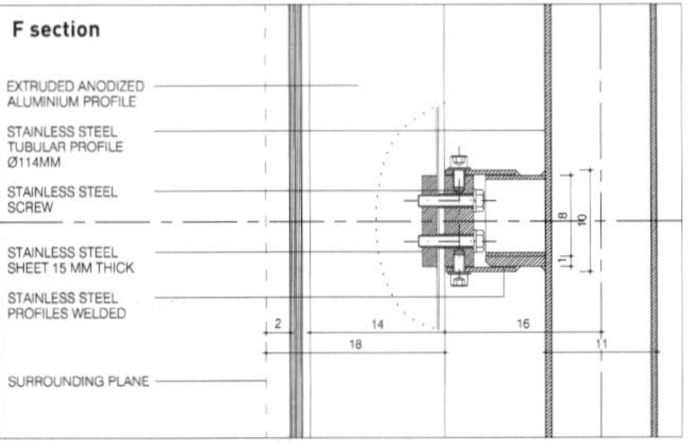

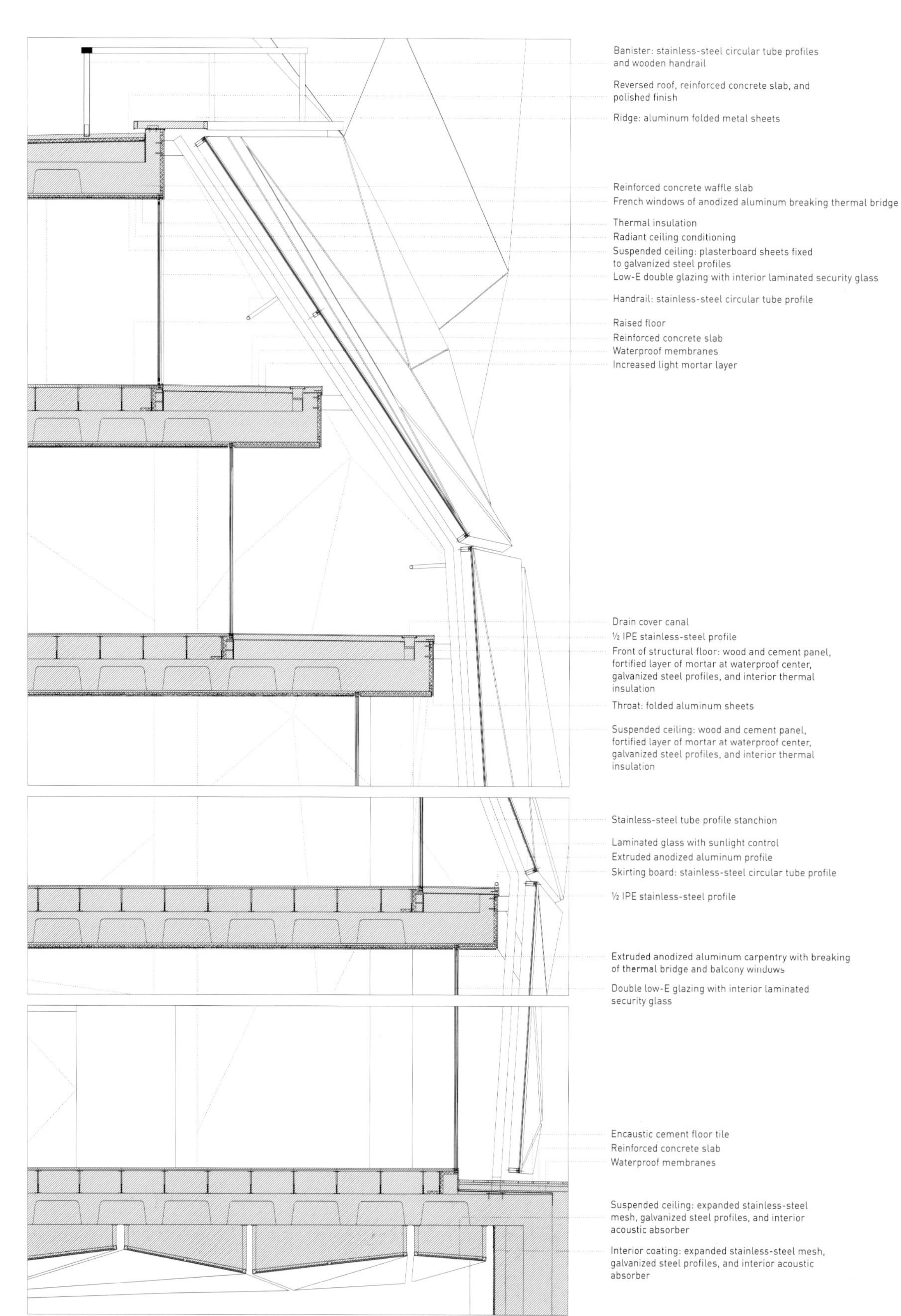
Banister: stainless-steel circular tube profiles and wooden handrail
Reversed roof, reinforced concrete slab, and polished finish
Ridge: aluminum folded metal sheets
Reinforced concrete waffle slab
French windows of anodized aluminum breaking thermal bridge
Thermal insulation
Radiant ceiling conditioning
Suspended ceiling: plasterboard sheets fixed to galvanized steel profiles
Low-E double glazing with interior laminated security glass
Handrail: stainless-steel circular tube profile
Raised floor
Reinforced concrete slab
Waterproof membranes
Increased light mortar layer
Drain cover canal
½ IPE stainless-steel profile
Front of structural floor: wood and cement panel, fortified layer of mortar at waterproof center, galvanized steel profiles, and interior thermal insulation
Throat: folded aluminum sheets
Suspended ceiling: wood and cement panel, fortified layer of mortar at waterproof center, galvanized steel profiles, and interior thermal insulation
Stainless-steel tube profile stanchion
Laminated glass with sunlight control
Extruded anodized aluminum profile
Skirting board: stainless-steel circular tube profile
½ IPE stainless-steel profile
Extruded anodized aluminum carpentry with breaking of thermal bridge and balcony windows
Double low-E glazing with interior laminated security glass
Encaustic cement floor tile
Reinforced concrete slab
Waterproof membranes
Suspended ceiling: expanded stainless-steel mesh, galvanized steel profiles, and interior acoustic absorber
Interior coating: expanded stainless-steel mesh, galvanized steel profiles, and interior acoustic absorber

07

Glass Townhouses

Venice, California, USA — Sander Architects
Translucent glass

DESIGN INTENTION

This building is divided in half vertically to create a pair of three-story condominiums that incorporate many sustainable design strategies and materials. The narrow corner site has a broad public elevation with a challenging southwest orientation. The homes' slender mass is exploited to reduce their environmental impact in two ways: extensive glazing on the long walls maximizes natural daylighting throughout, and operable windows facilitate natural cross ventilation and passive cooling.

MATERIALITY

The primary elevation of the building is a double layer of translucent materials. The inner layer is a multiwall acrylic panel that provides waterproofing and some thermal resistance, inside an outer layer of saw-toothed plates of glass. The effect from the interior is a double-height wall that fills the rooms with light during the day and allows the interior lights to glow toward the street at night. The use of glass continues through the house with detailing accents in living spaces, kitchens, and baths. This project showcases the many uses of glass and the different conditions that can be achieved in areas of the domestic setting.

TECHNICAL

Venice, California, has a hot, dry climate, with more than 260 sunny days in a typical year. It is near enough to the ocean to benefit from milder temperatures and fresher breezes than inland locations, but building design is dominated by a priority on minimizing heat gain. The broad southwest elevation was an obvious asset regarding daylighting, but was a potential liability regarding heat and glare, because afternoon sun would potentially shine into an already warm interior.

The translucent outer glass panels diffuse the beams of sunlight softly, but also convert some of the radiant energy into heat. The heat is then conducted through the glass panes to the outside air on both sides, and carried away from the enclosed spaces. By placing the glass pieces in a sawtooth configuration, the glass outer layer gains a 2" vertical vent every 28" of its length (50 mm every 710 mm). Air can naturally convect horizontally through these vents, and move vertically because the bottom and top of this zone between layers are not airtight. An earlier iteration of this elevation had a tightly packed series of channel glass as the outer layer, which would have diffused light similarly, but would not have dissipated heat nearly as well.

All materials in the outer layer are water resistant. Each plane of glass is held at the top and bottom in the saw-tooth configuration by a strip of wood-plastic composite, a material that is normally used as an alternative to wood in residential decks or similar applications. Here the product was adapted by simply cutting a groove at an angle to receive the glass. The composite strip is supported continuously by an aluminum angle. In these locations, the underside of the composite material was saw-cut laterally at 12" (305 mm) intervals along its length to create drips for water to drain toward the outside.

The 0.25" (6.3 mm) thick glass pieces were sandblasted to make them translucent. Although this coarsened the surface and made it more difficult to clean, for this application that was not a concern. The outer layer of glass decreases the amount of ultraviolet light that reaches the multiwall acrylic inner layer, prolonging the life of the polymer.

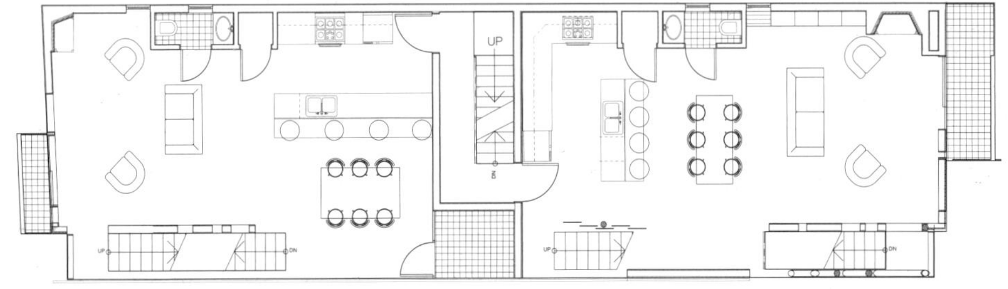

01

01 Second-floor plan

02 Exterior view from southwest

02

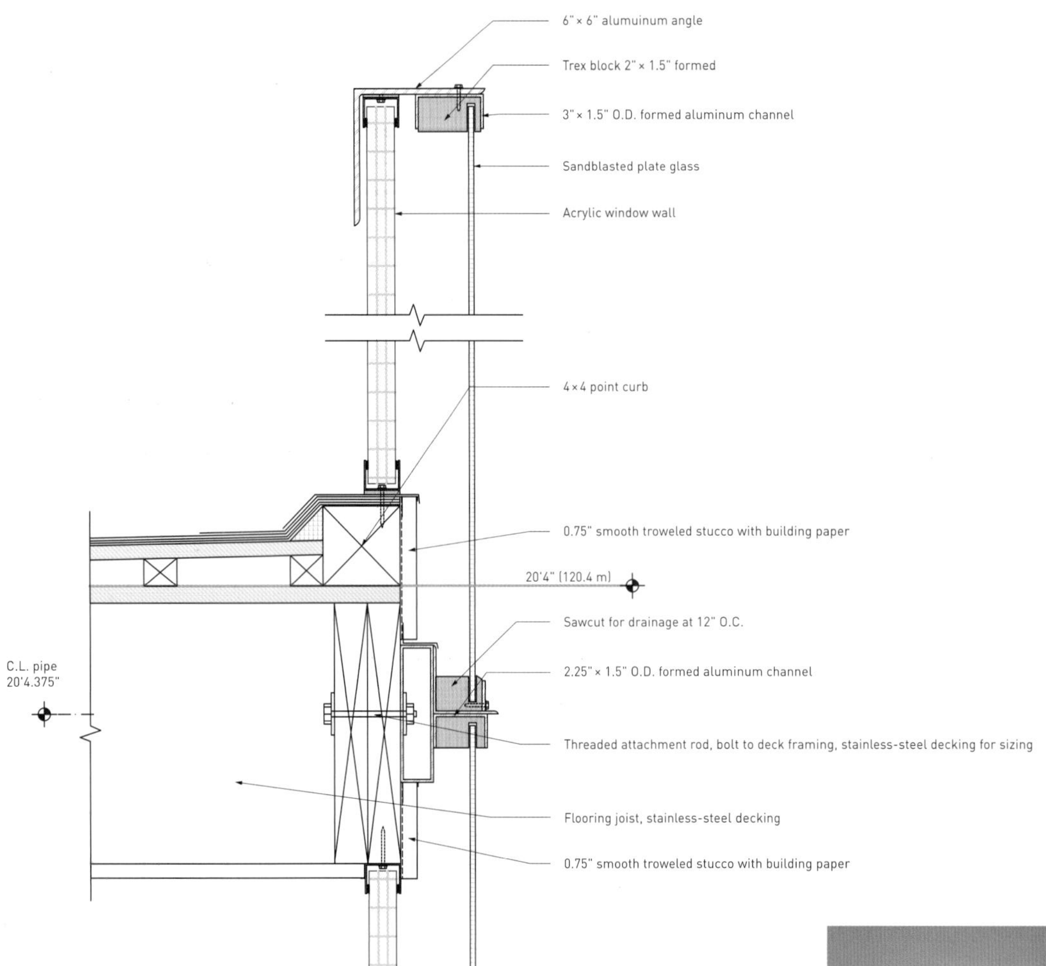
6" × 6" alumuinum angle
Trex block 2" × 1.5" formed
3" × 1.5" O.D. formed aluminum channel
Sandblasted plate glass
Acrylic window wall
4 × 4 point curb
0.75" smooth troweled stucco with building paper
20'4" (120.4 m)
Sawcut for drainage at 12" O.C.
C.L. pipe
20'4.375"
2.25" × 1.5" O.D. formed aluminum channel
Threaded attachment rod, bolt to deck framing, stainless-steel decking for sizing
Flooring joist, stainless-steel decking
0.75" smooth troweled stucco with building paper

03

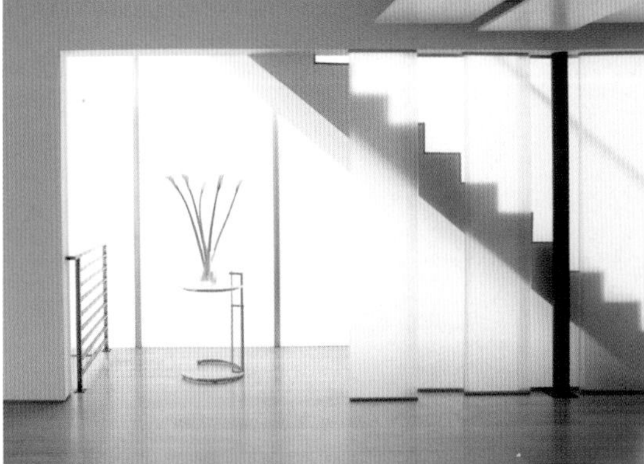

05

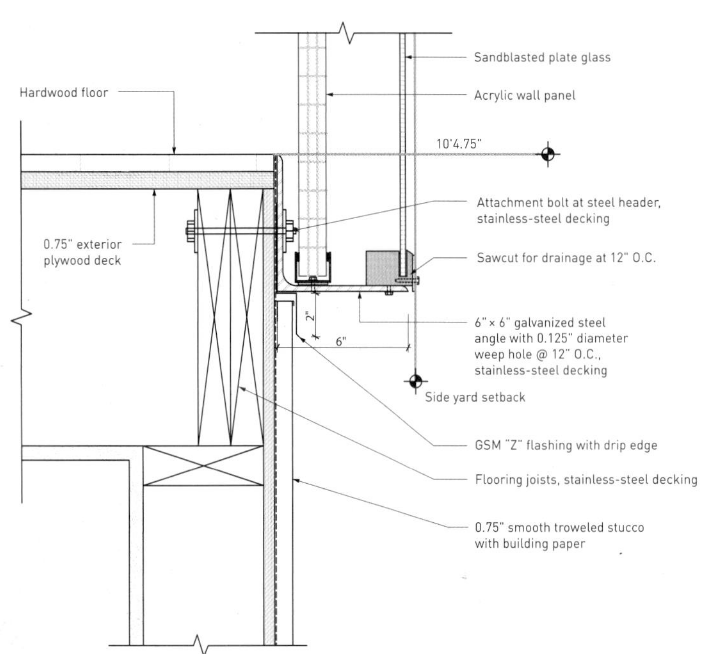
Sandblasted plate glass
Hardwood floor
Acrylic wall panel
10'4.75"
Attachment bolt at steel header, stainless-steel decking
0.75" exterior plywood deck
Sawcut for drainage at 12" O.C.
2"
6"
6" × 6" galvanized steel angle with 0.125" diameter weep hole @ 12" O.C., stainless-steel decking
Side yard setback
GSM "Z" flashing with drip edge
Flooring joists, stainless-steel decking
0.75" smooth troweled stucco with building paper

04

06

03 Glass curtain wall at roof

04 Glass curtain wall at floor

05 Glass layers soften light in living space

06 Nighttime view from south

07 Plan detail at corner

08 Daytime view from south

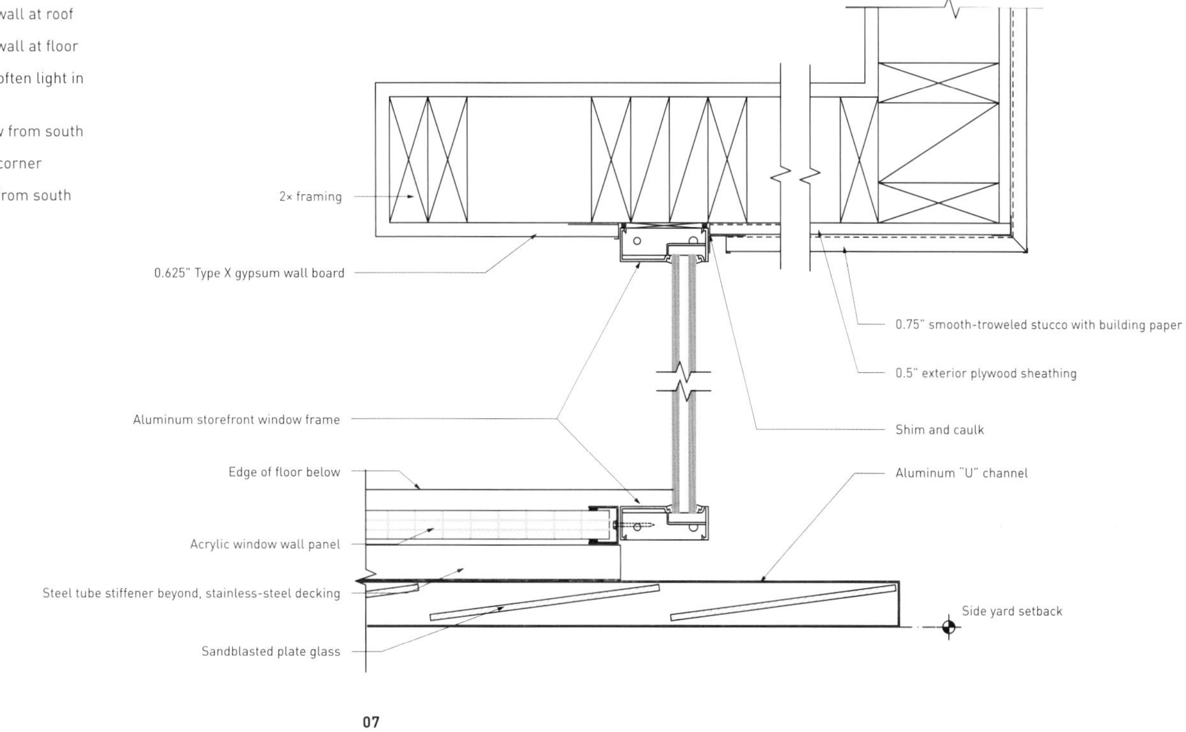

07

08

Factory Extension

Murcia, Spain — Clavel Arquitectos
Channel glass, translucency

DESIGN INTENTION

This project was for the sales offices of the firm Vigaceros, a company that manufactures and distributes industrial machinery and supplies to manufacturing and construction sectors. The concept was to expand the existing premises, located in the Oeste industrial district, so the facility projected a more contemporary identity and architecturally enhanced the formerly unattractive district.

Exposed steel trusses organize the upper office floor, where the individual offices are arranged. The ground floor has been left open and acts as the showroom and sales area. The new area is linked to the existing industrial building, permitting the showroom to dissolve into the factory space and establishing a symbiotic relationship between the two spaces.

MATERIALITY

The busy street front of the two-story building became a demonstration of the company's products—Vigaceros manufactures the primary cladding materials at the factory behind this showroom. Both the building's illuminated interior and the company's name over the galvanized metal will appear or disappear, depending on the natural or artificial lighting conditions.

The front enclosing system is made of overlapping channel glass, perforated metal sheets, and pieces of COR-TEN steel linked by flat surfaces and folds. These layers produce a set of visually complex and interesting conditions from one piece to the next, clearly suggesting that this building is not your typical factory.

TECHNICAL

The metal facade materials are fixed at points within each plane of material rather than at the corners, making the structure lighter and its boundaries more ambiguous. The perforated metal screen hovers above the ground plane and advances the appearance of levity.

The translucent facade of channel glass is set back from the front in an irregular zigzag line behind a screen of galvanized steel bearing the company name. An interesting play of light results in shifting degrees of transparency and translucency through perforations in the steel. In daylight the lettering dominates; at night the illuminated interior attracts the attention. This project shows that glass, but also metal sheets, can have transparent, translucent, and opaque qualities under controlled conditions.

The channel glass is 0.24" (6 mm) thick; each piece is one story tall and 11.1" (280 mm) wide. No metal mullions were needed with the channel glass because it is self-supporting in these dimensions. The perforated galvanized metal sheets are only 0.016" (0.4 mm) thick but the span between vertical ribs is narrow, approximately the same as that of the channel glass. Like the channel glass, the steel screen has no substructure, because the ribbed plane supports the construction.

01 Nighttime view
02 Transverse section
03 Exterior detail
04 Exploded perspective of construction assemblies
05 Construction sequence

01

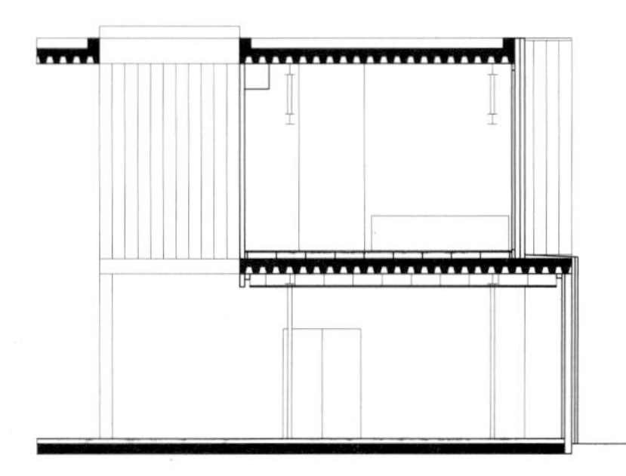

02

03

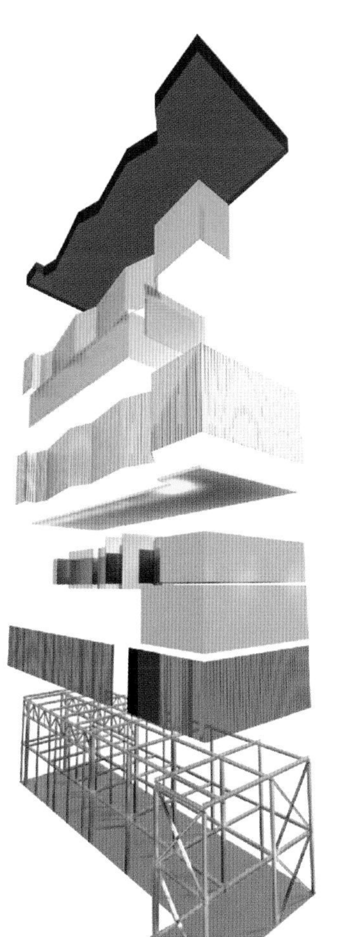
Gravel-covered flat roof
Composite floor
Concrete slab on steel deck
Facade interior
Extruded aluminum windows (2 mm)
Double glazing of two panes of glass, 6 mm thick, with layer of air
Facade exterior, bonded glass profiles of U-shaped section (U-glass) 6 mm thick, 262 mm broad
Composite floor
Partition wall of plasterboard and profiles of extruded aluminum
Interior facade, exterior microperforated metal sheet: galvanized, self-supporting, painted aluminum, 0.4 mm thick
Prefabricated metal structure

04

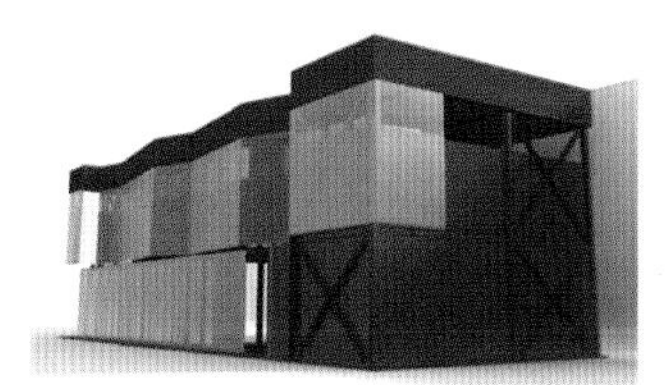

05

Diana Center at Barnard College

New York, New York, USA — Weiss / Manfredi Architecture / Landscape / Urbanism
Ceramic frit, shadow box glass assemblies

DESIGN INTENTION

Barnard College is an intimate campus compressed into the dense urban environment of Manhattan. Composed of an eclectic group of predominantly brick buildings, the campus is focused around grassy Lehman Lawn. The Diana Center is a 98,000 sq. ft. (9,100 sq. m) multiuse building that establishes a setting for campus life, bringing together spaces for art, architecture, theater, and art history, as well as faculty offices, a dining room, and a cafe. From the historic entrance gate at Broadway, the wedge-shaped building frames Lehman Lawn and unites landscape and architecture, presenting views to the campus and the city.

A diagonal void cuts the building, establishing sightlines through the gallery, reading room, dining room, and cafe. Anchoring the lower levels, a 500-seat multipurpose space and 100-seat black box theater house lectures, special events, and theatrical productions. On the campus side of the building, an unfolded glazed staircase encourages informal encounters at the heart of the project.

MATERIALITY

The building's enclosure establishes a reciprocal relationship between the campus context and the internal programmatic elements. Residing in a campus defined by brick and terracotta, the Diana Center translates the static opacity of masonry into a contemporary, luminous, and energy-efficient curtain wall. A total of 1,154 panels of varying widths calibrate gradients of color, opacity, and transparency to the Diana Center's diverse programs, allowing views into the building's public functions and limiting visibility where privacy is necessary. The translucent acid-etched fritted glass combines with colored metal panels to create constant shifts in hue and reflectivity under varied lighting and climate conditions.

As a LEED Gold building, sustainability motivated many design decisions, supporting Barnard's efforts to both teach and practice environmental principles. The Center's green roof offers a 2,800 sq. ft. (260 sq. m) ecological learning center for biology and environmental science students as well as a valuable new social space. The building maximizes daylight and views and incorporates operable windows, radiant flooring, and recycled materials. The lighting control system, occupancy sensors, automated shading, and high-performance MEP systems help increase efficiency and enable daylight harvesting.

TECHNICAL

The Diana Center employs a variety of construction materials and assemblies to achieve a coherent whole. The primary structure of concrete on a steel frame is altered in varied ways. For instance, it accepts a stair that engages the outer wall, is modulated in section to provide varied interior volumes, and has an accessible vegetated roof deck.

The building's stout structure reaches out to the envelope with members of diminishing mass and depth, permitting greater spatial connection to the exterior. The outermost layer is typically an aluminum curtain wall frame with a dominantly vertical orientation, fully wrapped by various glass and aluminum cladding elements. Great care is evident in the details to provide the necessary transitions between rough structure and refined finishes, but also between elements of low and high construction tolerances, and between materials that may be incompatible, such as aluminum and steel, or concrete and aluminum.

The anodized aluminum curtain wall frame is bracketed to the concrete or steel armature. Wall surfaces are typically wrapped with various glass products. Composite aluminum cladding is set flush with the glass at transitions, such as at copings and transitions between glass types. The aluminum transitions were made of copper anodized extrusions, with some bar stock and break metal pieces to match. Some aluminum panels were made with a metallic Kynar finish rather than being anodized.

Glass in this curtain wall is always insulated, using 5/16"–5/8"–5/16" (8–16–8 mm) cavity glass panels consistently to standardize details. At parapets and spandrels, where visibility through the glass is not desired, a shadow box is used. The shadow box's dark backing surface makes the unit uniformly opaque from the outside. Before the glass panel is fabricated, a ceramic coating is roller-applied to the surface of the inner layer of the outer plane of glass (the #2 surface). It is then baked on to permanently bond to the glass. Shadow box glass panels are never seen from the inside. The inner layer of glass in these units is simply clear glass, and chiefly contributes to thermal control. An air space separates the inner glass surface from the backing, assuring that no contaminants can migrate to the glass panel.

Vision glass in this project was made using a variety of ceramic frit patterns that were screen printed onto the glass. The ceramic frit is then baked onto the glass in the same manner as for shadow box glass units. The frit pattern offers permanent view and light controls to the envelope, and carries the hue of the shadow box glass units and metal cladding into the vision glass panels. The ceramic frit on many of these vision glass panels have a gradient of vertical colored stripes, making one edge of the glass panel nearly opaque, and the other edge clear. The result is a complex elevation that appears to be composed of diagonal wall pieces, when actually they are coplanar.

It is particularly challenging to produce the same color in both shadow box glass and screen-printed vision glass, because the ceramic coating is applied differently, and because the tint or reflectivity of the vision glass may differ from that of the shadow box glass units. A coordinated effort between architect and glass fabricator was used at the Diana Center to achieve a seamless visual result.

Most of the glass panels in this building's curtain wall are fixed in place, but in some locations operable awning lights were custom-fabricated to permit local control over ventilation. These operable sashes consist of a thin aluminum frame that is inside the insulated glass panel, and is not exposed to the exterior.

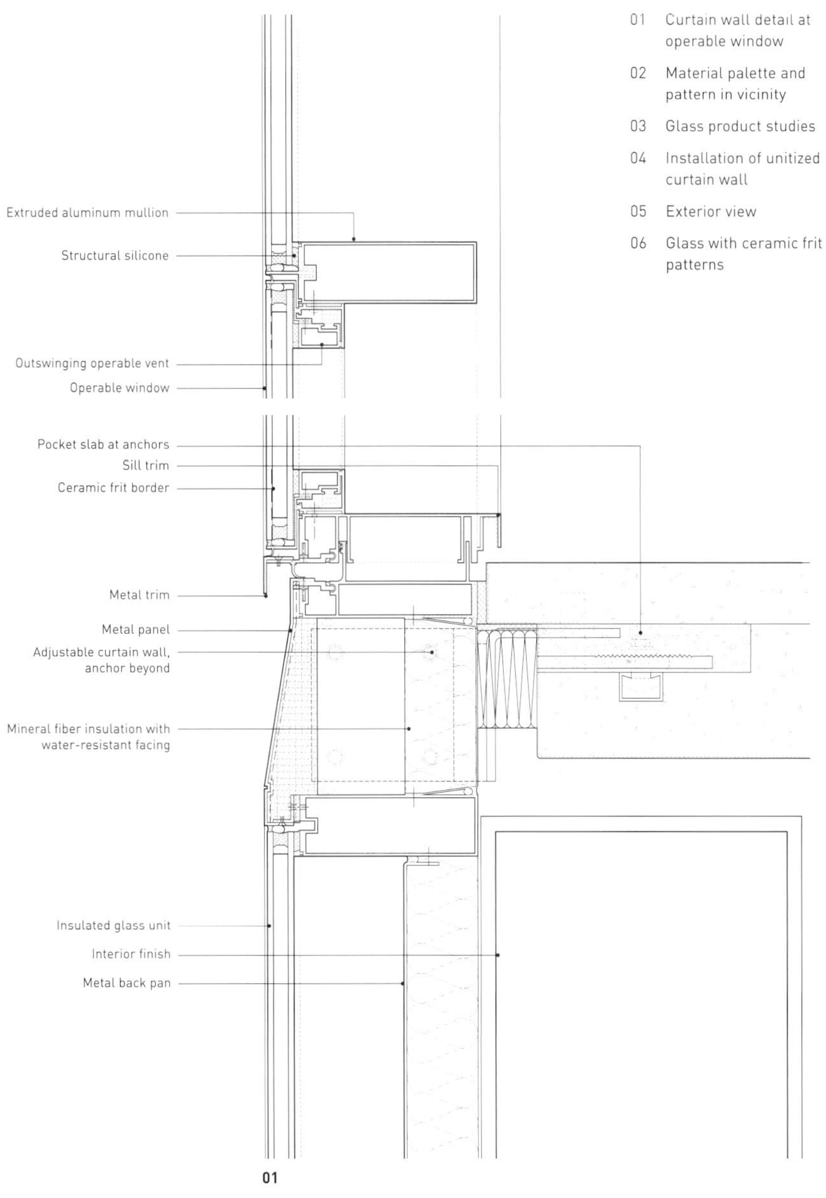

01

01 Curtain wall detail at operable window

02 Material palette and pattern in vicinity

03 Glass product studies

04 Installation of unitized curtain wall

05 Exterior view

06 Glass with ceramic frit patterns

05

02

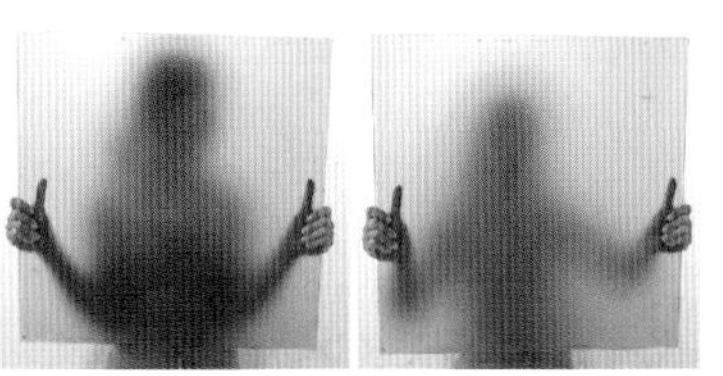

03

04

06

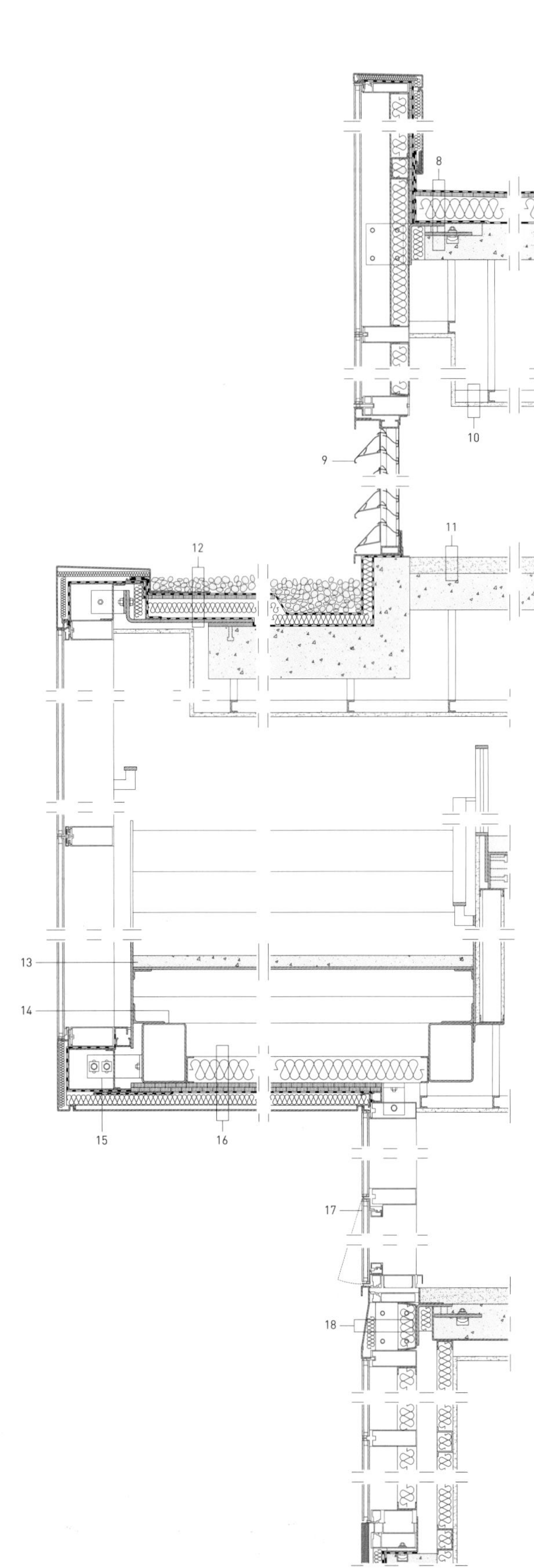

1. Curtain wall with 5/16"–5/8"–5/16" (8–16–8 mm) aluminum double-glazed units with opaque glass, air space, 2.875" (75 mm) sheet aluminum sandwich panel with insulation interlayer on frame of aluminum profiles, 0.5" (14 mm) waterproof plywood panel, double waterproofing membrane, sheet aluminum flashing, finish on inner face of parapet consisting of 1" (25 mm) sheet aluminum sandwich panel with insulation interlayer on aluminum brackets
2. Coping consisting of sheet aluminum flashing, 0.875" (22 mm) board insulation, waterproofing membrane, aluminum window frame
3. Parapet fixed by brackets to slab formed by 2.625" × 2.625" (65 × 65 mm) steel box profile uprights surmounted by 0.5" × 3.125" (14 × 80 mm) steel plate
4. Green roof comprising 8.5" (215 mm) topsoil, root-repellent membrane, 5.875" (150 mm) board insulation, waterproofing membrane, 8.25" (210 mm) reinforced concrete slab
5. 7.125" (180 mm) floating deck with 1.375" (35 mm) stone flags
6. Full-height curtain wall with 5/16"–5/8"–5/16" (8–16–8 mm) aluminum double-glazed units with low-E treatment
7. Facade formed by 2.375" (60 mm) sheet aluminum sandwich panel with rigid insulation interlayer and vapor barrier on interior face
8. Roof formed by waterproofing membrane, 0.5" (14 mm) waterproof plywood panel, board insulation of varying thicknesses forming slope, waterproofing membrane, structure of steel L-profiles, and steel plates embedded in concrete connecting facade to supporting structure, 5.875" (150 mm) reinforced concrete slab
9. Solar shading comprising fixed aluminum blades
10. False ceiling formed by 0.375" (10 mm) gypsum board, frame of aluminum C-profiles, and tie rods suspended from supporting structure
11. Floor with 2.625" (65 mm) honed concrete finish, 5.5" (140 mm) reinforced concrete slab
12. Roof formed by gravel layer, sheet aluminum, waterproofing membrane, 0.625" (15 mm) waterproof plywood panel, 3.125" (80 mm) board insulation, waterproofing membrane, 5.125" × 21.25" (130 × 540 mm) steel L-profile connecting facade to slab
13. Internal staircase tread consisting of steel frame and 1.75" (45 mm) honed concrete
14. Staircase supporting structure in 9.625" × 7.5" (245 × 190 mm) steel box profiles
15. 8.625" x 8.625" (220 x 220 mm) steel L-profile (parallel to plane of section) connecting facade to stairs
16. Sheet aluminum exterior finish, 1.75" (45 mm) board insulation, vapor barrier, double 0.75" (18 mm) waterproof plywood panels, 4.125" (105 mm) board insulation on structure of 1 × 4.125" (25 × 105 mm) aluminum C-profiles
17. Opening 5/16"–5/8"–5/16" (8–16–8 mm) aluminum double-glazed unit
18. Cladding consisting of shaped sheet aluminum and board insulation with average thickness of 1.75" (45 mm), 6.25" × 6.25" (160 × 160 mm) steel L-profile (parallel to plain of section) connecting facade to slab, 2.875" (75 mm) shaped sheet aluminum with insulation

07

WALL TYPE 1 & 1A PANEL TYPES

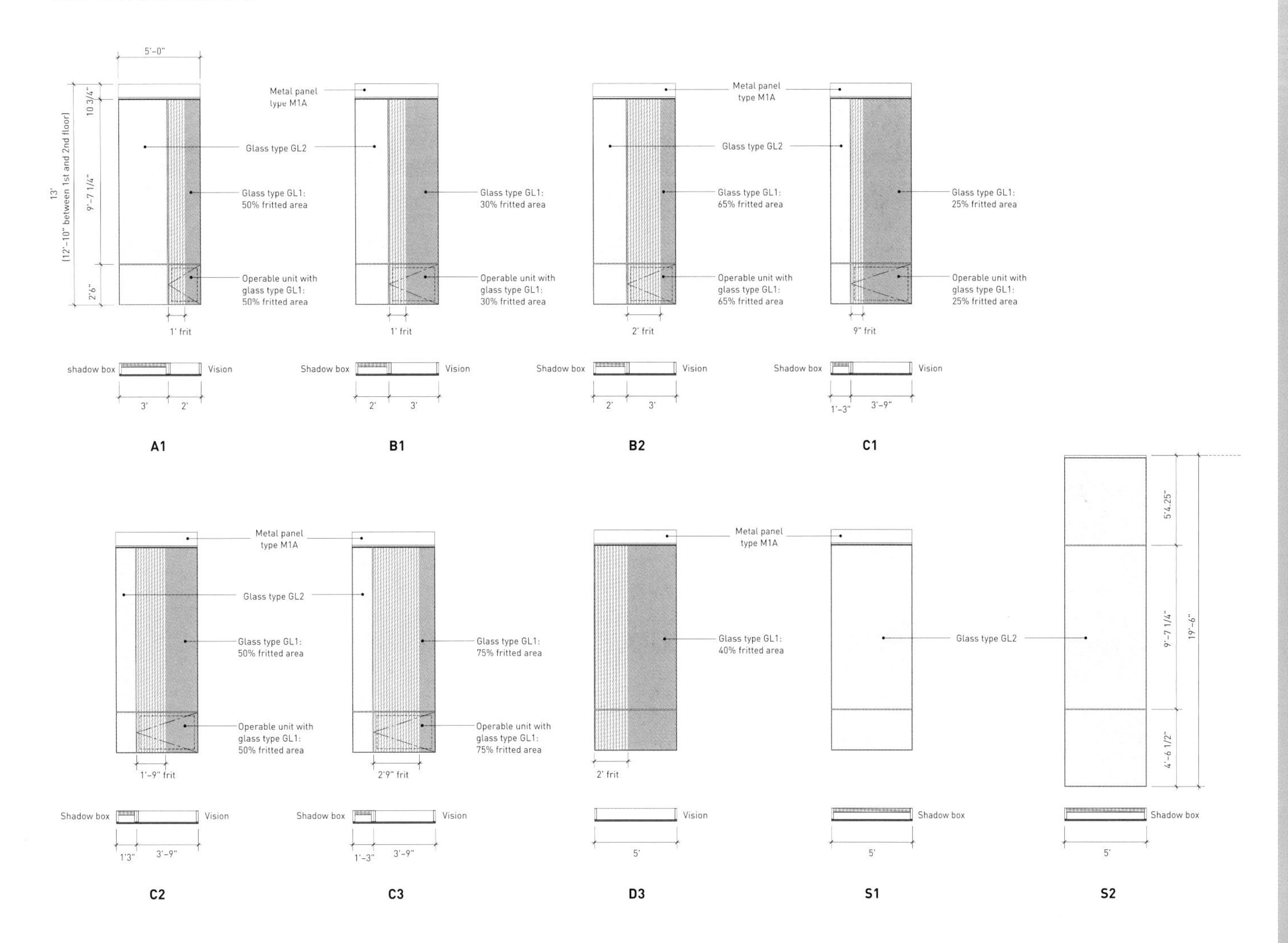

WALL TYPE 2 PANEL TYPES

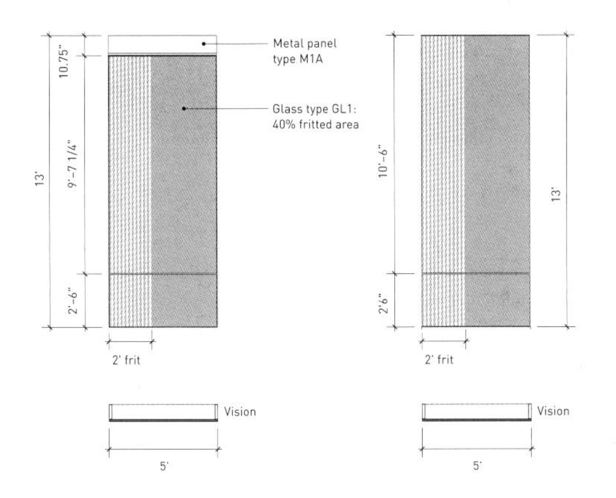

08

07 Detailed section at wall and roof

08 Unitized curtain wall types

Spiral Gallery

Shanghai, China — Atelier Deshaus
Curved tempered insulated glass

DESIGN INTENTION

This art gallery, located in a parklike setting, aspires to translate the beauty of the surrounding park to the confines of the gallery. The spiral shape is intended to open up views to the site's landscape while a visitor experiences the gallery. The interior space gradually transitions from public to private, creating two paths to the galleries from the scenic landscape. These interlocking arms of solid and void organize the public spaces and more private elements of the program, while an intentionally elongated path makes the 2,700 sq. ft. (250 sq. m) gallery seem even larger. The organic nature of the curved glass and spiral floor plan underlines the goal of synchronizing nature and architecture. The spatial compression of the entry experience heightens appreciation of the spatial release into the open gallery spaces. Using glass to curve this pathway achieves the goal of an unobstructed and continuous relationship with the surrounding landscape.

MATERIALITY

A concrete core anchors the building. From this core, steel beams were cantilevered to support the roof loads. With no need for vertical structural members in the galleries or outer walls, the latter could be made entirely of glass. A perforated, corrugated aluminum screen surrounds the glass exterior wall and acts as a curtain, eliminating the harshness of direct sunlight coming into the gallery. Using glass here to conform to the spiral floor plan visually and experientially gives the gallery visitor the desired experience of being aware of the landscape beyond but also appreciating the artwork within the space.

TECHNICAL

The insulated glass cladding panels are 12.9' (3.93 m) tall, with details that minimize the visual presence of the metal frames that hold them. Steel channels are concealed in the horizontal floor and ceiling assemblies so that the plane of the glass passes unobtrusively through the horizontal planes.

The channel at the head is tall enough to receive the glass panel as it is being installed, and to engage the glass when a panel is lowered into place onto setting blocks. Minor deflections of the roof assembly will not directly bear on the glass skin due to the accommodating details that permit the glass to move vertically within the steel channel at the head. Rubber gaskets isolate the glass from the metal at the top and bottom; vertical butt joints received silicone sealant.

The glass panels are curved, tempered glass pieces that are assembled into an insulated glass panel. The glass pieces are 0.59" (15 mm) thick, and the cavity between them is 0.47" (12 mm), for a total thickness of 1.65" (42 mm). The outer piece of glass has a low-E coating to improve thermal performance.

The curvature of the glass cladding varies from nearly flat to a radius of only 9.8' (3 m). The architect notes that the glass panels were hot-bent to the curved shape prior to tempering.

The design acknowledges that heat gain and glare would be a problem if glass alone were the exterior envelope. The perforated corrugated aluminum screen moderates this threat, and also softens views to the outside from the gallery spaces.

01 Transverse section through spiral
02 Section along length of spiral
03 Exterior
04 Exterior from above gallery
05 Ground-floor plan

1 Gallery
2 Studio
3 Office
4 Mechanical room
5 Kitchen
6 Toilet
7 Storage
8 Courtyard

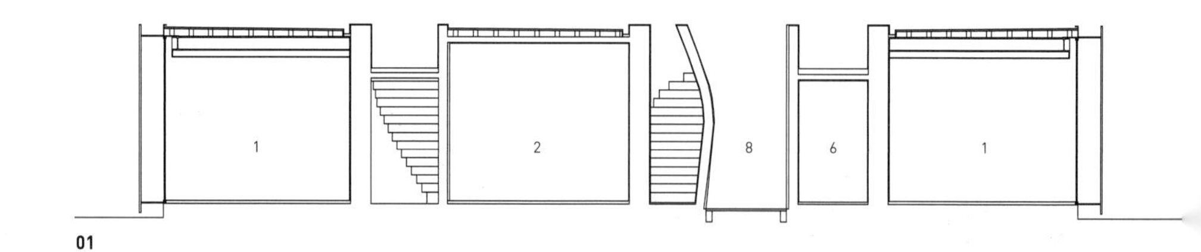

01

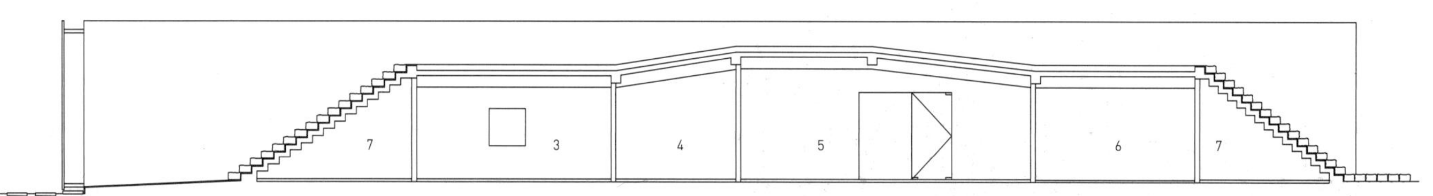

02

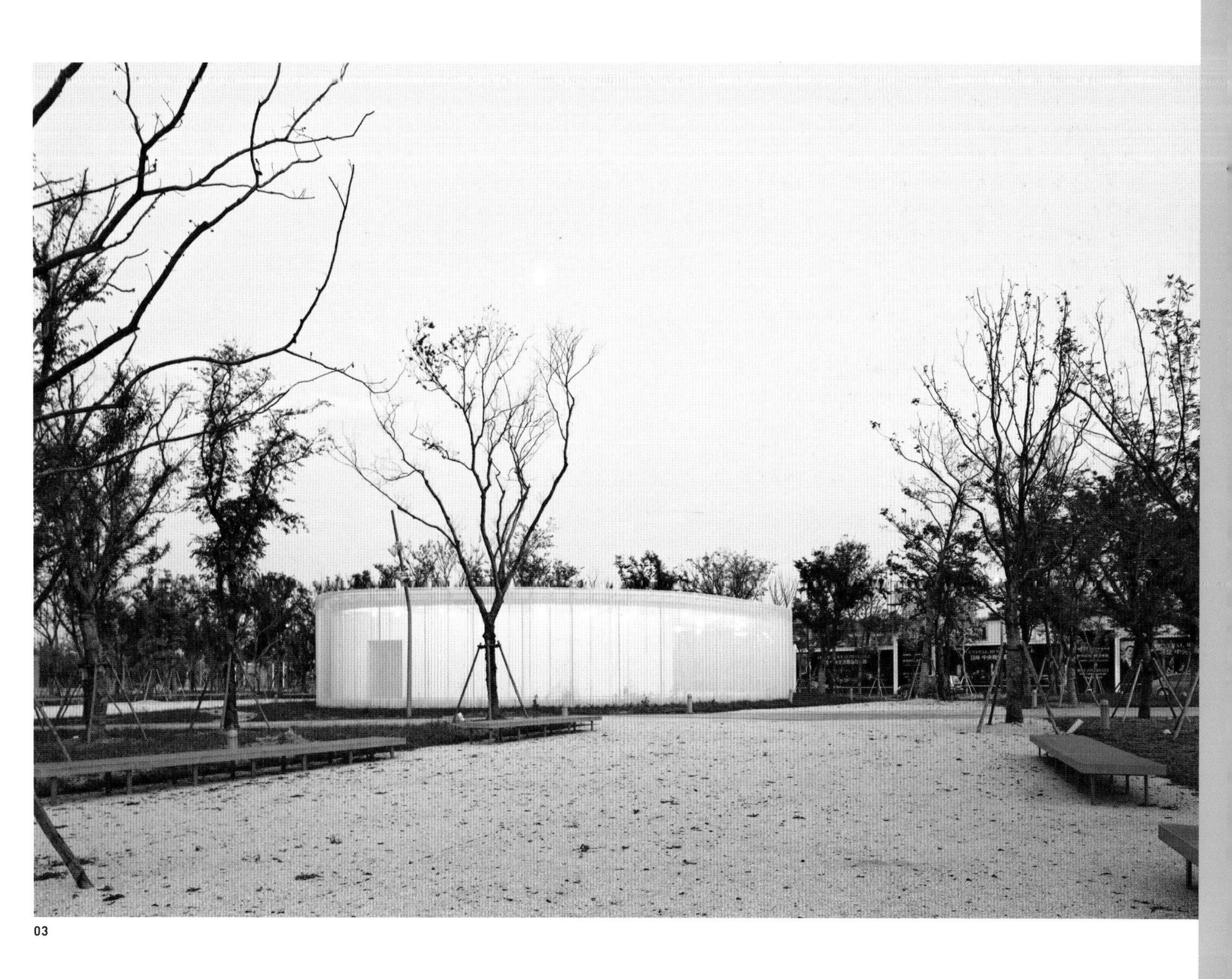

03

04

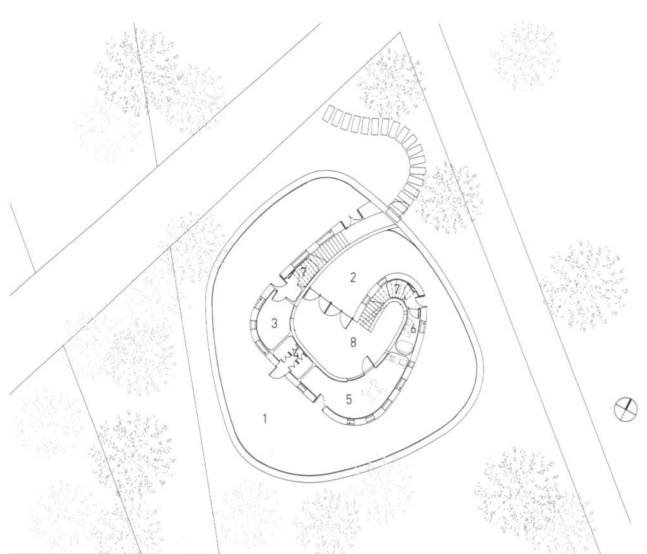

05

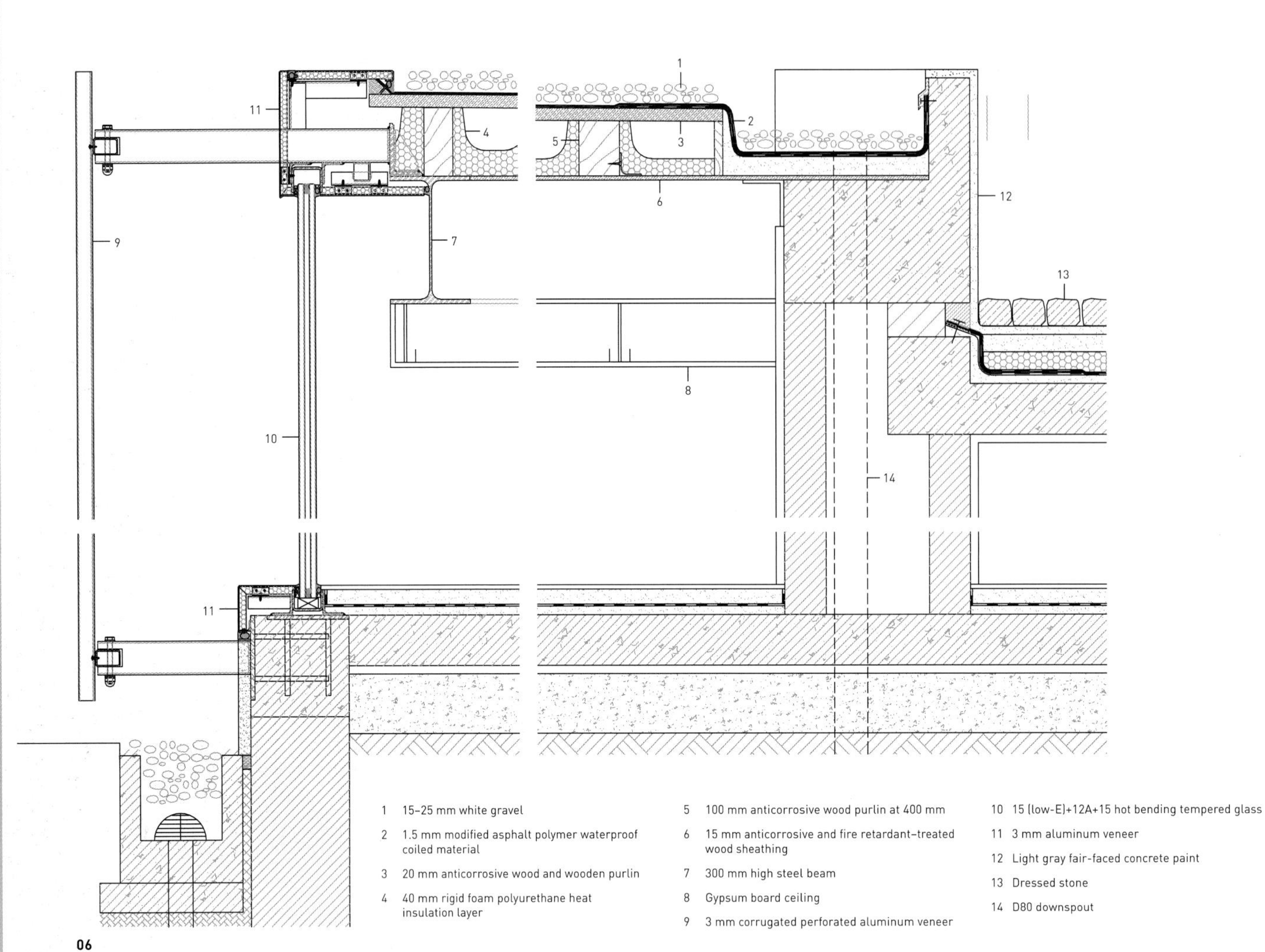

06

07

06 Detailed section at wall and roof

07 Gallery interior

08 View of space between curved tempered glass and perforated aluminum screen

08

The Crystal (Nykredit Bank)

Copenhagen, Denmark — Schmidt Hammer Lassen Architects
Ventilated double-envelope glass system

DESIGN INTENTION

The Crystal, a sophisticated new building for the Danish bank Nykredit, is sited northwest of the existing bank premises. Freestanding, it reads as a transparent, geometrical glazed form which, resting only on a single point and a single line, floats as a visually light, crystalline structure above its plaza.

In terms of both form and scale, the building is an intermediate between the city and the neighboring harbor, and harmonizes well with surrounding buildings. The Crystal's southern side rises to create space for the main entrance, where there is passage under the building and a clear view out toward the harbor and Nykredit's head office building, called the Glass Cube.

The demands of functionality, flexibility, and efficiency inform the interior of the building. The typical floor plan is Z-shaped, forming two atria and ensuring all workstations are well lit and enjoy great views. The disposition of the plan can vary from floor to floor and accommodate an open plan, separate offices, or meeting rooms as needed. All this is supported by the building's rhombic structural system, which is placed immediately inside the facade. The system functions as an architectural element while also allowing interior spaces to be column-free.

The Crystal is designed to interact with its environment, offering a subtle connection between the formal architecture of surrounding buildings and the more natural waterfront area. Its crystal form stands as a piece of sculpture in this urban setting, creating a place-making urban statement.

MATERIALITY

The building's faceted glass facade reflects daylight and the immediate surroundings, but the double-glazing also features an integrated sunscreen that allows the building to adapt to changing light conditions. In addition, the outer glazing system includes a subtle silk print design that mitigates sunlight and enlivens the ambience of the harbor area. The facade is insulated to prevent noise from the busy roads outside.

A holistic approach to the environmental strategy informed many features of the project, including its exterior cladding. The scheme combines a completely transparent office building with exceptionally low energy consumption: The building's operations consume only 22.20 kBtu/sq. ft. (70 kWh/sq. m) overall, 25 percent less energy than required by Denmark's existing energy legislation.

The roof is covered with highly efficient photovoltaic panels that generate up to 80,000 kWh/year. Rainwater runoff is repurposed into graywater for restrooms throughout the building, while circulating seawater provides additional cooling.

TECHNICAL

The glass cladding of occupied spaces uses a sophisticated double-envelope system with a ventilated cavity in the 2.62' wide (800 mm) space between the two glass envelopes, which is sufficient for maintenance access. This space also contains operable horizontal blinds in some locations and fixed glare control in others, as well as the secondary steel framing that supports the outer envelope. A sloping glass roof covers the top while thermal breaks isolate the outer frame from the steel interior assemblies. A gutter at the bottom of the cavity collects any incidental water that condenses within this space. The triple-layered inner glass facade provides extremely effective thermal insulation for this cladding type, with a thermal resistance of R 5.68 ($U = 0.7\ m^2K/W$).

The building operates an automated nighttime cooling strategy where natural ventilation is introduced into the double facade through numerous horizontal vents, then discharged through the atrium skylights, maintaining optimum internal temperatures. Small motors automatically control operable blinds within the double-envelope cavity.

Sunny exposures have a different configuration of fixed and operable blinds that optimize use of daylighting. A subtle silk-printed design on the outer glass facade functions as a sunscreen, creating a harmonious and versatile working environment for employees. The frit patterns vary between glass panels, but also within a given glass panel, giving the facade a visually complex reading of layers.

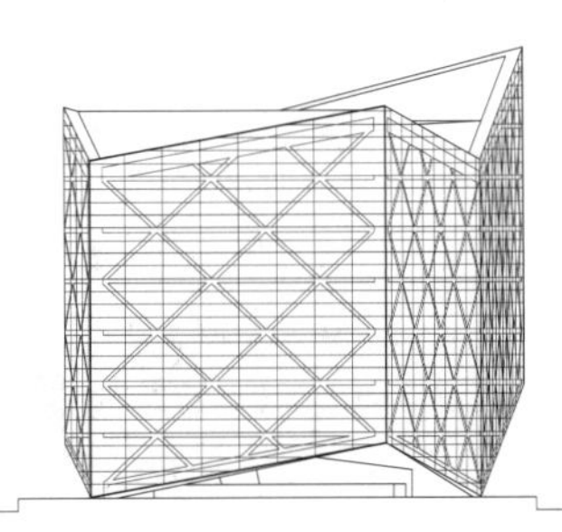

01

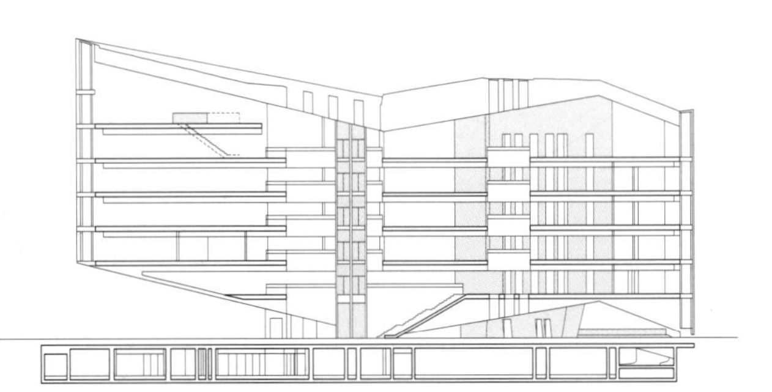

02

03

04

05

01 East elevation showing passage under building

02 Longitudinal section

03 Exterior view from south

04 Exterior view from southwest, with the Glass Cube at right

05 A corner during construction

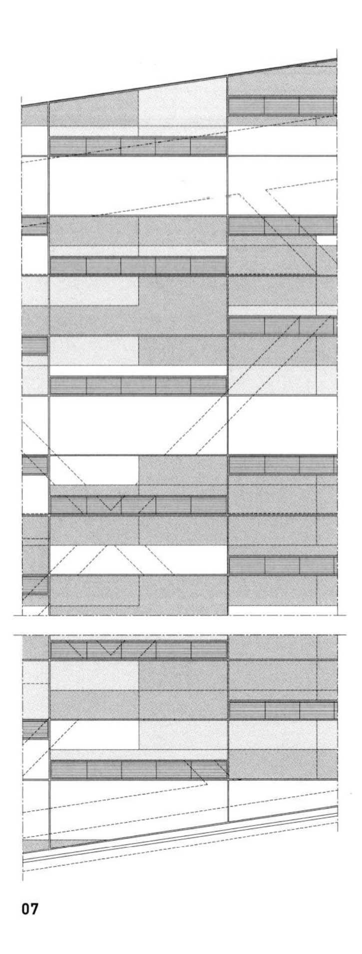

07

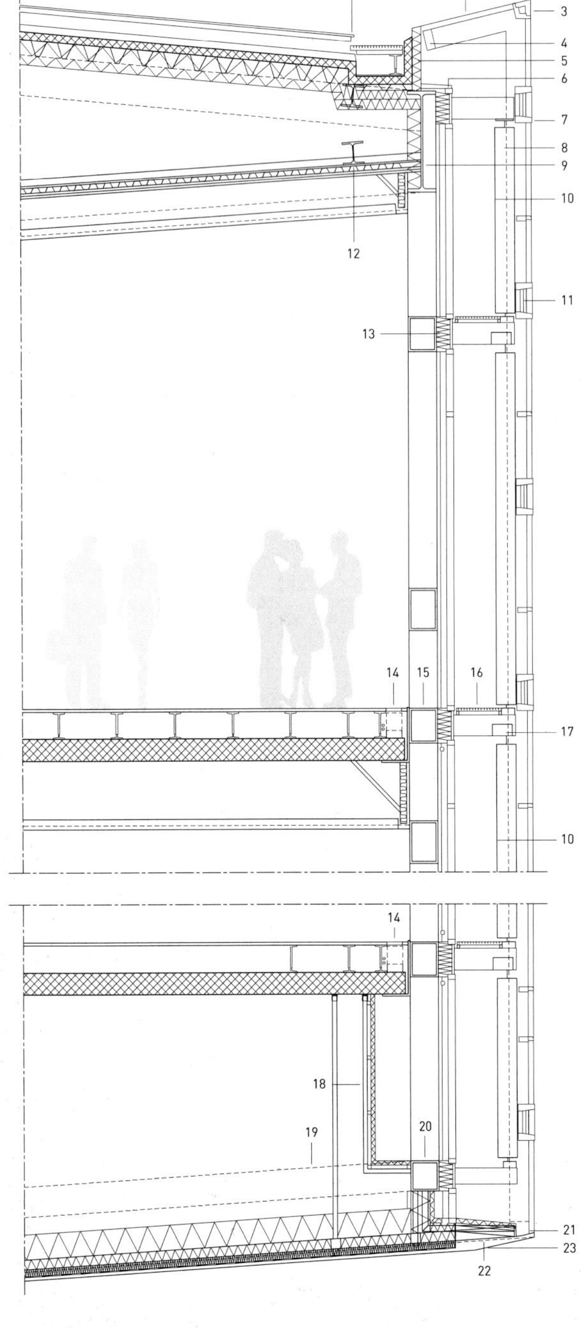

1 Roof construction / gutter
2 Glass roof
3 Top edge facade, silicone joint
4 Steel bracket
5 Insulated facade panel
6 Insulated facade panel
7 Horizontal profile
8 Blinds
9 Steel profile
10 Fixed glare control
11 Air-intake opening
12 Steel substructure of roof
13 Inner bracket
14 Steel panel
15 Horizontal steel profile
16 Insulation: carrying profile, support, maintenance grille, inner bracket, canted metal sheet with integrated rail for glare-control lamellas
17 Blinds wheel: facade illumination, bracket
18 Insulated facade panel
19 Steel substructure
20 Angular steel profile
21 Integrated gutter
22 Substructure for underside cladding
23 Cladding

06

06 Detailed section of wall, roof, and soffit

07 Facade details

08 Site plan

09 Interior at elevated corner

10 Double-envelope facade during construction

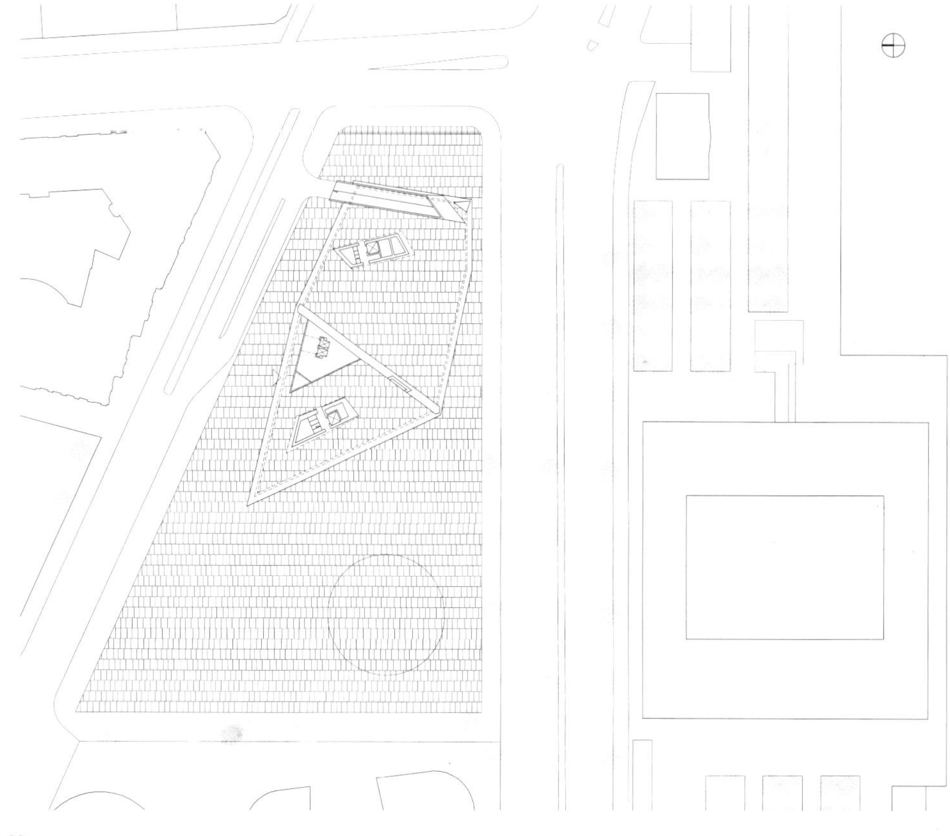

08

09

10

Cité du Design

Saint-Étienne, France — LIN Architects
Modularity

DESIGN INTENTION

The Cité du Design was designed to rejuvenate Saint-Étienne's centrally located but underutilized factory district. The project includes a new facility to nurture the economic and social properties of the existing factories and the city's International Design Biennial, held there since 1998. The 656' long (200 m) building occupies the former site of the city's armory. The placement of the new building acts as a mediating filter in the urban space between the existing Place d'Armes and the main factory building. Adjoining the new structure is an existing building for the École Supérieure d'Art et Design de Saint-Étienne, a school that was renovated to house workshops and classrooms. Glass modular panels gave the architect a flexible design palette that fittingly meshes with the overall materiality and the programmatic features of the new building.

MATERIALITY

A steel space truss spans the entire 102.4' (31.2 m) width of the building. Formed out of nominally equilateral triangles, the steel structural geometry is able to receive any of eleven interchangeable modules, each with varied visual and technical qualities, which can be arranged according to functional purpose, research requirements, or even seasonal preferences. These modular glass pieces fit neatly into the structural steel system and can filter light, control the view, absorb or transform energy, and regulate air ventilation and temperature. Each module demonstrates the sophisticated applications and level of flexibility glass can provide. Inside the long building, each programmatic zone is separated by glazed walls that offer thermal and acoustic control.

TECHNICAL

The single-story building has a concrete floor elevated above a service plenum. Hydronic heating is integrated into the floor slabs. The steel spanning structure has a crowned sectional profile, shedding water to the long edges of the plan.

The space truss spanning system is continuous with the space-trussed wall system and uses the same general kit of parts. Only at building corners, entries, and bases of walls does the fenestration break from the standard triangular geometry. The walls' steel structural members bear on the foundation only with the inner line of vertical supports, while the outer line of supports and the triangular skin overhang the foundation. At the perimeter of the building, the paved ground plane slopes down to the foundation wall, leaving a reveal below the wall assembly. Operable panels below the floor plane can be opened to permit outside air to sweep into the reveals and up through open floor panels into the interior spaces.

The building's envelope is composed of varying interchangeable units that let the triangular modules perform the ideal function for any particular location. In addition to the normal range of exterior envelope concerns like light transmission and thermal insulation, the modular envelope permits such innovative systems as photosynthesis modules and photovoltaic panels. The skin of the building reacts continuously to changes in climate. In the future the panels may be replaced or modified according to changing needs or new areas of experimentation.

The triangular modules come in two sizes: those used on the long walls are 41.3" (1.05 m) and those on the end walls are 47.3" (1.2 m). For vision glass infill panels, the smaller panels use 0.24" (6 mm) float glass, and the larger panels use 0.32" (8 mm). Most glazed modules use insulated glass, although an uninsulated version is also available. In one unit, fixed louvers reside in the cavity within the insulated glass assembly. In another unit, photovoltaic cells convert radiant energy into electricity, but the photovoltaic cells do not fill the triangular panel, permitting dappled light to pass through to the interior. Where light transmission is not important, insulated anodized aluminum panels are used. On the roof, thickly insulated hatches can be installed where appropriate.

Extensive analysis determined the distribution of the triangular modules to deliver optimum functionality to the interior space. There are more than 4,300 triangular panels on the roof alone. These tiny movable pixels making up the envelope constitute an infinite number of configurations for the researchers using the building. A research greenhouse occupies approximately 10 percent of the length of the building.

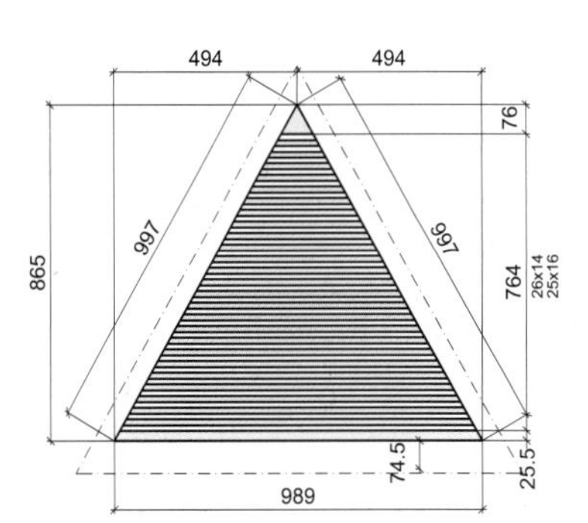

01

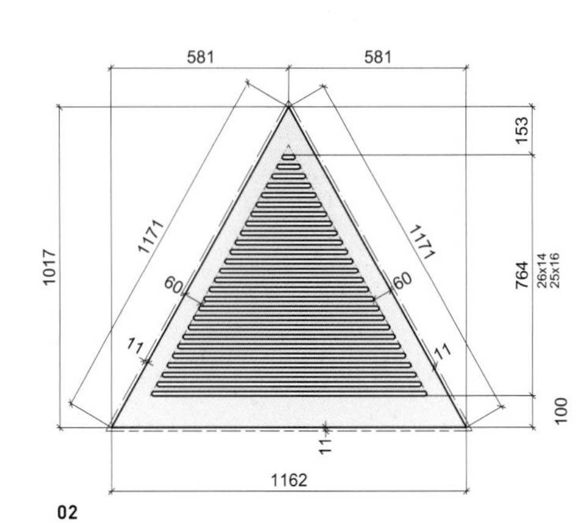

02

01 Plan detail of small glass panel

02 Plan detail of large glass panel

03 Exterior view from north end

03

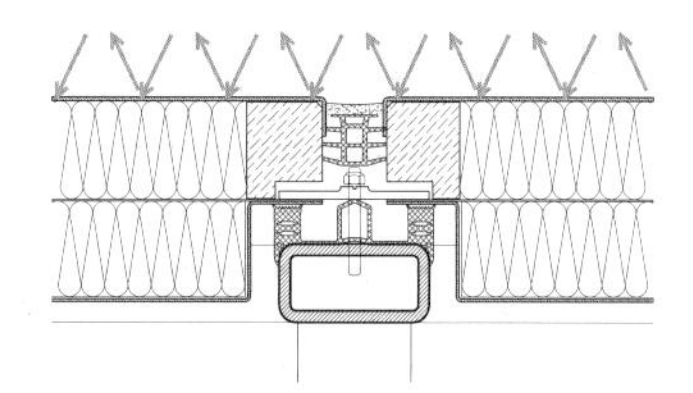

Opaque panels in natural anodized aluminum

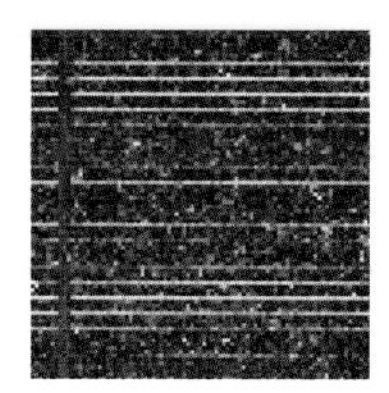

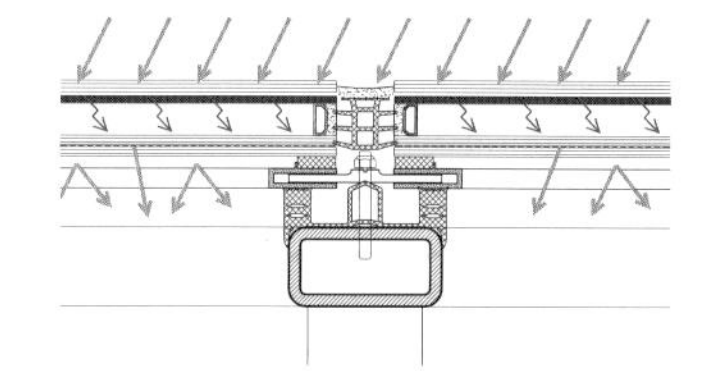

Photovoltaic panels

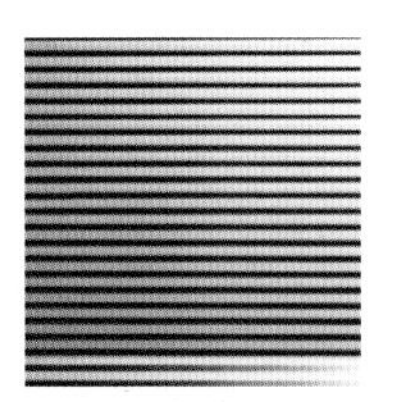

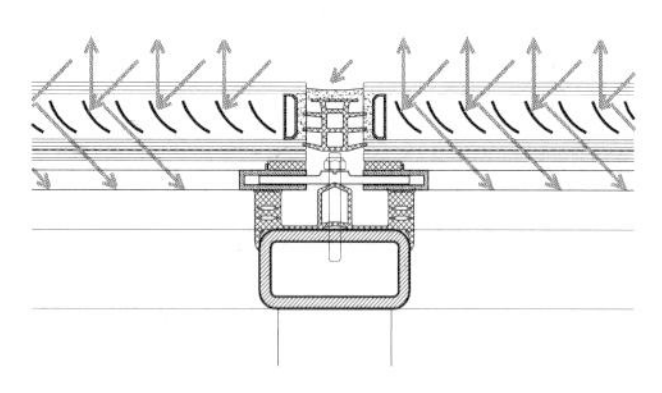

Insulating glass panels with fixed louvers

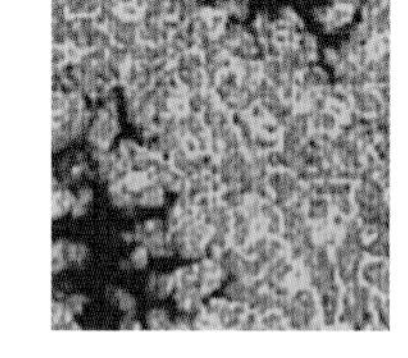

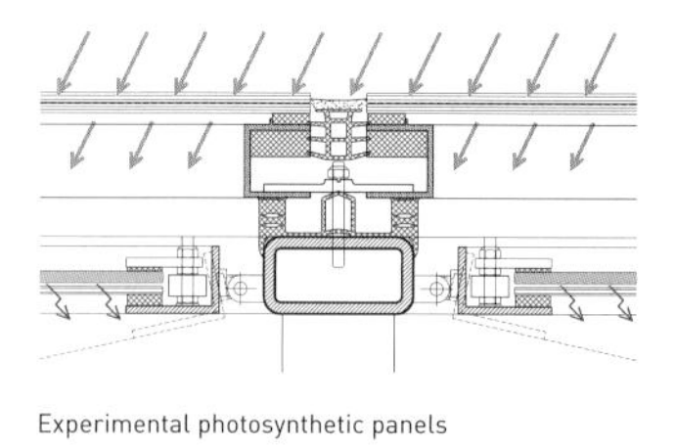

Experimental photosynthetic panels

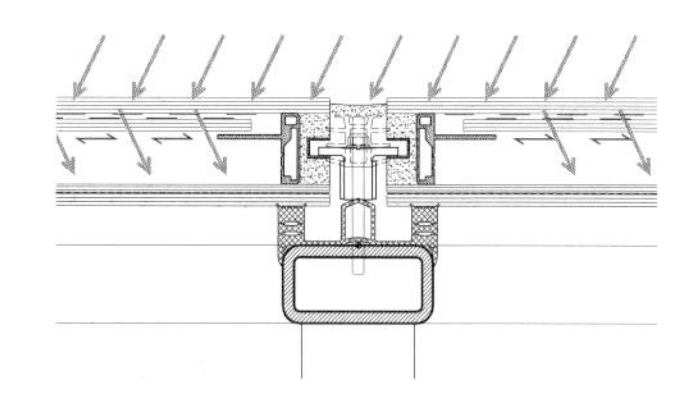

Glazed insulated glass panels allowing light (two sliding windows)

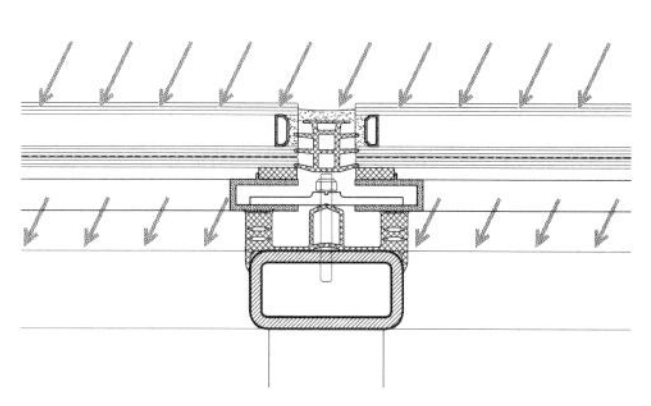

Insulating glazed panels in daylight

04

05

06

04 Sectional details of selected glass modular panels

05 Exterior view toward entry

06 Nighttime view from southwest

07 Triangular panels meet orthogonal boundaries.

08 Partial plan

09 Transverse section

07

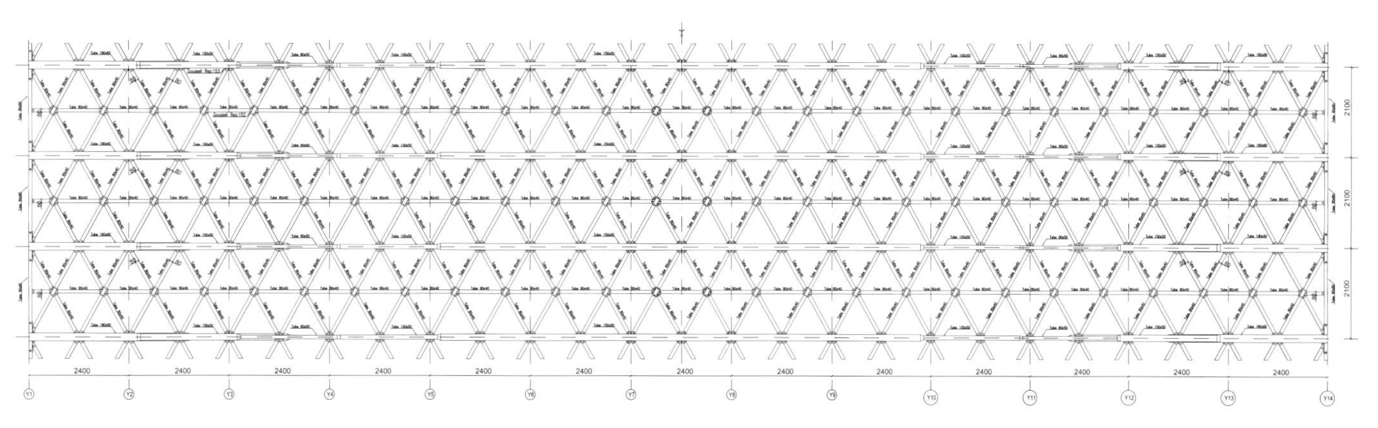

08

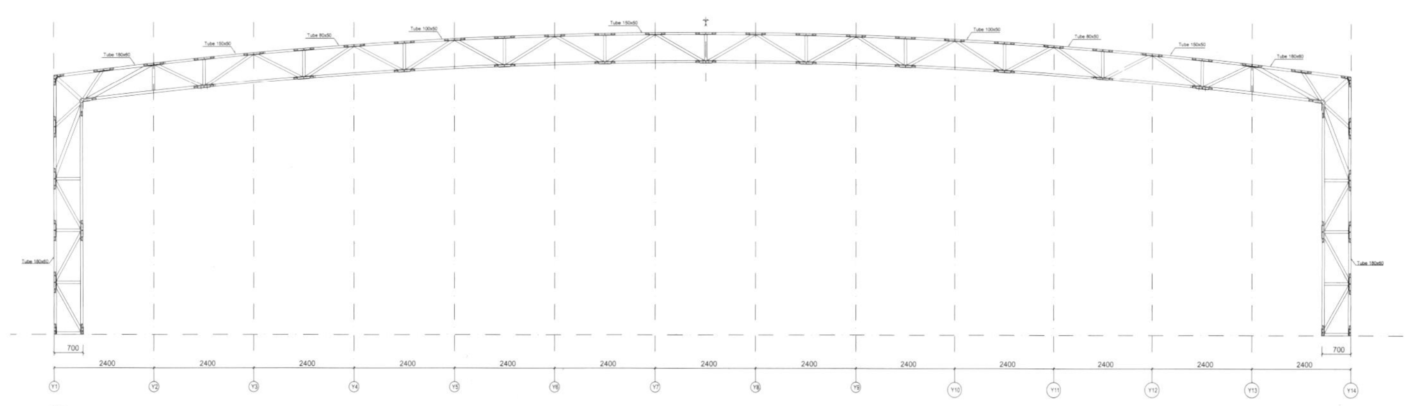

09

Ernst Koller Pavilion

Basel, Switzerland — Berrel Berrel Kräutler Architekten
Insulated glass panels, embossed glass

DESIGN INTENTION

A successful businessman, furniture designer, and film director, Ernst Koller (d. 2002) had great influence on the international aluminum and metal world. Among his most important inventions are double glazing, integrated wood and metal windows, light metal windows and facades, whole-metal facades, prefabricated building methods, exposed building styles, and minimalist skeleton building styles.

The Swiss School for Metal and Building Technology and Berrel Berrel Kräutler Architekten, along with current students (who were significantly involved), intended for the Pavilion to bestow Koller's innovative spirit on future generations of young architects and designers. The result, a modest glass box 430 sq. ft. (40 sq. m) in area, is a creative space for exhibitions and gatherings. The Pavilion is located near the school on a shaded street, where it stands in striking contrast to the natural canopy and an adjoining baroque garden. The Pavilion is snug against the sidewalk, allowing passersby to glimpse its interior details and exhibits. At dusk, the Pavilion is illuminated from the inside, like a glass lantern. The simple plan and modestly sized structure allowed the design to utilize the materiality and inherent characteristics of glass to create a remarkable space.

MATERIALITY

The Pavilion's structure was created chiefly using Koller's patented aluminum H-sections, with other profiles used in minor capacities. The H-sections are 6.8" × 2.4" (175 × 60 mm). Two such sections meet at the corners to frame square voids which conceal downspouts carrying water from the roof.

All walls are insulated glass; horizontal planes include a luminous glass ceiling and a finished floor of exposed black steel plates. The graphic patterns etched on the glass exterior were digitized cross-sections of Koller's patented work in metals. The digital images were printed onto film and embossed onto the cavity face of the outer glass layer as the insulated panels were fabricated.

The frame is a repetitive grid of aluminum members braced with diagonal steel rods. The glass wall panels are the enclosure system over the metal frame. With neither a heating nor cooling system, the Pavilion relies on an insulated floor and roof during the winter and deciduous trees for shade in the summer.

TECHNICAL

The Pavilion's custom-fabricated glass walls were made using 14.7' × 3.9' (4.5 × 1.18 m) insulated panels. Additional panels at the corners are 4.8' wide (1.46 m) to cover the corner assemblies. Each glass panel is made of 0.66" (17 mm) laminated safety glass for the outer layer, a 0.79" cavity (20 mm), and a 0.51" (13 mm) laminated safety glass inner layer, for a total thickness of 1.97" (50 mm)—about twice as thick as normal insulated glass.

The wall panels are supported by the same aluminum frame that they wrap. Angles from the frame cantilever to elevate the lower edge of each panel 0.5" (12 mm) above the stone base. This slender reveal not only visually separates the glass panels from the ground features, but also provides a space through which outside air can pass to the interior, naturally ventilating the interior space when the aluminum floor vents are opened.

The Pavilion aptly demonstrates applications of custom fabrication and the potential strengths of glass. In one instance, the designers were able to achieve minimal seams at the panels' vertical corners by extending the outer layer of glass beyond the inner layer of glass and the panel's sealed edge. This variation of a quirk miter corner minimizes the panel edge's exposure to weather. The small reveal between panels at the corners is not sealed; rather, the designers relied on the newly formed pressure-equalized cavity to deter water intrusion. A second example occurs at the seams of adjoining panels that meet at vertical aluminum mullions. The sealed edges of the insulated glass panels are recessed slightly into the cavity, which permits an aluminum flat bar to be inserted and screwed into the vertical mullion from the outside, pressing the inner glass layer uniformly against gaskets at the panel edges. The reveal between the outer layers of glass is made watertight using a backer rod and sealant.

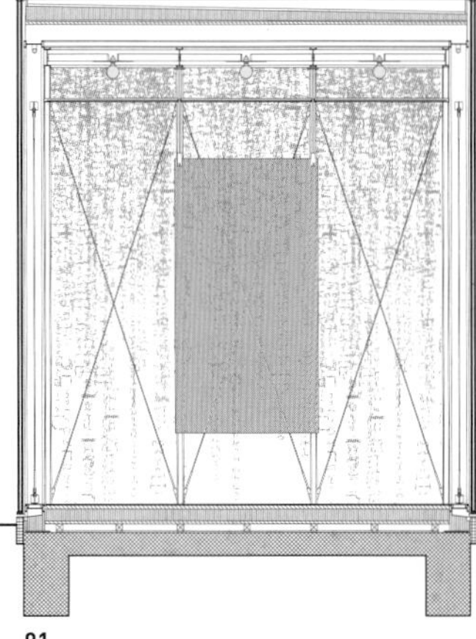

01

02

01 Transverse section

02 Glass facade from garden

03 Longitudinal section

04 Exterior view from pedestrian walkway toward entry

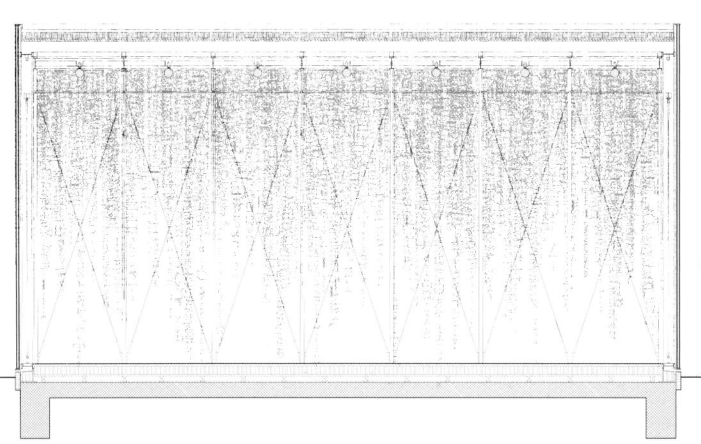

03

04

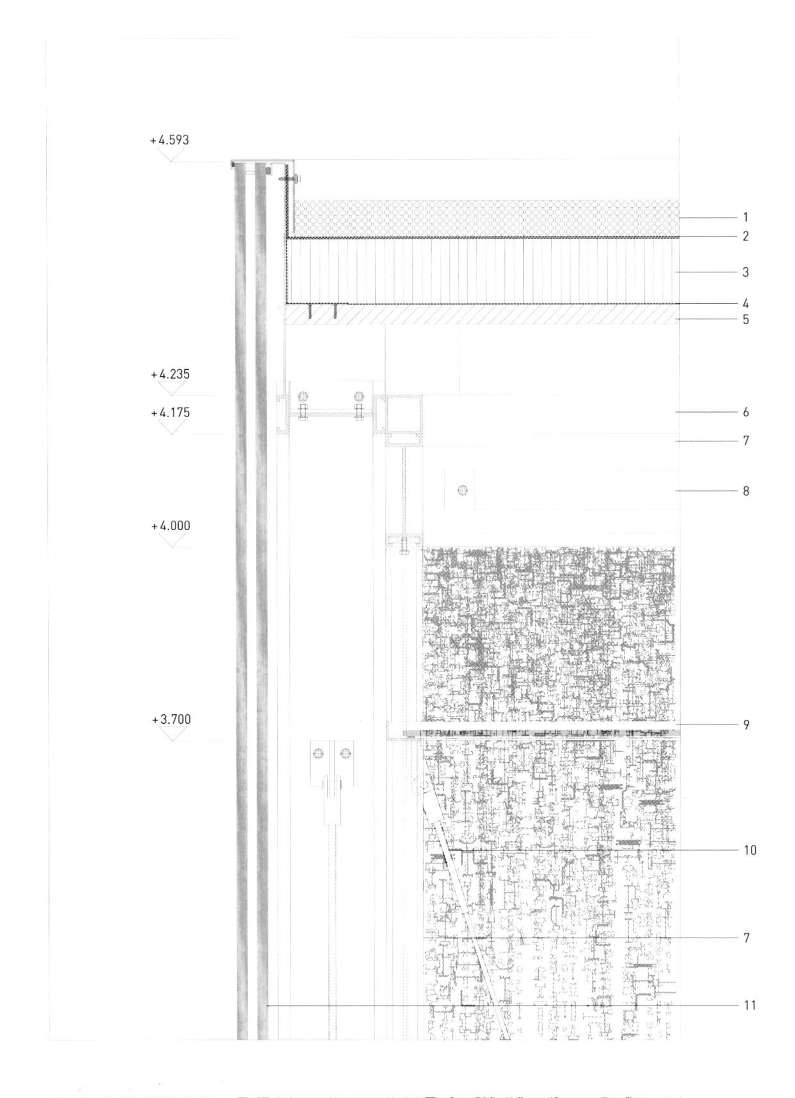

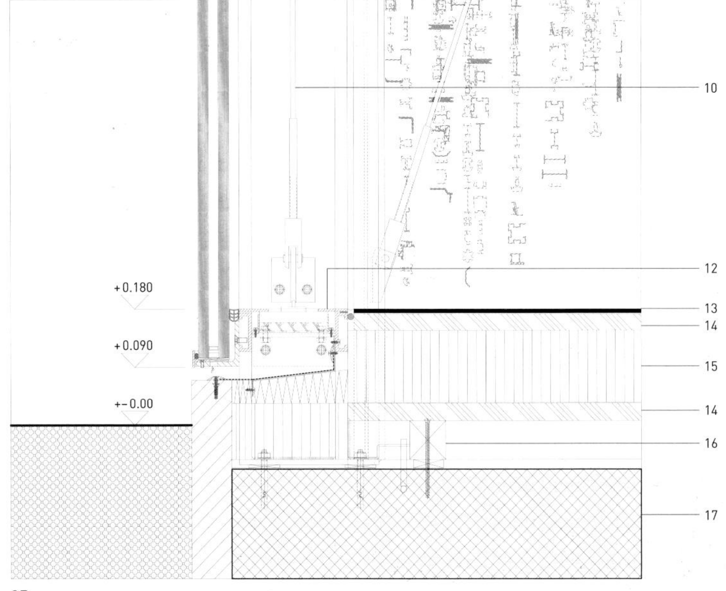

1 50 mm bed of gravel
2 Asphalt sheet sealing layer
3 100 mm thermal insulation
4 Vapor barrier
5 25 mm oriented strand board
6 60–60–6 mm structural hollow section
7 175 × 60 Koller naturally anodized aluminum H-section
8 60 × 8 mm at bar for light fixing
9 False ceiling with 6 mm toughened glass
10 Steel tension rod
11 Double-glazed 17 mm laminated safety glass with print, 20 mm cavity, and 13 mm safety glass
12 Naturally anodized aluminum cover to air supply duct
13 4 mm black steel sheet
14 25 mm plywood
15 100 mm polystyrene thermal insulation
16 60 × 60 mm wood strips
17 Reinforced concrete

05

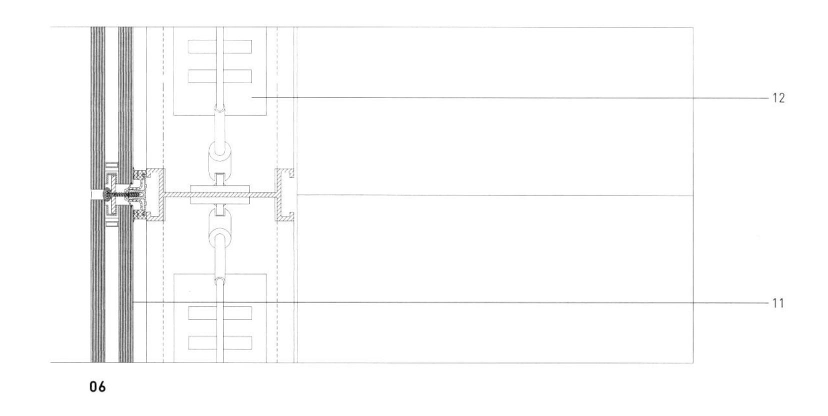

06

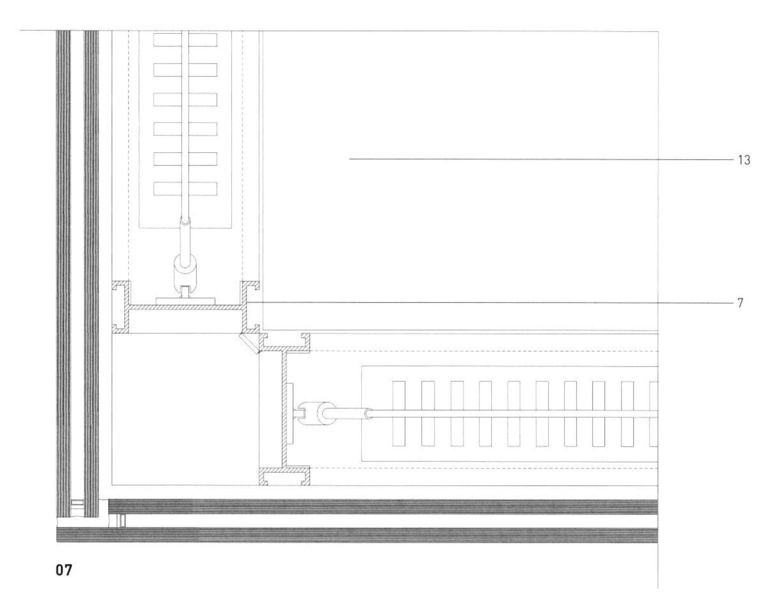

07

08

09

05 Detailed section at wall and roof

06 Plan detail at intermediate column

07 Plan detail at corner

08 Gallery interior

09 Entry facade

Apple Flagship Store

Shanghai, China — Bohlin Cywinski Jackson
Curved tempered laminated glass

DESIGN INTENTION

The design of Apple's flagship retail stores often display innovative uses of glass, especially for fixtures and stairs. The Shanghai store is no exception. A crystalline lantern, the store's prominent glass cylinder connects the surrounding urban plaza to the retail space below. Its prominence and high visibility in this location called for a unique and unprecedented structure. Transparency was the entry piece's primary design goal. Because polymers can fade, haze, or discolor over time, especially when exposed to ultraviolet light, glass was preferred whenever possible.

The space is arranged around a central circulation tower that suggested the radial geometry of a lantern, appearing here as a cylinder with a strong vertical axis. A 10'-wide (3 m) reflecting pool surrounds the cylinder, complementing the use of glass with increased reflectivity and light. The pool encircles the glass structure except at the entry, which is a 60-degree segment of the cylinder.

MATERIALITY

Glass, while beautifully transparent, also forms the building's hardworking exterior envelope. Featuring previously unrealized dimensions and shapes of glass products, the envelope functions structurally in novel ways.

Crystal-clear glass is sometimes undesirable for a particular application, such as the stair treads at the lantern's center. Imagine the privacy concerns of a see-through staircase, or the danger its smooth, impermeable surface might present on a rainy day. To eliminate both concerns, the layers of the glass treads are frosted and have a raised diamond tread pattern, like those commonly found on metal steps. Though still impermeable, the texture provides safer footing while maintaining the stunning ephemeral quality of glass.

Glass, like many dense, mineral-based materials, has a high level of thermal conductivity. In cold weather, this can lead to abrupt changes from a comfortable interior air temperature to the cool inner face of a glass skin, whose heat is quickly conducted to the outer surface. When the interior temperature falls below the dew point, condensation droplets may accumulate, detracting from the intended visual clarity. To mitigate the potential for condensation, air-conditioning supply grilles are located at the interior base of the lantern. Fan coil units propel dehumidified air toward the glass, preventing condensation by removing moisture.

TECHNICAL

The Shanghai Apple Store's cylindrical lantern is 41' tall × 32' in diameter (12.5 x 9.75 m) and is structured using laminated, tempered glass. The glass cylinder is composed of twelve vertical face panels, supported by triple-laminated structural glass mullions at 30-degree intervals. The panels run the full height of the building, an unusual and admirable feat; the only interruptions are two curved doors and their flanking panels.

The glass cylinder challenged designers and fabricators to find new processes to produce the glass elements, which had to be curved to very specific shapes. Because of the store's urban location, the designers anticipated various potential impacts, from toddlers to excited shoppers and errant equipment. To provide appropriate durability and load-bearing strength, the glass had to be tempered and then laminated. Of course, once it is tempered, glass cannot be altered in shape or size, so each layer in this project had to be given its final configuration beforehand. This labor-intensive process brought together curved glass pieces that differed slightly in radius and size, so that when the three pieces were finally laminated, their edges met in proper alignment. Using a process adapted from the automotive industry, a thin layer of polyester film was placed between layers of tempered glass, and the entire sandwich was then placed under high pressure and temperatures to melt the film without de-tempering the glass.

In an effort to maintain clarity throughout the lantern, the designers used custom-made metal hardware to join all finish wall surfaces and structural glass fins. The fins are composed of three layers of tempered and laminated glass. Glass panels are fabricated with holes to receive the stainless steel hardware, with dense rubber washers between them to soften the forces.

This hardware strategy is also applied to the structural glass elements that support the 16.17'-high spiral stair (4.93 m) with an outside diameter of 20.5' (6.25 m). The stair's central glass tube is anchored to the floor at the retail level below. It is composed of six pieces of glass of uniform height. Its outer curve is a ribbonlike stringer that is only supported where it touches the floor near the lowest tread, and where it is connected to landings and glass beams cantilevered from the central cylinder at 60-degree intervals. The treads themselves are composed of four layers of glass. One of the inner layers is recessed to accept inserts and hardware that connect the treads to the vertical supports. Each of these trapezoid-shaped treads has two such connections at the outer end and one at the inner end.

The cylinder's glass roof has a subtle slope and is supported by glass beams spanning the fins. All of the fittings are made of stainless steel or titanium. The joints between the exterior panels are sealed with structural silicone.

The glass innovations in this project were the result of diligent collaborations between parties on at least three continents. The project team included architects and engineers, but also glass systems engineers, specialized manufacturers, and fabricators. Separate interior and exterior assembly crews installed the finished glass products. The architects' drawings, including many 1:1 scale details, became federally registered patents owned by Apple.

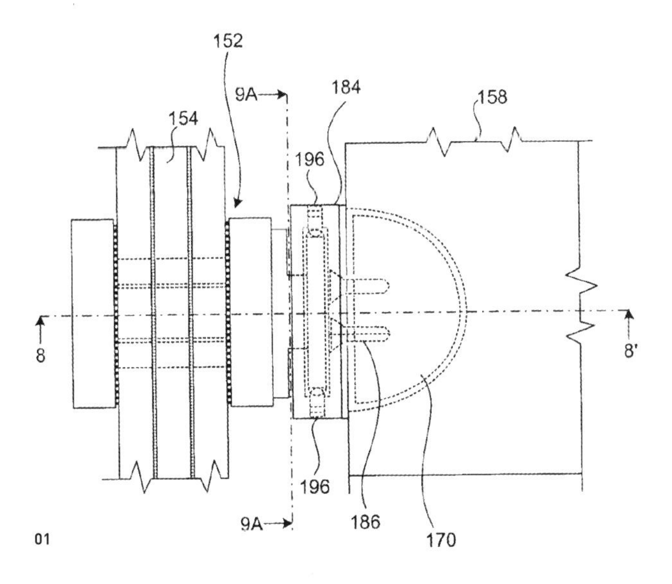

01

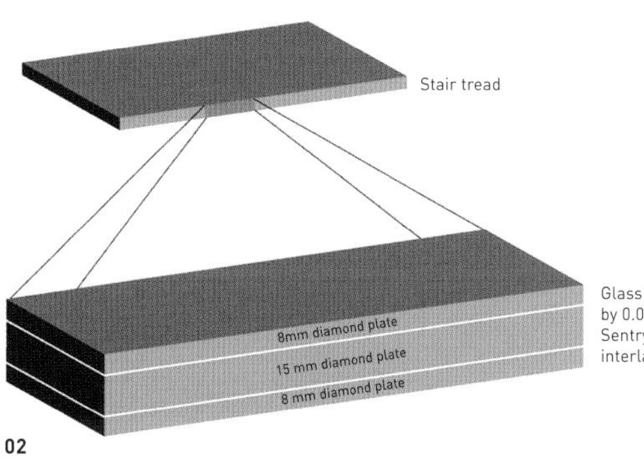

02

03

04

05

01 Plan detail of connection between laminated glass treads and structural glass supports. A full description is available in US Patent "Staircase" D478999 S, August 23, 2003.

02 Diagram of laminated glass treads

03 Exterior view at entry from urban plaza

04 Glass treads and structural glass supports

05 Curved glass stair and floor assemblies

Concrete

THE BASICS

Concrete's massive and monolithic quality results from a mixture of Portland cement, water, and aggregate (usually made up of crushed stone or gravel and a fine sand). As a material it is strong in compression, and when enhanced by steel reinforcement it can also have great tensile strength. Concrete can take any shape or form through casting, and can have a variety of surface textures, finishes, and colors.

Concrete's uses in architecture are numerous and diverse. It can be used for structural members including columns, beams, roofs, floor slabs, footings, and foundations, as well as for cladding and paving. It is a fireproof construction material, as it neither burns nor rots. It is also relatively low in cost. Perhaps its most advantageous quality is its sculptural malleability; it is a shapeless material in which form, size, and texture must be designed.

Concrete varies in quality according to the proportions and characteristics of the cement, water, and aggregate from which it is made. Its strength is determined by its water/cement ratio: generally, the less water, the more strength. This ratio also affects the material's water resistance and durability. *Admixtures*—materials added to the base of water, cement, and aggregate—can be mixed into the concrete to improve its workability or to change its characteristics, such as increasing its strength, speeding or slowing its curing time, or changing its color or texture (see pp. 54–55).

Aggregate makes up approximately three-quarters of concrete's total material volume, giving the material its main structural capability. Therefore the strength of a concrete mix also depends heavily on its aggregate. In most applications, the ideal is an evenly graded mix of fine and coarse aggregate. Portland cement is a fine gray powder, and is manufactured from a number of raw materials, including lime (derived from limestone, marble, or seashells), iron, silica, and alumina (all derived from clay or shale). When water is combined with the cement, an exothermic reaction forms chemical bonds with the aggregate and releases heat—known as the *heat of hydration*, or *curing*, which is a byproduct of the setting and hardening of the concrete. Concrete's specified compressive strength is generally developed within twenty-eight days after placement, but its strength continues to increase as the hydration process evolves.

HISTORY

The ancient Romans discovered concrete while quarrying limestone for mortar. They unearthed a silica- and alumina-bearing mineral that, when mixed with limestone and burned, produced a cement. This cement—which we now know was an early version of Portland cement—was much more adhesive and cured more quickly than any material they had seen, and it utterly transformed their construction technology. This early version of concrete can be seen in the unreinforced dome of Hadrian's Villa, a palace built near Rome between 125–135 CE. As the Roman Empire disintegrated, the knowledge of concrete technology was lost, not to be rediscovered until 1756, when a British engineer, John Smeaton, performed the first scientific investigations of cements. In 1824, Joseph Aspdin patented what he named Portland cement, after the English Portland limestone. Portland cement has remained the dominant cement used in concrete production ever since.

Reinforced concrete was invented and developed simultaneously by several engineers in different countries during the 1850s. In Paris in 1854, J. L. Lambot built reinforced concrete boats with iron bars, wire, and mesh. This technique of reinforcing concrete with steel did not become widespread, however, until after a French gardener, Joseph Monier, registered for a patent for reinforcing concrete flowerpots with iron mesh in 1867. He later adapted his process to build concrete water tanks, bridges, and eventually beams and columns. Also in 1854, William Wilkinson from Newcastle, England, began to use reinforced concrete in house construction, applying for a patent for the construction of "fireproof dwellings, warehouses, other buildings and parts of the same." A French builder named François Coignet built concrete houses using iron-reinforcing rods in France and the United Kingdom from 1850 to 1880. In the United States, Thaddeus Hyatt made and tested reinforced concrete beams during the 1870s. Hyatt's research is generally now credited as the basic principles of how we use reinforced concrete today. In 1875, a house with reinforced concrete walls, beams, floors, and stairs was built in Port Chester, New York, by W. E. Ward, and is considered the first reinforced concrete building in the United States. Also in the 1870s, a French builder named François Hennebique applied for a patent for a reinforced concrete system to build concrete houses. He established a franchising empire to build concrete houses in many countries, including France, Belgium, Italy, and South America. By the end of the nineteenth century, major structures were being built of reinforced concrete, and engineering design methods were established for its use. In the 1920s, French engineer Eugene Freyssinet created a scientific basis for *prestressed concrete*, an invention that allowed concrete to be used in large-scale structures. Freyssinet's research and design led to roads, bridges, and large harbor construction, as well as airplane hangars, such as one at Orly Airport in Paris.

As the twentieth century progressed, concrete's material qualities were employed in such remarkable structures as Frank Lloyd Wright's Unity Temple (1905) in Oak Park, Illinois, the roof of Le Corbusier's Ronchamp Chapel (1955) in France, Eero Saarinen's Dulles Airport Terminal (1962) in Virginia, and TWA Terminal at JFK Airport in New York (1962). In each of these projects, the architect used the material to achieve a very specific design goal by exploiting the inherent properties of concrete.

DESIGN CONSIDERATIONS

The biggest advantage to using concrete for designers is its range of possible forms and shapes, limited only by its formwork. Concrete's sculptural qualities and variety of surface textures, in addition to its structural capabilities, makes it a versatile design tool. It can take on linear forms in the shape of beams and columns, just like steel and wood; it can mimic the dense, wall-like forms of stone or masonry. Uniquely, concrete can also take on a planar form, such as a floor slab. It is a material that has such vast possibilities that magnificent designs can result—though magnificent failures are not uncommon. Craftsmanship and forethought are critical in concrete design in order to avoid the mundane character of which the material is also capable.

Executing a desired appearance takes a great deal of knowledge and foresight. Detailed specifications, drawings, and discussions between the architect and the contractor are necessary to achieve the desired quality, and material mock-ups and site visits may be required for a very specific appearance and outcome. For foundations and other purely functional purposes, where the concrete's appearance does not matter, detailed specifications are still vital to ensure the correct densities and ratios of concrete that will perform its function in the building.

However sculptural and moldable concrete is, minor imperfections in its surface are typical. Though part of the material's inherent character, it is difficult to get a perfectly smooth surface of uniform color. Using smooth, nonporous materials such as metal to line the formwork helps, but there are many factors to consider to achieve a desired surface texture. The concrete mix itself, the aggregate size within the mix, admixtures, the casting and finishing techniques, environmental conditions, and even the scheduling of the concrete trucks—all affect the material's ultimate appearance.

Concrete surfaces can have an wide array of textures or colors. Surfaces can be sandblasted to expose aggregates for a specific aesthetic; dyes and mineral pigments can be added to concrete to achieve almost any color, as in many concrete floors; polishers and coatings can also be applied after curing to achieve a smooth or coated surface. When still freshly mixed, concrete can be manipulated to achieve a preferred texture, or objects can even be cast into the concrete.

Concrete can fail as an architectural material if any component of its mixing, placement, or curing is incorrect. Other disadvantages include its weight and the complexities involved in the forming process. There are some recent advances in concrete technology, however, in which admixtures can improve these shortcomings. Recently developed admixtures can lighten concrete's weight without compromising its strength. For instance, *high-performance concrete* is an ultra-light concrete containing fibers that make the material self-reinforcing, eliminating the need for any steel components. This allows for thin concrete members to be manufactured without losing any structural capability. *Self-consolidating concrete* has admixtures that allow the concrete to stay extremely fluid during the pour without compromising the strength of the material. It does not require vibration after pouring and enables pouring into complicated molds or similarly constrained areas. Newly developed *transparent concrete* contains glass fibers or resin that allow varying levels of light transmission. These are just three of the many advances and areas of research in concrete technology. The desired appearance of the material is arguably limited only to the extent which a designer is educated about the material and the limits of that designer's imagination.

TYPES

Reinforced concrete

Reinforcing concrete with prefabricated steel components lends added strength to the material. This is an inspired marriage since the steel is protected from corrosion by the concrete and the concrete gains the metal's tensile strength, a quality it does not possess on its own. Reinforced concrete is well-suited to situations where both tensile and compressive strength is needed. Most commonly, steel reinforcement bars, high-strength steel cables, or steel mesh are placed in the concrete in areas where there will be tension. *Prestressed concrete* is created by applying a compressive stress to concrete by *pre-tensioning* it with steel strands. In prestressed concrete, the concrete is cast around stretched, high-strength steel strands, allowing it to cure, then the external tensioning force on the strands is released. Stress is then transferred to the concrete, taking advantage of its intrinsic strength in compression. Most precast concrete structural elements are prestressed. *Post-tensioned concrete* is made by stressing lubricated steel strands after the concrete is cured. Site-cast concrete spanning systems such as beams and floor decks are often post-tensioned. Both prestressed and post-tensioned concrete result in more slender, efficient assemblies than conventional reinforcement.

Reinforced concrete is most often used in structural beams, columns, wall panels, slabs, or any other structural project, such as bridges and roads. Designers of reinforced concrete buildings must take care to design and construct them well, or the steel can corrode and rust, and cracking can occur. In wet and freezing conditions, some building codes require epoxy-coated rebar and/or a sealer to keep water out and to prevent cracks and failure.

Cast-in-place concrete

Cast-in-place concrete, also called *poured-in-place* and *site-cast*, is defined as concrete that is poured directly on-site. An advantage to this site-specific method is that the concrete is cast specifically for one job, allowing for an unlimited sculptural quality with no restrictions on size or shape since it is cast exactly where it will remain. However, the construction process can be slow, as more time is needed to build or set the formwork at the site. Additionally, since the formwork is made on-site and in some cases is not used again, the costs can be higher. This cost can be defrayed if premade, reusable formwork is used. Cast-in-place is not without risk, since environmental conditions will affect the pour, and controlling temperature and moisture can add cost and difficulty.

The formwork into which the concrete is cast acts as a mold that holds the shape of the concrete until it has hardened and has developed sufficient strength to support its own weight. Formwork can be a major cost consideration. It can be either specially constructed for each project or purchased as reusable, prefabricated units of standard lumber, plywood, metal, fiberboard, or reinforced synthetics. The key to typical formwork is that it be strong and stiff enough to support the large weight and fluid pressure of wet concrete. Forms must also be tight to prevent loss of liquid or cement paste. Generally, the higher the quality of formwork, the better the resulting concrete. Formwork is usually coated with a release agent or other suitable material before the concrete is cast to prevent water absorption or unwanted bonding between the form and the concrete. *Form ties* are metal devices that are used to prevent the formwork from spreading as the lateral load of plastic concrete is imposed. When the formwork is removed, the wires or rods remain in place and are usually twisted, broken, screwed, or pulled off, depending on the type of form tie. The configuration of the form panels and the location of the form ties are important design considerations in wall appearance.

Precast concrete

Precast concrete is generally made at a factory before being moved to and installed at the site. It uses an automated system of mixing and casting in a controlled environment, which yields consistency in craft and materials. It can be cast as panels, slabs, and beams, as well as complex shapes for structural or enclosure elements, or any other form in the building construction. Precast building systems are a booming industry; their use can accelerate the construction process and can also be a timesaving and cost-effective method for projects that utilize a number of uniform or large-scale members, such as airports, parking structures, or stadiums. Precast concrete cladding panels that are attractively finished and contain insulation and some building services are becoming more and more viable.

The formwork in which precast concrete is cast is usually made of high-quality steel, coated plastic, or wood and can be used many times, yielding a more consistent and controlled concrete member. Since the formwork is not made on-site (or used only once), this reduces the unit cost of the concrete products. Time is also conserved since there is no formwork to fabricate or remove from the site. Precast units are usually treated with steam to create the ideal amount of moisture and heat for the concrete to cure quickly. Precast concrete products can be cast, cured, and removed from forms in twenty-four-hour cycles, with a high-quality result. On the construction site, precast members can be erected very quickly, much like steel. They can also be erected in poor weather conditions without having to wait for concrete to cure properly, in contrast to cast-in-place concrete.

Because precast concrete must be transported to the site, there are a number of practical limitations to consider. The concrete units can often be extremely heavy and large, making transportation to the construction site difficult, as the size of the units are prescribed by the legal highway or rail line capacities between the factory and the building site. The infinite sculptural qualities of concrete can similarly be constrained by these transportation restrictions. Some portions of a building cannot practically be precast due to the size or shape of the piece, or the logistics of transportation and erection. Foundations, slabs on grade, or other large elements cannot be precast. Repetitive, consistent, and manageably sized elements are the best choices for precasting.

Precast concrete can also be cast at the site and then moved with heavy machinery into its final location. One of the most common of these practices is called *tilt-up concrete*. This method eliminates the constraints of transporting precast members over roadways to the site, but climate considerations and proper formwork need to be addressed, as with cast-in-place concrete.

Concrete masonry units

Concrete masonry units (CMUs) are technically considered a type of unit masonry, but are made using special concrete that is precast into formwork. CMUs are typically manufactured as hollow-core 8" × 8" × 16" (200 × 200 × 400 mm) blocks. They are usually cast in metal molds, released immediately, and then steam-cured to a specific moisture content. The blocks can be made with different densities of concrete dependent on their intended use. They are often employed as back-up walls for brick or stone, but are increasingly used alone as an economical structural wall construction. Their hollow cores allow for reinforcing steel and grout to make the wall load-bearing.

The American Society for Testing and Materials (ASTM), which establishes standards for materials of construction, governs CMU use for load-bearing construction. C90 is the common, hollow load-bearing unit, and is the most economical masonry wall one can construct. Among others, the C129 is a hollow, non-load-bearing unit, the C145 is a solid load-bearing unit, and the C55 is cast in a common brick dimension. The ASTM also specifies different grades, types, and weights for each block. CMUs provide an economical way to build a load-bearing wall relatively quickly and easily. One can also achieve an insulated wall with CMUs when the hollow cores are filled or when a cavity wall is constructed. Strength can be increased by filling the CMU cells with concrete and steel. CMUs are available in an almost endless array of colors, textures, and sizes, giving a designer many options. Their disadvantages include the weight of the units and the dependence on skilled workmanship at the construction site. Unless a CMU wall is built well, it can be unattractive, leak, or have structural problems.

Autoclaved aerated concrete

Autoclaved aerated concrete (AAC), also called *autoclaved cellular concrete* (ACC), is a lightweight, thermally efficient, and structural concrete that has been in use in construction in Europe since the mid-twentieth century. Its use in North America is still much less prevalent, primarily because the investment in manufacturing equipment and infrastructure is quite costly. It is a silica-rich material that contains sand or fly ash (a byproduct of coal combustion), lime, Portland cement, aluminum powder, and water. AAC is often not made with fly ash due to availability and its quality control. The aluminum powder reacts chemically with the other materials and creates tiny hydrogen bubbles, causing the concrete to expand to approximately twice its original volume. The mix is then moved into an *autoclave*—an airtight chamber filled with pressurized steam—where the porous material gains strength, durability, and rigidity via chemical reactions over a twelve-hour period.

AAC can be used in load-bearing walls for shorter buildings and as curtain walls in taller buildings. It has a very high air content, causing it to weigh about two-thirds less than conventional concrete, and has nearly twice the thermal insulation values. It has approximately 1/5 the density of standard concrete and 1/10 the compressive strength. AAC can be manufactured with different densities; higher densities result in higher compressive strength but lower insulation values. Unlike normal concrete, which usually needs additional insulation, AAC can function as a structural insulating wall by itself. The overall insulation value varies, depending on the climate, the R-value, and the thermal mass effect. It can be formed into blocks, panels, lintels, or floor slabs, and has been utilized as an alternative to wood, as it can be shaped by conventional carpentry tools, is relatively lightweight, does not rot or burn, has fairly good sound absorbing qualities, and resists insects. One of the disadvantages of using AAC is that it has a high embodied energy due to the high energy demands of the autoclave. It also might not perform as well as more conventional types of construction in warmer climates. AAC needs to be protected from the environment and surface abrasion with siding, plaster, stucco, or other suitable finishes.

Rammed earth

Rammed earth construction is the forceful tamping to compact a mixture of earth and cement into a formwork system to create a dense and structurally stable wall. Professionally constructed rammed earth involves using heavy mechanized pneumatic equipment with a rubber or steel tip to efficiently compact the soil. The mix is approximately 8 percent water, 3 percent cement, and 89 percent soil. Ideal soil contains both sand and clay, but should not contain organic materials such as peat or loam, which would decompose. Formwork may be textured or smooth to give the final surface different qualities. It must be heavily reinforced to withstand the force of the compactor. Walls are typically made at least 1' (305 mm) thick to allow for the compacting equipment to reach each "lift" of earth of 4–12" (100–305 mm). Each lift can be differentiated if a striated final appearance is desired, or the appearance of each lift can be minimized for a monolithic effect. Rammed earth walls have a good thermal mass, and are energy efficient, fire resistant, and considered environmentally friendly. They have their disadvantages: it is difficult to ensure the correct earth mix, and the labor can be more intensive (and therefore costlier) than other construction types. Considerations for utilities and HVAC systems integrated into the walls must also be taken into account.

Fiber cement

Fiber cement is a manufactured product increasingly used as a siding material. It is a combination of cellulose fiber material, Portland cement, silica, sand, water, and other additives. This fiber material provides tensile strength and helps prevent cracking. It is made in sheets and autoclaved (a process described above). The intense steaming actually gives fiber cement a low moisture content, making it a stable product that has little warping or movement. It is a good product to use in place of wood where there is excessive moisture or a chance of termites. It can be made into boards for a horizontal lap siding or in a panel sheet, much like the proportions of standard plywood, for siding purposes. It can be applied in much the same way as wood siding; however, its higher weight makes it more unwieldy to manage relative to a wood product. Fiber cement products are usually available with a smooth face surface or an embossed texture that mimics actual wood.

Transparent concrete

Transparent concrete is concrete that allows partial light transmission through resin or other optic fiber additives. Resin concrete, for example, can have up to a 20 percent transparency and still retain its strength. The concrete uses a dry ready-mix concrete product with a thermoplastic polymer resin that does not crack or undermine the structure. This thermoplastic polymer has a light transmission factor of 92 percent and has moderate resistance to UV rays and chemicals. The mix also contains inorganic materials such as alumina, which allows the material to cure with out the use of water. The resins are very often clear, but can also be different colors. Transparent concrete can also be made with optic fibers, which often proves very costly. The advantage of transparent concrete is that it allows the filtering of light in a structural and thermally resistant wall.

Ultra high performance concrete

Ultra high performance concrete (UHPC) is high-strength concrete, also called *reactive powder concrete*. This type of concrete does not require steel reinforcement bars or mesh, nor does it require vibration during the placement process. The mix flows readily and easily into formwork without air voids. The reinforcement of the concrete is from high-carbon steel fibers (or polyvinyl alcohol fibers) within the mix, making it inherently strong. This gives the concrete a high tensile and compressive strength and allows for panels and wall thicknesses to be reduced by 50 percent or more. It contains cement, silica, sand, and water, as does most concrete, but it also contains the distinctive ingredients of ground quartz, wollastonite (a siliceous mineral fiber), and other fiber reinforcement. This type of concrete is resistant to chemicals and water penetration and also has a high resistance to abrasion.

Graphic concrete

Graphic concrete is a new technology; its primary feature is a custom-designed graphic that is integrally adhered to the surface of a precast concrete element. This process is only possible in a controlled manufactured precast setting. The process involves applying an inhibitor on a special membrane to which the designed patterns are printed. This membrane is then spread over the concrete mold where the concrete is cast. The membrane inhibits the chemical curing process in the only the locations of the image. After curing of the element, the slow-curing concrete in contact with the inhibitor is flushed away, revealing the design chemically etched upon the surface of the concrete. This design is permanently imparted to the concrete surface. In addition, the portion of the panel surface that was in contact with the inhibitor is slightly recessed from the face of the panel.

Fabric-formed concrete

Fabric-formed concrete is a reinforced concrete construction that uses flexible fabric membranes as formwork. The flexible, lightweight, and inexpensive qualities of the fabric membrane relative to traditional formwork makes this a newly attractive way to cast concrete for use in cast-in-place or precast members. Beams, panels, columns, and slabs—almost any shape can be cast using this method. The flexibility of the membrane allows for easy curves and smooth surfaces. This process also may result in higher-strength concrete as a result of the filtering action that allows air and excess water to pass through the fabric formwork. Because this formwork is flexible, the form of the resulting piece is determined by the interaction of the heavy concrete with the fabric. Weight distribution of the freshly mixed concrete must be carefully calculated and modeled to achieve the intended form. The resulting appearance of fabric-formed concrete can take on endless designs of forms, textures, and shapes.

Self-consolidating concrete

Self-consolidating concrete is a type of concrete that optimizes the aggregates, admixtures, and cements in its mix to balance strength with workability. *Superplasticizers* (a type of admixture described below) are especially useful to make the mix flow freely without compromising the concrete's strength. Because of its fluidity it can be poured into intricate formwork and produce a fine, smooth surface. The mix does not require vibration due to its fluid consistency.

Admixtures

Admixtures—materials other than water, aggregate, and cement that are added before or during the mixing process—can greatly improve the quality of concrete by increasing its strength, workability, and durability, and can help it cure under adverse environmental conditions. In addition to improving the performance of concrete, admixtures can also add color or change its final appearance.

AIR-ENTRAINING admixtures increase concrete's workability and are considered one of the most common and beneficial admixtures. They also protect concrete from freeze-thaw damage by having thermal insulating properties. In high concentrations, concrete containing these admixtures is lightweight and non-structural, given its proportion of air to mass. These admixtures reduce concrete's strength, so a consultation with engineers is important to ensure the concrete will withstand the stresses of the application.

—

ACCELERATING admixtures make concrete cure or harden more quickly, reducing construction time and project costs. These admixtures allow for formwork to be removed sooner and, in colder climates, may give the concrete much-needed strength before the onset of freezing temperatures. However, they can also cause shrinkage and discoloration of the concrete as it cures. Calcium chloride, a common ingredient in accelerating admixtures, can corrode any embedded ferrous metals (such as steel) in the concrete. Therefore use of this chemical must be carefully monitored.

—

RETARDING admixtures slow down the curing or hardening process, allowing more time to place and finish the concrete. Retarders are commonly used in massive engineering applications, especially in the construction of bridge decks, dams, and very large foundations. They offset the normally high temperatures given off during the hydration process and avoid complications when unavoidable delays between mixing and placing occur. Due to the longer timeframe for setting, concrete containing retarders may be vulnerable to environmental conditions during the curing period. It may also be more vulnerable to *creep*, a permanent deformation in a material caused by structural stress.

—

SUPERPLASTICIZERS are organic compound admixtures that transform a stiff concrete pour into a more fluid and workable mix. They also can permit a reduction of the water content to increase the concrete's strength. Slag cement, fly ash, and microsilica are some ingredients that can plasticize the concrete to make it more workable and keep the water content low without sacrificing the concrete's compressive strength.

—

WATER-REDUCING admixtures allow for a 5–10 percent reduction in the amount of mixing water needed while retaining the same amount of workability for the concrete. These different chemicals can produce a higher-strength concrete and aid plasticity, but may slow the hydration process and decrease the early strength of the concrete. Different types of chemicals added to concrete can be called water-reducing admixtures; their advantages and disadvantages vary depending on the particular chemical used.

—

FLY ASH admixtures are made from a powdered waste product of coal-fired power plants and can increase concrete's strength and decrease its permeability. They can also improve a mix's workability and reduce the required amount of mixing water.

—

POZZOLANS admixtures are mineral admixtures that include cementitious materials and natural pozzolans such as volcanic ash, fly ash, and silica fume. These admixtures improve the workability of the concrete and reduce the internal temperature during the curing process. If the internal temperature of curing concrete gets too hot, the pour will not cure properly, possibly compromising its structural integrity and causing shrinkage or cracking.

—

PIGMENTING admixtures can be added to concrete to achieve a desired color. There are three primary methods for coloring concrete. The *integral method* mixes the coloring agent throughout the concrete mix, usually done while the concrete is in the batching silo or mixing truck. The resulting colors are generally muted but are uniform throughout. The *dry method* of coloring is applied to exposed surfaces after the concrete has been placed. The coloring agent is troweled into the surface and forms a thin veneer of color on the slab. These colors are generally more vibrant than the integral method because the concentration of pigment on the surface is typically greater. Finally, concrete can also be colored with a chemical stain that penetrates cured concrete surfaces, generally producing an uneven and variegated color effect due to varying absorbencies of the concrete surface. Chemical stains react directly with the existing concrete's minerals and pore structure.

In addition to these admixtures there are many others, all of which have particular purposes. *Freeze-protection* admixtures allow concrete to cure at temperatures below 20 °F (11.1 °C). *Fibrous* admixtures—short fibers of glass, steel, or plastics—give the concrete added reinforcement at a micro-level. *Shrinkage-reducing* admixtures (SRAs) decrease the effects of drying shrinkage by reducing the concrete's surface tension, and *corrosion-inhibiting* admixtures contain calcium nitrite to protect reinforcing steel, and any other ferrous metal within the concrete, against corrosion.

Movement Joints

Buildings move due to many factors, including thermal change and environmental stress. Movement is often accommodated by separating sections of a building to move independently within a prescribed range. Building movement joints are the flexible connections between these sections. There are four basic types of concrete joints:

CONTROL JOINTS allow for controlled cracking along a formed, tooled, or cut joint. They allow for shrinkage of the sections of concrete.

—

CONSTRUCTION JOINTS occur when successive concrete pours abut one another. Seams between successive pours, called *cold joints*, are often a point of weakness; reinforcement bars and interlocking keys may be used to tie the two concrete members together.

—

EXPANSION JOINTS are engineered joints that allow two adjacent structural elements to move independently of each other when subjected to stresses. They allow for both contraction and expansion of the concrete sections.

—

ISOLATION JOINTS, which are a type of expansion joint, are used to separate concrete into individual structural elements or to isolate the concrete from other construction materials.

The size and frequency of joints varies depending upon many factors, including thermal and moisture conditions, loading conditions, and strength of the materials.

Hämeenlinna Provincial Archive

Hämeenlinna, Finland — Heikkinen-Komonen Architects
Precast concrete, graphic concrete

DESIGN INTENTION

The Provincial Archive is a public institution that preserves, displays, and makes accessible to researchers the records of the past. It was conceived as an important public building that should play a visible and recognizable role in the townscape. Much more than a place to store historic documents, it is the depository of the collective memory of this province, approximately 50 miles (85 km) north of Helsinki. The building is a dramatic departure from the typical anonymous warehouse or office block.

The Archive's different programmatic elements are housed in separate volumes, each of which expresses its purpose through its appearance. The public functions are in an open, transparent street level; above that, administrative functions are held in a simple aluminum-clad volume. The archives themselves, the most public faces, are contained in a volume clad with concrete panels etched with decorative figures, a contemporary take on ancient inscribed stone that was inspired by the historical documents, stamps, and writings stored within.

MATERIALITY

The exterior precast concrete panels are highly finished and exposed to view from the inside and out. They aesthetically and symbolically contribute to the building's surfaces, and also exclude unwanted ultraviolet light from penetrating the archival storage spaces. The patented graphic concrete method involves applying a surface retardant to a custom-printed template. The template is spread over the mold table, and the concrete is carefully cast against it. The template inhibits the chemical curing process as it proceeds normally in unexposed areas. After curing, the template and retardant are flushed away and the image or pattern remains—a result of the contrast between the concrete surface against the form (fair-face) and the slightly lighter eroded portion, where the fine aggregates within the concrete are exposed.

Any design that can be screen-printed can also be used in this method. It can be incorporated into any precast concrete elements, but cannot be used in cast-in-place. The manufacturer consults with designers, trains precast element fabricators, and urges all parties to experiment with concrete mixes, pigments, and aggregate colors to find ever more interesting results. This partnership of material manufacturer and designer achieves an allegorical and relevant meaning to the building.

Cast-in-place concrete columns support cast-in-place concrete floor slabs. The roof deck is made of precast-concrete-cored slabs covered with rigid insulation and a thick layer of lightweight concrete.

TECHNICAL

The graphic concrete panels were cast horizontally, upon templates already positioned in the form. At the time of construction, templates were limited to a maximum of 10.5' × 4.1' (3.2 × 1.25 m), so multiple templates had to be grouped together to form some of the images on the faces of the archives. The precast wall panels come in four sizes—with widths of 19.4' or 21.7' (5.9 or 6.6 m) and heights of 7' or 4.7' (2.1 or 1.4 m). The wall panels consist of a 7.9" thick (200 mm) structural concrete inner layer, 7" (180 mm) of rigid insulation, and the 3.5" thick (90 mm) graphic concrete cladding.

The exterior layers are mitered to fit together tightly at the corners of the building, permitting the detailed etchings to be continuous around corners, as they are across all horizontal and vertical seams in the plane of the wall. Horizontal and vertical seams between panels are only 0.63" (16 mm).

A continuous thermal envelope minimizes heat loss and protects the archival storage. It also encapsulates the thick inner layer of structural concrete and the floor slabs so that they serve as a thermal mass. Weeps occur in the horizontal seams between panels at intervals of approximately 4.7' (1.4 m). They are made of inverted U-shaped stainless steel and assure that any water within the precast panel can exit.

01

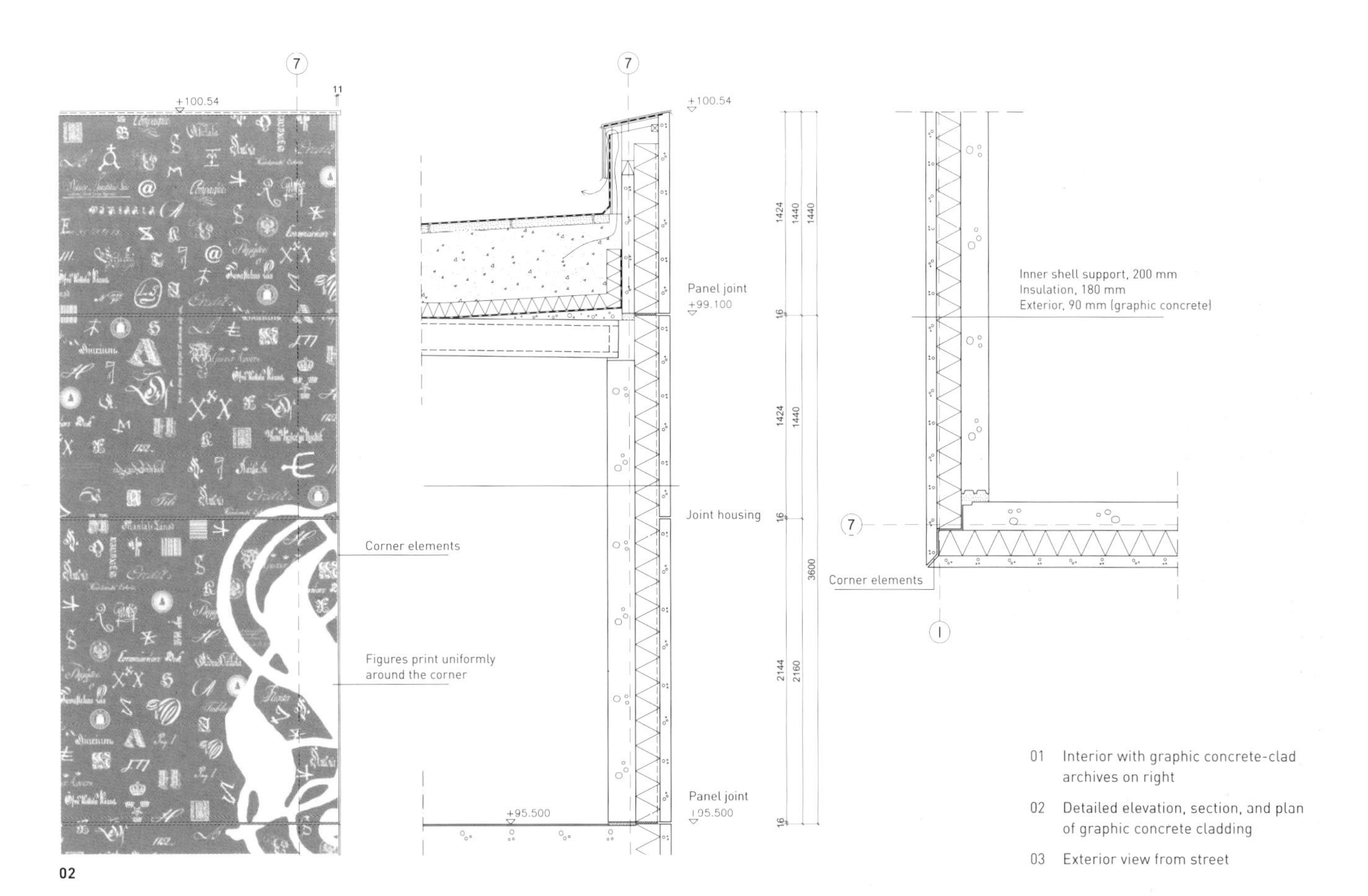

02

01 Interior with graphic concrete-clad archives on right

02 Detailed elevation, section, and plan of graphic concrete cladding

03 Exterior view from street

03

Casa Pentimento

Quito, Ecuador — José María Saez & David Barragán
Precast concrete modules

DESIGN INTENTION

The prime objective for this single-family home was to connect its occupants to their physical surroundings. With a limited budget, the designers searched for a solution through clarity, reduction, and simplification, preferring inexpensive or even free resources such as natural light, the temperate mountain climate, and common, locally available materials.

This was accomplished by designing a single prefabricated concrete form that would comprise the structure and include walls, furniture, ladders, and even enclose the garden. Economies of scale placed emphasis on the design of a versatile shape that could be assembled in varied ways for different functions. The walls of the house take on many functions: They can be camouflaged as a fence or hedge in some areas, and in others they become stacked flower pots—vertical extensions of the garden.

MATERIALITY

A darkly pigmented concrete slab serves as the foundation. It adapts to the topography, either bypassing or embracing the surrounding trees as they are encountered. The prefabricated system rests upon the slab, connected via vertical steel rods with epoxy to the slab and threaded through precast pieces. This tight structural network of small columns and short-span lintels is especially well suited to the area's seismic activity.

The precast concrete elements came in a standard size and configuration, but were easily placed in four positions within the assembly. Each piece is 39.3" long, and approximately 9.8" in height and width (1,000 × 250 × 250 mm). The interstices are left open at some points and closed in others, using either transparent/translucent acrylic or opaque wood as desired. Inside, these same interstitial connections sometimes conceal electrical services, and help to support wooden shelves, seating, tables, and steps.

Although the site is located near the equator, this Andean setting, at an elevation of more than 7,700' (2,300 m), is actually very mild. Temperatures vary from 53–86°F (12–30°C), with only minor fluctuations from day to night. Therefore the house required no thermal insulation nor any mechanical heating or cooling systems. The thermal mass of the precast concrete assemblies combined with natural ventilation options provides sufficient thermal control.

TECHNICAL

The precast concrete elements were fabricated less than ten miles (16 km) away. Steel formwork was used to yield elements with consistently smooth, almost polished surfaces. Each of the six forms could produce eight elements per cycle, for a total of forty-eight elements per day. The elements themselves were light enough to be placed by hand. All of the concrete aggregates came from the same local quarry. Consistency of mix was carefully monitored to give the concrete uniform appearance and physical properties. To increase its workability, a very fine aggregate size and limestone dust were used, as was a plasticizer admixture. The plasticizer also allowed the water / cement ratio to be somewhat lower, which increases strength and water resistance. A waterproofing additive was also used to reduce weathering on exterior exposures.

Welded wire fabric made of steel was embedded into each precast concrete element to increase their tensile capacity. The wire used was 0.16" diameter at 4" on center (4 mm at 100 mm on center). The four vertical steel rods that link the elements together were 0.39" (10 mm) in diameter, and were welded to a steel frame at the top of the walls. A cast-in-place concrete roof slab engages this frame and provides lateral support to the walls.

01

02

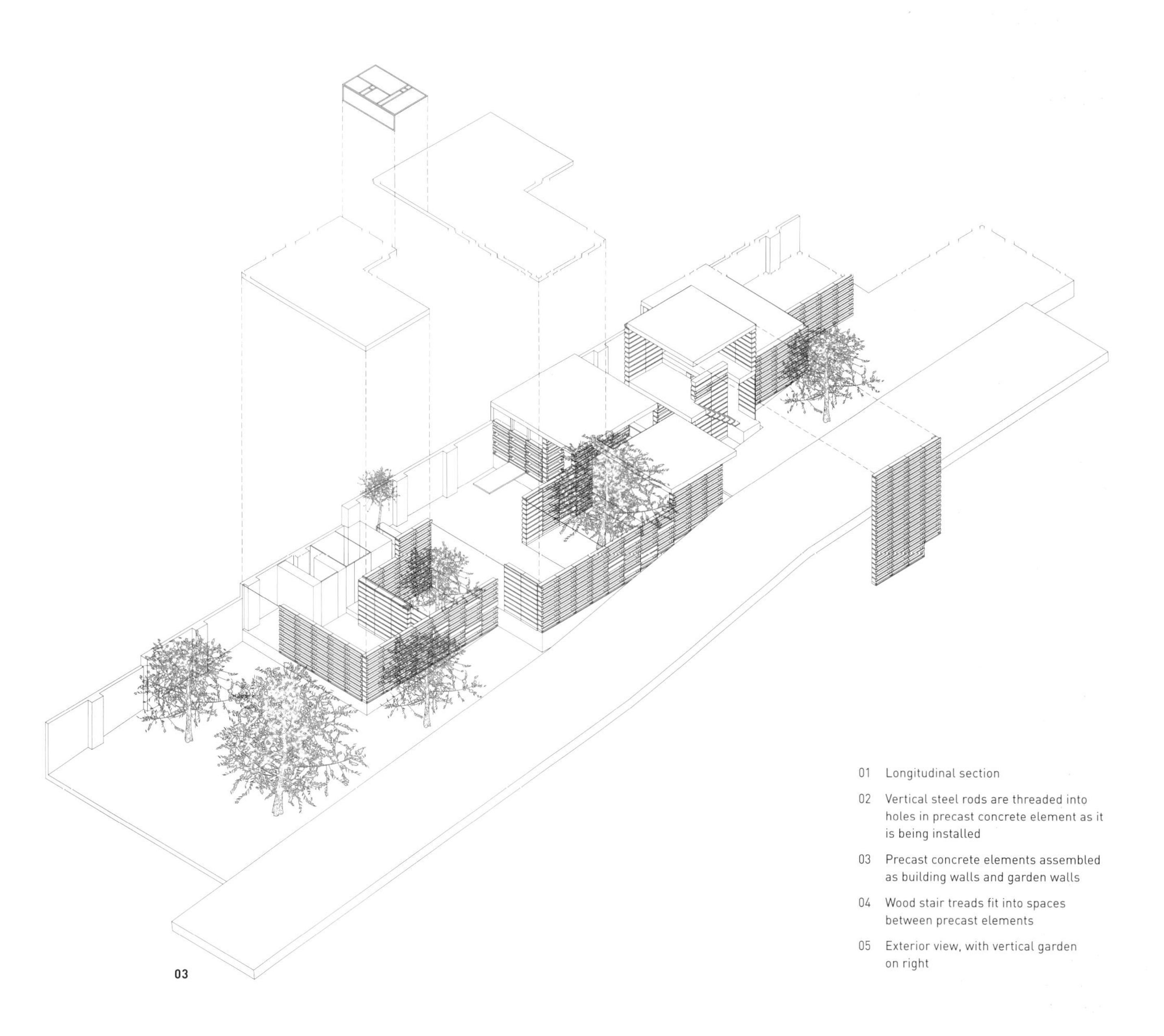

03

01 Longitudinal section

02 Vertical steel rods are threaded into holes in precast concrete element as it is being installed

03 Precast concrete elements assembled as building walls and garden walls

04 Wood stair treads fit into spaces between precast elements

05 Exterior view, with vertical garden on right

04

05

Design Indaba 10×10 Housing Project

Cape Town, South Africa — Design Space Africa Architects (formerly MMA Architects)
Cement-based stucco

DESIGN INTENTION

The 10×10 Low-Cost House was the entry of South African architectural firm Design Space Africa to an invited competition hosted by Design Indaba, a multidisciplinary design platform that supports creative spirit in a wide range of media. For the competition, ten South African architects were paired with international firms to design low-cost housing solutions for Cape Town's Freedom Park neighborhood. The project brief called for a dignified yet low-cost house of 450 sq. ft. (42 sq. m), in either a detached or duplex configuration, arranged in a grouping of ten such houses. The budget of approximately $6,480 (€4,200) per house prompted the designers' search for material innovation. This timber-framed structure filled with sandbags and plastered with stucco was an award-winning solution.

The architects also wanted to demonstrate that green technologies need not be expensive, but can be easily implemented and accessible to a wide market. The building components and materials were simple, readily available off-the-shelf products, but even with low-tech assembly methods the actual cost of the house was approximately $9,725 (€6,250). The cost, however, was ultimately acceptable to the developer. The other design teams failed to produce solutions that met such challenging objectives, so this design was adapted for use for all ten housing units.

MATERIALITY

The design emphasized local production of construction elements whenever possible. For example, the prefabricated wood-frame EcoBeam construction system was locally produced in Cape Town and the Freedom Park community helped to fill the sandbags and assisted in building assembly. By involving unskilled community members in the construction, the project both delivered affordable housing and economically empowered the local community, contributing to its sense of ownership of the houses. Cement-based stucco covers the structure. It contains chemicals that combine with the water in cement and waterproof the structure against hydrostatic pressure, and it was painted on both sides. The thermal qualities of the sand and the simplicity of the construction system, which is from abundant sources and low in embodied energy, make it an innovative and genuinely local design.

TECHNICAL

After the initial grading of the site, prefabricated EcoBeam frames were set in place. The frames were prefabricated for this specific project using a 35.4" (900 mm) module between verticals, which was adapted to frame window and door openings. The wood frames for the walls were 8.9" thick (225 mm), made using 1.5" × 1.5" (38 × 38 mm) wood elements in all three axes. It was erected on wooden "sole plates," which were secured to sandbag foundations stabilized with 2 percent cement. This frame became the armature that guide all subsequent steps in the construction of the walls.

The wood frames were filled with sandbags stacked in an overlapping pattern, like running bond in a masonry wall. Each course of bags was tamped to consolidate the minerals and remove air pockets. Chicken wire covered the sandbag-filled frame to provide reinforcement for the subsequent stucco coatings. Walls were covered with two-coat stucco, 0.8" thick (20 mm) on the inside, and 1.2" (30 mm) thick on the outside. Paint was applied on both interior and exterior wall faces.

A 3.94" deep (100 mm) reinforced concrete ring beam increases the strength of the wall assembly immediately below the joist and rafter bearing. It continues at that elevation around all of the perimeter walls as a unifying bond beam. Since sandbag construction had not been previously used in two-story applications, this concrete ring beam provides added structural integrity.

The exterior walls are extraordinary hybrids of several conventional wall typologies. Some are more commonly found in masonry assemblies (the ring beam, bonded courses of sandbags, and metal ties), while others (the prefabricated wood frame, its modular dimensioning, and wood siding exterior finish) are more typical of traditional wood frames. The cement-stabilized sandbags and trowel-applied stucco supplement masonry and wood features by contributing strength and durable finishes.

The walls remain vulnerable to water, which could deteriorate the wood frames in the walls, leach cement out of the mineral mixes, or corrode the mesh reinforcement in the stucco. To decrease water intrusion, the tops of walls were either covered with metal roofing, or if a parapet, capped with waterproofing. When water does manage to penetrate the walls, observation has shown that it passes through the stacked sandbags downward to the ground, rather than laterally toward the interior space.

01

02

01 Completed houses

02 Exterior view during construction

03 Ground-floor plan

04 Upper-floor plan

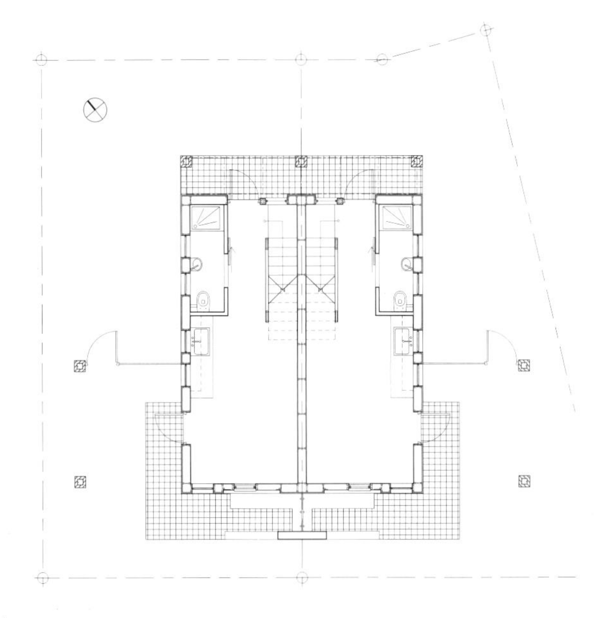

03

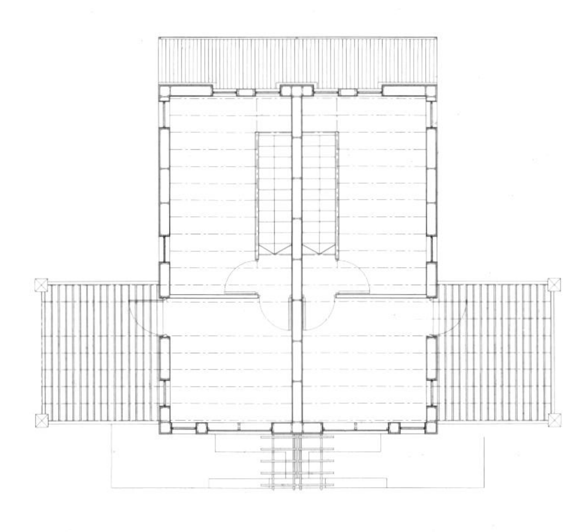

04

05 Plan detail of opening in wall

06 Elevation of wall construciton assemblies

07 Members of community prepare sandbags for construction

08 Sandbags stacked in EcoBeam frames, before chicken wire and stucco application

09 Typical wall section

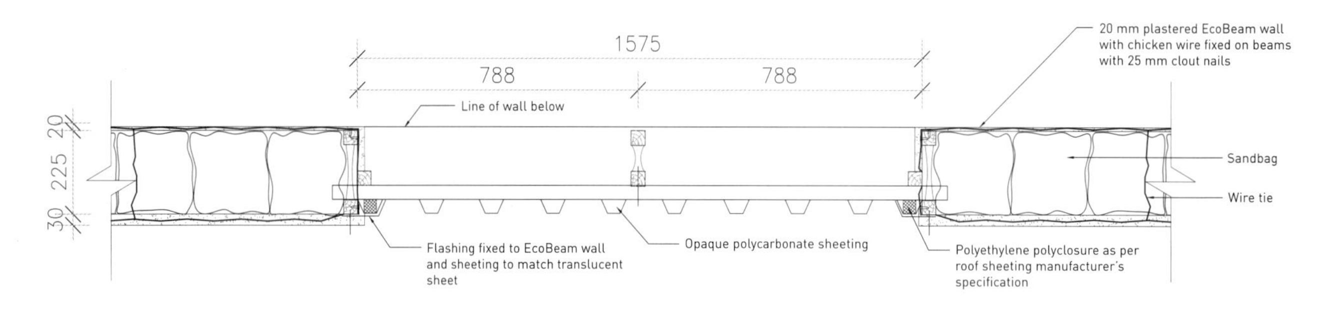

05

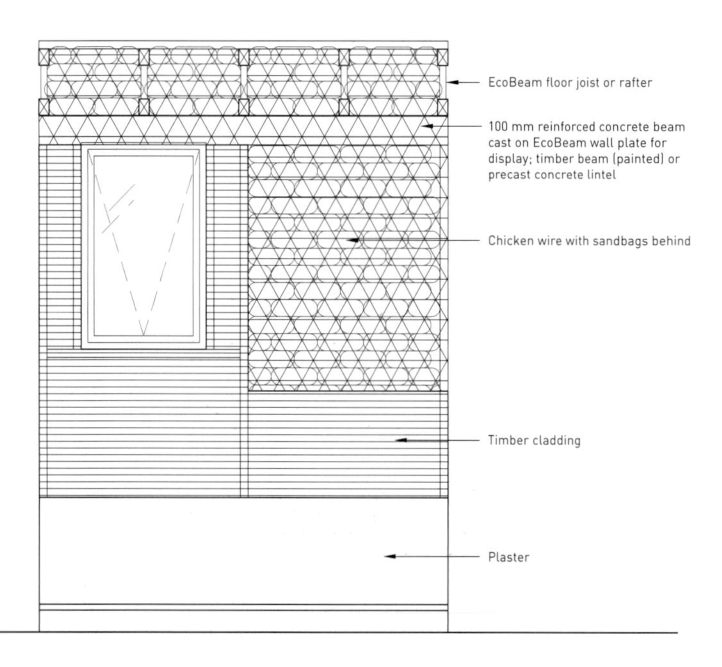

06

07

08

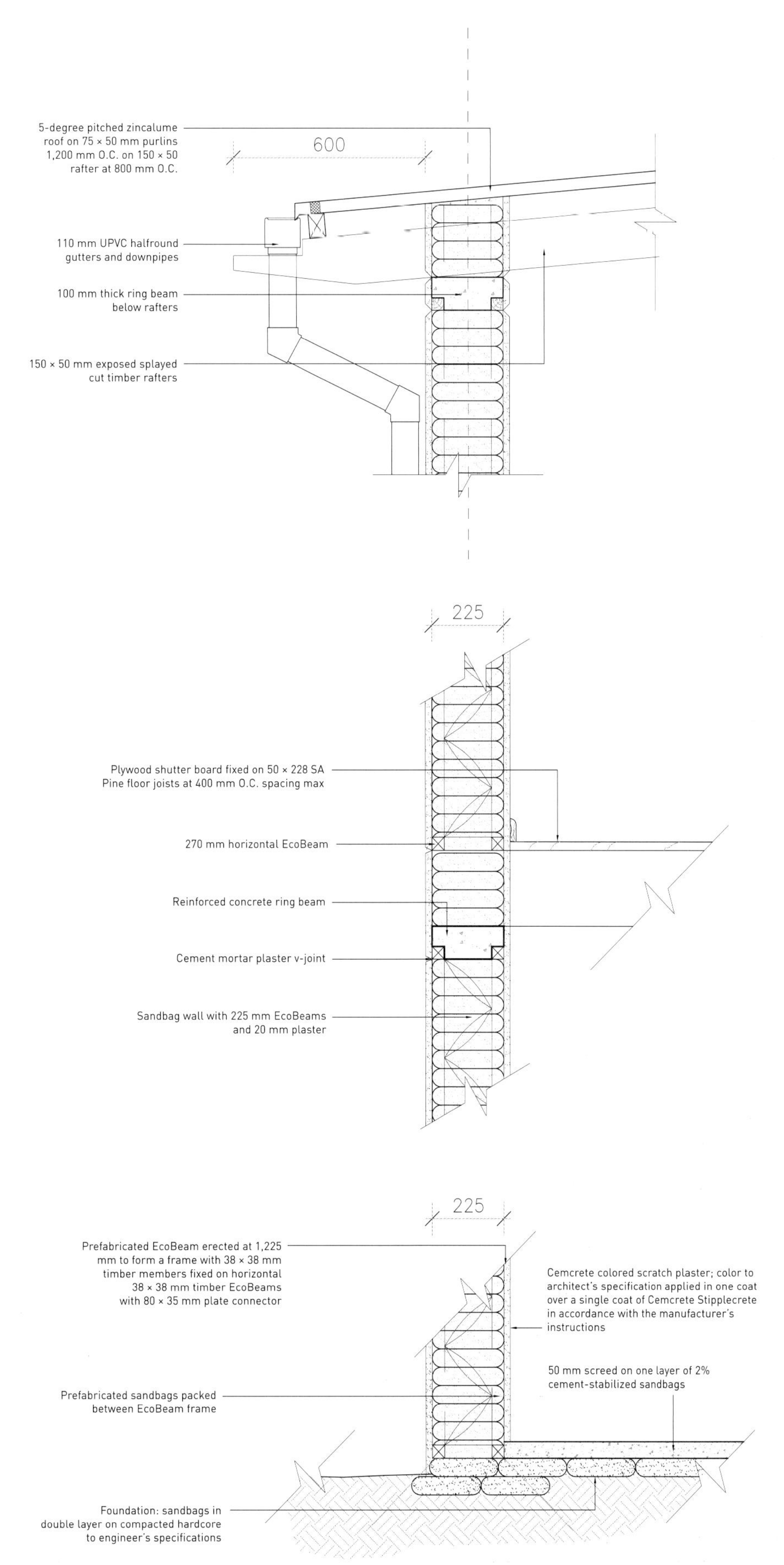
5-degree pitched zincalume roof on 75 × 50 mm purlins 1,200 mm O.C. on 150 × 50 rafter at 800 mm O.C.
600
110 mm UPVC halfround gutters and downpipes
100 mm thick ring beam below rafters
150 × 50 mm exposed splayed cut timber rafters
225
Plywood shutter board fixed on 50 × 228 SA Pine floor joists at 400 mm O.C. spacing max
270 mm horizontal EcoBeam
Reinforced concrete ring beam
Cement mortar plaster v-joint
Sandbag wall with 225 mm EcoBeams and 20 mm plaster
225
Prefabricated EcoBeam erected at 1,225 mm to form a frame with 38 × 38 mm timber members fixed on horizontal 38 × 38 mm timber EcoBeams with 80 × 35 mm plate connector
Cemcrete colored scratch plaster; color to architect's specification applied in one coat over a single coat of Cemcrete Stipplecrete in accordance with the manufacturer's instructions
50 mm screed on one layer of 2% cement-stabilized sandbags
Prefabricated sandbags packed between EcoBeam frame
Foundation: sandbags in double layer on compacted hardcore to engineer's specifications

09

Hanil Visitors Center and Guesthouse

Chungbuk, Korea — BCHO Architects with CAST (Center for Architectural Structures and Technology)
Fabric-formed concrete

DESIGN INTENTION

The Hanil Visitors Center and neighboring Guesthouse are at the edge of a cement and concrete plant, on a site that adjoins the beautiful Mt. Sobaek National Park. Damaged over the years by the passage of heavy trucks, the project reclaims the quality of the site. It is estimated that many such dilapidated reinforced concrete buildings in Korea will be replaced in the coming years, and the Center urges owners and designers to utilize the residual value from the older buildings for future construction purposes. The structure is an advocate for, and demonstration of, the various ways concrete can be recycled. The Center displays a wide range of formal expressions, including crisp planar, curving sculptural, and small-scale, fragmented concrete elements.

MATERIALITY

BCHO Architects asked the University of Manitoba's Center for Architectural Structures and Technology (CAST) to develop a formwork method for a unique facade for this building. After considering conventional methods, a design using flexible fabric molds was chosen for the entry elevation, where thirty fabric-formed precast elements are intended to resemble the tree trunks of the nearby forest. The elements were cast on the site horizontally, allowed to cure, and then tilted up and secured to the cast-in-place concrete building wall.

Unlike most precast concrete elements, these are not entirely repetitive. Repetition is normally associated with economical precast concrete fabrication, because engineering analysis of element configuration is expensive, as is formwork preparation. These elements support themselves but nothing else, thus their engineering design was less critical. Flexible-fabric formwork uses substantially less material than conventional formwork, making formwork preparation faster and less expensive, and producing little landfill waste. The use of flexible-fabric formwork also produces structurally efficient flowing shapes and complex curvatures with little expense.

Gabion walls were installed over the load-bearing cast-in-place concrete walls on the south side of the facility. They were made using irregular 3.94–7.87" (100–200 mm) pieces of fractured recycled concrete, placed inside rectangular cages of steel mesh. The textures are attractive, and the surfaces will weather and become moss-covered over time, which will further enhance its appearance without detriment to the facility. Material for the gabion wall came from the concrete slab upon which the fabric-formed concrete elements had been cast.

TECHNICAL

The flexible fabric-formed elements used tilt-up construction methods. On top of an unreinforced slab on grade, wood-framed partitions were set up to isolate each of the thirty elements. Plastic tubes of two different diameters were positioned and secured in place to give convex and concave profiles to the fabric skin. Reinforced synthetic fabric was draped over the tubes and on top of the slab, and the fabric's upper edges were secured to the partitions. Conventional form-ply covered the upper edges of fabric.

The two ends of the forms were enclosed with form-ply that was scribed to meet the varied shapes of curved fabric. A grid of reinforcing bars was set in the concrete to provide tensile strength, chiefly needed to lift the elements out of the formwork and move them to their final vertical position against the cast-in-place concrete building wall. Steel embeds needed to lift and secure the elements were also set in place. Workers carefully vacuumed the form cavity before casting concrete, since any residue left behind would be a permanent blemish on the face of the concrete.

A permeable formwork fabric produced both improved surface finishes and higher-strength concrete as a result of a filtering action that allowed air bubbles and excess mix water to bleed through the membrane. The fabric imprinted subtle features as the curved shapes morphed along the length of the concrete pieces. The unexpected juxtaposition of fabric shapes and textures onto hard concrete reminds the viewer that past experiences with these two materials were never so integrated.

The concrete facade elements are generally 3.3' wide (1 m) and up to 23.8' tall (7.26 m), and are secured with metal brackets at the footings, at roof level, and at the midpoint. Variations in element width and length were not uncommon, taking advantage of the flexible formwork system.

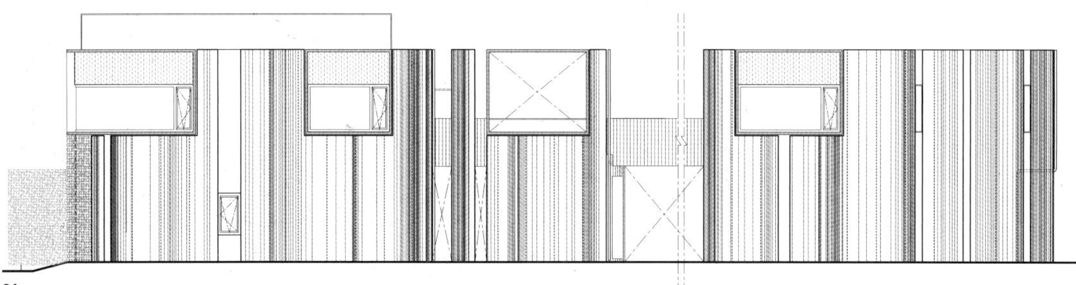

01

02

03

01 East elevation of fabric-formed wall

02 Exterior view

03 Detail view of fabric-formed wall at entry

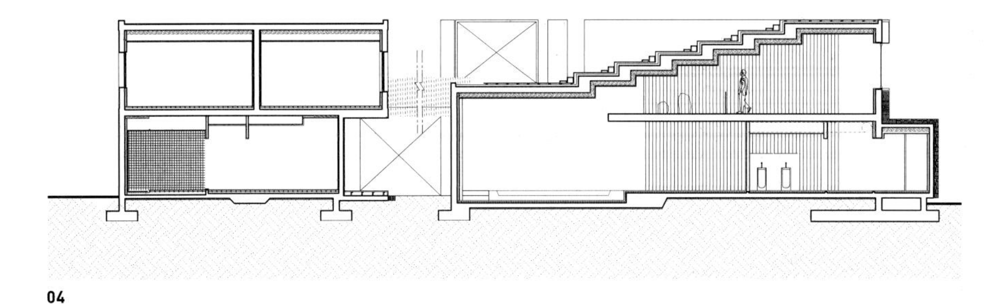

04

04 Longitudinal section

05 Wall section where precast fabric-formed concrete elements meet cast-in-place concrete wall

06 Wall section where gabion wall abuts cast-in-place concrete wall

07 Ground-floor plan

08 Plan detail of fabric-formed concrete wall

09 Varied tilt-up precast elements

10 Preparation of fabric-lined forms using plastic tubes and form-ply over a concrete slab

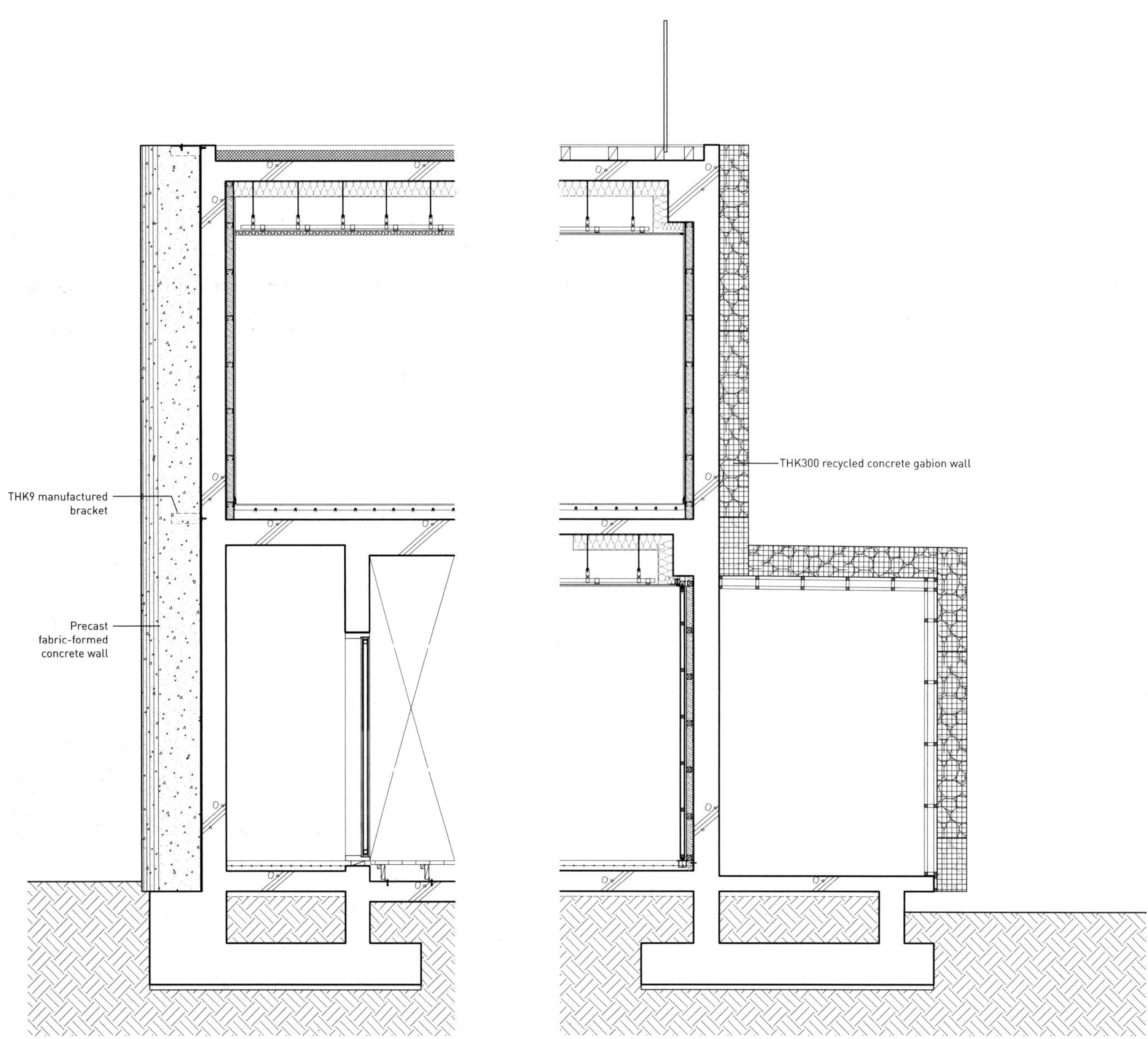

05

06

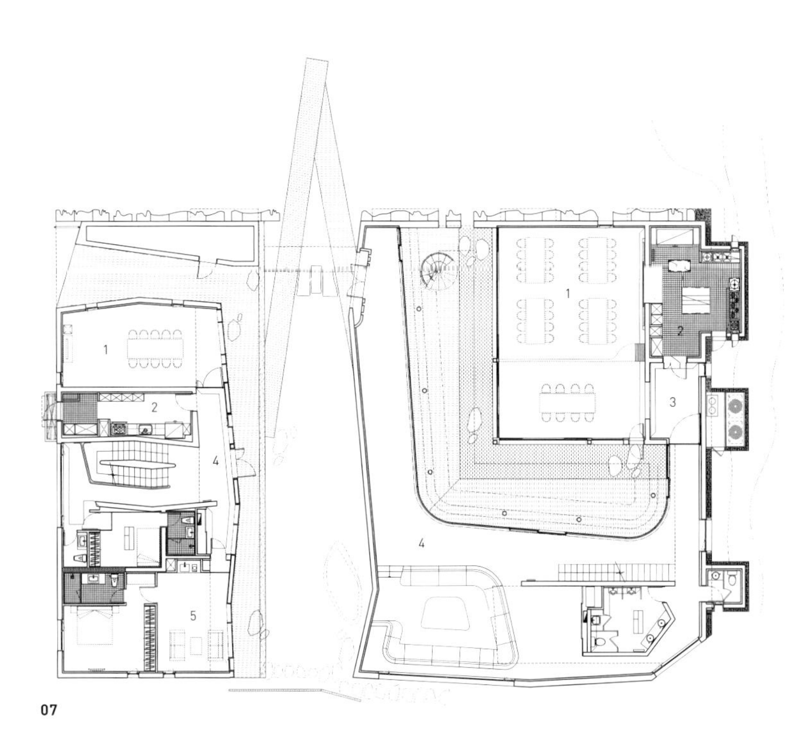

1 Dining room
2 Kitchen
3 Service
4 Hall
5 Vice-president's room

07

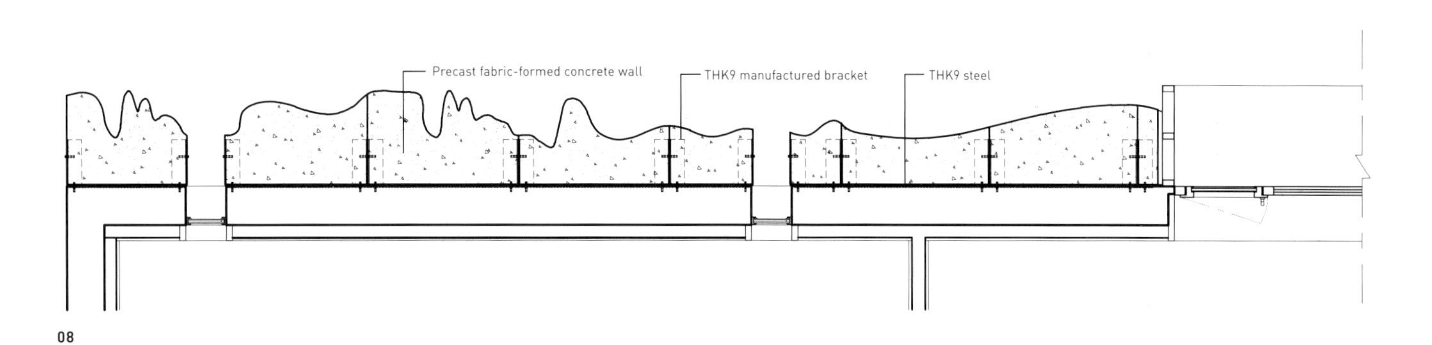

08

09

10

Harmonia 57

São Paulo, Brazil — Triptyque
Cement-based stucco

DESIGN INTENTION

Harmonia 57 is an office building located in a vibrant arts district on the west side of São Paulo. The public paths and streets in this district have become renowned galleries of artistic expression where even the graffiti is often considered high art. The design intention was to give the building surfaces a life of their own. They are meant "to breathe, sweat, and grow," and are covered by a planted outer layer that works as the building's epidermia. The roof surfaces are planted as well, with space reserved for occupied terraces. An exposed irrigation system of tanks and pipes became part of the building elevation, and produces a visible cloud of mist when active. Rainwater is collected and stored in roof-level cisterns to supply the irrigation system.

MATERIALITY

The tectonic system is a reinforced concrete frame and floors, in-filled with brick masonry cavity walls. The concrete frame and masonry walls are enveloped in a lightweight concrete wrap that contains voids where plants can root. The neutral gray of the building's exterior is animated by the leafy and colorful vegetation, which sways in the breeze. The building's interior spaces are flexible and have refined finishes. With its exposed structural frame and masonry walls, the exterior organic expression is not reflected on the interior; however, the building's large openings and ample terracing foster visual engagement between the inside and out.

TECHNICAL

The cast-in-place concrete structural frame is in-filled with a 9.5" thick (240 mm) brick cavity wall. A 0.3" thick (7.5 mm) waterproofing layer was applied to the outer surfaces of the concrete structure and masonry. A thin 3.5" (90 mm) layer of lightweight concrete was applied to the concrete and masonry substrate. This cement-based coating contains vermiculite, a naturally occurring igneous mineral sometimes used in potting soil for its exceptional capacity to hold water and nourish plants during dry periods. In construction applications, it also increases workability of the trowel-applied cement product. A hand-drawn stencil located numerous voids or "cribs" on the surface in an irregular pattern to receive the plantings. Within an hour of application, the cribs were carved into the fresh cement-based outer coating to a depth of 1.97–3.54" (50–90 mm).

São Paulo receives around 51" (1,300 mm) of rain per year, which is sufficient to meet the exterior's demand for nonpotable water. The challenge, however, has been to maintain a stable water supply in times of drought, since 60 percent of the annual volume occurs between December and March. In other words, almost two-thirds of the rain falls in only one-third of the year, leaving it relatively arid in the interim. The designers' estimated 792 gallons (3,000 L) of non-drinking water continues to be accurate and sufficiently met using the project's water management system.

The roof is also planted, which reduces the need for air-conditioning inside. The rainwater it collects and stores also happens to reduce the stormwater burden on the adjacent municipal infrastructure during rainy periods. The rainwater is filtered and treated with ozone as it enters cisterns and later winds up as graywater in toilets, as water for the irrigation system, or used for general cleaning. The irrigation of plants on the building surfaces is managed by a fully automated electronic controller, programmed to optimize the time and frequency of irrigation, and regulated to disconnect programmed irrigation when rainfall is adequate.

01 Longitudinal section through site and below-ground parking, with elevation showing irrigation system mounted on building walls

02 View of front, with operable screens opened and closed; roof-level cisterns and irrigation system on right

03 Corner view with ground-level cisterns and irrigation system

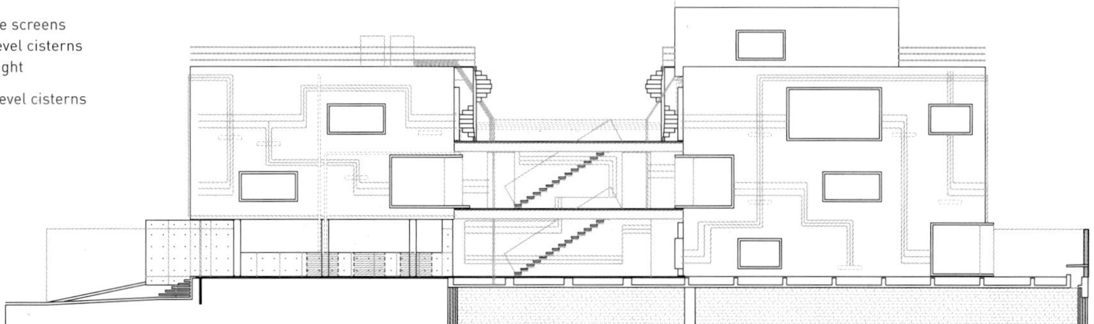

01

02

03

Hiroshi Senju Museum

Karuizawa, Nagano, Japan — Ryue Nishizawa
Cast-in-place concrete

DESIGN INTENTION

Renowned Japanese painter Hiroshi Senju wanted an open, luminous gallery space to best display his work, but also give visitors a relaxing space in which they could spend time in contemplation. The design for the museum, with its gentle curves, takes its inspiration from the rolling hills and lush vegetation surrounding the site.

Inside, site-specific exhibition spaces provide opportunities for personal experiences with the artwork, conjuring scenes encountered during a stroll through the woods. Large-scale nature paintings, often vivid depictions of water falling into pools, are mounted on freestanding panels within a sinuous path of the continuous gallery. The museum walls are made of laminated glass without mullions, to minimize the separation between inside and outside.

MATERIALITY

The museum demonstrates the fluidity of cast-in-place concrete, embodied in the undulating shapes of the floors. The museum foundations and ground floor are made of reinforced concrete, the columns and roof structure of steel frame. The roof structure is concealed by continuous, unarticulated plaster ceilings. The topography of the site is re-created in the concrete floor, and again in the ceiling. For practical reasons the roof assemblies were not made of concrete, but they mimic its appearance. The overall effect is a minimalist calm that permeates the galleries, making surfaces abstract and featureless. Even necessities such as light fixtures, switches, and air supplies are discreetly concealed from view.

TECHNICAL

The architect's drawings indicate the subtle shape of the concrete floor in 2" (50 mm) contours. Highly skilled concrete finishers were hired to shape the architect's vision by hand. The exposed floor slab was finished with metal trowels to produce a smooth surface and then coated with a surface hardener. Paths through the galleries are lightly delineated along the floor.

The concrete floor is 3.94" (100 mm) thick, but the 7.87"-thick (200 mm) reinforced concrete structural slab is actually located about 1' (350 mm) below the finished floor slab, under a layer of gravel and sand; along the perimeter, an insulated air supply cavity appears instead. A continuous 2" (51 mm) slit louver delivers controlled air to the base of the exterior glass cladding. The concrete floor itself does not directly contact the cladding system. The steel roof structure is supported by 3.15" and 3.94" (80 and 100 mm) diameter steel tube columns with a fire-resistant coating. These columns pass through the finished floor slab to bear on the structural slab, where loads are supported by deep footings.

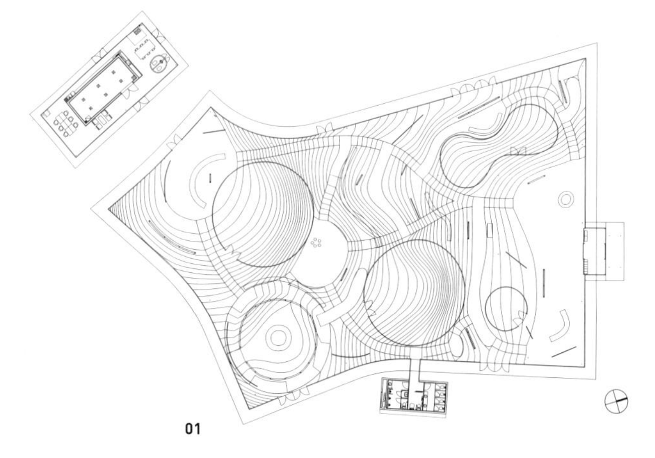

01

02

03

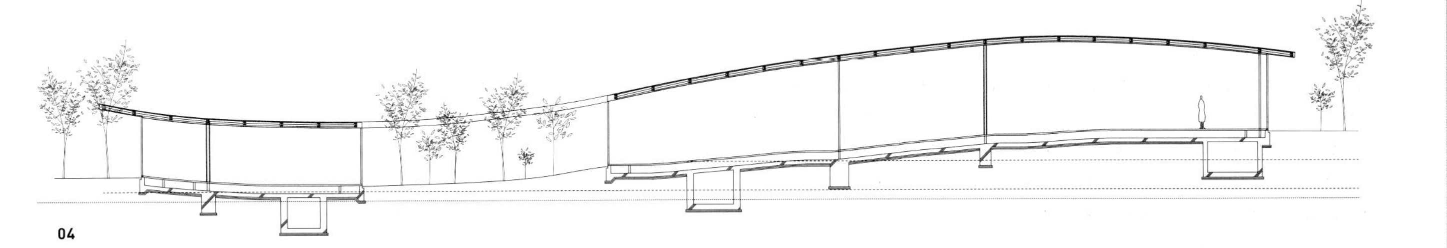

04

01 Floor plan with concrete floor slab contours at intervals of 2" (50 mm)

02 Interior view of gallery and natural court

03 Undulating floor of gallery, with path subtly marked in foreground

04 Section through building and site

05 Detailed section of exterior roof, wall, and floor assemblies. The concrete slab and substrates are slightly sloped. (Horizontal red lines added for reference.)

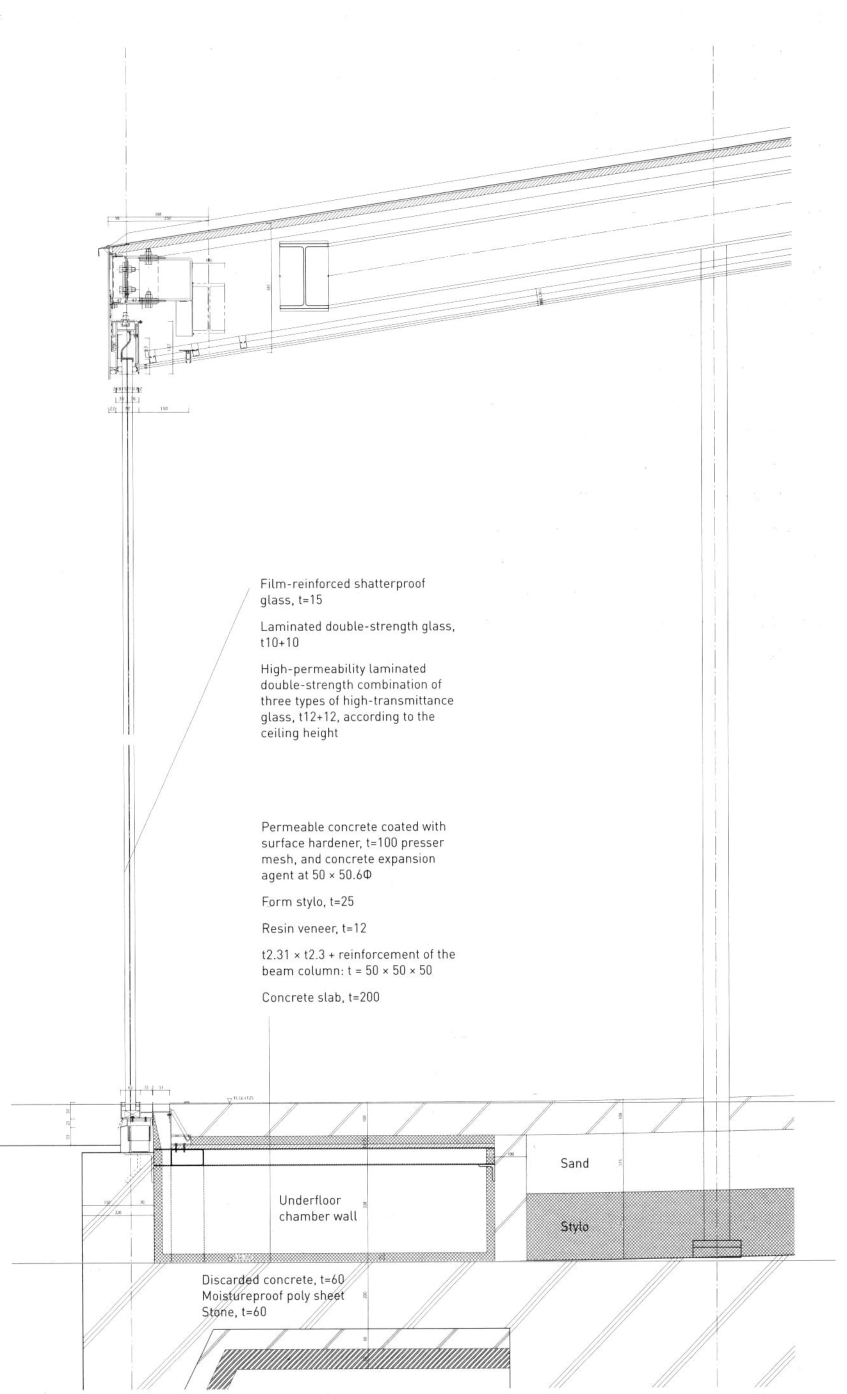

05

Italian Pavilion at World Expo 2010

Shanghai, China — Iodice Architetti
Light-transmitting precast concrete, photocatalytic concrete

DESIGN INTENTION

This pavilion was inspired by the game of pick-up sticks, called Shanghai in Italy. The imaginary sticks segment the pavilion into twenty spaces, representing the twenty regions of Italy. Each of these spaces could easily stand alone, but the pavilion is best understood as an integrated whole. The building plan simulates that of a typical city, with many short, narrow roads that open into a large square, an urban morphology common to both Italy and China. The pavilion was intended to provoke positive interactions between visitors and fulfill the Expo's theme, "Better City, Better Life."

Though large and technically sophisticated, the pavilion was built to be easily dismantled at the Expo's close, with each of the twenty spaces designed to potentially be re-established as independent small buildings elsewhere. During the Expo, the pavilion received more than twenty offers to be relocated to various cities in China. It remained in Shanghai, and was reopened as an exhibition gallery featuring Italian artwork and consumer brands.

MATERIALITY

It is documented that concrete was invented in Italy more than two millennia ago. Honoring that legacy, the Italian pavilion featured the debut of i.light, an adapted and innovative light-transmitting concrete, also developed in Italy. Approximately 40 percent of the pavilion's outer walls are made of this light-transmitting precast concrete product. Under low light conditions, walls appear to be solid concrete, but when more brightly lit from the outside, the walls appear to glow as light passes through resin embedded in the concrete matrix. At night the walls softly illuminate the exterior.

The 40,000 sq. ft. (3,800 sq. m) pavilion has walls that rise obliquely 65' (20 m) above the floor. The concrete walls are made up of more than 3,700 panels, each measuring 20" × 39" × 2" (500 × 1,000 × 50 mm) and weighing 110 lbs. (50 kg). The light-transmitting panels are made of a mix of proprietary concrete embedded with tiny pieces of resin, created by Italian firm Italcementi. The panels come in three degrees of transparency, with the most luminous composed of 20 percent resin on its surface. The entering natural light, even in angular paths deep inside the pavilion, evokes the sort of lighting found between buildings in a dense cityscape. Other light-transmitting concrete products rely on embedded fiber-optic glass and acrylic rods. The i.light panels not only transmit more natural light, but are more economical to produce as well.

TECHNICAL

The concrete mix contains proprietary cement and admixtures to produce a concrete that bonds to the thermoplastic polymer, and is strong enough to not crack along the plane of the aligned resin pieces. Type I high early-strength cement was used to accelerate the cure and strength. The aggregate was a graded siliceous/calcareous sand that produced a compact, granular pattern. Stainless-steel fiber reinforcement added tensile strength and ductility, and polypropylene fibers minimized cracking as the concrete cured. Chemical admixtures were added to improve workability and flow of the mix. The resulting panels have an impressive compressive strength of 9,400 psi (65 MPa). Fabricators were able to produce approximately two hundred panels per day. To reduce the cost of transport and handling, the panels were readily cast at the construction site. The resin was securely positioned in grooves during the pour to ensure it was exposed on inner and outer faces of the panels.

In construction, the panels were stacked and bolted to a steel inner grid by two stainless-steel anchors in each horizontal edge. All connections are bolted, permitting easy disassembly. A 2" (50 mm) blanket of insulated translucent ETFE adds thermal resistance to the internal walls and lets in sunlight. The pavilion interiors are illuminated by natural daylight when it is available, and by artificial lighting at night, powered by photovoltaic cells that are integrated into the glass cladding.

The thermoplastic polymer pieces are only 0.08–0.12" (2–3 mm) thick, but have a light transmission factor of 92 percent and good resistance to ultraviolet light and alkalis in the concrete, as well as acids. In the pavilion, the i.light's resin elements are clear, but the process could be adapted to add color. The manufacturer guarantees that the panels are as durable as traditional precast concrete panels, and after years of usage, no degradation of the precast panels has been observed.

Other portions of the pavilion were made of Italcementi's TX Active photocatalytic cement. Sometimes called "anti-pollution" or "smog-eating" cement, when exposed to light and air, concrete made with this ingredient accelerates the natural chemical oxidation process, which leads to faster decomposition of organic and inorganic substances in the atmosphere. The resulting exterior surfaces are slower to soil in urban atmospheres, and contribute to improved air quality.

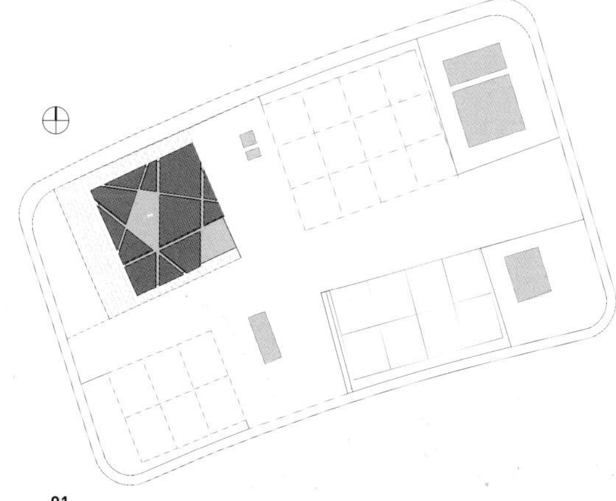

01

01 Site plan
02 South elevation
03 West elevation
04 Exterior view from southwest

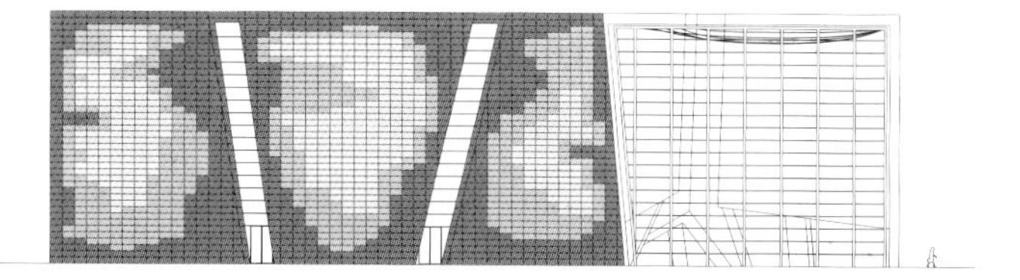

02

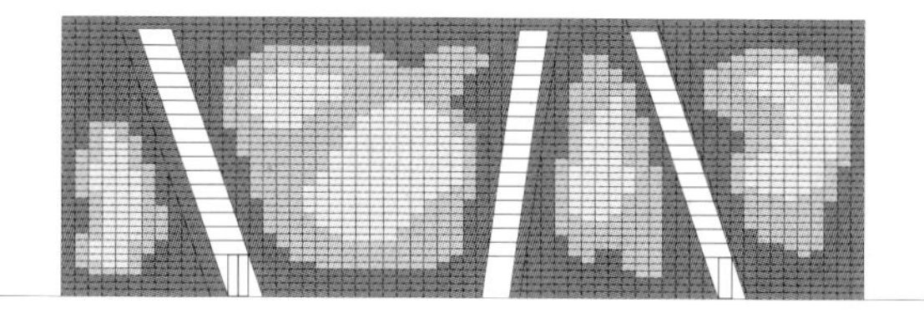

03

04

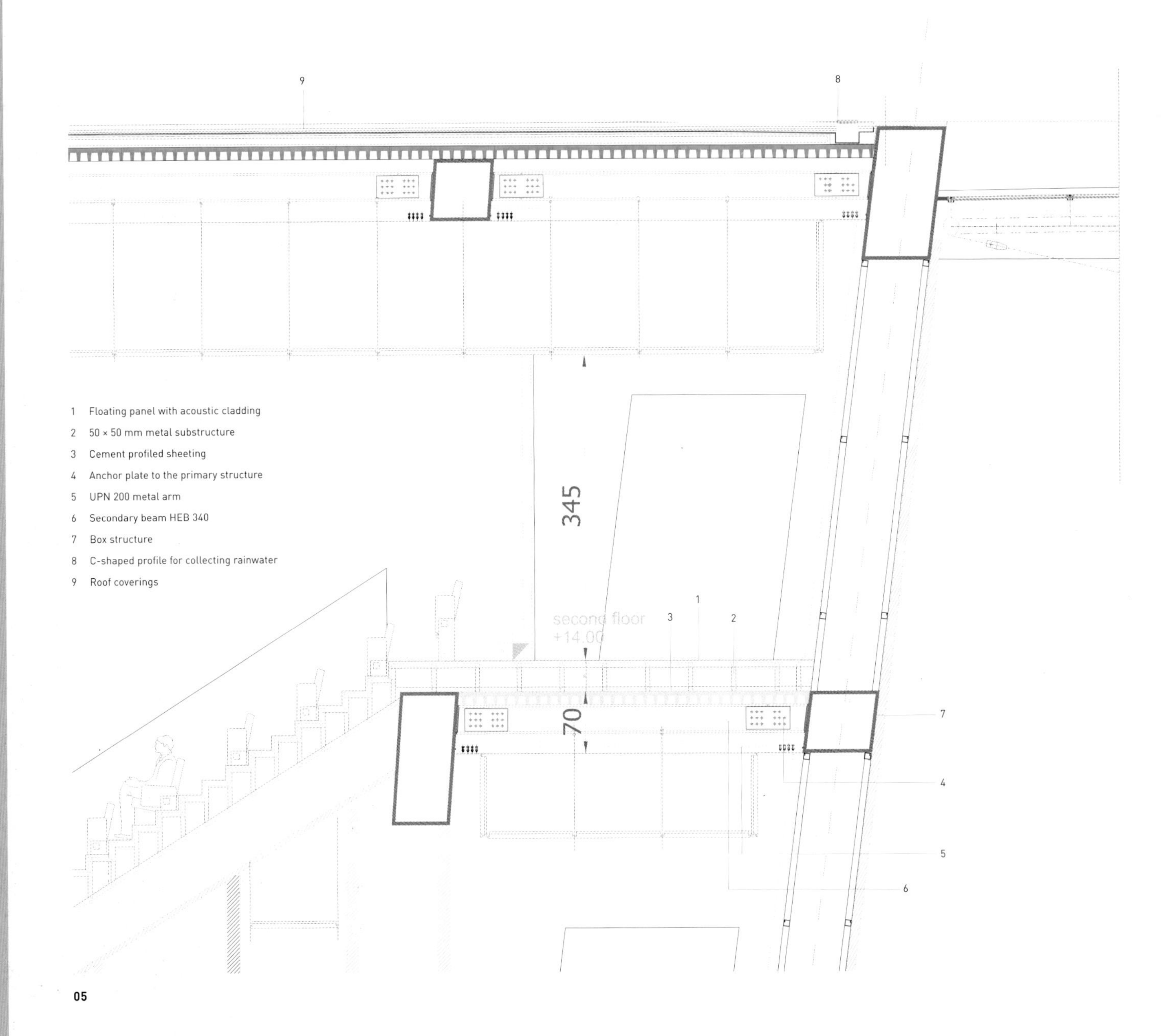

1 Floating panel with acoustic cladding
2 50 × 50 mm metal substructure
3 Cement profiled sheeting
4 Anchor plate to the primary structure
5 UPN 200 metal arm
6 Secondary beam HEB 340
7 Box structure
8 C-shaped profile for collecting rainwater
9 Roof coverings

05

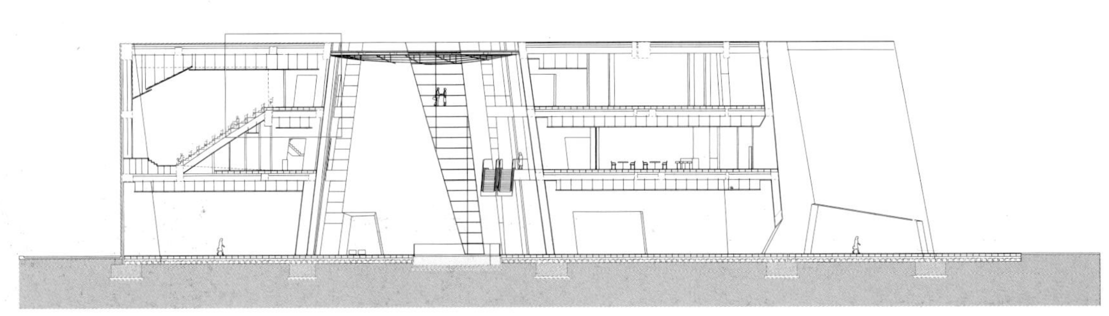

06

05 Detailed section

06 Building section

07 Detailed section through exterior wall assembly

08 Day view of light-transmitting concrete panels

09 Night view of light-transmitting concrete panels

1 Horizontal metal structure (180 × 70 mm)
2 Halfen-type profiles to anchor trim panels (70 × 50 mm)
3 i.light cement panels (1,000 × 500 × 40 mm)
4 Vertical metal structure (180 × 70 mm)
5 Anchor plate
6 Box structure
7 Aluminum profile for anchoring the membrane
8 ETFE isolation membrane
9 UPN200 metal arm
10 Floating floor (600 × 1,200 mm)
11 Lightweight concrete on trapezoidal sheet
12 HEB340 secondary beam
13 Anchor plate to the primary structure
14 Air pump (0.3 bar)
15 Plasterboard
16 HVAC systems
17 RCK200 cement
18 Cupolex crawlspace
19 RCK300 cement
20 Waterproofing membrane

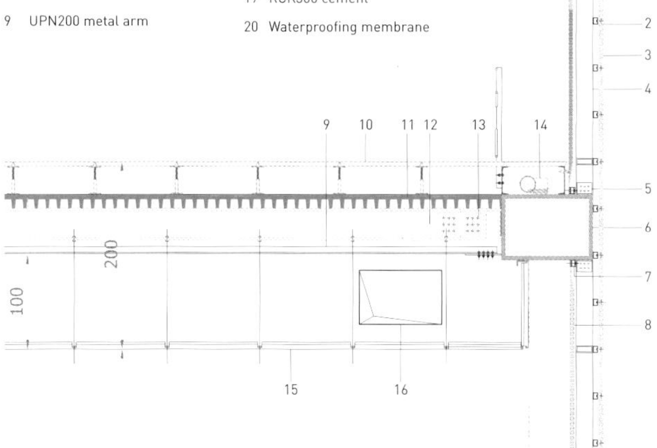

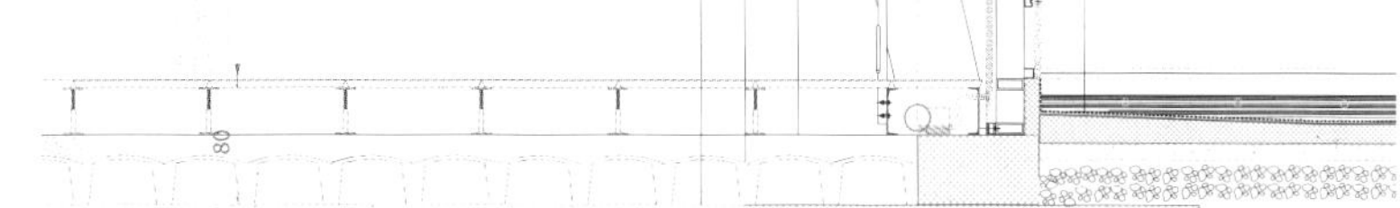

07

08

09

Nk'Mip Desert Cultural Centre

Osoyoos, British Columbia, Canada — DIALOG (formerly Hoston Bakker Boniface Haden)
Rammed earth

DESIGN INTENTION

The Nk'Mip Desert Cultural Centre is located in the South Okanagan Valley, adjacent to the Great Basin Desert, a 1,600-acre (650 hectare) preserve and conservation area. The building is an extension of the remarkable surrounding site, and reflects the native Osoyoos Indian Band's stewardship of the desert landscape. The fragility of the environment prompted rigorous concern for sustainability, in line with the ancient values of the Osoyoos Indian Band. The desert landscape flows over the building's green roof, and provided material for its rammed earth walls. The partially submerged building creates a layered view of the desert as it recedes into the adjacent riparian landscape framed by mountains in the distance. The land is dry year-round, and has cold winters and hot summers, with average temperatures ranging from 0–91°F (-18–33°C), often reaching 104°F (40 °C) on summer days.

MATERIALITY

Two affiliated companies, SIREWALL and Terra Firma, collaborated with the architects to implement modern analytical design practices for the building's rammed earth construction. The result was substantially improved performance, and at 262' long, 18' high, and 2' thick (80 m long, 5.5 m high, and 600 mm thick), the largest rammed earth wall in North America at the time of construction. Rigid insulation occupies its center, providing an estimated effective thermal resistance of R33 (RSI 5.81) and stabilizing temperature variations. The walls are constructed from local soil mixed with cement and color additives. The building effectively retains warmth in the winter, while its substantial thermal mass moderates and offsets peak temperatures in the summer.

Rammed earth construction is an economical option in dry regions where other materials are not readily available, and is a means to reduce embodied energy otherwise spent manufacturing and transporting conventional materials. Exposed rammed earth wall surfaces can resemble sedimentary soils, but are compacted and often stabilized with cement to reduce abrasion and erosion. They are intrinsically strong in compression, and durable if erosive forces are not extreme. Here they are reinforced throughout, and have additional reinforcement above windows and doors.

The subtle layering of the rammed earth walls evokes geological stratification, appearing natural and yet precise—its layers may be irregular, but its overall form is crisply geometric. All of the wall's faces have the same appearance and texture and contain a record of the horizontal wooden formwork used in construction.

Sustainability considerations included the involvement of the Osoyoos Indian Band in the main wall's construction, which contributed to the long-term ecological sustainability of the area and the community, and provided an opportunity to advance an authentically South Okanagan building technique. The project also created the opportunity for the Osoyoos Indian Band to develop artisanal construction skills as rammed earth contractors.

TECHNICAL

The earth-based wall system combines two 10" (250 mm) walls of compacted soil, sand, and cement with 4" (100 mm) of rigid polyisocyanurate insulation sandwiched in the center, for a total wall thickness of 24" (600 mm). Successive layers of differently tinted local soils were placed into the wide wooden formwork and compressed by a pneumatically powered tamper to 50 percent of its untamped height, approximately 125 lbs./ft.^{3} (2,000 kg/m^3). The architect specified that the lift heights for each layer would be 5–7" (125–170 mm), but was intentionally vague about aesthetics, letting the builders achieve the desired natural appearance on their own.

Traditional rammed earth walls use clay to bind fine mineral particles. In these walls, strength and durability are enhanced by adding 6–10 percent Portland cement to the mineral mix by weight, less than half that of normal concrete. A small amount of water, 5–10 percent by volume, was added to the mix to fully evolve the hydration process. Bond beams with higher concentrations of cement were used above and below windows, and as the parapet that ties the two wall planes together.

The wall is reinforced with #5 rebar at 16" on center vertically and horizontally (16 mm diameter, at 406 mm) in the center of both planes of rammed earth that make up the thick wall. Tamping around the rebar is especially critical. The rammed earth walls are constructed upon a reinforced concrete foundation. The rammed earth is elevated above finish grade on the concrete foundation to avoid abrasion near the ground. The concrete ground slab and roof slab below the vegetated roof both contain a radiant heating and cooling hydronic system.

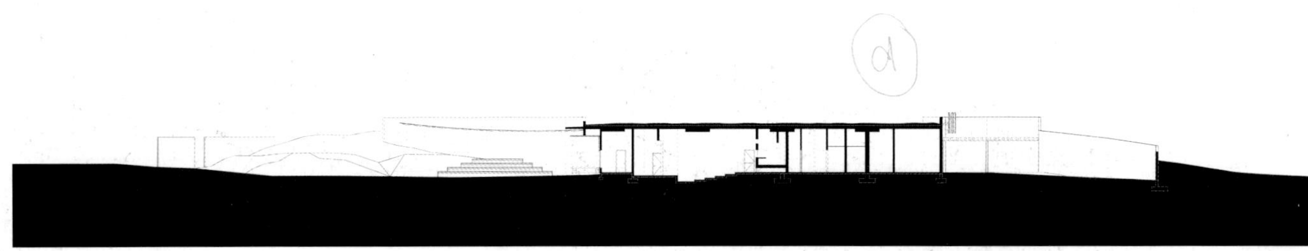

01

02

01 Longitudinal section through building and site

02 Exterior view from west

03 Ground-floor plan

04 Detail view of exterior materials

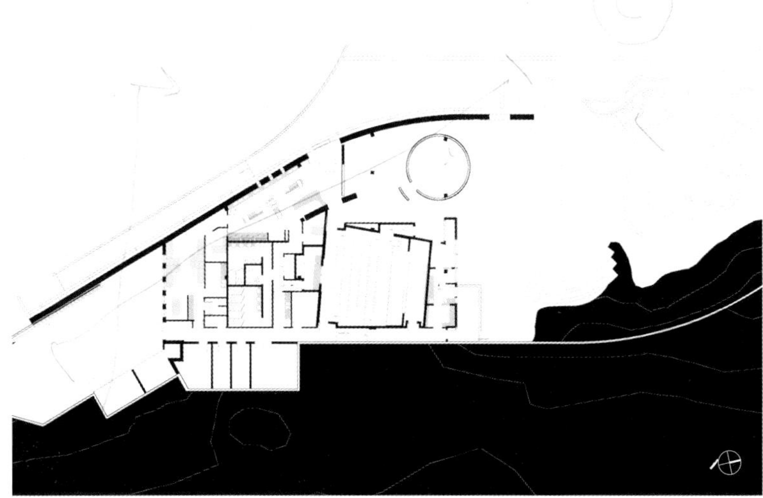
03

04

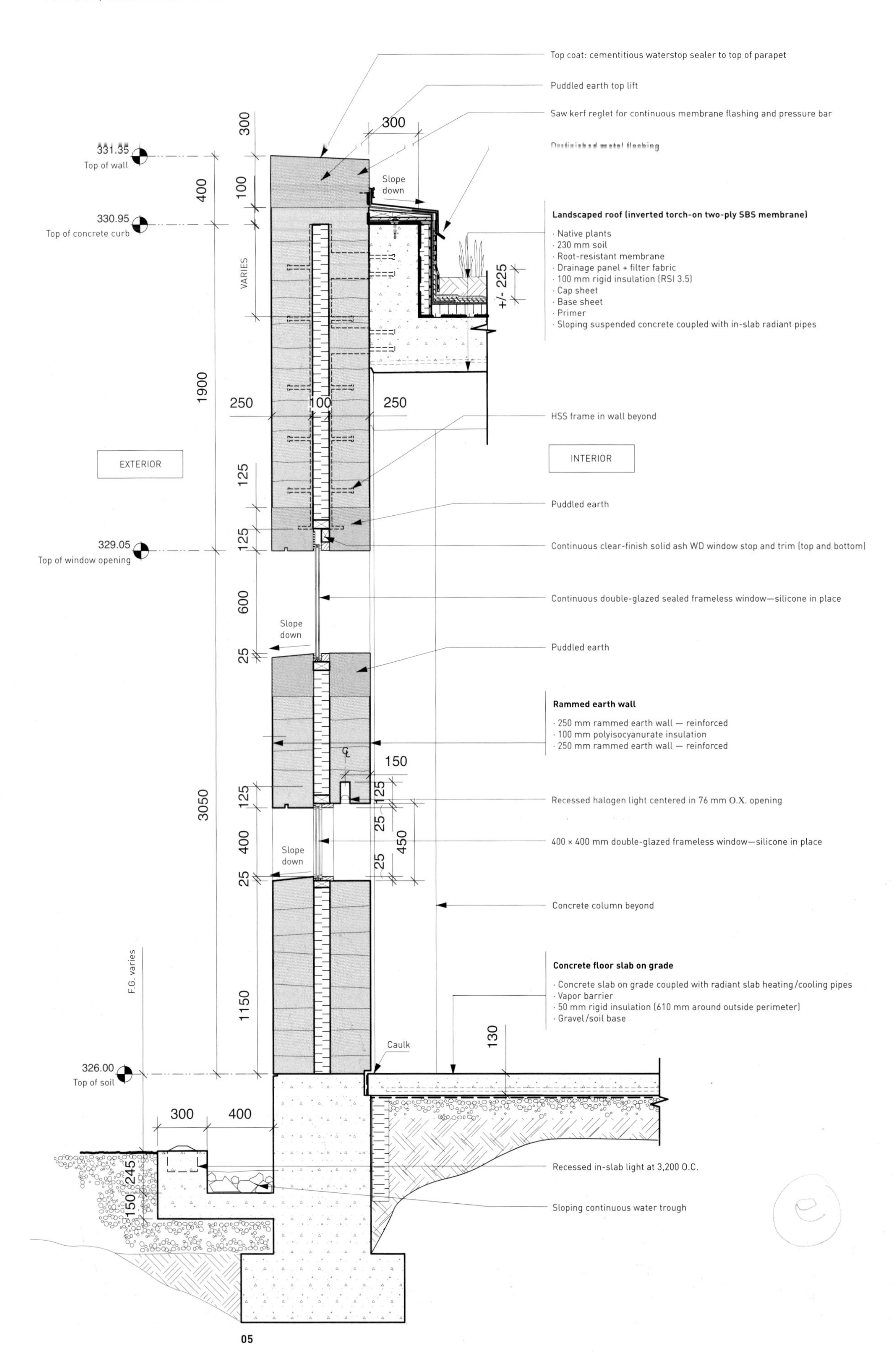
Top coat: cementitious waterstop sealer to top of parapet
Puddled earth top lift
Saw kerf reglet for continuous membrane flashing and pressure bar
Prefinished metal flashing
Landscaped roof (inverted torch-on two-ply SBS membrane)
· Native plants
· 230 mm soil
· Root-resistant membrane
· Drainage panel + filter fabric
· 100 mm rigid insulation (RSI 3.5)
· Cap sheet
· Base sheet
· Primer
· Sloping suspended concrete coupled with in-slab radiant pipes
HSS frame in wall beyond
Puddled earth
Continuous clear-finish solid ash WD window stop and trim (top and bottom)
Continuous double-glazed sealed frameless window—silicone in place
Puddled earth
Rammed earth wall
· 250 mm rammed earth wall — reinforced
· 100 mm polyisocyanurate insulation
· 250 mm rammed earth wall — reinforced
Recessed halogen light centered in 76 mm O.X. opening
400 × 400 mm double-glazed frameless window—silicone in place
Concrete column beyond
Concrete floor slab on grade
· Concrete slab on grade coupled with radiant slab heating/cooling pipes
· Vapor barrier
· 50 mm rigid insulation (610 mm around outside perimeter)
· Gravel/soil base
Recessed in-slab light at 3,200 O.C.
Sloping continuous water trough
331.35
Top of wall
330.95
Top of concrete curb
329.05
Top of window opening
326.00
Top of soil
EXTERIOR
INTERIOR
Slope down
Slope down
Slope down
Caulk
VARIES
F.G. varies
300
300
400
100
1900
250
100
250
125
125
600
25
150
125
125
25
450
3050
400
25
25
1150
130
+/- 225
300
400
245
150

05

05 Detailed wall section

06 Preparation of formwork and reinforcement for rammed earth wall construction

07 Rammed earth wall soon after formwork was removed

08 Exterior view of completed work

06

07

08

RATP Bus Center

Paris, France — ECDM
Ultra high performance concrete, reactive powder concrete

DESIGN INTENTION

The RATP Bus Center is a facility located in Thiais, an industrial suburb of Paris, which serves the operations of all bus lines south and east of the city. The daily flow of more than eight hundred bus drivers and three hundred buses energizes the site with nearly constant movement. The program includes administrative, maintenance, and security offices.

With the high usage demands in mind, the architects took cues from the site's expanse of asphalt and designed a building that appears to be a highly refined extension of the site. The building is clad with a durable material that is resistant to staining and weather. Large voids clad with colored and transparent glass contrast with the structure's hard, dark shell.

MATERIALITY

The building is clad with darkly hued precast concrete panels, the result of an added mineral pigment. Each elevation is subdivided according to a rational grid, giving order to the building surfaces in this industrial site. CNC-milling machines were used to create the flat, curved, and sometimes double-curved panel shapes. Digital tools also articulated exposed surfaces with nubby LEGO-like reliefs, taking full advantage of the plasticity of the concrete that would later fill the forms.

The precision of the panels and the thin joints are only possible with this unusual form-making process and special concrete mix. The quality of each piece was verified after removal from the forms and before being installed. Unlike conventional concrete, the finished precast panels are uniformly smooth in color and texture. The wall surfaces are armor-like, punctuated only by the brightly colored windows corresponding to the functions inside. Though composed of many programmatic functions, the building is reduced to a single dark, polished monolith with rounded corners, fused to the land. This appropriate choice of material meets programmatic goals and thrives in the given site.

TECHNICAL

The proprietary concrete mix used for the cladding panels is alternately called by the generic "reactive powder" or ultra high performance concrete (UHPC)—here French company Lafarge's Ductal brand was used. Compared to normal mixes for precast concrete, UHPC does not require vibration during placement, nor does it require steel reinforcement bars or mesh. Here, the concrete was reinforced using non-corrosive high-carbon steel fibers or polyvinyl alcohol fibers. These factors, combined with the concrete's high tensile and compressive strength, made it possible for panel thickness to be reduced by 50 percent or more.

UHPC resembles normal concrete in that both contain cement, silica, sand, and water, but it also contains some unique ingredients, including ground quartz, wollastonite (a naturally occurring mineral), and fiber reinforcement. Small aggregate sizes and a super-plasticizer admixture achieved extraordinary workability. The resulting concrete is self-consolidating—it readily flows without vibration to fill even complex formwork without forming pockets.

These one-story-tall precast panels are only 1.18" thick (30 mm), yet they manage to provide excellent security, weatherproofing, and durability. Joints between the panels are only 0.5" wide (12 mm), placed at intervals of 73" (1.86 m) horizontally, and they do not disrupt the uniform spacing of nubs on surfaces of adjoining panels.

Despite the thin section, UHPC is considered impermeable to water and chemicals and highly resistant to abrasion, making it an appropriate cladding for this industrial context on the ground level and above. The precast concrete cladding panels are connected to the cast-in-place structural substrate using stainless-steel hardware. Brackets are bolted to the back of each panel at four locations, matching the location of hardware that is bolted to the faces of the cast-in-place walls. The precast panels were installed from bottom to top, while the top two connections of each panel remained accessible for the installation of shims and nuts.

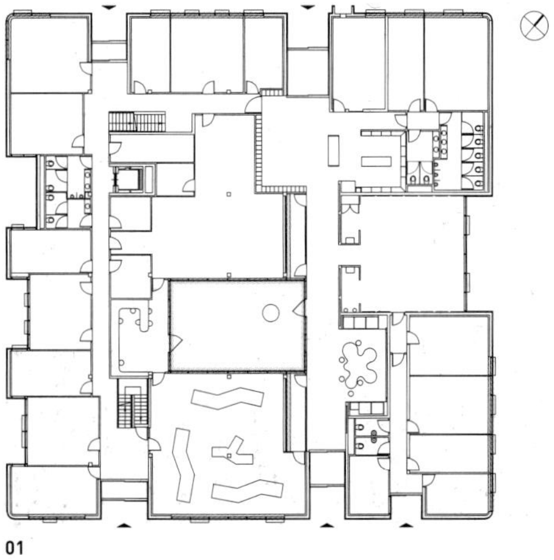

01

01 Plan of ground floor

02 Exterior view from east

03 Exterior view from south

02

03

04 Detailed section at roof and parapet

05 Detailed section at window sill

06 Formwork for casting simple-curved elements

07 Simple-curved and compound-curved precast concrete elements

08 Detailed view of facade elements

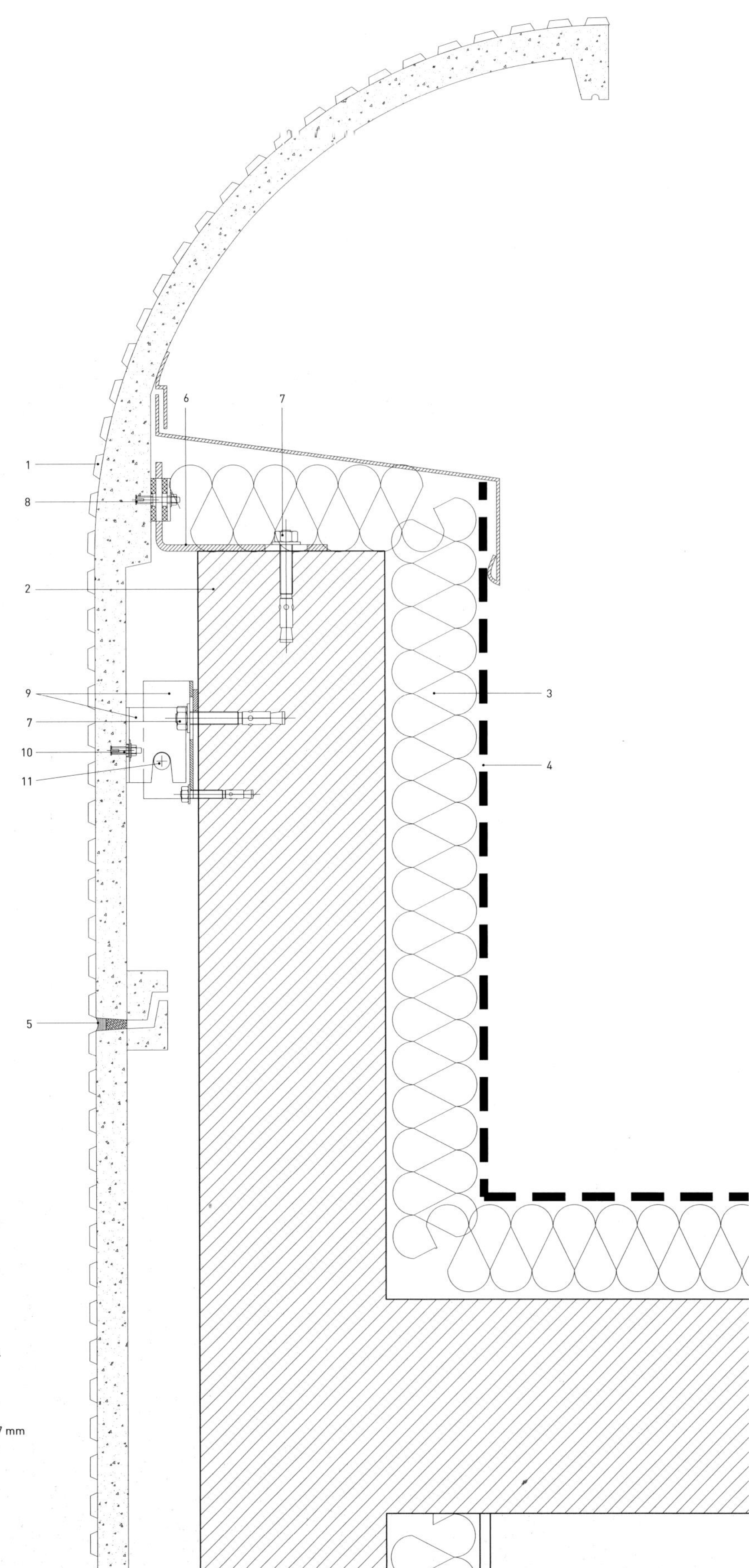

1 Precast concrete element

2 180 mm reinforced concrete

3 100 mm thermal insulation

4 Vapor barrier

5 12 mm high joint

6 6 mm stainless-steel brace

7 12 × 100 mm stainless-steel dowel

8 Insert KEIL:
Cartridge O.C. 15 × 7 mm
Shank O.C. 6 × 40 mm
Nut O.C. 6 mm
Plaque 40 × 40 × 3 mm, hole O.C. 7 mm
2 EPDM 40 × 40 × 5 mm, hole O.C. 12 mm

9 3 mm stainless-steel brace

10 Insert KEIL:
Cartridge O.C. 15 × 7 mm
Shank O.C. 6 × 35 mm
Nut O.C. 6 mm

11 Shank O.C. 16 × 130 mm

04

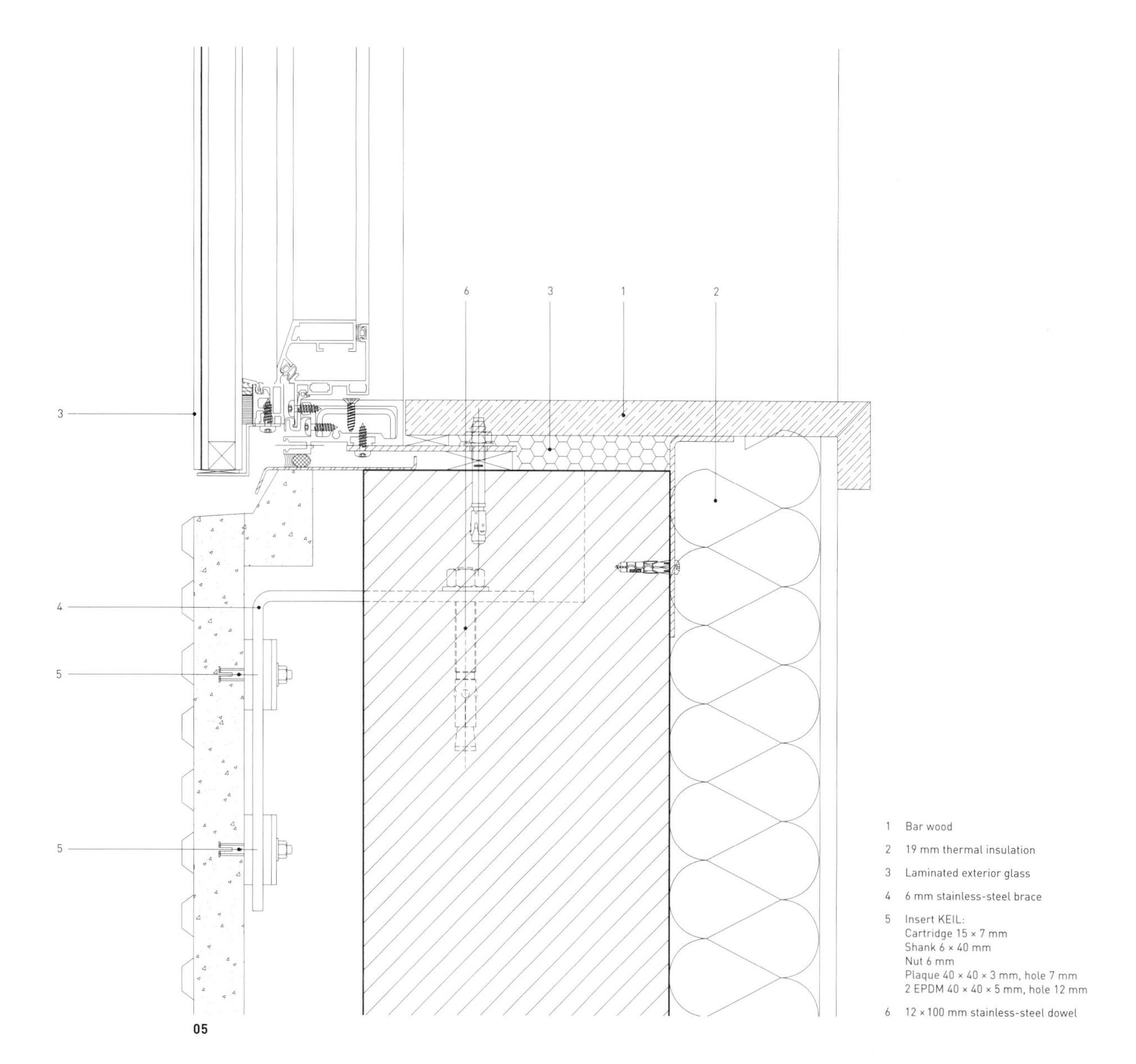

1 Bar wood

2 19 mm thermal insulation

3 Laminated exterior glass

4 6 mm stainless-steel brace

5 Insert KEIL:
Cartridge 15 × 7 mm
Shank 6 × 40 mm
Nut 6 mm
Plaque 40 × 40 × 3 mm, hole 7 mm
2 EPDM 40 × 40 × 5 mm, hole 12 mm

6 12 × 100 mm stainless-steel dowel

05

06

07

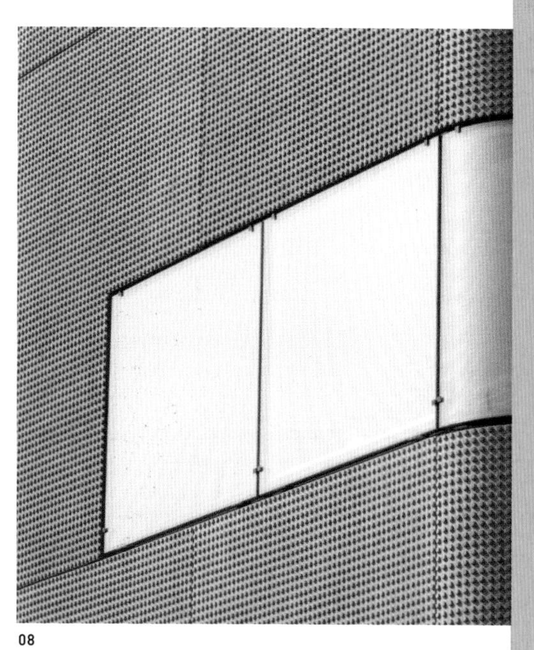

08

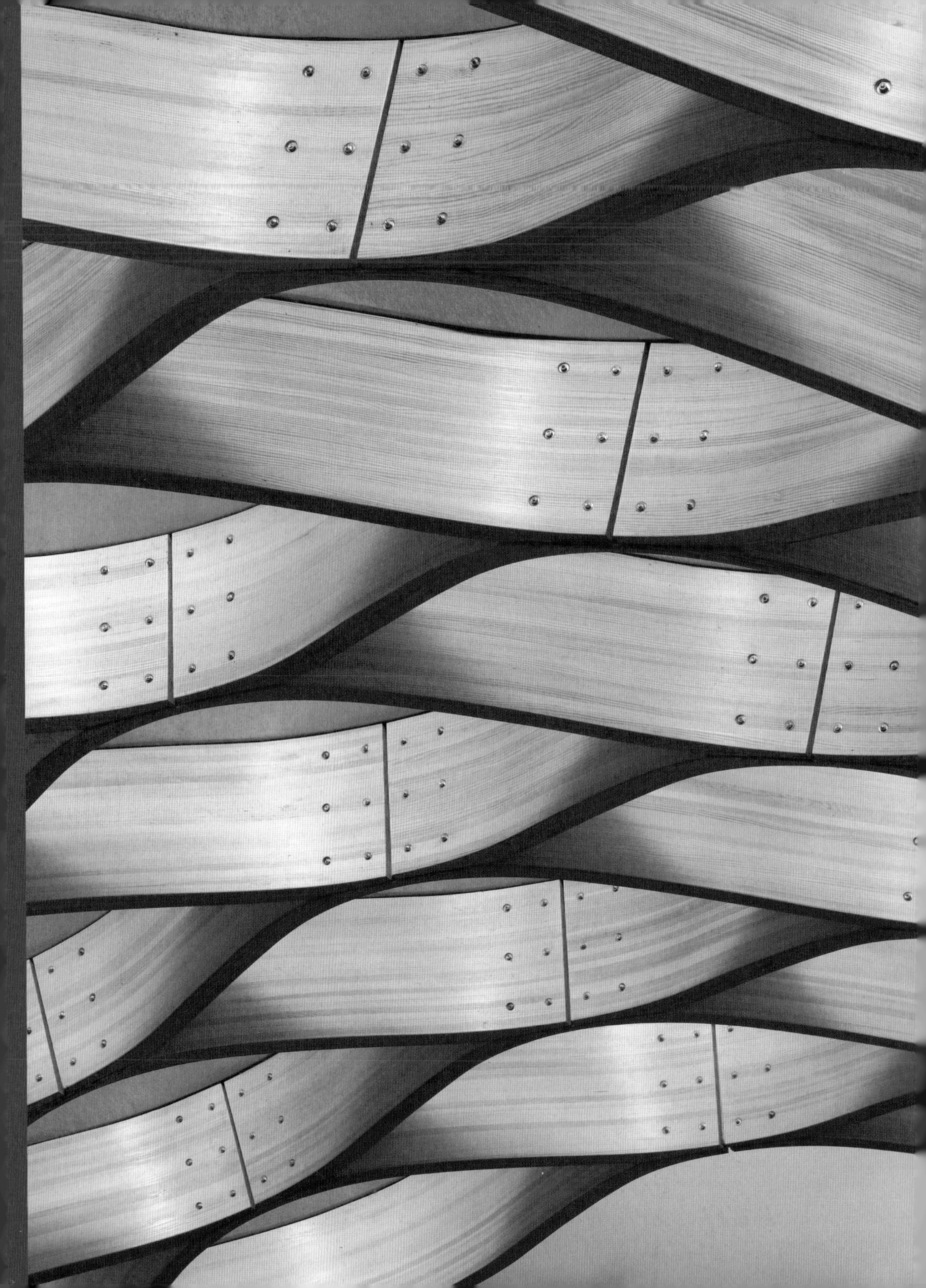

Wood

THE BASICS

The tree has always been, and remains, one of humanity's most critically needed plants on Earth. Throughout our species's evolution, the tree has provided fruit for food and wood for shelter, protection from the elements, and a source for a wide range of tools. Wood is natural, organic, lightweight, strong, readily accessible, and simple to work with in construction. Its wide variety of colors, textures, grain patterns, and fragrances give designers a versatile and adaptable expressive tool for construction. Its warm aesthetic and easy workability has made it an appealing architectural material for centuries.

The basic anatomical structure of wood includes fibers and cells. This structure, along with its chemical composition, determines the strength and technical characteristics of a particular type of wood. Wood is *anisotropic*: its inherent qualities are dependent on the direction of the grain. For example, its strength is one hundred times greater in tension and four times greater in compression in the direction with the grain than it is at a right angle to the grain, while shear strength is greater across the grain than it is in parallel, making it more vulnerable to horizontal shear than to vertical shear. Solid wood members are strongest when cut and used with the grain of the wood, while cross-grain pieces are weaker. A weaker piece of wood will typically withstand one-third more force in compression than it will in tension parallel to the grain. Perpendicular to the grain, the compressive force is only about one-fifth to one-half of the allowable compressive force parallel to the grain.

Most wood used in structural framing is softwood, while hardwood is generally used for finish woodwork, furniture, and the finer details in construction. Softwoods, such as pine, fir, spruce, or cedar, are less expensive and more plentiful, while hardwoods, such as oak, cherry, ash, walnut, poplar, or birch, generally have a finer grain, a better appearance, and are more expensive. Such a generalization is difficult to make, however, as literally thousands of types of wood are used for different purposes around the world, depending on locale, availability, and quality.

Before a piece of wood leaves the mill it is graded for both its structural strength and stiffness or for its aesthetics, depending on its intended use. *Lumber*—a sawed piece of wood—is sold by size, by species, and by *grade*, its ranking based on standards regarding structural strength or appearance. Structural lumber is graded either by a trained inspector or machine and is judged on its density and strength. The wood is then stamped with an industry-wide standard indication before leaving the mill. Grading allows a designer to discriminate among different qualities of woods to economically employ them for a particular use. The way in which a piece of lumber will be used can determine what grade is most viable. For example, structural members with a long span demand a different wood product than lumber for blocking or minimal structural needs. For this reason, it would not be uncommon to use several different species or grades of wood in one project, depending on their applications. Other factors to be considered when selecting lumber for structural purposes are the environmental conditions (temperature and moisture levels) in which the wood is to be located, the size and shape of the wood members, and the estimated loading cycles on the wood member.

The way in which wood is cut to become a piece of lumber also affects its ultimate strength. *Plainsawn lumber* is cut in a series of parallel planes through the log; this is a sawing method that gives the maximum yield and greatest amount of cut wood from the log. Plainsawn lumber can have a raised grain or a variety of grain patterns in each piece, tends to cup or twist more, and can shrink or swell in width. *Quartersawn lumber* is made by cutting quadrants of a log on the diagonal, at an angle generally radiating from the center of the log. This gives a more even grain pattern but leaves more waste in the cutting, making it more costly than plainsawn. Quartersawn wood is less prone to cup, twist, or warp, has less of a raised grain than plainsawn lumber, and is usually desirable for flooring and finish details because of its tight, consistent grain and fine appearance.

Flaws in a piece of wood such as knots, splits, checks, or warps affect its strength, grading, and appearance. These defects are largely due to natural characteristics, with some influence by the preparation process. This in turn affects where and how individual pieces of wood are used. Almost every piece of wood has some sort of discontinuity or flaw resulting from its growth process or how it is manufactured. *Knots*, indicating where branches were once attached to the wood member, are the most common wood defect. *Knotholes* are holes that are a result of knots that have dropped out of the wood. Both knots and knotholes compromise the structural integrity of a wood member; their size and number affect the grade of a piece of wood. Processing wood can also cause many defects, many as a result of *seasoning*—the controlled method of reducing the moisture content in wood members—in which shrinkage stresses cause distortions such as bowing, cupping, twisting, and crooking. Knowledgeable carpenters are able to judge a piece of wood to determine whether the level of defects in a wood member is allowable for its intended use.

The amount of moisture in a piece of wood affects many of its characteristics. Wood expands as its moisture content rises and shrinks as it lowers. This must always be taken into account when designing and detailing any wood structure, since inevitably wood will shrink or swell depending on its moisture content. Dry lumber has increased strength and resistance to decay, fungi, and insects. This can be done either through the relatively slow process of air-drying or through the use of kilns, as is typical for most wood products today.

Many of today's advances in the wood industry, such as *glue laminates*, plywood, and other engineered wood products, were invented to compensate for some of the material's natural faults and limitations. Wood is highly resistant to acids, bases, and salts, and chemical treatments can increase its resistance to fire, decay, and insect infestation. But connection materials that are often used in wood buildings must also be considered, for they may react to chemicals and should sufficiently resist corrosion. There is also an ever-growing industry of plastics and synthetic wood products that attempt to mimic its aesthetic, such as products for flooring, trim, and siding. These products have emerged as the ethical and environmental issues surrounding the cutting and clearing of trees are the subject of ongoing debates concerning the preservation of many wood species and other animals' natural habitats.

HISTORY

As an architectural material, wood is one of the most diverse and abundant in the history of construction. It is also the only truly organic major architectural material. For thousands of years wood was the most conventional building material along with stone and clay. It has typically been plentiful and readily used by man for construction. Today wood is the primary source of energy for 40 percent of the world's population, particularly in the developing world. For decades wood has played a key role in the construction of road systems, bridges, railroads, and the construction process of most buildings. In the United States almost all of the 1.25 million houses built each year are constructed of light wood framing, according to a recent study conducted by the Society of American Foresters.

Wood construction can be traced to the beginning of civilization through archaeology in the crude structures of the pit dwellings, simple earth structures covered with wood members for shelter. Other early wood structures include yurts, teepees, and lean-tos. Early structures in Greece, India, Northern Europe, and Japan were later typically constructed of masonry walls with a timber roof. Vitruvius, the Roman architect and author of *De Architectura* (27 BCE), talks about the primitive hut in his writings, which perhaps is the first written historical record of the use of wood in a structure. It was not until the Middle Ages that braced wood frames began to be used for walls. The hand-hewed practice of the cruck frame and the braced frame were two early timber framing methods that evolved in Europe, which laid the foundation for the framing methods we still use today.

For over 2,000 years timber framing was the method of choice for building with wood. It began with the realization that timbers from the forest could be hand-hewed into square log shapes and joined with mortise and tennon, dovetail, or pegged joints. In latitudes with thick forests, such as Europe, Japan, China, and India, the method of building with timber became a craft, with each geographic area developing its own style and process. For example, during the Middle Ages in England, in order to conserve wood, shorter wood members were used with in-filled masonry, a technique now identified with the Tudor period of the sixteenth century. By the 1600s craft guilds developed, teaching the art of timber framing and wood joinery, with apprentices taking great pride in their profession.

When British colonists arrived in North America in the seventeenth century, they brought with them their various regional methods and traditions of timber framing. The abundance of trees provided the early settlers with an almost limitless supply of construction materials, as forests covered an estimated 46 percent of the continental United States in the year 1600. (Today that number has dropped to about 33 percent, due in large part to the clearing of land initially for farming and later even more so for the development of growing suburban communities.) By the mid-1800s large timber framing began to disappear due to the invention of the wire nail and circular saw, and the existence of sawmills that could inexpensively produce smaller pieces of lumber. In the 1830s in Chicago, a new method of building called balloon framing evolved, which required less skill to construct and less time to build than timber framing.

It also utilized smaller trees that are more common. With the quickly growing population and the need for faster construction, balloon framing gained in popularity. It has been argued that this method also evolved due to the easy construction methods for barns and outbuildings. Eventually balloon framing evolved into *stud framing*, more commonly known as *platform framing*, which we use today, and which allows for even smaller trees with a modular system of dimensions. Compared to traditional timber framing methods, this construction method was seen as fast, efficient, and economical.

In recent decades, the use of wood has given rise to ecological debate. On the one hand, it is a renewable resource; on the other, awareness of clearing forests and how we harvest wood can be cause for concern. The growing sensitivity to environmental responsibility, as well as the ever-rising palette of material alternatives, has contributed to a waning dominance of wood. Plywood, particleboards, and wood-simulating plastics are now a large segment of the wood industry.

Despite such competition, wood remains the most popular building material for many reasons. It is completely natural, recyclable, endlessly replenishable, and if harvested responsibly does not disturb the ecological balance of the environment. Its use can also lend a sense of connectivity to the landscape through its warmth and naturalness. This tactile material can appeal to the psyche and senses and also fulfills the sustainability requirements of those who seek to address environmental concerns in construction.

DESIGN CONSIDERATIONS

There is a wide range of choices and issues that can inform designing with wood. These can include the particular construction method, structural criteria, and load requirements. Choices of the type of wood species or products and their grades and ratings also affect a design's outcome. The range of wood species available is seemingly great, with choices that determine the grain, color, size, sustainability, cost, and availability of the wood itself, which varies significantly over different geographic locations. Different species have colors that can range from black to tan to red to pale cream, and no individual member ever has the same exact appearance as the next. However, there are, of course, some wood types that are typically used for specific purposes—fir, pine, and spruce are most often used for structural members, while more refined woods such as cherry or birch, which are richer in appearance, are used for furniture and finish carpentry. Still other woods, such as California redwood, cypress, and red or white cedar, are more decay-resistant and therefore are often used for exterior exposures, such as roofing and wall cladding.

Wood construction is often categorized into four methods:

LOG CONSTRUCTION is one of the oldest building construction methods in history and was used not only for dwellings but also for other structures such as churches, towers, and bridges. Today it is rarely used unless there is a desire to obtain the distinct aesthetic of a log structure. Log walls are either stacked with solid logs or spaced and filled with other insulating materials such as mud or plaster chinking. The log itself can either be left as a round shape or can be edge-sawed for a more solid stacking connection. Log construction is characterized by its corner joints, which interlock with either a dovetail or cross-lap connection. These joints were historically carved by hand, though in log house kits today they are precisely cut by machinery to achieve uniformity and economy.

—

TIMBER-FRAME CONSTRUCTION is built story-by-story with sills, posts, beams, and struts erected at each level. This method historically consisted of oversized handmade mortise and tennon joints in which a large portion of the interacting wood members is subtracted to fit one inside of the other. Today most of these connections are computer processed, making them more accurate and economical. Today steel connectors are oftentimes used in place of the traditional mortise and tennon and pegged connections.

Timber-framed buildings cannot span the same distance with the same amount of material as steel, nor give a smooth continuity of material as concrete can, but they can give a unique aesthetic, a natural fragrance, and a general "environmental" connotation unlike any other material by leaving a natural material exposed in a recognizable state. It is more exceptional today to see a heavy timber-framed building because heavy timber must compete economically with a wider range of structural materials. Additionally, the environmental implications of destroying our older growth forests have given the timber industry limited supply of raw material. Recently there has been a rejuvenation of the timber-framing craft where centuries-old methods of joinery and the art of historical construction methods have been revived and put to practice. Building codes have a classification for heavy timber (type IV) that allows greater height and area than is the case for light wood frame (type V).

—

BALLOON FRAMING involves using wood members that continue through two or more stories in height. The roof and floor members attach to continuous members or studs running from sill to roof. The length of these studs makes them difficult to erect efficiently, and the spacing between them can act as multiple unintended fire and smoke flues, increasing the risk of more rapidly spreading a fire to upper floors. This method is often found in older structures and is not commonly used today.

—

PLATFORM FRAMING is a floor-by-floor process traditionally used for buildings no higher than three stories, and is the most common method of wood construction in North America today, accounting for almost 95 percent of wood construction. The wall frame is formed with story-height studs that are joined together with a sole plate at the bottom and double wall plates above, and then covered on both sides with plywood or another wood sheathing product to stiffen the frame. The walls are then most often covered on both sides with finishing materials. One of the advantages of platform framing is the use of shorter, standardized pieces of lumber, such as 8' (2.4 m) "studs," which are more available, less expensive, and easier to handle. Another advantage is that each floor is constructed one at a time, allowing for the floor below to act as a framing platform for the next. Other advantages are that it uses simple nailing connections. Today the majority of homes are built with a platform framing, though there is a huge range of new products available in the wood industry, including the panelized construction industry, which includes structural insulated panels (SIPs) and other types of wood panel products.

Wood has its disadvantages. Wood structures are susceptible to damage by fungi, insects, and especially fire. The threat of insects and fungi both increase due to the level of moisture content of wood and duration of time in which the wood is exposed to moisture. The best protection against both of these damaging elements is to use dry wood products and ensure that the wood is kept dry during construction and thereafter. In a living tree, the sapwood contains approximately 30 percent or more moisture. Certain species of wood, such as redwood, cedar, bald cypress, black walnut, and black locust, are naturally resistant to decay and fungi because they have chemical extractions that combat biological attack. Others, such as redwood, red cedar, and bald cypress, are also naturally resistant to insects due to natural oils in the wood that act as preservatives. Most wood-attacking organisms need both oxygen and moisture to survive. To reduce the problems caused by these organisms, wood must be kept away from the ground, crawlspaces and attics should be ventilated, and wood should be kept clear from any water near drainage areas and areas where there could be possible moisture from leaking pipes.

For decay and insect resistance, areas that are close to the ground, or outdoor structures such as fences, decks, docks, or porches, wood can be impregnated with preservatives through a high-pressure injection process. To protect against moisture, a pressure treatment is the most effective means. There are also preservative treatments that can be applied without pressure to the surface of a piece of wood to protect it from decay and insects. There are three types of preservatives that can be applied to wood:

WATER-BASED PRESERVATIVES leave the wood odorless and ready to be painted and also do not leach out or leak into the environment.

—

OIL-BASED PRESERVATIVES, which are highly toxic, may alter the color of wood, but can be painted to offset this.

—

CREOSOTE PRESERVATIVES are usually used in marine and saltwater applications. They give the wood a dark-colored, oily surface, and a strong odor that remains for a long period of time. Environmental restrictions greatly limit use of this method today.

For a fire-retardant treatment, lumber is placed in a pressure vessel and impregnated with chemical salts, which reduce its flammability. Fire-retardant lumber is usually not used in detached single-family home construction but is used most often in nonstructural partitions and other interior locations of constructions needing fire resistance.

TYPES

Wood as a material is classified into two major categories: *softwoods* and *hardwoods*, which actually do not refer to the materials' relative hardness or strength. Most softwoods have spiky leaves or needles and are usually evergreens, although there are exceptions to the rule, such as western larch, which loses its needles every year. Softwoods are usually also *coniferous*, which means that their seeds (conifers) are enclosed in cones. They generally grow much quicker, are softer, and are easier to work with than hardwoods. Some common softwoods include fir, pine, cedar, Douglas fir, redwood, hemlock, and spruce. Hardwoods generally have flat, broad leaves and seeds that are enclosed in fruit or nuts, such as acorns. Hardwoods are typically *deciduous*, and lose their leaves each season (although there are a few exceptions such as the Pacific madrone and tanoak, both found in the northwestern United States). Another distinction between the hardwoods and softwoods is that the former contain a more complex system of pores or vessels while the latter have a simple structure of large cells. Both hardwoods and softwoods have examples of strong and durable species, but hardwoods are generally more durable as a reflection of their slower rates of growth and tighter annual ring patterns. Some common hardwoods include beech, oak, ash, elm, sycamore, birch, balsa and walnut.

Softwoods are typically used for general construction purposes while hardwoods are usually used for flooring, paneling, trim pieces, and other finishing elements. Hardwoods are sometimes sliced into thin veneers and joined to lesser expensive woods for cost savings.

Lumber

Lumber in the United States is sized in inches by *nominal dimensions* rather than actual dimensions; nominal dimensions are not written with inch marks while actual dimensions are. For instance, a 2×4 is approximately 1.5" × 3.5" (38 × 90 mm), although slight variation is standard. Those in the construction profession simply refer to the nominal dimension, with the understanding that they are not actual measurements. In fact, because there are so many variables affecting the condition of wood, such as moisture and manufacturing techniques, it is never wise to assume that even the actual dimensions are to be taken literally. The best detailing specifies a wood detail with a *tolerance*, or allowed deviation, so that the wood members can have slight variation in dimensions. When a designer specifies wood for a construction project they must designate the species, the grade, the seasoning (moisture content percentage), the surfacing (how a piece of wood should be finished on its surface), the nominal size, and if there are any treatments to the wood. The construction manager or contractor will then order the wood from a lumber resource by specifying the lengths and the number of pieces of wood for each length. The following are some common terms for wood members:

BOARDS are pieces of lumber that are less than 2" in nominal thickness. They are usually graded for appearance rather than their strength and are used for trim, siding, and sub flooring purposes.

—

DIMENSIONAL LUMBER ranges from 2–4" (50–100 mm) of nominal thickness. These are usually available in 2' (610 mm) increments in length, with common lengths ranging from 8–16' (2.4–4.9 m). This lumber is usually graded for strength rather than appearance and is used for general construction needs.

—

TIMBER is wood members that are nominally 5" × 5" (127 mm) or larger in thickness. These are typically graded for their strength.

—

STRUCTURAL SOLID WOOD is a load-bearing wood that is rigorously graded with capacity requirements. Spruce, fir, pine, and larch are some of the common wood species used for structural wood members.

Laminated wood

Laminated wood is a structural type consisting of built-up layers of wood that have been glued together to form an engineered and stress-rated member. Laminated wood is often preferred to solid wood members due to its consistent appearance, availability in different sizes, and water resistance. *Glue-laminated wood* (or *glulam*) is composed of many small chips of wood glued together in different directions to create a girder or other structural members. The different orientations of these wood pieces provide greater strength than a single piece of wood of the same size and also allow for sizes and lengths unlimited by log sizes. The wood is fully seasoned (dried) before being laminated to ensure a high-quality member. Glulams are specified by their quality and size much like typical timber. High-quality glulams will use a specific type of wood and have a greater strength or size. The development of glulams was a significant advancement in the twentieth-century wood construction industry, allowing for longer spans and for shapes that the natural material cannot provide.

Panel products

Panel products are an efficient use of wood and are easy to install. They are also less vulnerable to swelling and shrinkage due to moisture and temperature changes. There are three general groups of wood panel products: plywood, composite panels, and non-veneer panels. These categories are classified as structural wood panels, which are specified either by their thickness or a span rating, both indicated on a stamp that is placed on each wood panel. The span rating is an indication of a structural panel's load-bearing capacity and gives a common industry marker for the many different types of panels made of different wood species.

PLYWOOD is made up of multiple wood veneers glued together, alternating grain direction ninety degrees for each adjacent veneer. There are always an odd number of veneers, with the grain of the front and back always parallel to the longer dimension of the sheet. Plywood is generally made from wood veneer sheets that were rotary sliced from logs and then kiln-dried to an approximate moisture content of 5 percent. These sheets are then glued and pressed together under elevated temperatures and high pressures to create a solid board. The plywood sheets are then trimmed, sanded, graded, and stamped. Plywood grades are rated by the American Plywood Association with the letters N, A, B, C, or D, with N being a smooth, natural finish; A, a smooth, paint-grade finish; B, a smooth finish with knots and plugs; C, a sheathing grade, unsanded; and D, a grade limited to interior panel use. The standard plywood sheet is 4' × 8' (1.2 × 2.4 m) and can range in thickness from 0.25–1.125" (6.4–28.6 mm).

One of the main advantages of plywood is its high uniform strength in relation to its weight. Its unique cross-layered structure in addition to the adhesives used give it a high strength. It is also less susceptible to shrinkage, swelling, and warping than a solid wood member. Plywood is readily available and is an economical way to frame a building. It also affords a way to create curved shapes to be framed in a project. Disadvantages include its weight and unwieldiness, and unless a high grade is selected plywood can have voids or inconsistencies in its structure. It is an environmentally friendly material in that it puts waste and wood scraps from mills to good use. It is also an attractive material because it is 100 percent biodegradable and has an environmentally friendly manufacturing process. Chemicals used to treat and glue in the products are of concern because they may give off unwanted gases inside a building and may have other adverse effects on the environment.

—

COMPOSITE PANELS have two or more parallel veneer sheets that are bonded together with a core of reconstituted wood fibers through a synthetic adhesive using heat and pressure. Composite panels are available in a vast range of different types. Panels can differ by the type of wood used to construct them, their thickness, and their structural capability. Some composite panels are available with insulation inserted into the sheet or with a different material, such as aluminum, attached to one side to construct an all-inclusive wall panel.

—

There are three basic **NON-VENEERED WOOD PANELS** available, each having different classes or grades: **ORIENTED STRAND BOARD (OSB)** is made up of long strands of wood particles that are glued and compressed together in a resin into three to five layers; **WAFERBOARD** is made up of large flakes of wood, also glued and compressed together; and **PARTICLEBOARD** is made up of smaller wood particles than OSB and waferboard and has a finer appearance.

Manufactured wood components

Manufactured wood components combine dimensional lumber, structural panel products, wood connectors, and other wood products to create a more efficient building component that is a complete wood member.

TRUSSES are structural roof and floor components that usually combine 2×4s or 2×6s with toothed plate connectors (see p. 92). An advantage of using a truss structural system is that it uses less wood than a conventional rafters-and-joists structural system. Additionally, they are usually engineered by the manufacturer after a designer submits the span, roof pitch, and the desired overhang detail. A disadvantage of using trusses is that their struts can make attic spaces unusable.

—

PLYWOOD I-BEAMS and **BOX BEAMS** can be used in place of traditional rafters or joists for long-span framing. These manufactured components can be custom designed and use timber resources more efficiently than conventional wood components.

—

PANEL AND BOX COMPONENTS have become more and more prevalent in the construction industry as entire walls, floors, and roofs can be prefabricated off-site. Some panel components can also be prefabricated to include insulation, windows, wiring, and exterior or interior finish material. The panel industry has expanded rapidly, making a wide range of options and variations of panel components available for different construction types. This customization of panels not only addresses a building's more particular needs but also allows a designer more affordable yet varied options in the prefabrication industry. Panelization places more of the work in a factory than at the construction site. Designers need to adjust their approach toward materials and construction details accordingly.

Thermally modified wood

Thermally modified wood (or *torrefied wood*) comes from the process of taking kiln-dried wood and heating it in a kiln to chemically and physically change the wood. The wood is dried slowly and then baked again in an air-tight kiln at a higher temperature that makes the sugars and tannins in the wood unattractive to insects. The wood becomes a darker color with a very low moisture content. The wood also hardens and has improved dimensional stability after the baking. The wood is steamed and cooled slowly again under close control to minimize stress within the wood as it returns it to ambient temperature and humidity levels. The resulting wood is resistant to biological decay. The advantages of thermally modified wood are is that no paint or stain is needed and it requires almost no maintenance. Another advantage is the resistance to biological attack. Depending on the wood species, the dark color of the torrefied wood will lighten to a gray and will become more brittle comparable to regular wood.

Bamboo

From China to India, bamboo has been a prime material for wood construction for centuries. Bamboo can be harvested in three to six years, a relatively short time period comparable to traditional wood, which usually can take ten to twenty years to mature. One of the fastest growing bamboos can grow up to one meter a day and reach its full mature state in two months. Bamboo is very rigid and dense, making it a strong material with a high tensile strength, which increases as the material ages. Bamboo has its limitations in construction: The material shrinks with temperature and moisture changes, and like many other wood products, bamboo is attractive to insects and is vulnerable to fungal rot if not treated. The material is economical and efficiently renewable.

CONNECTORS

Nails, screws, bolts, toothed plates, and adhesives are used to connect wood. Wood fasteners are often noted as the weakest component of wood construction, rarely being as strong as a monolithic material or the wood member itself. Historically, pegged or mortise and tennon connections were used to connect wood, both of which compromised the strength of a wood member due to the removal of material from each member.

NAILS are available in a wide range of sizes, materials, and shapes, geared to a particular use or purpose. Fastening with nails is the fastest and easiest way to connect wood members, requiring no pre-drilling or preparation, as they are driven into wood members with a hammer or a pneumatic gun. Nails are most often made of mild steel, but are available in a variety of other metals such as aluminum, copper, zinc, brass, or stainless steel. While the rest of the world measures a nail's diameter and length in millimeters, in the U.S. they are measured in a term called *pennies* and designated as *d*. A 2d nail is 1" (25 mm) long, a 6d nail is 2" (51 mm) long, and a 10d nail is 3" (76 mm) long. The three types most often used in construction are *common*, *galvanized*, and *finish* nails. Common nails have flat heads, are used in most construction framing, and are not intended to be exposed to the environment. Galvanized nails have a protective zinc coating on them to inhibit rust and corrosion. Finish nails are not meant to be seen; they have a tiny head and are used in finish woodwork such as casework and interior detailing. Other types of nails are box nails, casing nails, brad nails, roofing nails, cut nails, and concrete nails, each shaped differently in terms of its head, shaft, and point, to suit their particular use.

—

SCREWS generally yield a stronger and tighter connection than nails due to their threaded shaft, which is placed directly into wood or into pre-drilled holes and then screwed into place. Wood screws take longer to install than nails, but because they have threads they have more holding strength and are somewhat easier and less damaging to remove. The more threads they have, the stronger they are. They are typically used for light framing, finish work, cabinetry, furniture, or drywall. Drywall screws, which are typically used for connecting drywall to wood or light steel members, are small in size but can be inserted with a power screwdriver without pre-drilling. Screws should be approximately 0.125" (3.175 mm) less in length than the combined thickness of the two elements being joined. Screws are classified by use (wood, metal, drywall, set screws, machine), type of head (flat, round, oval, slotted, Phillips, pan, hex socket), finish (steel, aluminum, stainless steel, brass, bronze), lengths (0.5–6" [13–153 mm]), and diameter (up to 24 gauge).

—

BOLTS are threaded connectors that have round heads on one end and receive a threaded nut on the other. *Nuts* are threaded to receive the end of the bolt. Bolts are typically used for major structural connections when screws and nails are insufficient. They vary in length from 0.5–30" (13–762 mm), with diameters up to 1.25" (32 mm), and can have flat, round, square, or hexagonal heads. Different types of nuts include cap, wing, square, or hexagon nuts.

Washers are flat metal disks sometimes used with bolts to distribute the compressive forces across a larger area of the connected wood members. Washers can also be used as spacing devices or to provide a seal between two materials. While most standard bolts use a nut to secure the end of the connection, *lag bolts* can be used when one end of the bolt is not accessible.

—

TIMBER CONNECTORS increase the load-carrying capacity of bolts and are typically only used in heavy timber construction. The most common timber connector is called the *split ring connector*, two rings placed in pre-drilled holes in the two connecting members and secured with a bolt to increase its strength. The split ring not only spreads the load but also allows the wood to adjust for shrinkage and expansion.

—

TOOTHED PLATES are most often used in the manufacturing of trusses and other prefabricated roof and floor members. These toothed fasteners act as a plate of multiple nails that splice wood members together. They are inserted into wood by hydraulic presses, pneumatic presses, or mechanical rollers, and form a strong connection with the fibers of a larger volume of the wood than would be the case with a nail or screw, thus minimizing splitting.

—

ADHESIVES are most often used in the manufacturing of plywood, cabinetry, some wood structural elements, laminated woods, and other panel wood products. Adhesives may be used on the construction site in conjunction with nails or screws to make a more permanent connection or to minimize minor movement or squeaking in flooring. Adhesives that are used on a construction site include sealants or other glues that are dispersed from a gun in mastic form. The nail or other fastener secures the connection while the glue cures.

—

METAL PLATE FASTENERS serve a variety of uses, the most common being the *joist hanger*, which creates a strong connection at a right angle between joists and beams. These fasteners can be made of steel but are typically made of galvanized steel sheet metal. There are a wide range of sheet metal connections that join wood members for light frame construction.

Stork Nest Farm

Dvůr Semtín, Olbramovice, Czech Republic — SGL Projekt
Oak screen, glue-laminated arches

DESIGN INTENTION

A nineteenth-century farmstead that had been abandoned for thirty years was newly renovated as a venue for conferences and recreation. The farm's old distillery, replete with chimneys, had become a popular roost for some local storks, whose nest became the farm's symbol and now informs the design of the equestrian arena. For ninety years generations of storks have returned to the farm; the architects wanted to bring people back here too.

The architects intended to build with a stork's attention to shape and materials, with no desire for originality or vanity. The residential program consists of a reception area, hotel, conference hall, restaurant, pool, and recreation garden. A barn, stable, and outdoor exercise yards accompany the equestrian arena, which hosts a variety of cultural and social events.

MATERIALITY

The new complex's arena exhibits wood in both its raw and refined states. The glulam frame demonstrates the potential of modern manufacturing and engineering while the tangled oak wrap shows the beauty of wood in its natural state.
The arena has an external diameter of 111.5' (34 m) and height of 41' (12.5 m). The supporting structure is made of glulam timber beams clad with translucent polycarbonate. Approximately 200 tons of oak logs make up the external expression, which recalls the stork nest. The natural deterioration of the logs will not harm the performance of the structural or enclosure systems, but will hopefully enhance their symbolic value in the project, and can be easily replaced.

The equestrian arena's riding surface is made of sand with capillary irrigation. A removable wood floor can be installed for other events. The riding area is surrounded by a protective barrier and seating for approximately two hundred people, with additional seating on an upper level.

TECHNICAL

Twenty-four glulam arches were anchored to the concrete foundation ring; at their tops they are joined to a 26' diameter (8 m) steel compression ring. Since all arches have the same dimensions, the jigs to make the first arch were efficiently used to make the others. The clear span of the frame is more than 93' (28 m). Pinned connections join the arches at top and bottom, and wood purlins, placed at 3.3' (1 m) intervals, fix them in place laterally and support the polycarbonate cladding.

The purlins and polycarbonate cladding are installed below the upper edges of the glue-laminated arches so the upper edges are available to receive a galvanized steel truss. The skeletal steel truss does not contribute at all to the structural spans of the arena, but supports the hundreds of oak logs that give the building its identity. Brackets secured to the top chord of the truss support the heavier logs, while steel cables secure them to the bottom of the truss. The logs' irregularity is counterpoint to the highly rational construction systems below.

The compression ring supports a suspended grid containing lighting, audio, and other equipment. The oculus is covered by a dome-shaped translucent cover that lets in light and conceals ventilation equipment. A screen of oak members intercepts excessive light and radiant heat before it enters the enclosure system. Natural ventilation effectively controls interior temperatures.

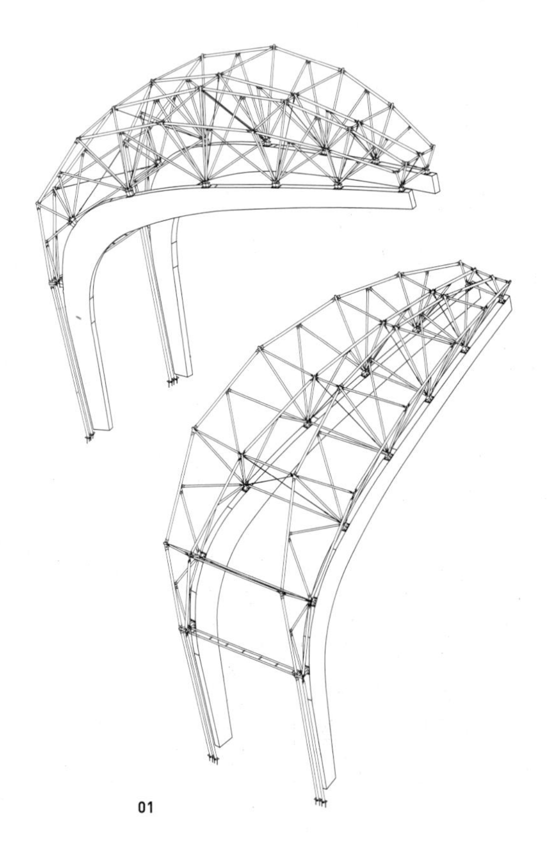

01

01 Glue-laminated arches and galvanized steel supporting frame

02 Building section

03 Oak logs attached to supporting frame

04 Exterior view from outdoor exercise ring

05 Entryway

06 Interior

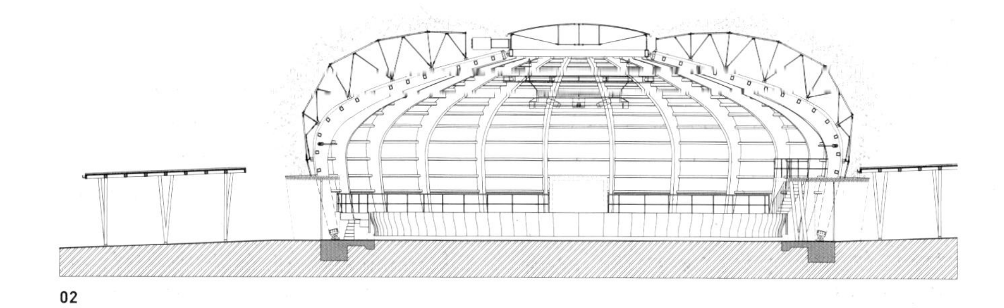

02

03

04

05

06

Private Residence in Riedikon

Uster, Switzerland — Gramazio & Kohler
Pine slats, CNC fabrication

DESIGN INTENTION

With a wooden slat system covering its elevations, this three-level house is a modern update of the gable-roofed houses and barns surrounding the site. The client offered two conditions: maintain their neighbor's view of Lake Greifen to the west and restrict parking to the east of the house. The local building codes required that all windows be vertical rectilinear openings.

The solution is a wedge-shaped house, similar to a truncated gable in plan and form. The architects used pine fins to conceal and cover the house elevations to achieve desired levels of transparency. Subtle adjustments made to the slats optimize oblique views to and from the windows of the house, controlling daylight penetration into the spaces as well.

MATERIALITY

The house is wrapped with 315 CNC-milled pine slats, created using a specially developed program to control the mass-customization fabrication process. These slender wood fins articulate the surface of the house as a counterpoint to its basic mass. Their cross-sections modulate in relation to the windows to control sunlight and view. Where there is no cladding, sliding glass doors open to a terrace with open, unrestricted views of the lake. The undulating shapes of the machined slats embody the gentle curves of the wood grain, which is left unfinished to expose the warm hue of the natural wood. The structural system of reinforced concrete is fully enveloped by the well-insulated timber-framed walls. Fiber-reinforced cement panels clad the building walls, and the concrete-reinforced floor contains the building's radiant heating system.

TECHNICAL

The 1.2" × 5.9" (30 × 150 mm) pine slats were CNC-milled to produce highly varied viewing and lighting conditions using the simple fin-like system. Using CNC technology a modest material like pine could be precisely manipulated to achieve results not possible with traditional methods, allowing the profile of was each fin to be changed along its length as it was being created at the fabrication shop. Many of the elements were milled at an angle, increasing the space for light to pass through. The slats are all continuous, so there are some splice joints within a given member. The roof overhangs the tops of the slats, protecting the vulnerable pine end-grain from the weather. The bottoms are elevated above the ground to reduce contact with water from below.

The CNC mill was used to bore holes into the center of the edge of each fin, through which the fins were screwed into the face of the building wall by hand. Horizontal battens, made of 3.15 in. square (80 mm square) wood, had been installed at prescribed elevations inside the fiber-cement cladding to receive the screws. Bushings were used to hold fins at least 1.57" (40 mm) off the face of the building wall, where they are consistently spaced 5.9" (150 mm) on center, equal to the fin's depth before being milled. Manipulation of the fin profiles was required the most when crossing windows.

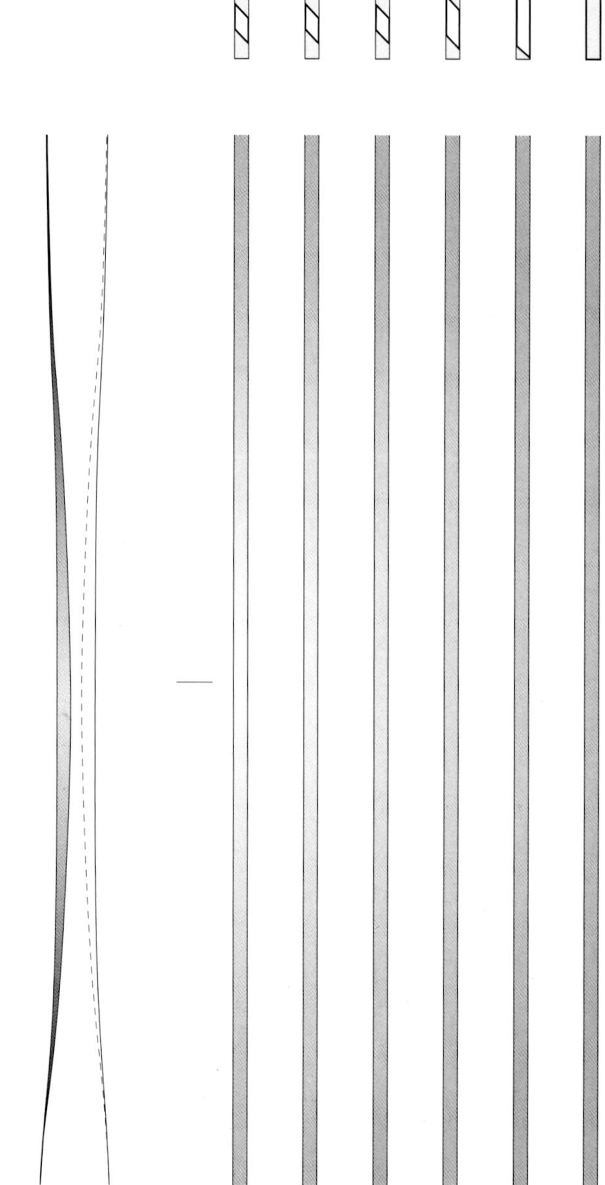

01

01 Wood slats from side, in plan, and in elevation

02 CNC-milled slats over windows and solid walls

02

03 Detailed section and plan at window on upper floor

04 Exterior view from northeast

05 Ground-floor plan

06 Exterior view from north

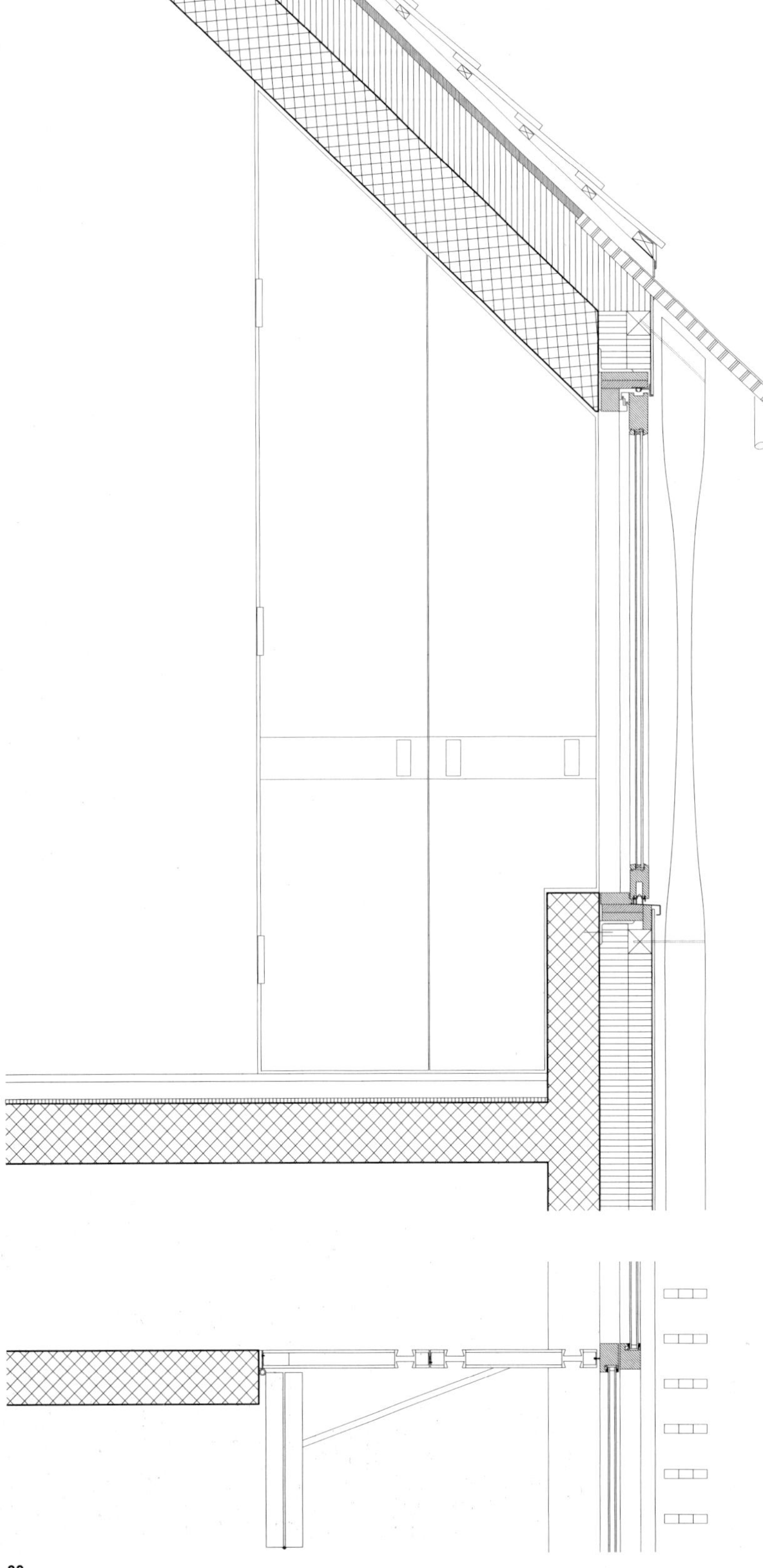

03

04

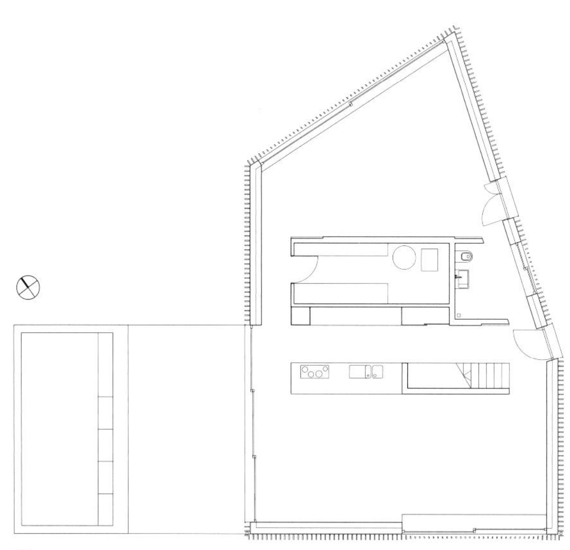

05

06

Viikki Church

Helsinki, Finland — JKMM Architects
Prefabrication, wood shakes

DESIGN INTENTION

Evoking the sanctity of the ancient Finnish forests, the Viikki Church is the result of an invited competition to design new worship and parish halls, offices, and meeting rooms. With a town square planned nearby, the church also connects the eastern and western parts of Helsinki's Latokartano neighborhood. The building can accommodate five hundred people, of whom four hundred fit in the worship space. With only sixteen months allotted for construction, a collaborative team of architects, engineers, wood industry representatives, and academic researchers relied on prefabricated components to address the tight schedule. The objective was to integrate prefabricated components into an architectural whole, so architectural objectives were sometimes placed ahead of structural efficiency to achieve the highest-quality wood construction.

MATERIALITY

The sanctuary facades are covered with mechanically split aspen shakes, the office facilities with horizontally spaced aspen boards, and the belfry with vertical aspen battens. Natural weathering has patinated the unpainted cladding of the facades to a fine silver. To ensure quality the design team paid special attention to the origin, correct felling, drying, and working of the wood, as well as its transport, storage, and installation.

The exterior surfaces of the windows and doors are oak and the interior walls and floor are whitewashed spruce. Custom machine-pressed wood veneer ceiling elements serve as air diffusers and acoustic control elements. The spruce flooring was radially sawn for increased durability, which also exposed a more subtle grain pattern. The goal was to create a harmonious and unified appearance, despite the different surface orientations. In terms of upkeep, it is easy to restore these treated surfaces with lye, even years later.

TECHNICAL

Glue-laminated beams form the primary girders for the church hall and the parish hall. Ten beams span 28.5' (8.7 m) in the main parish hall. The beams were reinforced with a tension rod for the longer 43.3' (13.2 m) spans in the worship hall. The spacing between the girders in all three halls is 3.94' (1.2 m).

The mechanical strength-grading of the spruce lumber was augmented by visual inspection out of concern for its appearance. Finger joints were developed that were unnoticeable on both sides of the joint, preserving the aesthetic features of the wood. During design, moisture modeling of the wall panels was performed to ensure that the surface plies of the laminated veneer plywood panels did not buckle as the wood became wet, or that gaps between elements did not become too great as they dried. Regular moisture, humidity, and temperature measurements were made at the building site to maintain optimal construction conditions. Radial cutting of the wood minimized movement and distortion as the moisture content changed.

The spruce trunks used for the cladding were selected while still standing in the forest. The logs were radially sawn into planks before the lumber was dried in a kiln to reduce the moisture content to roughly 8 or 9 percent of its dry weight. While cutting the lumber to size and milling the tongues and grooves, the carpenters simultaneously graded the wooden slats. It was specified that the radial-sawn lumber was to be cut to size and glued together with the laminated veneer plywood panels on the same day. The panels then were wrapped so that they would not be exposed to any moisture during the trip to the construction site.

As aspen ages the cellular structure hardens and its surface begins to glisten. A sample wall was built on the site to monitor the aging of aspen shake cladding. The wall turned a desired shade of gray over the eighteen-month construction period, confirming the choice of this species. The cellular structure of the shakes was preserved by splitting rather than sawing, because fewer pores are exposed on the surface. These shakes were split radially to minimize bending and cracking, because their annual rings are oriented perpendicular to the surfaces. The shakes are between 2.75–5.5" wide (70–140 mm), and are approximately 1" thick (25 mm) on the exposed edge, which was cut at a 60-degree bevel. The hidden edge is only 0.20" (5 mm) thick. The shakes taper along their 15.7" (400 mm) length, less than half of which is exposed to the weather, to ensure that there are at least two courses of shakes between the inside and the outside at any point on the wall surface. Stainless-steel nails secure the covered upper end of each shake to their batten / counter-batten substrate. Only one nail per shake secures it in place, allowing some degree of movement according to climate conditions. No surface treatments were used on any of the exterior aspen or oak facades.

Solutions to protect the underlying wood elements included a factory-applied waterproofing treatment. These protective layers later served either as permanent vapor barriers or as the final waterproofing material. Thermal insulation was also installed in the exterior wall elements at the factory. In this way, the prefabrication process addressed many of the final assembly needs.

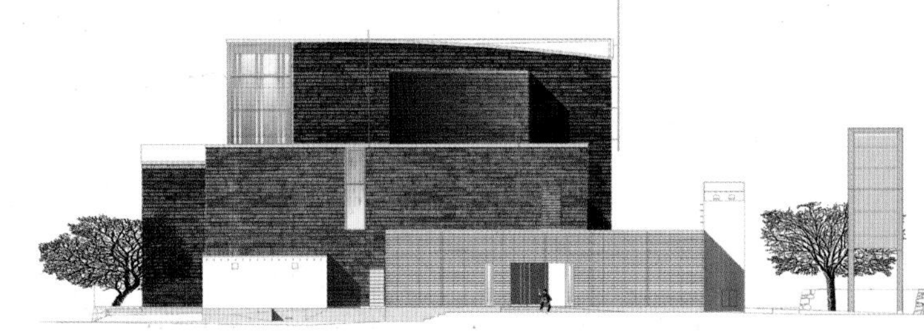

01

01 East elevation study

02 Section and plan through exterior wall; detailed instructions for processing the wood shakes

03 Exterior view from south

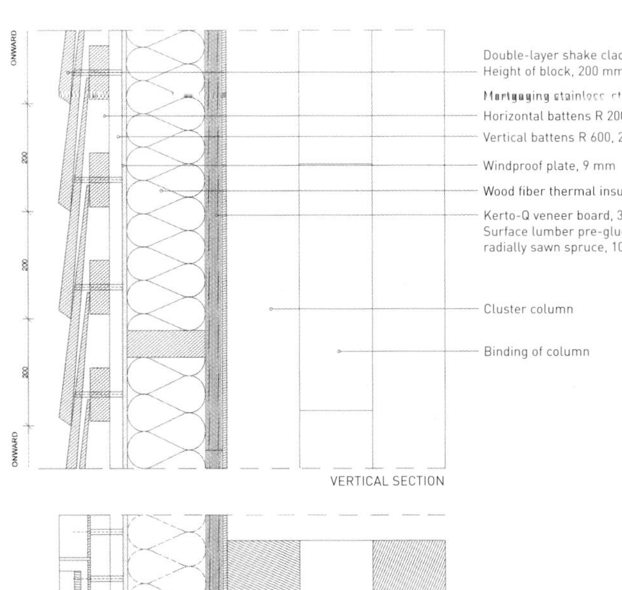

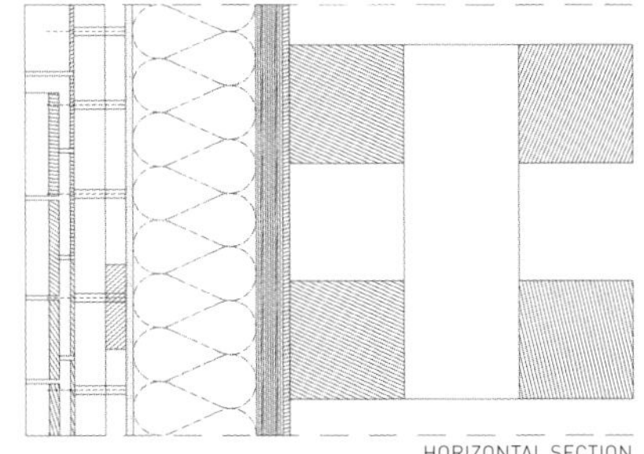

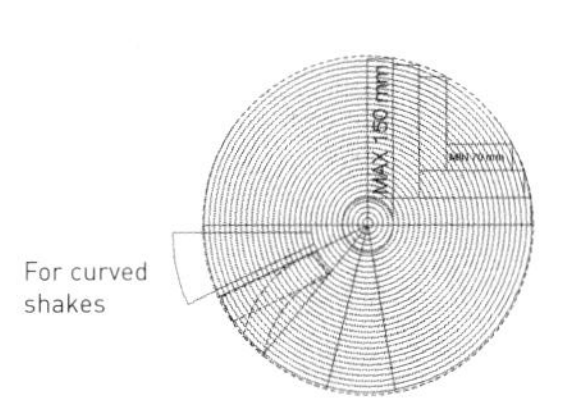

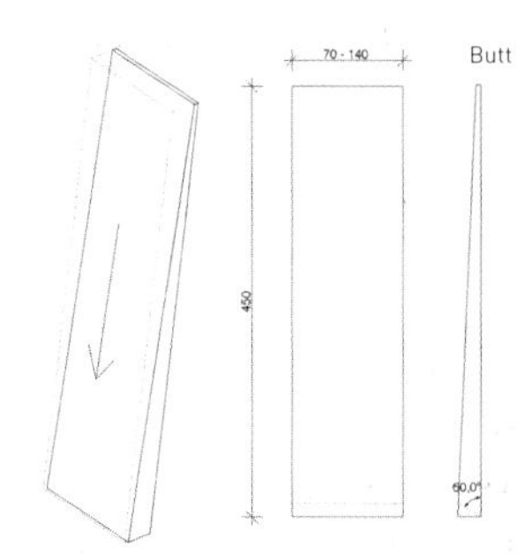

02

03

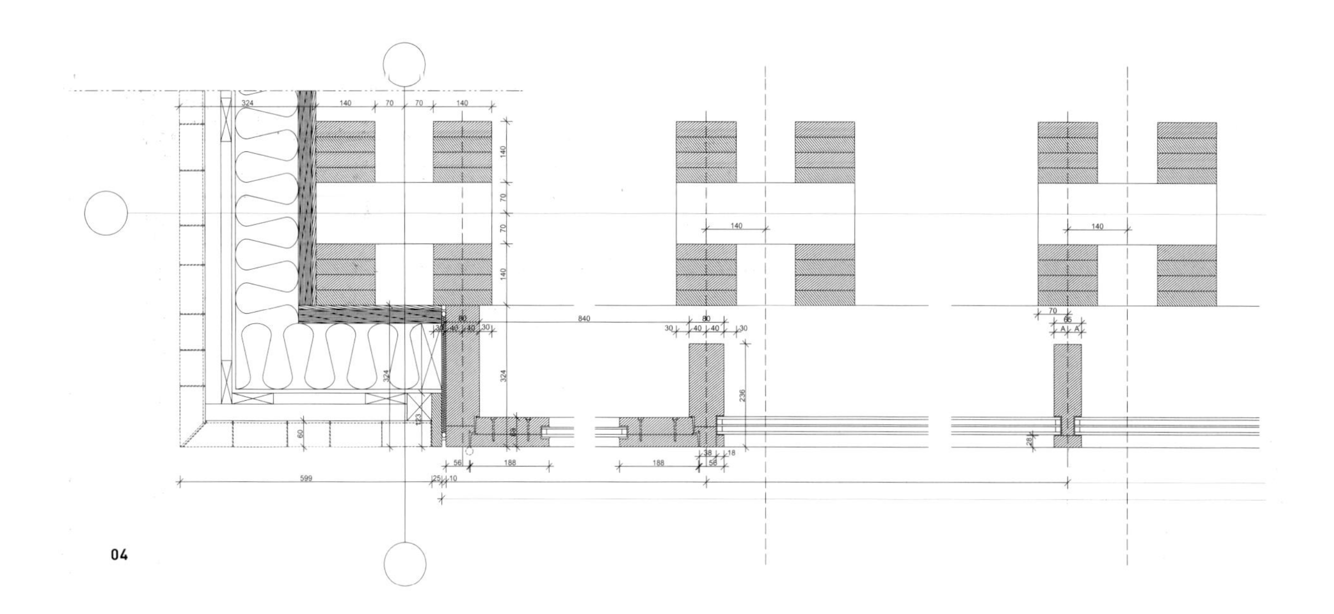

04

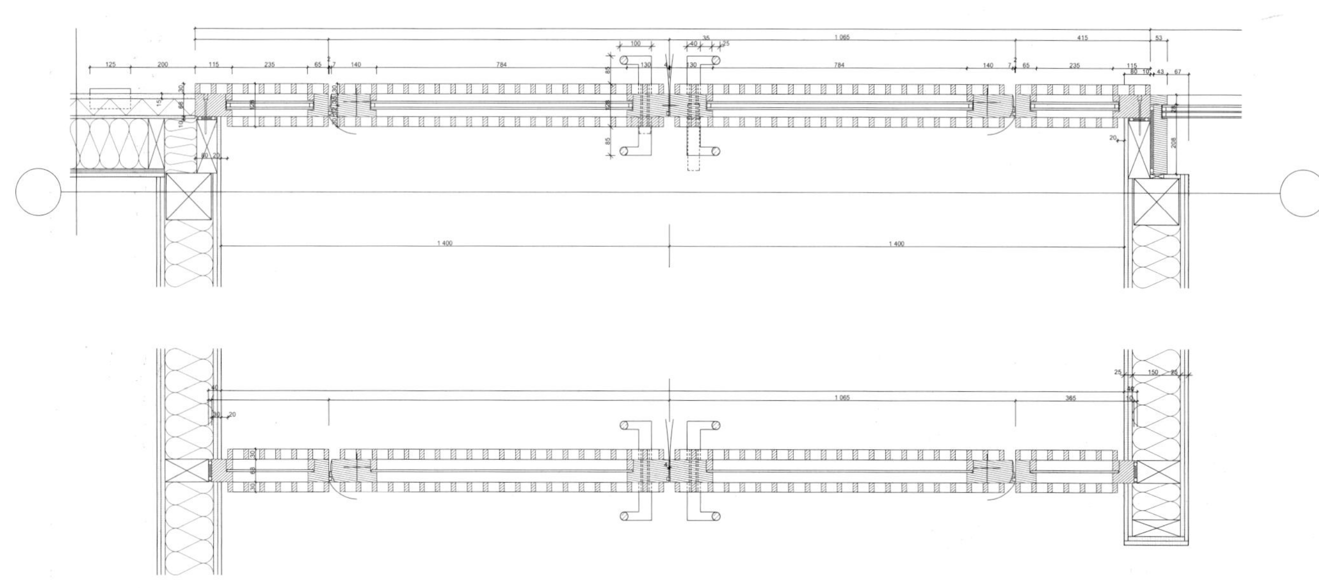

05

04 Plan detail at exterior corner of worship hall

05 Plan detail of wood doors at entry vestibule

06 Installation of tension rod-reinforced wood beam above worship hall

07 Worship hall interior

08 Worship hall interior

09 Section through glazed portion of exterior wall

06

07

08

C
+19.900
+19.740
170
61.5°
28.5°
+19.207
2,648
+15.900
2,648
226
130
102
28
+14.416
+14.340
+14.194
+14.000
75
75
141
61
300

09

Soe Ker Tie House

Noh Bo, Thailand — TYIN Tegnestue Architects
Bamboo

DESIGN INTENTION

Noh Bo is a small village in Thailand, near the border with Myanmar / Burma, where the sixty-year-long conflict in the region has forced several hundred thousand people to flee from their homes. The conflict has left many of the local ethnic Karen refugee children orphaned and in need of shelter. In 2006, a sympathetic Norwegian, Ole Jørgen Edna, built an orphanage in Noh Bo that housed twenty-four children. By 2009, Edna sadly was in need of more beds, and wanted to add units to house up to fifty children.

The Soe Ker Tie House—so-called in the Karen language because of its resemblance to a butterfly—was to provide the children with personal space for informal interaction and play. Six 4-person sleeping units were built using a process that can be replicated in the future. Together the houses also form a small community group. With a budget of only $12,300 (€9,500), the project is a case study in resourcefulness and efficiency.

MATERIALITY

Almost all materials used were of local origin. Only a few materials were from more than a few miles away, such as the cement used in the concrete, corrugated metal roofing, cables, and joining hardware. Even the brick pavers were locally produced.

The project's most prominent feature is the bamboo weaving technique used on the side and back facades of the houses. The same technique can be found within the vernacular style of nearby houses and traditional craftwork. All of the bamboo was harvested within walking distance of the site, and as a rapidly renewable resource it will replenish itself quickly.

To prevent problems with moisture and rot, the sleeping units are raised off the ground on four concrete foundations that were cast inside of old tires. The houses' specially shaped roof promotes natural ventilation within the sleeping units and serves as a means to collect and store rainwater for use in the dry season. The surface rhythm of the woven bamboo cladding resembles that of the corrugated metal roof material overhead.

The Soe Ker Tie Houses blended local skills and TYIN's architectural knowledge. By imparting a working knowledge of important principles like bracing, material economization, and moisture prevention, this project will hopefully lead to a more sustainable building tradition for the Karen people in the future.

TECHNICAL

The primary structural frame was made of a native dense wood called ironwood. All structural wood frames were joined with lapped, sliding-fit connections, which were bolted once the positions were verified. The wood frames were triangulated in one axis with wood struts, and steel diagonal cables were used to impart stability in the other axis.

The metal roofing provides generous overhangs, protecting much of the wood and bamboo assemblies below, and allowing the walls to remain relatively open for ventilation. The end-grains of wood elements were sheltered by overhanging roofing or other elements, protecting the most vulnerable surface of the wood. When lumber was lapped at splices, the end grain of the exposed member was oriented toward the ground, not the sky, reducing the likelihood of end-grain absorption.

Bamboo was used with its tubes (culms) intact as flooring. With the diaphragms removed the tubes were packed to form a screened opening in the wall. Bamboo was split and woven into a mesh, taking advantage of the stiffness of the material. The springiness of bamboo makes each piece press against others in the woven mesh with enough force and friction to form a plane of post-tensioned forces at equilibrium.

Cladding materials were often woven or sandwiched between other elements, minimizing the need for conventional metal fasteners.

01 Perspective of ironwood frame, bamboo deck, and cladding

02 Exterior

03 Weaving split bamboo to form side wall cladding

04 Detail of completed project

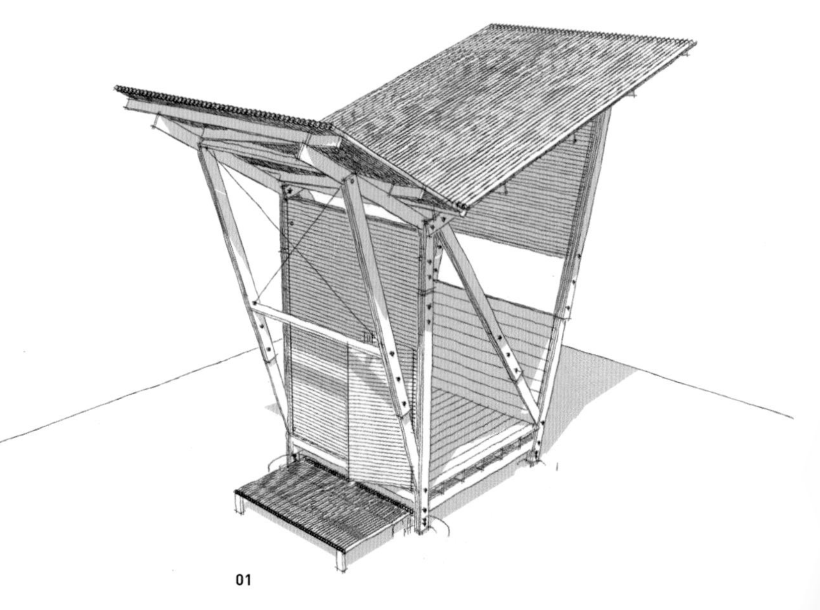

01

02

03

04

05 Transverse section

06 Bamboo floors, wall finishes, and platforms were applied to the completed ironwood frame

07 Varied types of openings, including one with stacked bamboo culms

08 Interior view showing culms on front wall and platforms, and woven split bamboo for side walls

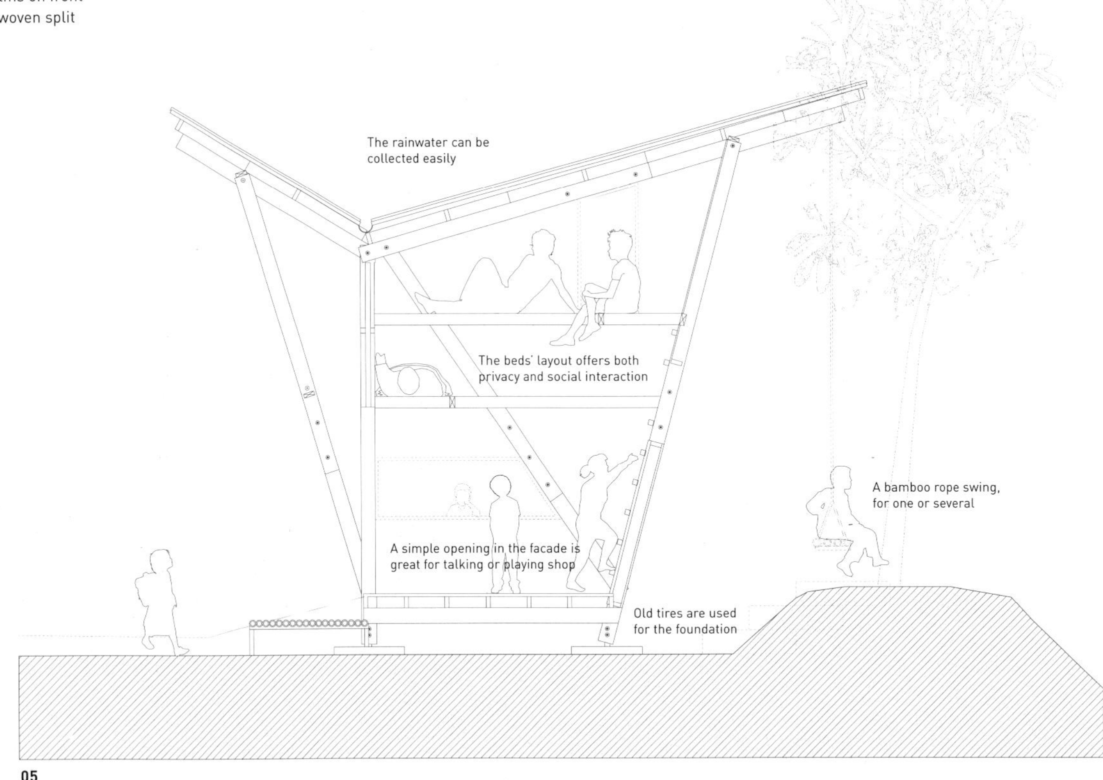

The rainwater can be collected easily
The beds' layout offers both privacy and social interaction
A simple opening in the facade is great for talking or playing shop
A bamboo rope swing, for one or several
Old tires are used for the foundation

05

06

07

08

Harry Parker Community Boathouse

Boston, Massachusetts, USA — Anmahian Winton Architects
Composite resin-core wood panels

DESIGN INTENTION

The 30,000 sq. ft. (2,790 sq. m) Harry Parker Community Boathouse is a long, horizontal floorplan that sits comfortably along the Charles River. The acclaimed building has not only enhanced Boston's urban riverfront, but also offers lessons about sustainable design. The project exemplifies how design and architecture can positively affect a community by attracting new involvement and energy.

The design is inspired by regional precedents such as old covered bridges. The traditional New England tobacco barn with its operable slat cladding is the precedent for the large building's ventilation. References to wooden oars are clearly visible in the boathouse's cladding, which was cleverly adapted to function as louvers, vents, and daylight controls where needed.

The large facility is home to over 170 boats, some of which are as long as 60' (18 m). It also contains a repair shop, training facilities, classrooms, and offices. The structure could just as easily become a barrier between the river and the community, but its segmented construction stacks some of its program on an upper level, and it sits back from the river edge to provide a continuous public path along the water.

MATERIALITY

Varied configurations of wood-veneer resin-core panels give the building its unique material character. These panels offer several advantages compared to standard plywood: they are dimensionally stable, colorfast, and typically demand little maintenance. Used here as a rainscreen, the panels are faced with sustainably farmed obeche (*Triplochiton scleroxylon*) veneers and protected with a factory-applied acrylic finish. The panels were installed in standard-sized large sheets fixed to 18' (5.5 m) tall operable bi-fold aluminum frames, so the wall can be opened for natural ventilation. In other locations the resin-core panels appear as undulating "gills" through which mechanical ventilation equipment brings in fresh air. Over some upper-floor windows, they are shading louvers, reducing glare and heat gain while permitting daylighting and a view to ground-level activity. Each cladding treatment satisfies functional needs, but their experiential effects are more varied: The surfaces of the building transform with visitors' movement around it, not unlike the rhythmic punctuations of the river.

TECHNICAL

The resin-core panels are ventilated rainscreen facades. It was important to maintain equal temperature and humidity conditions on both sides of each panel, so the ventilated cavity behind the panels achieves this goal and reduces environmental stress on the underlying assemblies. The design was tested using full-scale, working prototypes of the wall assemblies that included the kinetic elements. The architect's working drawings, which included exploded axonometrics of the various component assemblies and efficient cutting patterns for the 4' × 8' (1.2 × 2.4 m) sheets of paneling, were provided to the fabricators.

On fixed wall sections, a 2.75" (70 mm) insulated metal panel system is the primary weather barrier. The undulating louvers on the front (southwest) elevation are held by angled aluminum frames placed at 30" (762 mm) intervals to set the angle and receive the staintess-steel screws that secure each louver. The wavy pattern repeats every 30' (9 m) along this elevation. The large bi-fold vents along the 200' (60.9 m) length of the bays are manually operated with a chain pull with gear reducers. Like a good rowing shell, this building derives gratifying performance from human exertion.

In addition to natural ventilation and daylighting, the entire facility is heated and cooled with ground-source heat pumps to meet sustainability objectives. By expanding the thermal comfort boundaries for this building's hearty users to 68–84 °F (20–29 °C) from the typical 72–76 °F (22–24 °C), it was possible to reduce the size of the mechanical equipment. Low-flow plumbing fixtures mitigate water consumption, and stormwater runoff is managed by a hardscape of permeable pavement and crushed stone. Bioretention swales recharge groundwater rather than directing the rainwater into the river.

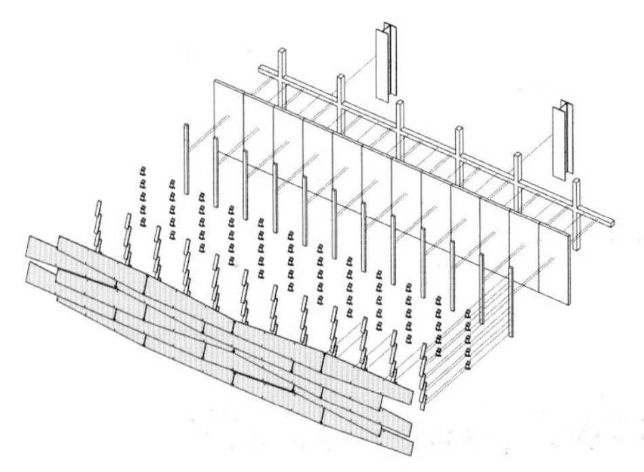

01

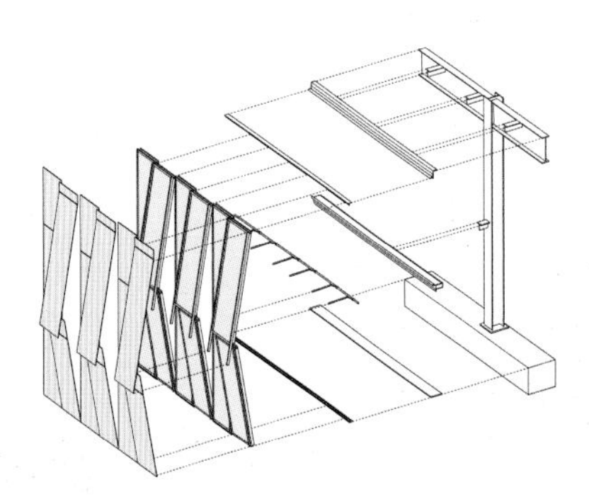

02

01 Exploded axonometric of louver assembly

02 Exploded axonometric of operable vents

03 Vents in open position

04 Resin-core plywood louvers, vents, and fixed wall cladding near boathouse entry

05 Exterior wall section, plan, and elevation

03

04

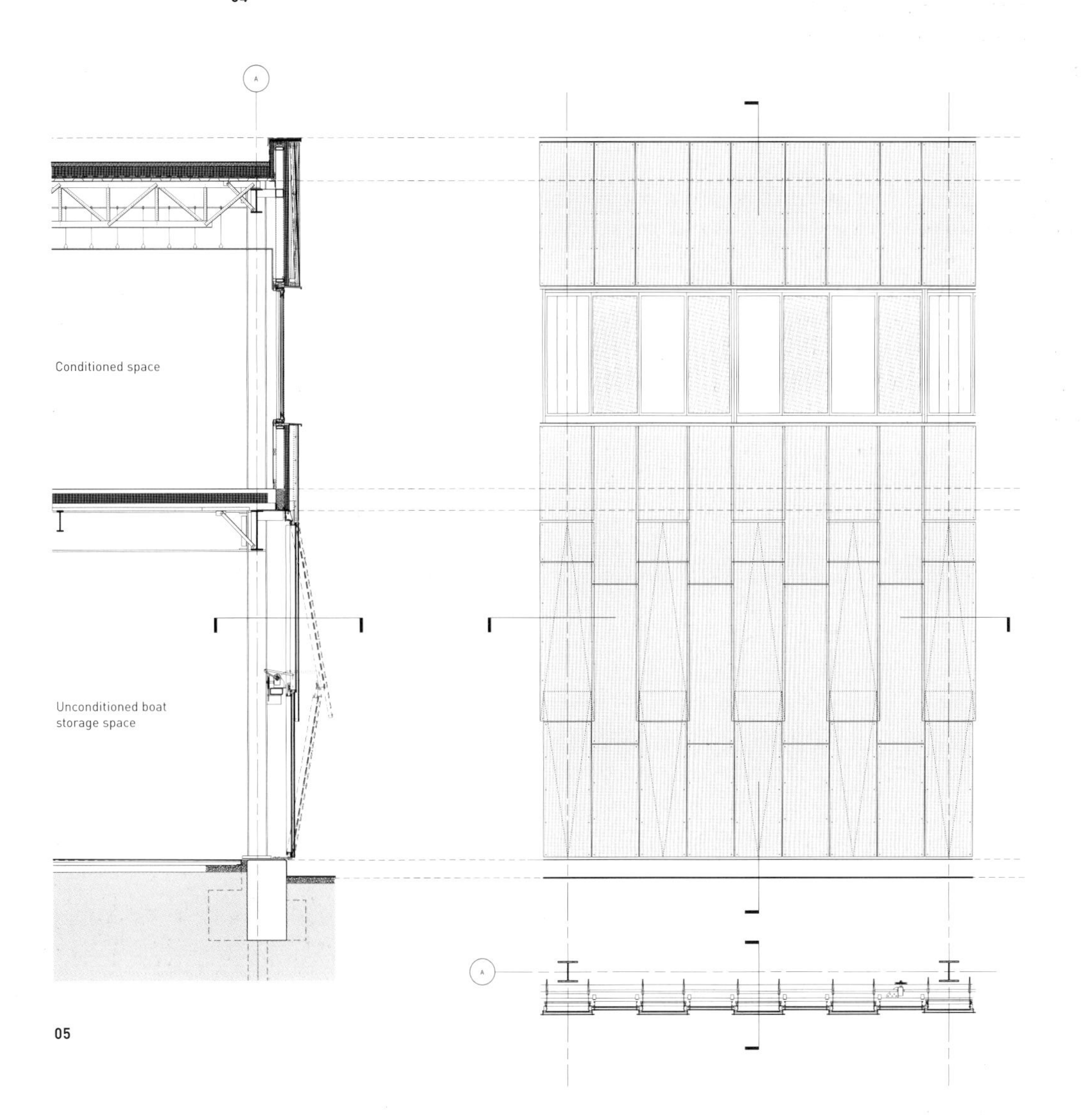

05

06 Section detail at edge of elevated floor; fixed louvers installed over solid wall and over exhaust grilles

07 Section detail at edge of elevated floor; wood veneer resin-core panels shown in closed and open position (dashed)

08 Model of operable vent assembly

09 Exterior view with boat storage and repair bay open

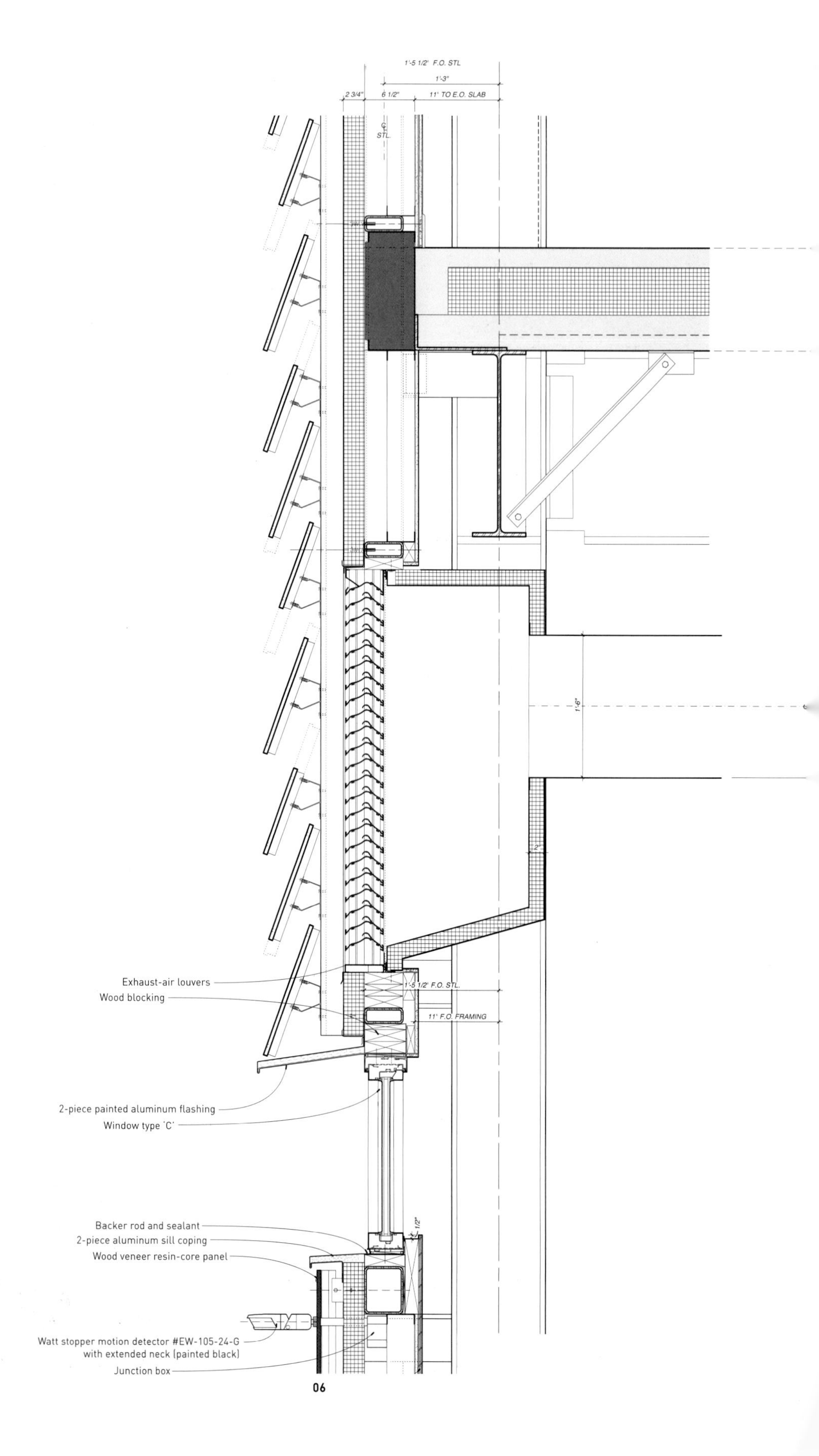

06

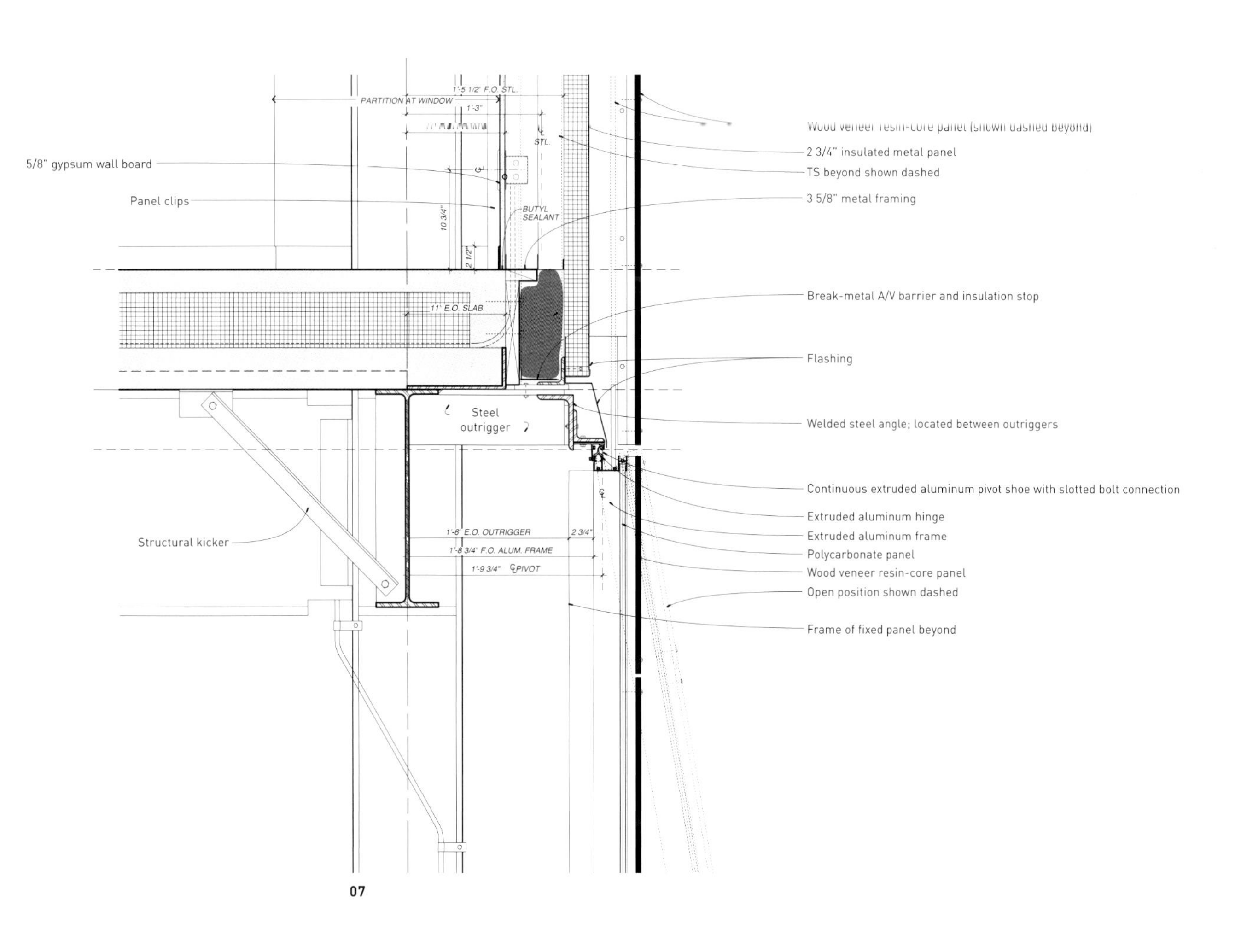
Wood veneer resin-core panel (shown dashed beyond)
5/8" gypsum wall board
2 3/4" insulated metal panel
TS beyond shown dashed
Panel clips
3 5/8" metal framing
PARTITION AT WINDOW
BUTYL SEALANT
11' E.O. SLAB
Break-metal A/V barrier and insulation stop
Flashing
Steel outrigger
Welded steel angle; located between outriggers
Continuous extruded aluminum pivot shoe with slotted bolt connection
Extruded aluminum hinge
Extruded aluminum frame
Polycarbonate panel
Wood veneer resin-core panel
Open position shown dashed
Frame of fixed panel beyond
Structural kicker
1'-6" E.O. OUTRIGGER
1'-8 3/4" F.O. ALUM. FRAME
1'-9 3/4" ℄ PIVOT

07

08

09

EcoWoodBox Kindergarten

Hanover, Germany — Despang Architekten
Thermally modified wood

DESIGN INTENTION

The project brief called for the facility to be didactic and to create a "sensual union of space, form, and nature," but children's activities determined the spatial arrangement of this community kindergarten. All of the service spaces run along the building's northern edge and are connected by a linear circulation space, which is also wide enough to serve as a play-street, leading to the living rooms to the south.

This internal hierarchy responds to thermal logic, transitioning from closed in the north to open in the sun-exposed south. The exterior walls on the north side are solid, largely opaque, and juxtaposed against an undulating glass skin to the south that creates intimate alcoves inside and outside for small group activities. The classrooms and outdoor activity areas merge with the open landscape to the south, whose deciduous trees shade the glass during summer months. East and west walls are constructed with wood much like the north elevation, but with larger window openings. In addition to accommodating learning space for children, the building also provides a setting for occasional community dinners and social functions.

MATERIALITY

The walls are made of prefabricated panels framed with more economical Trus-Joist TJI wood trusses, rather than conventional wood studs, to produce very thick wall cavities. The thick walls are filled with 16" (400 mm) of cellulose insulation made from recycled newspapers. The roof is insulated with 16" (400 mm) of rigid insulation.

Thermally modified, or torrefied, pine wood slats were secured to thermally modified plywood panels to form a lattice on the outside of the solid walls, recalling the surrounding neighborhood's weathered pine fences. These special wood elements were manufactured nearby and then fabricated into panels to be installed as a rainscreen over a batten / counter-batten frame. A well-ventilated rainscreen is essential to keep the moisture content of the wood acceptably low in this climate zone.

The torrefied wood offers many advantages in exposed applications outdoors. Though it is usually made from inexpensive species, this process enhances its color and texture, and afterward it requires very little upkeep to stay presentable. No paint or stain is needed because the wood is not vulnerable to biological attack. Even very slender wood elements treated in this way are unlikely to warp or bend out of alignment, an important advantage when selecting material for slats of these dimensions. Over several years, the dark gray wood will lighten a little.

TECHNICAL

The batten / counterbatten frame provides sufficient space between the rainscreen and the outer face of the sheathing to conceal the gutter at both the eave and its leader. The vertical slats march repetitively along the length of the project, looking more like a fence than a building facade. The wood framing module sets a cadence for window and door openings, as well as for the important spaces inside the building. The battens and counterbattens on the upper portion of the wall are 2.3" × 2.3" (58 × 58 mm). On the lower portion of the wall they are 1.2" × 2" (30 × 50 mm).

The vertically oriented torrefied wood slats extend from the torrefied plywood above the window 7.5' (2.3 m) downward toward the concrete plinth. They create a lattice over the windows and continue down in front of a solid wall, despite not being anchored to a firm substrate along this length. With at least five years of weathering thus far, this project has demonstrated that torrefied wood is uniquely capable to span this far without distortion.

Fasteners securing the slats to the plywood substrate were installed from the building side of the plywood before the rainscreen panels were installed on the building. This minimized harmful corrosion of the fasteners and staining of the exterior finishes. The project used thermal mass and very high levels of thermal resistance in the walls and roof, in addition to its orientation and configuration, to earn the first Passive House designation for a kindergarten in Hanover.

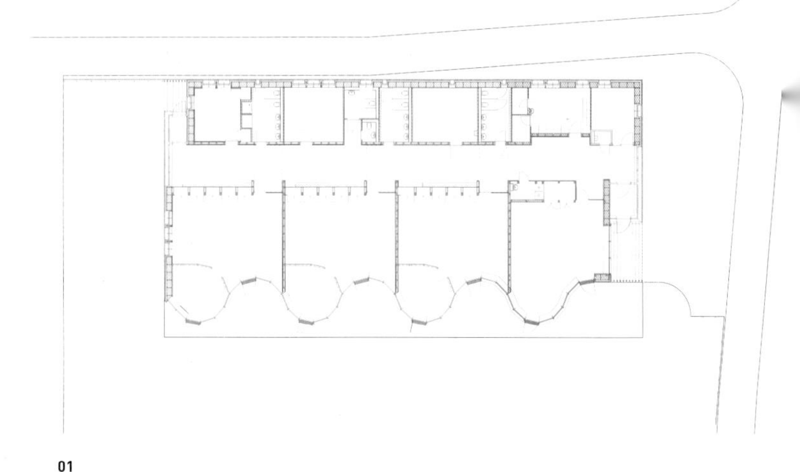

01

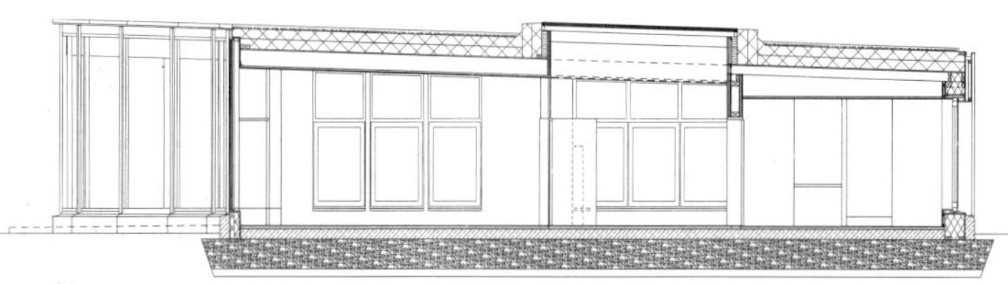

02

03

04

01 Ground-floor plan

02 Transverse section

03 Exterior view from south toward classrooms

04 North facade with vertical wood slats over walls and windows

05

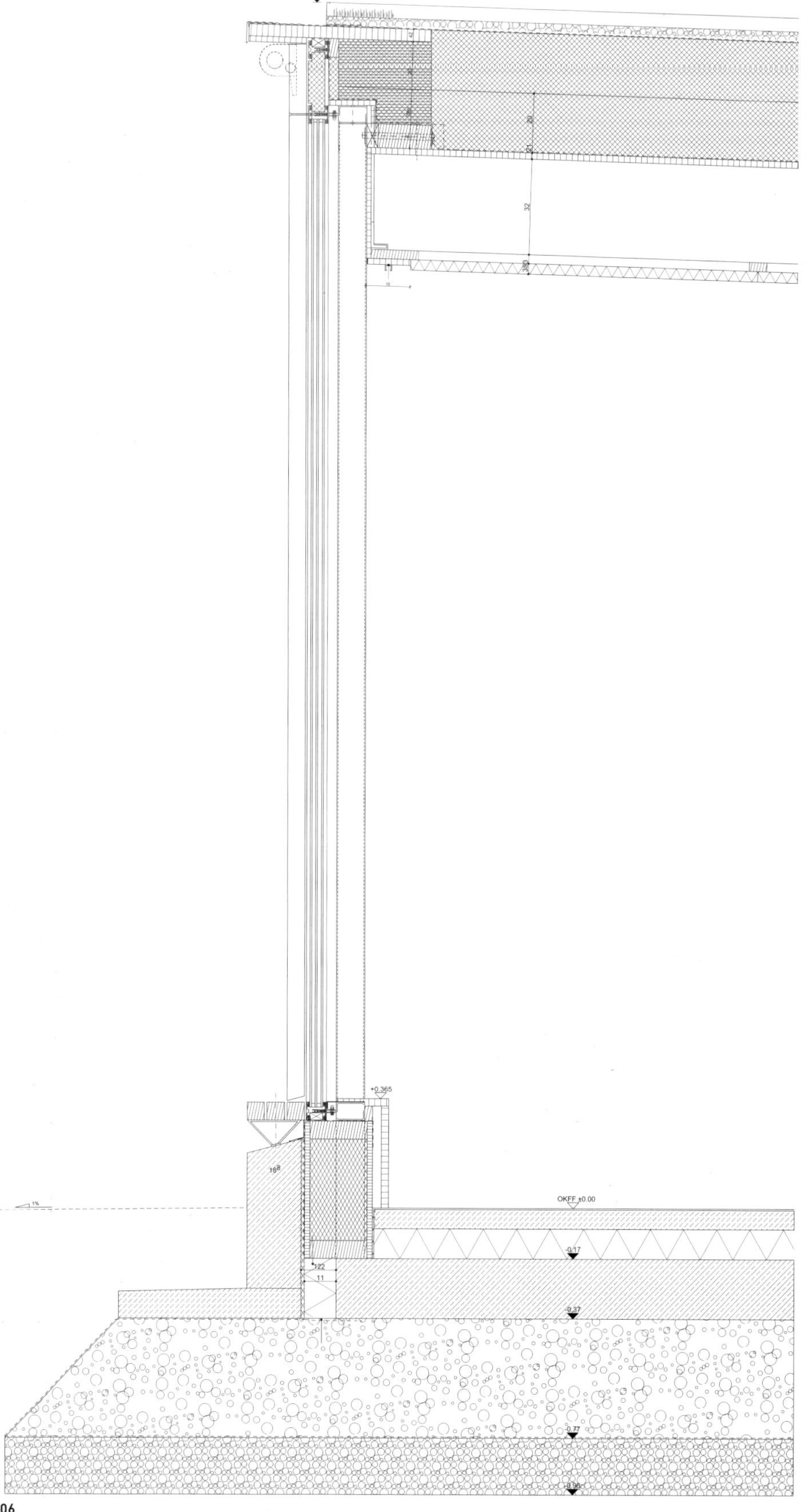

06

05 Installation of prefabricated wall assemblies; cladding and finishes installed in situ

06 Section through glazed south (classroom) wall

07 Existing wood fence in neighborhood used as a contextual reference

08 Torrefied pine slats

09 Section through north wall, with thermally modified wood slats and plywood rainscreen assembly

07

08

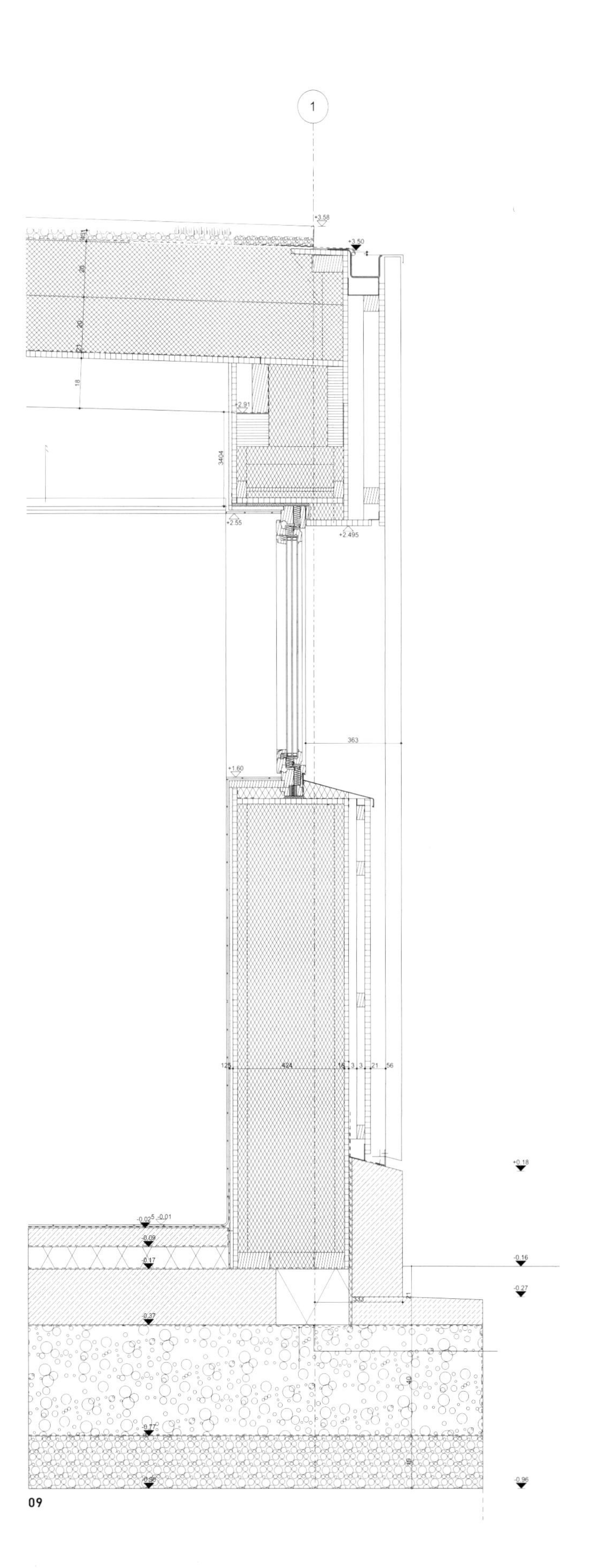

09

Nature Boardwalk at Lincoln Park Zoo

Chicago, Illinois, USA — Studio Gang Architects
Laminated wood

DESIGN INTENTION

The design intention of this project was to create an outdoor classroom for the Lincoln Park Zoo. The project consists of a new boardwalk that circumscribes a pond and passes through educational zones where visitors may study different animals, plants, and natural habitats. This pavilion was integrated into the boardwalk to act as a shelter for open-air classes. When not in use for educational purposes, it is used for yoga classes and other park activities. The laminated structure is constructed of prefabricated, bent-wood members topped by a series of interconnected fiberglass pods, which give the surface an organic curvature that was inspired by the tortoise's shell.

MATERIALITY

Douglas fir, the primary material for the pavilion's technical and aesthetic features, was chosen for its abundance near the fabricator, located in the Pacific Northwest. Among American softwoods, Douglas fir is the strongest per pound; it is also straight-grained. Both of these assets are important in this application. The design demonstrates the inherent pliability of thin wood elements. Curved and assembled in an open lattice, the small, light elements can form a strong structure. The region's environmental regulations strictly manage forests and natural habitats, also making their wood well matched with the client's land stewardship objectives.

Douglas fir has some natural resistance to mold and decay. While the structure was not painted, a lightly pigmented stain was applied to further protect the elements. Fiberglass pods cover the lattice elements, significantly reducing their exposure to precipitation. The pavilion's curved wooden lattice elements are bolted together with steel plates at their milled connections.

TECHNICAL

Similar to laminated veneer lumber (LVL), the pavilion's structural elements are made of multiple thin plies of wood adhered under pressure. But unlike LVL, each 15" (380 mm) ribbon of laminated wood was molded into a custom-designed sine curve during fabrication; they also curve three-dimensionally into a structure with a 15.25' (4.6 m) radius. Hand-operated jigs held the veneer sheets in the desired shape during fabrication. The architects explored CNC-milling machines but found traditional jigs were more cost-effective and desirable for this scale of project. Cutting across the longitudinal grain of the wood to make curved shapes would have significantly weakened it.

The lattice elements are milled at each end to pair with others using custom-fabricated toothed plate connections. The connecting plates are sandwiched between wood elements and bolted into structurally rigid connections. Pinned connections join the lattice to the foundation. Splices in the lattice are staggered so that at each connection, one curved member is continuous and able to receive up to two spliced elements on the other side of the plate. The lattice is constructed of 144 of these identical pieces, which made fabrication more efficient. When assembled, they form a barrel-vault-shaped lattice that is 43' long, 33' wide, and 17.5' tall (13.1 × 10 × 5.3 m).

The exterior surface's fiberglass pods are screwed in place from the top into the wooden structure. A weatherproof gasket seals the joints between the wood and the fiberglass shells. The pavilion is open on the ends and near the base of the vaulted shape.

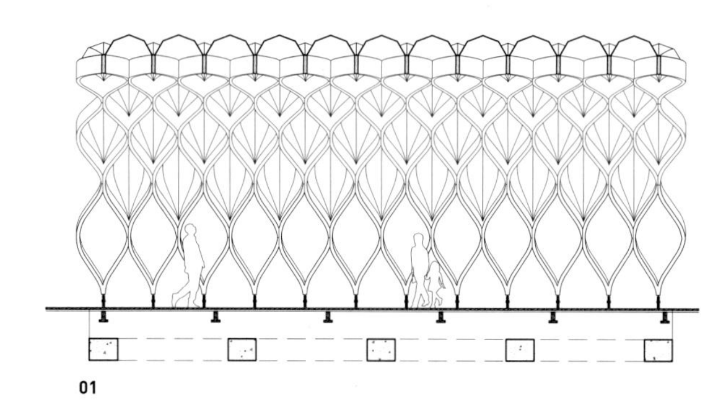

01

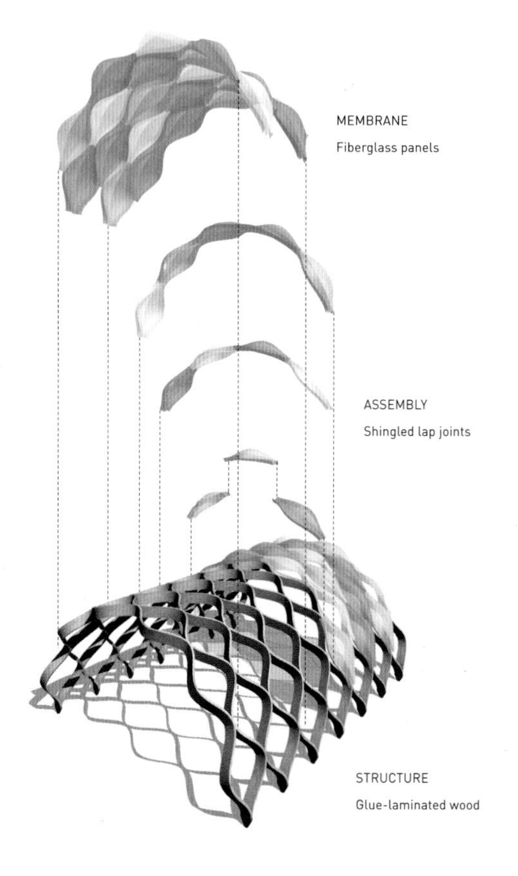

A. The First Lamination

This is the resultant stock first lamination beam.

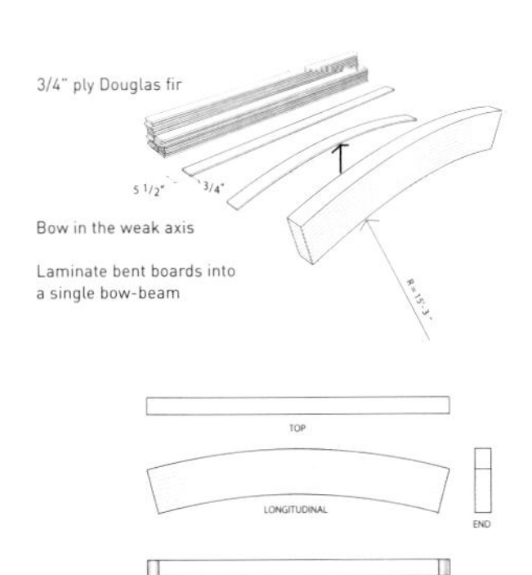

B. Slice Longitudinally

This creates strong, thin laminates that can be bent in the weak axis for the second lamination

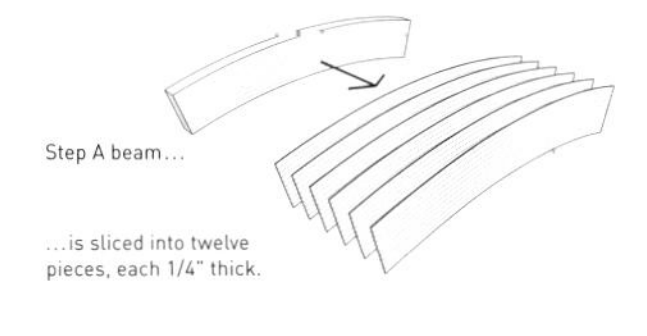

C. The Second Lamination

This is the resultant basic structural beam-unit...

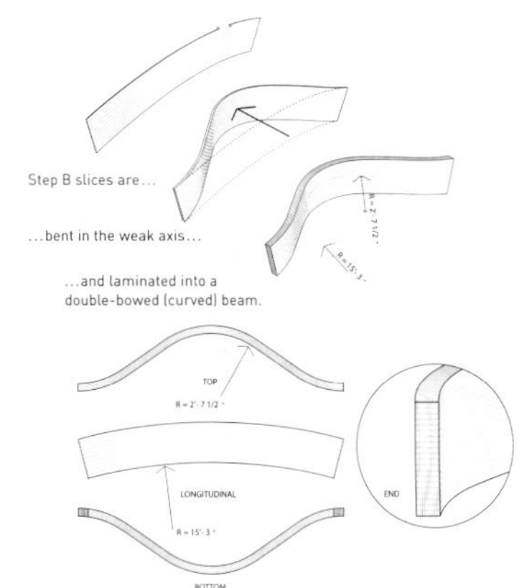

D. Construction

...which, when joined with other, identical beams, creates the barrel-vaulted pavilion structure

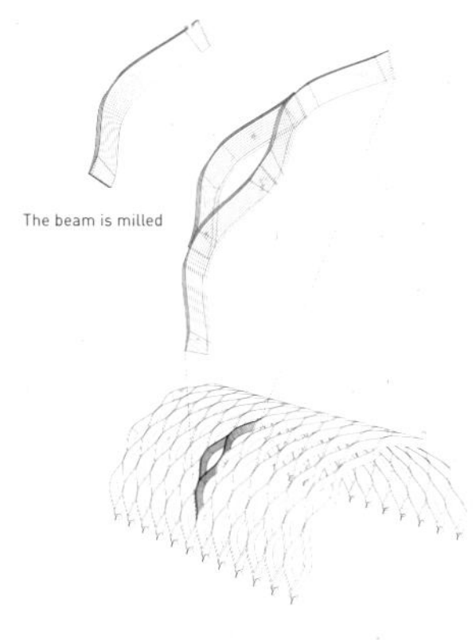

03

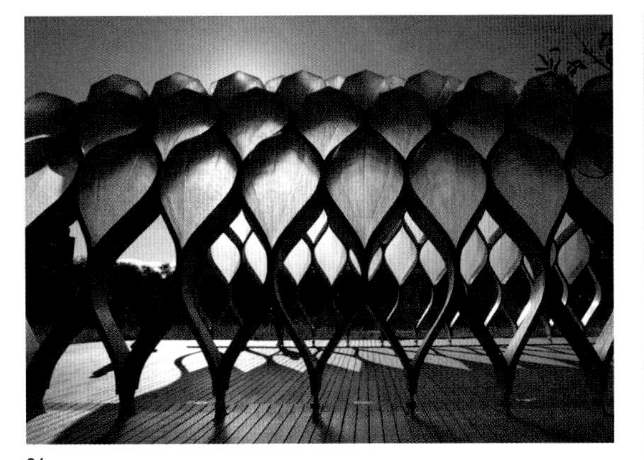

04

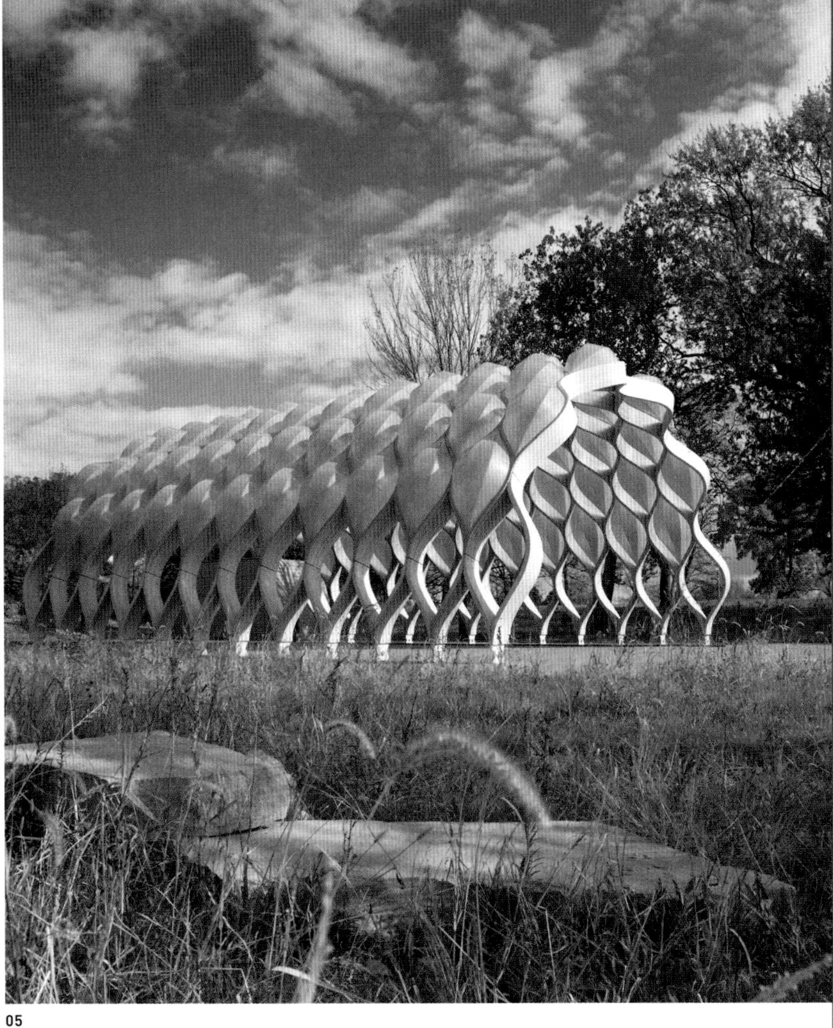

05

01 Longitudinal section at center line of barrel-vaulted pavilion

02 Exploded perspective of glue-laminated structural frame and fiberglass pod membrane elements

03 Steps to transform Douglas fir lumber into laminated barrel-vaulted lattice

04 Wood lattice and translucent fiberglass pods

05 Completed pavilion

Dairy House Annex

Hadspen Estate, Somerset, England — Skene Catling de la Peña
Oak timber

DESIGN INTENTION

This project renovated and converted a historic dairy and cheese-making building into a five-bedroom house and retreat. The intention was to create a natural interpretation of the original dairy building that preserved the structure's significance on the bucolic 850-acre estate. The house is approximately 2,000 sq. ft. (186 sq. m) with a new adjacent pool and garden that overlook the landscape. The dairy's original interior walls were all removed during the renovation, leaving a stone shell. An oak and glass annex containing a study and baths was added to the rear, inspired by the character of a nearby wood barn on the estate.

MATERIALITY

The architect (and owner) gave priority to the use of local materials wherever possible. Oak timber was harvested, planked, and patiently seasoned in storage barns on-site. After the wood was sufficiently dried over several years, it was cut and finished by a local cabinetmaker, whose shop is located very near the estate.

The construction alternates the stacked layers of oak slabs and laminated glass plates. Both the wood and glass blocks were left unfinished on the exterior but were carefully aligned on the inside. The oak was milled on the two horizontal faces and on the inner face, but not on the outer. By not cutting the outer surface, the natural wane of the log makes each piece unique, while protecting the wood's natural pores from the weather. The laminated glass blocks act like a prism, projecting multicolored sunlight over the floors and walls. Inside the house the walls seem lightweight because so much daylight passes through, while from the outside it appears much more heavy and rustic. The opposite is true at night, as artificial lighting makes the house glow from the inside. The height of the wood and glass layers increases toward the base and decreases toward the top, reinforcing a sense of weight and rustication.

TECHNICAL

This project combines ancient principles of log construction with contemporary materials. In traditional log construction, the horizontal pieces interlock at corners, with material from each piece subtracted to receive the next piece. Here the horizontal wood elements overlap at corners but are not notched, creating the open space between slabs of wood that is now filled with glass. The full width of the wood slabs do not extend to the corners; instead, the ends of each piece were cut to create what appears to be a square-shaped column at the corner, but is actually the alignment of the cuts in more than two dozen oak slabs. No exposed fasteners appear on the interior or exterior at these connections.

Oak slabs in the walls are approximately 13' wide (4 m) between corners, exceeding its spanning capability, especially high on the wall where the wood slabs are thinner. The span is reduced to approximately 3.9' (1.2 m) by inserting oak blocks into the spaces between continuous slabs in lieu of glass. Like the corners, these also appear to be columns because of their precise alignment, but are actually stacked pieces of wood. By using this method, the designer assures that cross-grain shrinkage of the wood assemblies will be equalized across the whole building. In addition to thoroughly drying the wood pre-construction, this detailing strategy accommodates the material's tendency to shrink and swell slightly as its moisture content changes. The corner detail originally called for holes to be bored in the intersecting oak slabs to receive a vertical threaded rod that would limit warping of the wood pieces and finely tune the compressive stresses on them. The rod was ultimately not needed because the seasoned oak was very stable.

A manufacturer generously donated float glass plates to the project. The plates were stacked and laminated by a nearby specialist using interlayers of polyvinyl butyral to make them into strong and watertight blocks. The blocks not only act as the building's skin, but also can carry compressive loads if needed, since they were laid horizontally instead of on the more typical vertical axis. Placed on rubber gaskets, the blocks then sit directly on the oak planks. Foam seals at the top provide weatherproof movement joints on the facade; clear silicone is added to form a final weather seal.

Wood trim pieces such as fascia are also made of oak and secured in place with brass screws to minimize staining. Fastener locations align with the structural rhythms of the elevations.

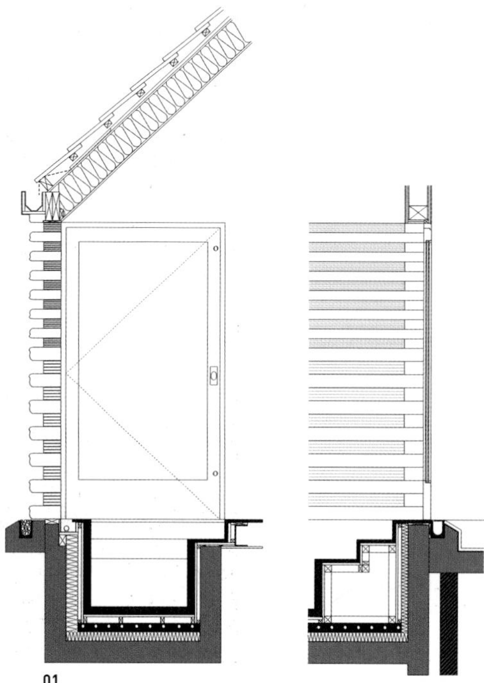

01

02

03

04

01 Transverse section at bath

02 Exterior view from north

03 Transition to pool showing natural wanes of oak timbers and laminated glass infill

04 Exterior view from northwest in recessed court; existing building to the right

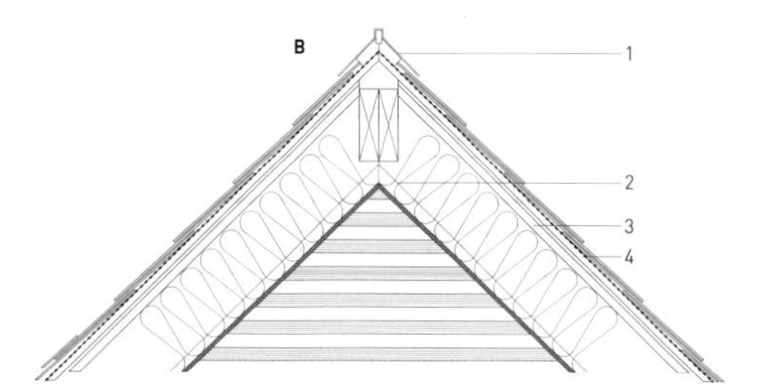

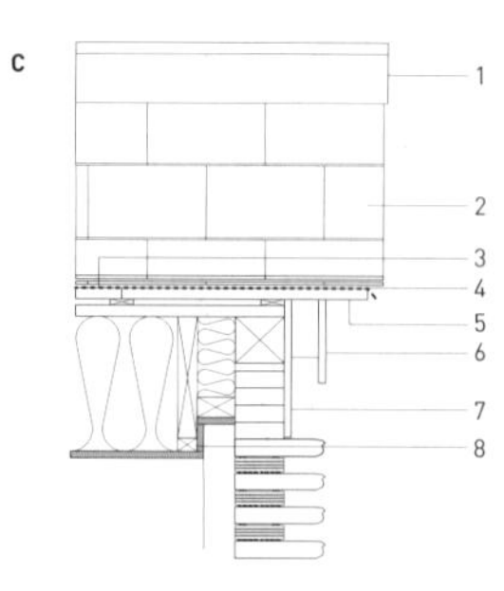

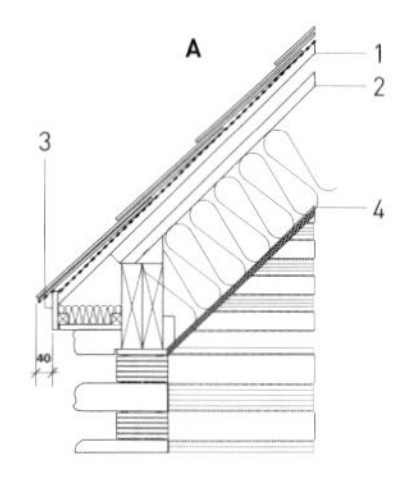

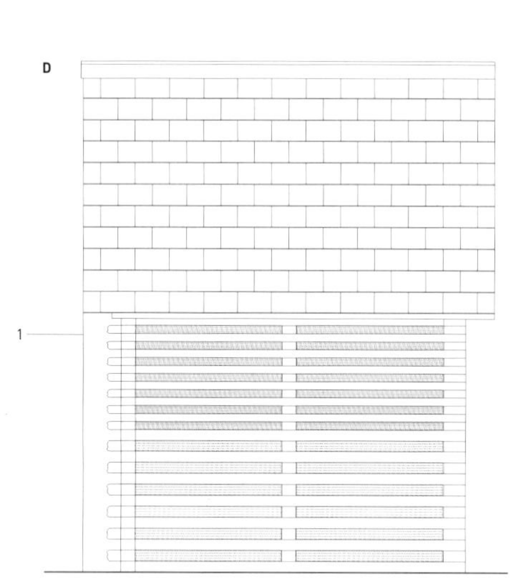

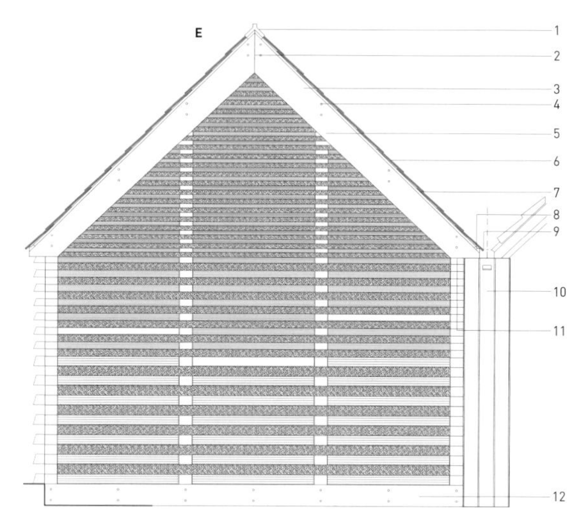

05

A Wall section

1. New decking
2. Existing decking
3. Painted pelmet
4. Firing piece to adjust level of soffit to required angle

B Roof section

1. Lead ridge
2. Firing piece to adjust level of soffit to required angle
3. Existing decking
4. New decking

C Wall and roof section at rake end

1. Lead ridge
2. Slate
3. Ply decking
4. Roofing felt
5. Oak decking
6. Oak fascia, lined up with edge of Waney board
7. Oak fascia
8. Firing piece to adjust level of soffit to required angle

D Side elevation

1. Edge of roof lines up with wall of old building on south elevation. Overhang replicated on north elevation.

E End elevation

1. Lead ridge
2. Discrepancy between pitch of facade and roof equally divided between the two fascia boards
3. Oak fascia
4. Unlacquered brass screws
5. Oak fascia
6. Slate
7. New decking
8. Solid oak edge piece
9. Edge of tile, symmetrical along center of steel column
10. New steel channel with slot and spout
11. Edges of fascia board line up with timber "column"
12. Oak fascia

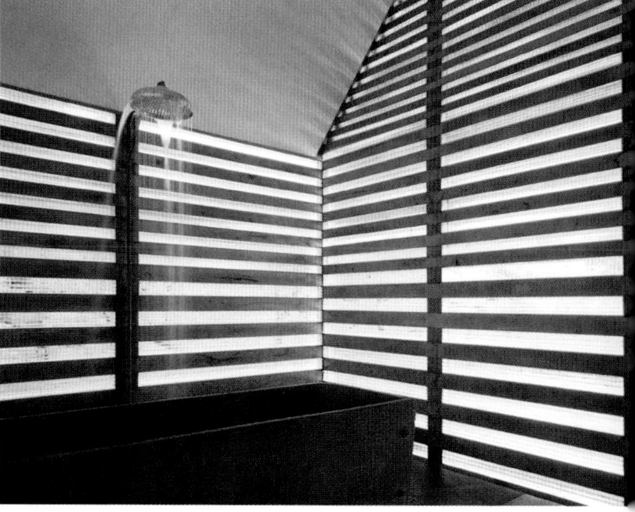

06

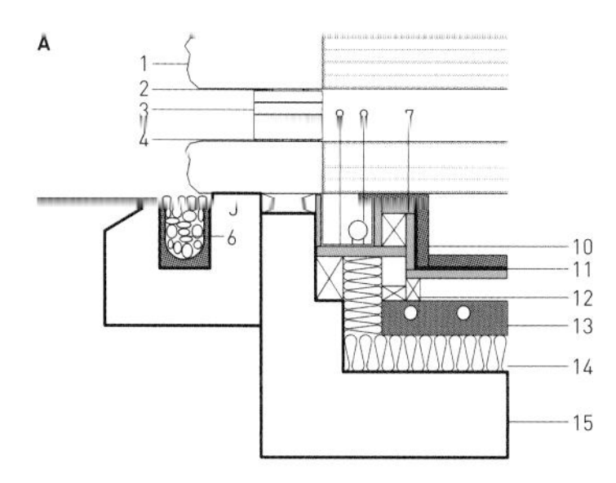

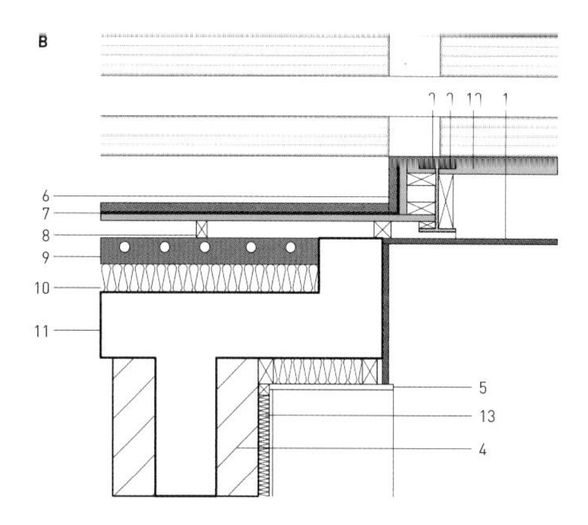

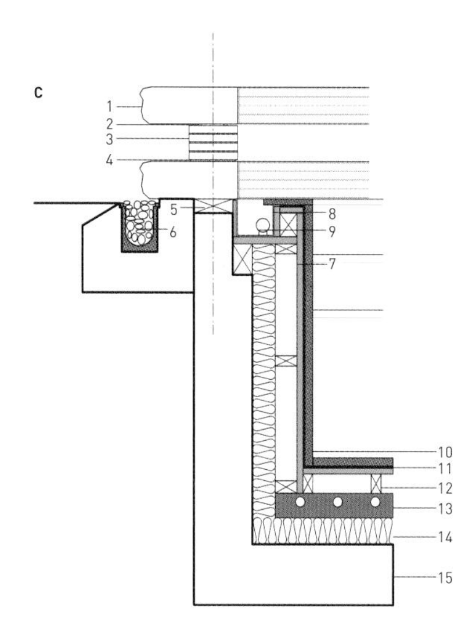

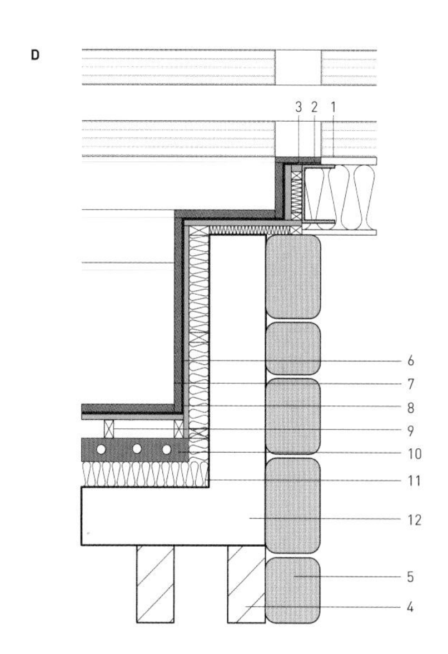

07

05 A–C: Transverse section through wall and roof; section through wall and roof at rake end

D–E: Elevations of side and end

06 Oak timbers lapping at corner, supported by stacked wood blocks

07 Detail sections where oak timber walls meet foundation in bath

DETAIL A: Bath

1 Waney board
2 Illmod 600 10/3–7 compriband
3 Laminated glass block
4 GSP02 gasket by Euroseal
5 Timber packer
6 ACO channel filled with pebbles
7 18 mm formed ply trench and shower
8 Code 6 lead covering to trench
9 Light extrusion
10 Concrete/slate slabs
11 Fiberglass
12 SW furring pieces
13 65 mm screed with underfloor heating
14 65 mm rigid insulation
15 Concrete pit

DETAIL B: Shower

1 12.5 mm plasterboard, skimmed and painted
2 89 × 152 mm steel beam
3 Rubber pad
4 100 mm blockwork
5 18 mm painted MDF shelves
6 Concrete/slate slabs
7 Fiberglass
8 SW furring pieces
9 65 mm screed with underfloor heating
10 65 mm rigid insulation
11 Concrete pit
12 25 mm ply support to slab
13 30 mm thermaboard

DETAIL C: Bath

1 Waney board
2 Illmod 600 10/3–7 compriband
3 Laminated glass block
4 GSP02 gasket by Euroseal
5 Timber packer
6 ACO channel filled with pebbles
7 18 mm formed ply trench and bath
8 Code 6 lead covering to trench
9 Light extrusion
10 Concrete/slate slabs
11 Fiberglass
12 SW furring pieces
13 65 mm screed with underfloor heating
14 65 mm rigid insulation
15 Concrete pit

DETAIL D: Bath

1 20 mm oak flooring
2 90 × 150 mm steel channel
3 Rubber pad
4 100 mm blockwork
5 Dry stone wall
6 18 mm formed ply trench and bath
7 Concrete/slate slabs
8 Fiberglass
9 SW furring pieces
10 65 mm screed with underfloor heating
11 65 mm rigid insulation
12 Concrete pit

Metropol Parasol

Seville, Spain — J. Mayer H. Architects
Laminated veneer lumber

DESIGN INTENTION

The Metropol Parasol created an iconic contemporary urban center at Seville's Plaza de la Encarnación, formerly intended for a parking garage. After Roman and Moorish remains were discovered at the site, a new design called for a series of six intersecting parasols to grow out of the archaeological excavation and become a contemporary landmark. These intersecting parasols are prominent points of access to the museum below ground and to the plaza above, defining a tangible relationship between the historical and the contemporary city.

Below ground is an archaeological museum housing the site's discoveries. The ground floor remains the site of the city's central market, while the roof space is used for civic events. At the very top, amid the beams of the Parasol's roof, a restaurant is located next to a public promenade. The mixed-use character is a dynamic catalyst for culture and commerce in the heart of Seville.

MATERIALITY

The primary material used is MetsäWood's Kerto-Q, a laminated veneer lumber structural element with a polyurethane coating. The parasols themselves are a composite structure; steel threaded rods were glued into the wood with an epoxy at the connection nodes to transfer the forces to the wood. These wood elements are typically used to strengthen walls in existing buildings, but the Parasol uses composite action to take greater advantage of the compressive strength of the engineered wood products. The architects initially conceived of a structure made of thin steel, but found that Kerto-Q was a more appropriate material choice.

Made from kiln-dried spruce, Kerto-Q was chosen for its intrinsically high strength-to-weight ratio and its straightness. Thin veneers of wood are dried in an oven, and then glued using a non-toxic and water-resistant adhesive. Once glued, they are hot-pressed while the adhesive cures, then cut into pieces and stored. The LVL members were manufactured in Finland and fabricated in Germany before being assembled in Seville.

The project takes advantage of Kerto-Q's available long spans. Since one-fifth of the veneers are glued crosswise, the material has improved lateral bending strength and stiffness, increasing its stability when used as a beam. Cross-bonded veneers also reduce moisture-driven variations in size across the width of the member.

TECHNICAL

Metropol Parasol is one of the world's largest timber engineering constructions, measuring approximately 492' long, 246' wide, and 92' high (150 × 75 × 28 m). It has 3,400 individual wooden elements and over 3,000 connection nodes, most of which are under considerable stress.

Kerto-Q is available in continuous pieces reaching up to 75' (23 m) in length—much longer than natural lumber—and unlike timber, its physical properties are known with greater certainty. The maximum length of an element in the Parasol is 54' (16.5 m). One piece located in the "trunk" is 54' × 11.5' × 0.46' (16.5 × 3.5 × 0.14 m). Analytical design optimized the size and shape of each piece, reducing the timber resources needed and minimizing waste. Elements in the Parasol vary in thickness between 2.7–12.25" (70–310 mm).

An orthogonal grid based on a 59" (1,500 mm) square module was used. High structural strength and deep structural members result in an exceptionally strong frame. The intersecting tall, slender elements produce an excellent moment of inertia and high flexural resistance. The wood planes are held together by tabs on one plane being inserted into a slot in the intersecting plane, all of which are secured with steel bolts.

Computer-aided design allowed remarkably accurate design and engineering analysis. These digital data drove manufacturing robots that precisely cut each element to interlock with others. These methods led to fewer pieces and fewer joints. The weight of the structure was also reduced, as was the amount of labor and construction time, lowering construction costs.

The Parasol has no roof, which would be problematic for normal wood element, that are vulnerable to surface weathering and possible loss of adhesion between plies. A two-part polyurethane finish was applied to extend the structure's service life and reduce maintenance needs, while bringing uniform color to the structure. This coating is a new type of polyurethane that is waterproof yet diffusion-permeable. It allows the wood to breathe, and like the wood itself, releases no hazardous fumes when burned. The wood elements also were certified by the Finnish Forest Council of Certification.

Kerto-Q is considered renewable and has residual value at the end of its life cycle. The ability to disassemble the frame at the end of its service life, perhaps to be reused, was another environmental consideration that set this material apart.

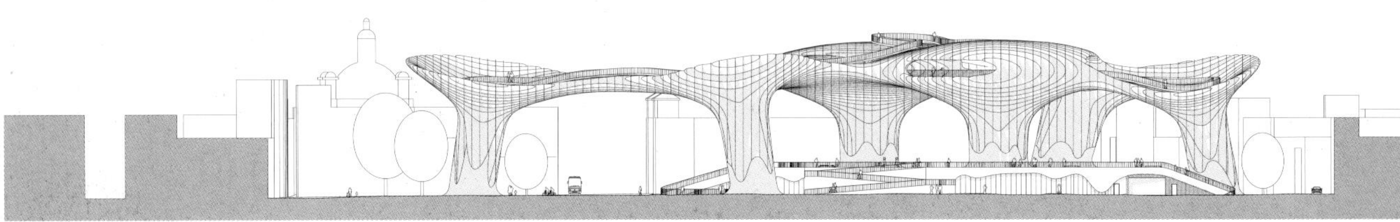

01

02

03

01 Longitudinal section through Parasol and context

02 Exterior view from street

03 Aerial view of the site's urban context

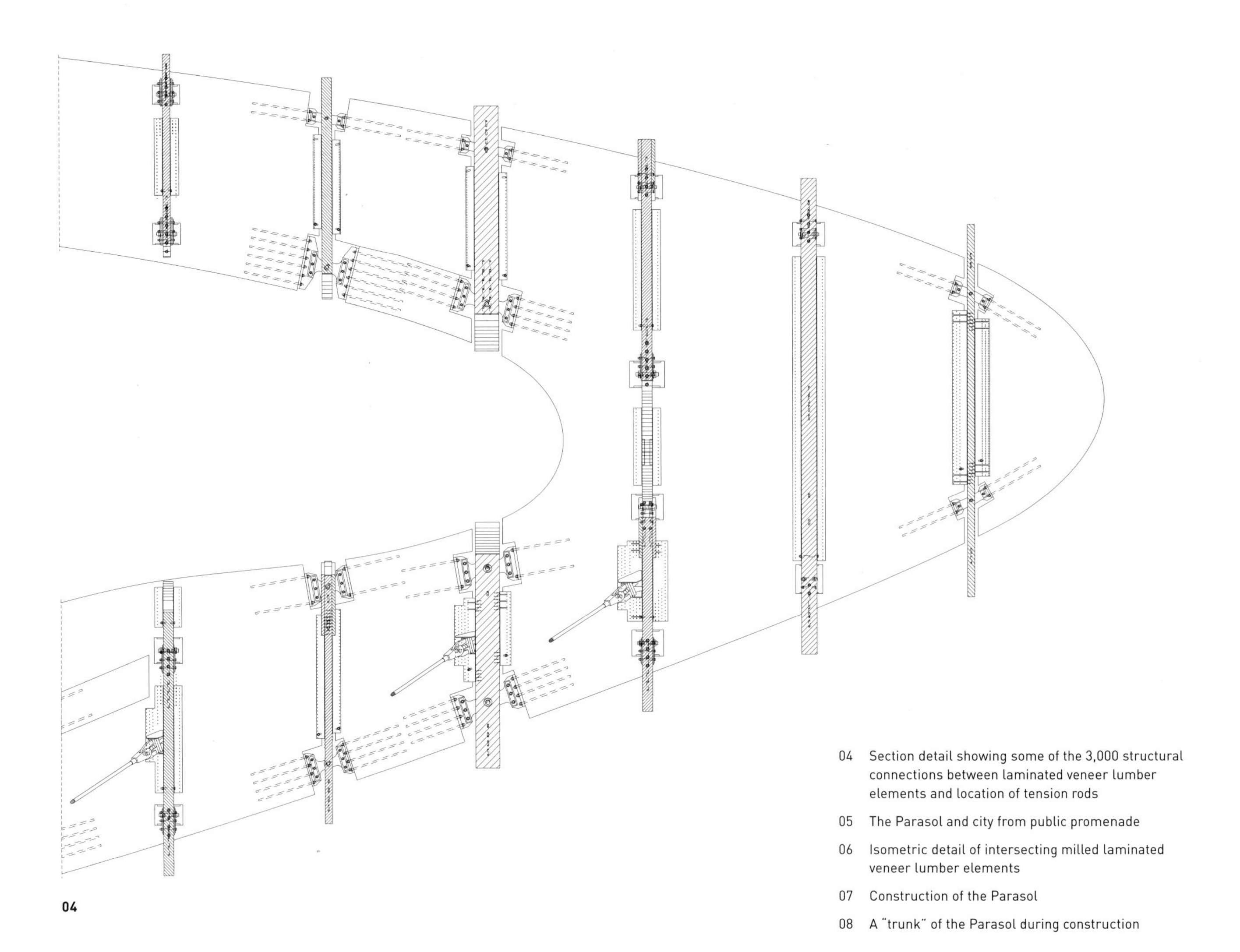

04

04 Section detail showing some of the 3,000 structural connections between laminated veneer lumber elements and location of tension rods

05 The Parasol and city from public promenade

06 Isometric detail of intersecting milled laminated veneer lumber elements

07 Construction of the Parasol

08 A "trunk" of the Parasol during construction

05

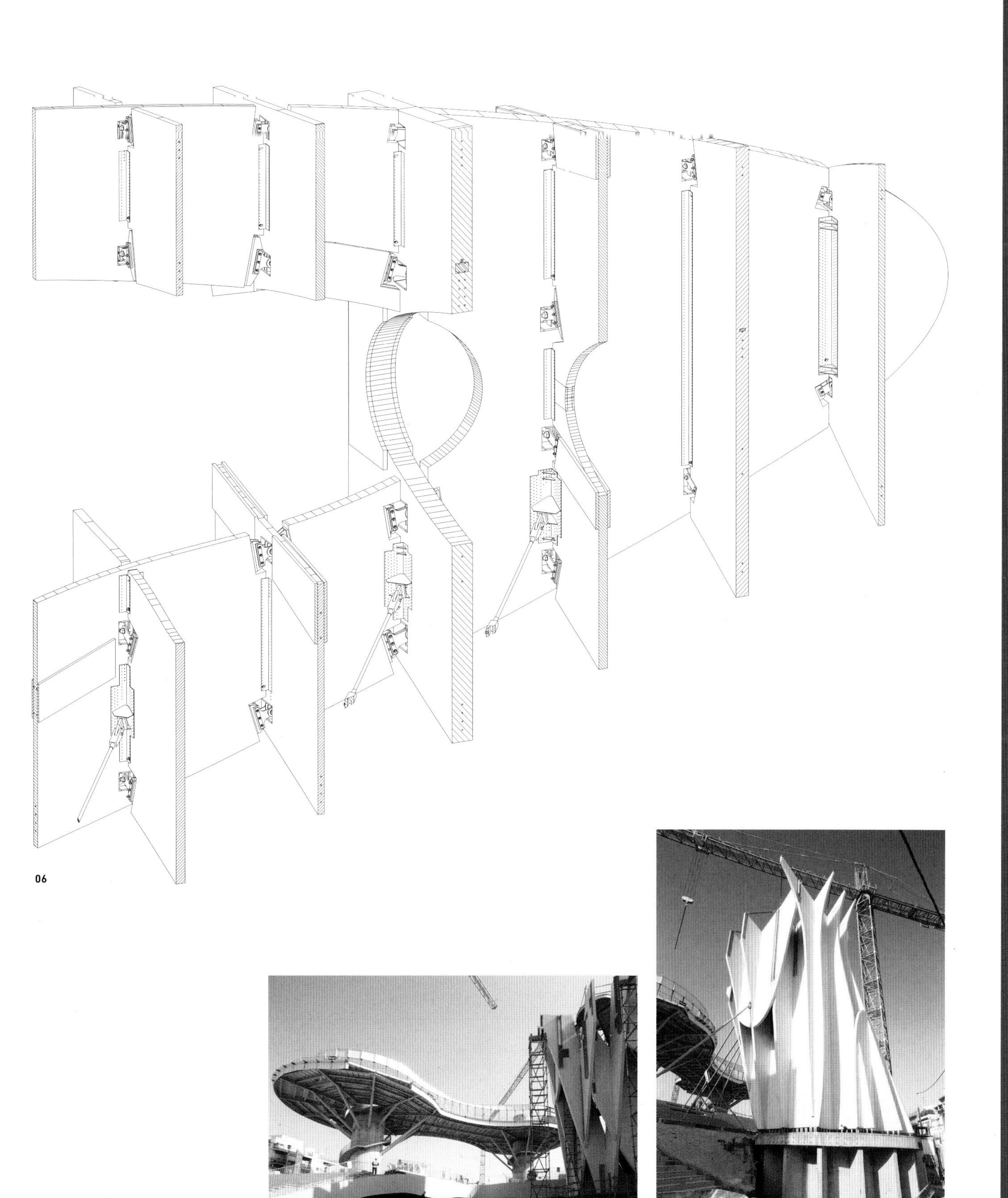

06

07

08

Skating Shelters

Winnipeg, Manitoba, Canada — Patkau Architects
Bendable plywood, integrated design and fabrication

DESIGN INTENTION

Winnipeg is located on the Canadian prairie, and is the coldest city of its size outside of Siberia. There, where winter can last for six months, it is important to learn to take advantage of cold weather's recreational opportunities. One way is river skating, where the Red and Assiniboine meet in the center of the city. When frozen and plowed of snow, the rivers become incredible skating trails many miles long, but when the wind chill makes it feel like -50°F (-46°C), these temporary shelters provide safe harbor during the winter skating season.

The installation consisted of a cluster of six intimate shelters, each of which accommodates only a few people at a time. They are grouped in a small "village" with their backs to the prevailing wind, seeming to have life and purpose as they huddle together, shielding each other and their occupants from the elements.

The six shelters have a total area of only 108 sq. ft. (10 sq. m.), but have a significant presence on such a featureless white landscape. They were grouped into a cluster to optimize their entrance access in a practical way. This apparently casual arrangement is actually a precise 120-degree rotation between pods, some of which went through a secondary 90-degree rotation to define a sort of interior space within the larger grouping.

The shelters set forth varied relationships to the changing sun and wind directions, giving skaters choices that can be matched with environmental circumstances.

MATERIALITY

Thin skins of 0.2" (5 mm) thick flexible plywood were cut into patterns and attached to a timber frame with a triangular base and wedge-shaped spine. Each plywood sheet was bent to give each shelter its structure and spatial character. The architects built full-scale prototypes in their workshop to fine-tune the curved shapes to plywood's properties. The shape is only stable when the flexible planes are curved and stressed, then secured. Stress points were relieved by a series of cuts and openings. The project illustrates the benefits of direct experimentation and seamless integration of design and fabrication.

These structures are delicate and alive. They move gently in the wind, creaking and swaying at various frequencies, floating precariously on the surface of the frozen river, shaking off any snow that might momentarily adhere to their surfaces. Their fragile and responsive nature makes those sheltered by them more aware of the ferocity and beauty of winter on the Canadian prairies.

TECHNICAL

The architect's drawings identify the skin material as 0.2" (5 mm) mahogany "rubber ply," but these are actually made of three layers of mahogany, assembled to be flexible in one direction. The two outer plies are each 0.08" (2 mm) thick; the inner layer is oriented perpendicular to the outer layers and is only 0.04" (1 mm) thick. The material allowed curvatures of less than 16.7" (425 mm) radius to be achieved. Bending the flexible plywood in plane (its weak axis) makes it stable. Unlike rubber-core plywood, this product has a more durable, crisp edge where cut or drilled, and fasteners will not compress its thickness. The product was used for all of the plywood surfaces, assuring consistent appearance.

Bendable plywood was not available in exterior- or marine-grade products, so the architect specified interior-grade plywood, intending to encapsulate it in two coats of polyurethane. During fabrication the finish was changed to an oil-based stain, since the shelters were temporary and would not be exposed to liquid water. Some plywood surfaces were CNC-milled with 0.2" holes at 1" on center (5 mm holes at 25 mm) in a staggered pattern. The strategy permitted ventilation, and gives occupants a veiled glimpse to the outside.

Care was taken when joining the thin, post-tensioned plywood elements to spread the stress of their connections over a large area of plywood using multiple small fasteners. When the plywood sheets were joined in the same plane, they were typically lapped approximately 4" (100 mm), adhered, and fastened with aluminum dome-head rivets and washers. At the sharp upright corners opposite the entry of each pod, the plywood skin elements were screwed to a wedge-shaped spine of wood, and faced with plywood that is scribed to the curved faces of the skin. A similar element joined the plywood at the ridge. Galvanized steel 25-gauge sheet metal gussets were used to reinforce some connections.

The floor of each pod was a cross-laminated board assembly, durable under the wear of skaters walking and standing on it wearing sharp skates. The bulbous equilateral triangle shape of the floor set forth the curves of the walls. The floor edge was notched to precisely receive the lapped joints between sheets of plywood with no gaps, assuring full contact between the fragile skin and the sturdy base.

The pod floors rested directly on the frozen surface of the river. To anchor them, augers were used to bore 7" (180 mm) holes into the thick ice below the three corners of each pod. An anchor bolt attached to the floor extended down into the hole with a plywood disk on the end. Water was poured into the hole to fill it, which promptly froze solidly until spring.

01 Elevation views of bendable plywood panel layout

02 Aggregation plan of six pods

03 Pods on frozen river alongside skating trail

04 Bendable plywood pods are anchored firmly to the ice and deflect cold wind

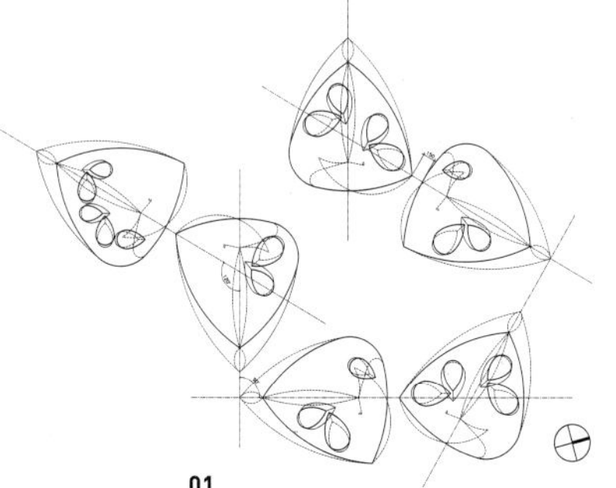

01

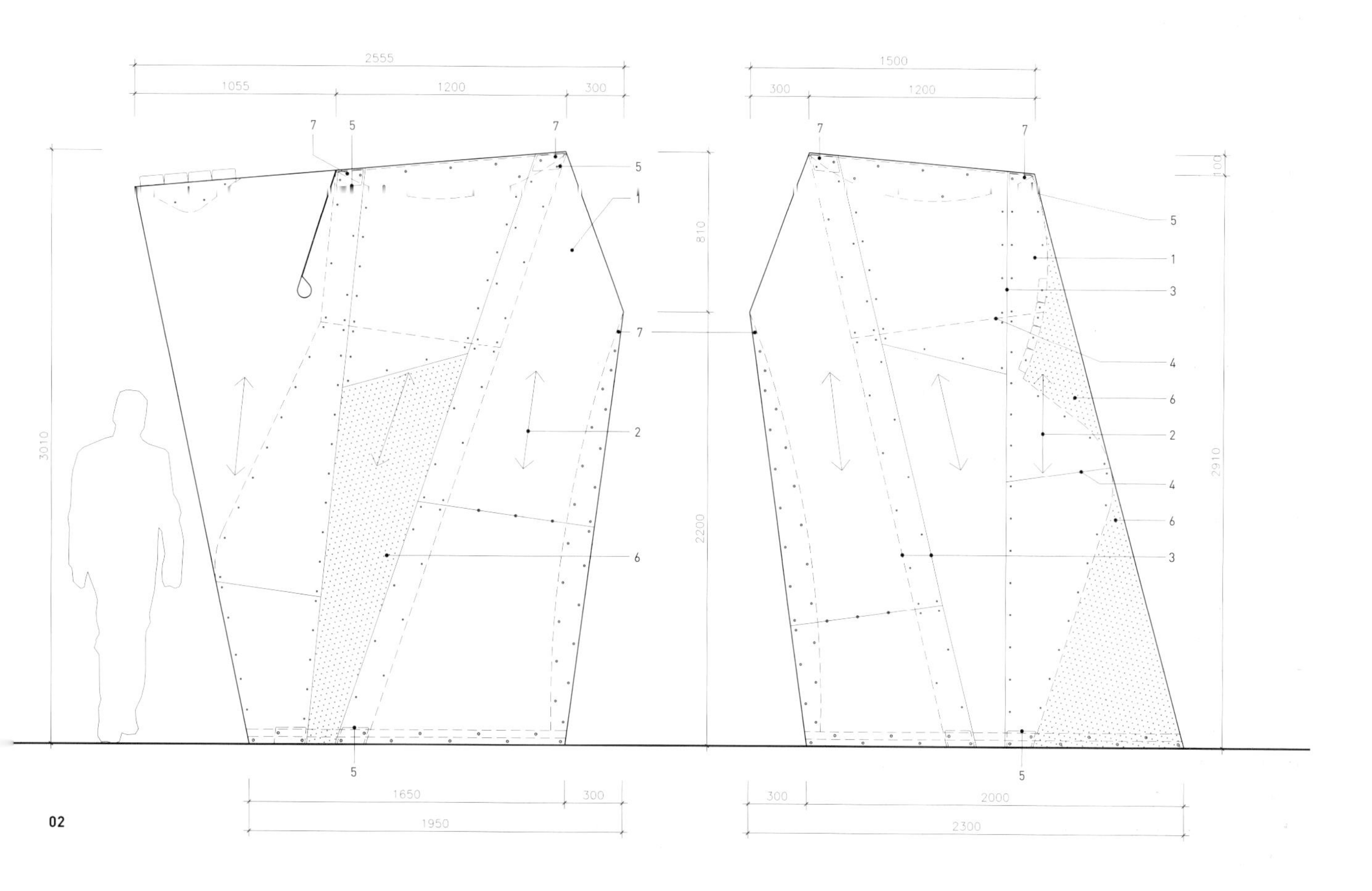

02

Key notes

1. Rubber ply panels: 5 mm mahogany rubber ply from 1,219 × 2,438 (4' × 8') long-grain sheets
2. Direction of face grain
3. Lap joint: fasten and adhere as indicated
4. Butt joint: fasten with 5 mm aluminum dome-head rivets and 5 mm stainless-steel fender washers
5. Galvanized steel sheet metal strapping as required, minimum thickness 25 gauge
6. Round staggered perforation pattern with 5 mm diameter holes at 25 mm offsets. Offset pattern 20 mm from edge and align as indicated.
7. 8 × 0.75 stainless-steel flat socket-head wood screw and #10 countersunk finishing washer

Additional notes

Fasten and adhere base with 10 × 2.5 stainless-steel flat socket head wood screw and #10 countersunk finishing washer

Fasten and adhere wood corner post and ridge with 8 × 1.5 stainless-steel flat socket head wood screw and #8 countersunk finishing washer

5mm diameter aluminum dome head rivets with 5 mm aluminum washers

Base plate assembly: 38 × 286 (2' × 12') lumber, lap and adhere and fasten with 8 × 2.5 socket head wood screws

Ice hole: drill with ice auger and flood with water after installing round plywood plate

Notch base assembly to suit rubber ply panels

Taper base to suit rubber ply panels

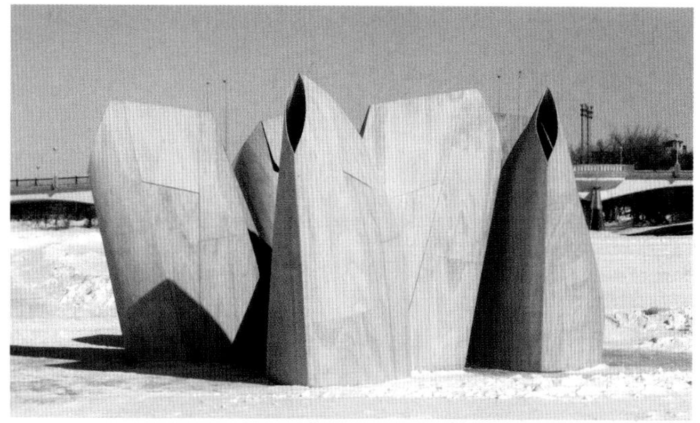

03

04

Metals

THE BASICS

Metals are elements made by the refinement of minerals, each with unique qualities derived from their constituents and the process used to produce them. Unlike wood or stone or many other materials, metals are entropic—they can be re-covered, re-formed, or mixed together to form totally new metal types. Metals that contain iron are called *ferrous* metals, such as steel, cast iron, and wrought iron. Ferrous metals are generally the strongest metals but tend to oxidize easily. *Nonferrous* metals contain no iron, such as aluminum, copper, and lead. These metals are usually easy to work with and are considered more attractive. Generally nonferrous metals are more costly; however, they tend to form a protective oxide layer on their surface to prevent excessive corrosion. Most architectural metals are alloys or mixtures of various elements, controlled to yield optimum qualities for a particular application. Metals have a great range of properties. They can be lustrous, ductile, conductive of heat and electricity, corroded by oxidation, vulnerable to heat, and are considered the strongest architectural material.

Minerals that contain a mixture of metallic elements and various impurities are called *ore*. The process of extracting metal from ore is called *smelting*. Combinations of metals, or a base metal mixed with traces of others, are called *alloys*. The predominant elements used in architecture are iron, aluminum, copper, zinc, and titanium. Metals are seldom used in their pure state, but rather as alloys that offer more strength and durability. Most often these elements are alloyed with others to yield optimum qualities for a particular application.

Metals can be worked with the following methods and processes:

CASTING, in which molten metal is poured into a mold to achieve a desired shape

—

FORGING, in which hot metal is forced into a die to achieve a desired shape

—

ROLLING, in which hot or cold metal passes through a series of rollers to give it a profile

—

EXTRUDING, in which metal is pushed through a die, squeezing it to a desired cross section

—

DRAWING, in which metal is pulled rather than pushed through the die, to produce wires, tubing, or rods

HISTORY

Metal is one of the oldest materials to be manipulated by man, and has been used for its strength and versatility. For centuries metals have been shaped into tools, weapons, and different practical objects. Copper, one of the harder historic metals, was first used for tools, followed by bronze, which is a copper alloy. Gold and silver, which are soft metals, were only used for decorative purposes as they primarily are today. The Greeks used bronze and iron for tying stone blocks together without mortar, and the Romans used lead and copper for water pipes and roofing. But it was not until the eighteenth century when iron could be processed economically enough for metal's role in architecture to become significant, as it was manufactured for structural beams, columns, and machinery. By the nineteenth century, structural iron and steel were becoming common. When reinforced concrete was invented in the 1860s, the marriage of steel and concrete revolutionized the construction industry: longer spans and taller buildings were possible as never before.

Copper is thought to be one of the first metals ever used—archaeologists have found evidence of its use stretching back as far as 6000 BCE. In fact, for most of recorded history, copper was the prevailing construction metal due to its combination of strength and durability. The first evidence of copper production techniques appeared in 6000–4000 BCE in the eastern Mediterranean area (present-day Turkey), where copper was extracted and forged into finished tools. In 5000 BCE, the Egyptians became very skilled in working copper by smelting in wood-fired furnaces and creating tools, jewelry, and other ornaments.
It was the Romans, however, who first used copper in a major architectural application. They mastered soldering and brazing techniques and created some different fluxes to clean and remove oxides from copper's surface. The Pantheon, built by Marcus Agrippa in 27 BCE and later rebuilt by Hadrian in 120 CE, had a copper roof and cornice, which remained intact until the beginning of World War II. As history progressed, copper's use increased, primarily for the roofs of many Renaissance buildings and the steep roofs of the Gothic cathedrals and churches. More recently, the Statue of Liberty was constructed of copper sheets over an iron framework. Copper's primacy did not fade until the second half of the twentieth century, when iron, as a steel alloy, became the most common construction metal, followed by aluminum, with copper falling into third place.

Zinc was first used by the Romans in 200 BCE as a copper alloy to make brass, but was not commercially produced as an architectural metal until the 1650s. It is a blue-white-colored metal that is relatively brittle and will oxidize to a self-protecting gray surface. The first production method for zinc was in a sheet form, but the result was extremely brittle and cracked easily. The hot-rolling process reduced zinc's brittleness and increased its strength as an architectural metal. It was first used architecturally in Europe during the Industrial Revolution, primarily in roofing and details. Brass, developed in the seventeenth century, contains up to 40 percent zinc and is most often used for finishes, fixtures, and ornamental objects. It was most commonly seen in the form of roof tile or ornamentation. The United States, where copper was much more widely used, did not develop zinc sheet production until 1838, relying on imports to meet modest demand for this metal.

It can be argued that the development of steel was one of the most pivotal moments in the history of architecture, giving a freedom of design and space and opening up structural possibilities in countless new ways. With the construction of Joseph Paxton's Crystal Palace in London in 1851, cast iron and wrought iron, later refined to what we know today as steel, was shown to be a new construction material with capabilities like no other.

Iron, which is not abundant in pure form in the earth's crust, was historically a metal used only for tools. The largest source of pure iron, in fact, can be found in meteorites—not a particularly reliable source. The most common way to obtain iron was the smelting of iron ore, which is very common all over the world. In the Middle Ages, most of the refined iron was extracted in a contraption that acted somewhat like a blast furnace. A mix of crushed iron ore and charcoal were placed in a stone vault and molten iron (also called pig iron) would sink to the bottom and release into molds. The charcoal added traces of carbon to the iron, which altered its workability. Interestingly, the use of wood to produce charcoal for iron smelting was one of the main causes of world deforestation during the Industrial Revolution. Late in the nineteenth century, charcoal was replaced by coke, a residue of coal used for fuel. The iron produced at this time was almost a pure iron—it was very malleable since it had little carbon. It was called *wrought iron* and was used mainly for tools and weapons for centuries. Large amounts of wrought iron were produced in Europe after the 1300s. While wrought iron is almost pure iron, metal produced in a blast furnace with 2 to 4 percent carbon is called *cast iron*. The Chinese discovered cast iron in the sixth century BCE, but the process of production did not fully evolve until the twelfth century in Europe. Cast iron is much more brittle, difficult to work, and has a lower melting point than wrought iron. A malleable, low-carbon iron alloy was sometimes produced in a blast furnace. This metal, which was approximately 1 percent carbon, was historically the closest metalworkers came to producing what we know today as steel. In the early 1800s cast iron structural members became a viable alternative to load-bearing masonry walls, but iron remained an expensive alternative until the late eighteenth century, when cheaper manufacturing processes emerged. Whether these advances spurred the Industrial Revolution or vice versa is debatable.

In the mid-1800s steel was only used for very specific non-architectural applications, such as swords or scissors. Early production of steel was unpredictable, not very homogeneous, and thought of as a very demanding process. Only in certain geographic areas such as some parts of Asia were these select batches of steel produced with any success. In 1855 Englishman Henry Bessemer designed the first converter for processing steel, which by today's classifications was really cast iron. Steel began to be produced in large quantities after Bessemer discovered how to add and control the amount of carbon. It was first produced by either adding carbon to molten wrought iron or by preventing carbon from oxidizing in the pig iron. In the United States, Andrew Carnegie of U.S. Steel and Edgar Thompson of Bethlehem Steel both helped feed the Industrial Revolution by producing large quantities of steel in the 1800s. Steel began to be used in railroad tracks, bridges, shipbuilding, and eventually skyscrapers.

Aluminum is refined from bauxite, one of the most abundant metallic ores in the earth's crust, and was unknown to the ancient world. It was first sold in 1845 as a precious metal, but did not become widely used in construction until the past century. Prior to the twentieth century, purifying aluminum, which is not naturally available in a usable state, was a very expensive and lengthy process. Today, it is second only to iron as the most commonly used metal in construction.

William Gregor, an English chemist and mineralogist, first discovered titanium in 1791. His discovery was not widely known until 1795, however, when it was "rediscovered" by Martin Klaproth, a German chemist. Klaproth named the metal *titanium* after the Titans, the family of giants that was overthrown by the gods in Greek mythology. Interestingly, he named it so because of the difficulty in removing the impurities and oxygen to reduce titanium to a pure state, not because of the high strength with which we associate it today. Initially, titanium was only used in paints as a pigment supplement. The metal has many tiny impurities that made it a brittle material and difficult to work. It first became commercially available in 1951 and was developed into a product four times harder than steel. Mass production of titanium began in World War II by Dr. William Kroll, a German who fled Nazi Germany and came to the United States. In the early 1950s titanium was considered purely an aerospace material, given its light weight and high strength. It was not until the 1990s that titanium was considered a realistic architectural material, when its price dropped and its production techniques were refined.

DESIGN CONSIDERATIONS

In architecture, metals have developed and grown into a huge industry that produces materials for an unprecedented range of applications. It is too general to speak about "metal" as if it were one simple material, given its enormously wide range of types, colors, qualities, and properties. In architectural applications, metals are relatively lightweight and malleable, in addition to being strong. They can be used sculpturally, allowing for free-form designs. Metals are available in a variety of surface finishes—the range of color, texture, and luster allows architects an immense degree of design flexibility. With today's variety of finishes and coatings, a designer can almost prescribe exactly how a metal should appear on a building, then find the product that will yield that appearance.

Beyond aesthetics, however, there is a long list of functional considerations when choosing a metal for a building. Despite the many product options and technological advances in applying metals in architecture, designers must be mindful of limitations associated with each material. How will it perform as a structural component? How will it react to different temperatures or to adjacent materials? How will it weather? How will its color, luster, and reflectivity endure? *Oil canning*, the waviness that, sometimes occurs in large stretches of metal and can be an inherent characteristic of metal products, should also be considered in the design process, or measures must be taken to prevent it.

The qualities of reflectivity, weathering, and finish can create a wildly diverse amount of design possibilities. Weathering and aging are important considerations, because as metals mature, they develop a patina, which is often seen as an inherently beautiful quality of the material. The familiar image of the vernacular barn and its rusted, colorful metal roof is a common architectural expression of the venerable and of a particular material culture. Architectural appreciation is often linked to a building material's expression of maturity and aesthetic age. In other circumstances, retaining a metal's original luster and finish and suppressing any declaration of age is a clear design intention.

The process of bimetallic corrosion (weathering) is complex and can be affected by a number of factors, including the surrounding environment, variations in composition, any coatings and finishes, and contact with other materials, the principle being that different metals expand at different rates as they warm. *Galvanic action*, which is the corrosion process that occurs when two unlike metals and moisture are present, is an electric current flowing from the *anode*, which corrodes, to the *cathode*, which gives the ions to the atmosphere. When two metals are in contact, the one that is higher in the galvanic series will become the anode and will corrode. The current flows from the positive (high end of the table) to the negative (low end of the table). For instance, when iron and copper are in contact, iron will become the anode and will quickly corrode (see Table 1, p. 140).

Metals, like other materials, expand and contract due to changes in temperatures. These changes are quantified and are represented numerically as *coefficients of thermal expansion*. These are ratios that give the amount of change per length of material per degree of change in temperature. The coefficient of thermal expansion for structural steel is 0.0000065 in./in./°F (0.000017 mm/mm/°C), and for stainless steel is 0.0000099 in./in./°F (0.0000173 mm/mm/°C). The greater the difference in thermal coefficient of materials being joined, the greater the need for details that accommodate thermal movement (see Table 2, p. 140). If not relieved, these stresses may cause a loss of integrity of the enclosure or structural system.

TYPES

The metal industry is a mammoth enterprise that continues to grow and evolve. Research yields new alloys and uses for metals constantly, and prices and manufacturing processes are always changing—all critical factors when architects make selections of materials. Whether the choice is as banal as an aluminum window frame or as expressive as the patina of a copper wall panel, metals are potent design tools.

Iron and Steel

Steel, one of the strongest and most affordable materials, is a ferrous metal, meaning it contains iron. It is used in all types of buildings and in all aspects of construction. Compared to other building materials, steel has a favorable strength-to-weight ratio, and it offers the greatest strength per volume. It combines optimum strength with elasticity and is most often used for light and heavy structural framing, in addition to other building elements such as windows, doors, and hardware. It is easily drilled, tapped, welded, fastened, and shaped. Its most important architectural characteristics are its strength, stiffness, and fire and corrosion resistance, all properties that can be further influenced by alloying and coatings.

Most steels today are produced and categorized as *standard* steel, which is then categorized further as *carbon* or *alloy* steel. The more carbon content a steel has, the greater its strength and hardness, though the more difficult it is to cold-work or weld. Alloy steel contains more than 1 percent carbon or other elements than the standards set for carbon steel. Construction steel is a combination of carbon and iron (98 to 99 percent iron and 0.16 to 1.7 percent carbon). More common and more affordable, carbon steels are used for structural and mechanical applications, while alloy steels are most often used for fixtures and finishing parts such as door handles, pulls, or countertops. The most common alloy steel is *stainless steel*, which is harder, stronger, and more corrosion-resistant than others. *High-strength, low-alloy steel* (HSLA), more commonly known by the trade name *COR-TEN*, is also a common alloy steel. It is not only extremely strong but also has a high resistance to progressive corrosion due to a layer of dense red/orange-colored oxide that develops on its surface. COR-TEN steel is an alloy metal in which a small amount of copper (0.25–0.55 percent) and other elements are added to steel. The yield strength of COR-TEN steel is greater than that of mild steel. It is considered a weathering steel because the exposed surface quickly oxidizes in the atmosphere, forming a dense, shallow, passive barrier against further corrosion. It does not require painting or other treatment, though it does tend to stain materials adjacent to it with reddish-brown ferrous residue as the rusty surface is eroded slightly by precipitation.

Wrought iron has a low carbon content (0.02 percent) and is almost a pure iron. It is a ductile material and is easily worked and forged when red-hot. It is highly resistant to corrosion, yet cannot be welded or cast. Wrought iron is made when iron ore is heated on a charcoal fire until it turns into a soft spongy state, not entirely melted. The spongelike iron can then be worked or wrought into a form in what is called a *white heat* state. Wrought iron is most commonly used for ornamental work such as grilles, hardware, gates, and railings. A small amount of wrought iron is still made today in the traditional fashion, but most metal called "wrought iron" is really mild steel with a low carbon content that can be formed into shapes by machine—putting many blacksmiths and their trade to rest.

The most commonly used steel is called *mild steel* and has a carbon content of 0.15–0.25 percent. A common strength-grade of steel as determined by the American Society for Testing and Materials is ASTM A36, with a *yield point*—the point at which a material begins to permanently deform—of 36,000 psi (248.2 MPa). A typical higher-strength steel, ASTM A572, which is a low-alloy, has a yield point of 50,000 psi (344.7 MPa).

Cast iron has a higher carbon content (approximately 1.8 to 4.5 percent), making the metal more brittle and difficult to work or forge when hot. Cast iron is an alloy of iron and iron carbide and is considered corrosion resistant and strong in compression. Due to its high amounts of carbon, cast iron is very easily cast, allowing for intricate molds. However, once it has solidified it cannot be worked. It is very hard and has good compressive strength but inferior elasticity; it also provides a tough surface that is less prone to rust than steel, despite its brittleness and low tensile strength. Originally, cast iron was made for both structural and decorative purposes, but its low melting point and lack of elasticity make it undesirable as a structural material. It is still made and used often today, more often for architectural decorative details, piping, plumbing fixtures, grates, street furniture, and rainwater fixtures.

Stainless steel is an alloy steel that contains between 12 and 20 percent chromium and other elements such as nickel, copper, molybdenum, and aluminum. It may be cast into slabs; hot-rolled into plates, bars, or sheets; cold-rolled into thin sections; welded; and otherwise readily formed. Because of its strength and low maintenance requirements, stainless steel is often used for curtain walls, sanitary fixtures, sinks, hardware, flashing, and trim. Its high corrosion resistance makes it suitable for masonry accessories as well. Since the cost of stainless steel usually precludes its use structurally, it is more often used in smaller or visible applications such as fasteners, hardware, and building products like kitchen appliances and limited areas of cladding.

MANUFACTURING STEEL

The raw materials for producing steel are iron ore, coke, and limestone. There are two standard processes for manufacturing steel: the *basic oxygen process*, used to make the bulk of standard-grade steel, uses an oxygen point to blow pressurized oxygen into a furnace containing pig iron and scrap metal; and the *electric arc furnace process*, which produces high-quality special steels like stainless steel, uses carbon electrodes to create a powerful electric arc that melts the metal. Both processes allow for the removal of unwanted elements and the addition of desired elements, carbon being the most common additive. Steel usually contains trace elements of other byproducts from refinement, such as sulfur and silicon.

Steel can be heat-treated to form alloys with other metals to change its quality. Metals that are alloyed with steel and their added qualities include:

ALUMINUM, which improves surface hardening

—

CHROMIUM, which increases corrosion resistance and hardness

—

COPPER, which increases corrosion resistance and strength

—

MANGANESE, which increases corrosion resistance and hardness

—

MOLYBDENUM, which increases corrosion resistance and strength

—

NICKEL, which increases tensile strength and corrosion resistance

—

TUNGSTEN, which increases strength at higher temperatures

After being manufactured, steel can be shaped in many different ways. Architecturally, this is classified under two main categories: *hot rolled* or *cold rolled*. Hot-rolled steel is rolled out of the casting area to a specific thickness. Cold-rolled steel, the most common architectural metal, is a product of the hot-rolling process. After being hot rolled, the steel is run through cold rollers, stretching the grains, smoothing the surface, and making the metal more dimensionally accurate.

There are a number of ways of working steel to increase its hardness and strength. One is by a process called *cold-hardening*, which is the method of hammering or compressing steel to make it harder. Another frequently employed method, *quenching*, heats the steel and then quickly cools it in water, oil, or air, creating a very thin layer of metal crystals on the steel's surface that is harder and more brittle than the rest of the metal, thereby increasing its strength. *Tempering* is another way to increase the hardness, ductility, or strength of steel by a heating and controlled-cooling process. *Annealing* is the process of heating steel and cooling it very slowly to make a hard steel soft, usually to improve cold-working, cutting, and forming methods. Steel can also be cast, forged, extruded, drawn, and rolled.

Galvanization is the application of a zinc coating onto steel or iron to prevent rusting. There are two methods of galvanization. *Hot-dipped galvanizing* involves a coating that is applied by immersing the metal in a bath of molten zinc, forming a protective layer of zinc on the outside and zinc/iron alloys bonding to the steel. Repeated dipping produces a thicker coating, increasing durability. Zinc is a brittle metal, dictating that complex shapes such as corrugations should be formed before being galvanized. The surface of the zinc coating freezes into a crystalline or spangled pattern that oxidizes to a self-protecting matte gray color. If this coating is scratched or marred to the steel beneath, zinc compounds form in the scratch and heal the discontinuity, preventing oxidation. *Cold-dipping*, or *electro-galvanizing*, is a less durable process in which a thin coating of zinc is electrically created on the steel member, resulting in a shiny surface finish that is less durably bonded to the iron or steel core.

APPEARANCE

In its most common and inexpensive form, new steel has a plain gray appearance that will quickly react with oxygen and then scale and rust. To improve its appearance and to prevent corrosion, steel can be finished in many different ways. It can be painted, galvanized, or chemically treated to prevent oxidation and corrosion. Although it is not combustible, it will lose strength and become ductile under high heat conditions. Building codes therefore require most primary structural steel to be fireproofed. Some of these methods include enclosing steel in layers of gypsum board, encasing steel in concrete, or covering the steel with spray-on fireproofing, all of which conceal it from view.

High-quality stainless steel has an aesthetically appealing appearance but is also more expensive than carbon steel or other alloy steels. Stainless steel can be finished in a variety of ways. It can be polished, brushed, textured, patterned, or made reflective with optical effects using an electrochemical finish.

WEATHERING

Mild steel and low-alloy steels are highly susceptible to reacting with oxygen and causing rust, with accelerated corrosion occurring in coastal and marine locations. Corrosion resistance of steel can be improved by applying paint, galvanizing, copper alloy, or various coatings such as powder. These can also improve the appearance by adding color or a shiny, uniform surface. Stainless steel, on the other hand, is highly resistant to atmospheric corrosion and will retain its original luster. Its corrosion resistance is due to a thin oxide film that continually forms on its surface. This film may be permanently colored bronze, blue, gold, red, purple, or green by a chemical and cathodic treatment.

JOINING

Steel can be joined by most of the common metal joining heat processes—welding or soldering—mechanically joined with bolts, rivets, pins, and most other mechanical fasteners. Steel is very easily welded and produces a strong bond. It can be welded using an oxygen/acetylene gas mixture or an electric arc, which is more suitable for large steel sections such as structural steel. Smaller sections of steel can be welded with an electric arc and a metal inert gas (MIG) using a semiautomatic tool and argon gas. A similar tool using a tungsten electrode (TIG) is also available. *High-strength bolts* are bolts that are heat-treated during manufacturing to give them extra strength. Their strength is a result of their shear resistance, as opposed to how tight they are turned to prevent slippage of the two materials. Bolting is quicker, easier, and cheaper, can be done on site, and is reversible, but is sometimes not as strong.

Aluminum

Behind steel, aluminum is the most commonly used metal in construction. It is one of the lightest and easiest metals to manipulate, bend, shape, cast, fasten, and weld, and is also very ductile, often extruded into shapes for architectural purposes. It can easily be drilled, tapped, sawed, planed, and filed with hand tools, making it a yielding material for tradesmen to use.

Aluminum is used in many different functions and locations in architecture, the most common being roofing, cladding, flashing, curtain wall and glazing systems, insulation, ductwork, hardware, and lighting. It is typically used for secondary building elements, but high-strength aluminum alloys are also used for structural purposes. This list continues to grow as the construction industry becomes more comfortable and creative with the material's capabilities and as it becomes more appealing to users.

Aluminum's resistance to corrosion is high, much better than steel's. It is also lighter than steel, copper, and most other metals. Aluminum's strength in relation to its weight is also better than steel. There are disadvantages to aluminum, however, including its higher cost, greater thermal expansion, and lower fire resistance compared to steel.

MANUFACTURING ALUMINUM

Aluminum can be manipulated using all the same methods for working steel, including casting, hot rolling, and cold rolling, although it can be worked at a much lower temperature than steel because its melting point is more than a thousand degrees lower, making it a cheaper and safer material to produce. Refining aluminum takes a significant amount of electricity, which has consequently made the business of recycling the material an extensive secondary trade for the aluminum industry.

For construction purposes, aluminum is almost always turned into an aluminum alloy. It is most often alloyed with copper, manganese, zinc, silicon, magnesium, or magnesium and silicon together. Each of these alloys are designed for specific purposes, such as for casting, added strength, or aviation purposes. The wide range of aluminum alloys are classified into three types:

NON-HEAT-TREATABLE ALLOYS are manganese and magnesium alloys. They are stronger than other aluminum alloys and are generally used for corrugated and troughed sheet roofing and cladding.

—

HEAT-TREATABLE ALLOYS are aluminum-magnesium-silicon and aluminum-copper-magnesium-silicon alloys. They are not as strong as non-heat-treatable alloys and have a lower corrosion resistance, but they are more resistant to fire. They are typically applied to structural and fastening uses.

—

CASTING ALLOYS are silicon, silicon-copper, and silicon-magnesium alloys. They are used for casting.

Aluminum's strength varies depending on the alloy used. Pure aluminum is too soft for structural use, and is therefore used only in fully supported roofing and flashing. Depending on the alloy it is married with, aluminum can be extruded through a die, allowing for a wider and more complex range of shapes and forms.

Aluminum is further classified for its tempering designation. *Temper* is the strength and hardness produced by thermal treatment and mechanical working. It is directly related to an alloy's overall strength. The temper designation is based on heat treatment, aging, and the annealing of the alloy. Aluminum is available in a large range of alloys, each created for specific purposes. These alloys are designated from 1,000 to 7,000 in seven categories. The number is followed by a letter that indicates the tempering designation—the most common stable series being "T" and usually designated from T1 through T10. The most common aluminum we see is 6061-T6, which contains trace elements of silicon and magnesium and is suitable for casting and fabrication.

APPEARANCE

Aluminum is naturally a clean silver/white color, but there are also an abundant variety of finishes, such as anodized, surface texture, plastic-coated, or painted, that can result in a transparent or colored appearance. These various finishes can be mechanically or chemically applied and are not only meant for aesthetic purposes but also for protection from the environment.

The Aluminum Association created a broad designation system for aluminum finishing processes. The labeling system recognizes that almost all finishes used on aluminum can be subdivided into three major categories: mechanical finishes, chemical finishes, and coatings. Coatings are further divided into five subcategories:

MECHANICAL FINISHES can be produced at the mill during the initial rolling or extruding processes, or by subsequent finishing techniques that include polishing, grinding, or brushing. It is typically a hand-operated process in which parts and components are finished dependent on their shape and form. The mechanical finishes applied to aluminum are standardized by the Aluminum Association into four classifications: fabricated, meaning the aluminum is used directly from the manufacturer with no additional finishing; buffed, where the surface is polished; directional textured, referring to a texture applied to the surface in one direction; and non-directional textured, where any range of textures are applied to the surface.

—

CHEMICAL FINISHES alter a metal's surface through one or more chemical solutions. There are three purposes for using a chemical finish on aluminum: to create a clean surface for a future finish; to provide a uniform electrochemical reactive surface for an anodonic coating; or to etch the surface to achieve a specific reflectivity. Because chemical finishes are applied in a batch, it is one of the least expensive processes. The Aluminum Association has labeled a chemical treatments designation into two classifications, non-etched and cleaned-and-etched chemical treatment.

—

COATINGS are subdivided into five categories: anodic coatings, resinous and other organic coatings, vitreous coatings, electroplated and other metal coatings, and laminated coatings. The most common in architectural applications are described here. When aluminum is exposed to air and has no chemical finish, a thin, protective oxide film forms on its surface, which over time becomes chalky and thick. Anodizing aluminum is a controlled process that makes this oxide film thicker and harder, thus increasing its corrosion and abrasion resistance. Most exterior applications using aluminum alloys are anodized surfaces. Anodizing is an oxidizing process in which the metal is immersed in sulfuric acid and electrolytically made anodic by converting the surface to an oxide film. It is then sealed by boiling the metal in water. This process increases the metal's durability, traps dyes, and adheres to other finishes. The finish appearance can range from clear to a wide variety of colors, but most important is the aluminum's increased hardness and durability after anodization.

—

CLEAR-COAT ANODIZING is the most common and economical process of anodizing. Today's technology has allowed for computerized monitoring equipment to help the anodizing process.

—

PLASTIC COATINGS, which are usually polyesters and fall under the "laminated coating" category, are applied electrostatically as a powder and then heat-cured to a self-cleaning finish. This is done for glazing systems, cladding panels, and rainwater components in buildings. Plastic coatings can give aluminum a range of colors, as can other finishes such as enamel or lacquer finishes. These finishes give a durable protection layer and a color to the metal, and often disguise the metal with the appearance of a more uniform, flat color and texture. When aluminum is painted, it should have an appropriate primer, and no lead-based paint should be used to avoid a galvanic reaction.

WEATHERING

Aluminum is generally resistant to corrosion due to a thin, invisible film of oxide on its surface, which forms immediately and continuously. In normal atmospheric conditions, the metal ages well, becoming a darker gray over time. Anodizing its surface or applying another protective coating may further improve it.

While aluminum can resist harsh weather conditions, corrosion can occur through contact with other materials such as plasters, mortars, uncured cements and, most significantly, copper. Aluminum can corrode any adjacent zinc- or iron-based materials. Aluminum therefore needs to be separated from other metals to prevent a galvanic reaction. Timber that contains preservatives like water-soluble copper or mercury can also aggressively react to aluminum. Water can stain its surface, causing it to oxidize and create dark stains that do not damage the material structurally but are extremely difficult to remove. When designing with aluminum, it is wise to think about how rainwater flows over a building and whether it flows over an affecting material (especially copper) before running over aluminum.

JOINING

Aluminum is difficult to solder because of oxide formation and heat dissipation. Aluminum alloys can be welded using *metal inert gas* (MIG) or *tungsten inert gas* (TIG) techniques, which are welding processes in which electricity is used to generate heat necessary to melt and attach separate metal parts. MIG welding, also called *gas metal arc welding* (GMAW), is done by sparking an electric arc between the welded parts and a consumable electrode. It uses an aluminum alloy wire as a combined electrode and filler material. TIG welding, also called *gas tungsten arc welding* (GTAW), uses a tungsten electrode and separate filler rods, making the process more flexible. Unlike MIG, the electrode is not the filler material and is a stationary rod. It is also possible to weld without a filler material with TIG. Aluminum is often mechanically fastened with, for instance, aluminum alloy (A-1) bolts and rivets, or with non-magnetic stainless steel. It can also be bonded with a strong adhesive on a prepared surface.

Copper

Copper is usually used as an alloy combined with zinc when used in building construction. Its important advantage over ferric metals (those with iron) is its resistance to corrosion, making it a wise choice for areas in which the metal is in consistent contact with water or severe atmospheric conditions. Today, copper is primarily seen in sheet form in roof systems and cladding. It is also used for finish details, gutters, and downspouts. Both brass and bronze are copper alloys, but there is an imprecise distinction between the two based on the concentrations of each element. The copper-zinc alloys that yield a more yellow surface are usually brass, while the more red and brown alloys are bronze. Brass and bronze are harder than copper and not as easy to form, yet are far softer than steel. These alloys are most commonly used externally on doorframes, balustrades, window surrounds, fasteners, and other fittings. In addition to their high corrosion resistance, copper alloys are also able to take on oxidized patinas, which can create a wide variety of surface colors.

Copper is a soft and easily machined metal, yet is also strong. It is relatively dense, with high electrical conductivity. However, copper's strength-to-weight ratio is low, making it a poor structural metal. Its malleability makes it easy to fold and seam edges on thin sheets, allowing for a clean and fitted cladding skin. It is ideal for outdoor use given its corrosion resistance, but attention should be given to water that runs over the material. Runoff from copper roofs or siding can prevent the growth of plants (though it does not affect animals); additionally, copper nails or fasteners drilled into tree trunks or branches can kill the trees. Copper runoff, in the form of green copper sulfate, will stain adjacent porous materials such as limestone, stucco, concrete, and other light-colored materials. This problem can be prevented by careful consideration of how details are designed.

Despite an overall decrease in the use of copper through the years, it is used more than ever today in electric power transmission, lighting, and wire circuitry; next to silver, copper is the most conductive metal. Since copper is a heavy material and is relatively expensive, it is usually used in thin sheets. Copper cannot carry its own weight and is usually supported by other materials such as a wood or masonry backing.

MANUFACTURING COPPER

In North America, most copper is obtained from sulfide ores in Arizona, Utah, Montana, Michigan, and Canada. It is also mined in Chile, Germany, South Africa, New Guinea, and Russia. Copper production today is similar to its ancient manufacturing methods, though it is predictably much more efficient and purifying techniques have now been mastered. Copper is produced by first concentrating mineral ore that has been crushed and ground through a flotation or separation technique. The ore is then roasted (but not melted) in a furnace to remove contamination and other volatile materials before being fully melted, which removes the major contaminate, iron. The result is what is called a *matte*, which is approximately 30 percent copper in block form. The next step is a conversion process where the matte is oxidized with air to form what is called a *blister copper*, which is approximately 99 percent pure copper. The blister copper can be purified further through a process called *electrolysis refining* (or *reduction*), where it is submerged in an electrolyte solution of copper sulfate and sulfuric acid, making the blister copper an anode (electronically positive), and yielding the final, 99.9 percent pure copper. In the 1960s, another technique called *flash smelting* replaced the roasting step, in which the ore is smelted with fluxes such as silica and limestone. This process produces a high-grade copper matte more efficiently and is environmentally safer.

Copper has the highest recycling rate of any engineered material—approximately 75 percent of copper used in architecture is recycled. In fact, the rate at which copper is recycled is actually equal to the rate at which it is mined. Disadvantages to copper production include the huge amount of energy and fuel needed to power the equipment used to mine copper.

APPEARANCE

No other metal has such unique color variations and textures as copper. Its distinct red/orange/brown hue and naturally aging surface make it an attractive design element for architects. Its longevity, lasting for decades and sometimes centuries, also makes it an appealing material choice. The progression from its natural burnish to an ultimate blue-green color has made it a pleasing material to watch transform over time. It is no surprise that copper is often used for ornamental metalwork, due to the range of color options that can be achieved through its different alloys, as well as chemical treatments. Both brass and bronze are available in an endless number of varieties. Yellow brass contains 70 percent copper and 30 percent zinc, while a more brown or red bronze is usually the result of copper alloyed with aluminum, tin, silver, or nickel. Different alloys have a diverse range of physical properties, and these can be exploited to meet a variety of needs.

WEATHERING

Copper is most commonly seen as a roof material that patinas to an aqua-green color over time. New copper has a characteristic metallic, dark brown color. Depending on the atmosphere and location, it begins to patinate to a distinctive green/blue over five to ten years. The patina is produced from sulfur compounds in the atmosphere and occurs more quickly in industrial and marine environments or in areas with higher temperatures or high moisture. In polluted areas with acid rain, dark streaks sometimes appear on the surface of the metal. This staining will then mature to the green patina, bypassing the rust stages. The metal fully stops mineralizing after approximately seventy years. If desired, there are finishes to prevent this patina process and retain the original dark brown color, as well as a pre-patinated finish to achieve the green color immediately.

Copper is compatible with most building timbers, but it will corrode quickly when it is in contact with moisture and red cedar. Copper corrodes most other metals upon sustained contact. In the presence of moisture, it will corrode metals that are higher on the galvanic series table, including steel, lead, aluminum, zinc, and cast iron.

JOINING

Copper is a very malleable metal and can be easily brazed, soldered, or welded at low levels of heat. When fastening mechanically, as with all materials, an allowance for expansion must be made—otherwise stress will build up in the metal and buckling and cracking will occur.

Titanium

Titanium is the fourth most abundant mineral on earth, after aluminum, iron, and magnesium. It is primarily mined in the Americas, with Brazil producing 65 percent of the world's supply of *rutile*, its primary ore. Titanium used in the United States typically originates off the coast of Australia, where it is mined from the ocean floor. Interestingly, old Soviet submarines from the Cold War are also a source of titanium.

Titanium is just beginning to mature as an architectural material. Given its high production costs, it is prohibitively expensive for most building projects. It is telling to note, however, that this was also the case for aluminum just over a century ago. As production increases, the cost will likely decrease, allowing for more architectural applications.

MANUFACTURING
Titanium is produced by mixing the primary ore, rutile, with coke and then charging it with hot chlorine gas. The ore then goes through further purification to create a metallic sponge of titanium. It is then converted into an electrode, melted, and formed into a slab. (Alloying the metal would occur at this stage, once it is melted.) The slab is then reduced to desired sheets or coils varying in thickness from 0.015–0.25" (0.381–6.35 mm). While titanium can be cast and extruded, for architectural purposes it usually is not.

APPEARANCE
Titanium is typically a light gray color and retains its tone for years without changing. When exposed to oxygen, a very thin film forms on its surface, preserving the surface color. One unique quality of titanium is that it can be developed into shades of silver, gold, blue, or purple through an electric charge. By changing the voltage, a different shade or tone of color is created on its surface. Different tones can also be achieved through an electrolyte bath.

WEATHERING
Titanium has the highest corrosion resistance of any architectural metal. It is a durable material with a low coefficient of thermal expansion, causing it to be very weatherproof and resilient. Even in marine and coastal uses, titanium is unaffected by all of the more typical weathering conditions affecting other metals.

JOINING
As in typical sheet-metal techniques, titanium can be formed and joined. It can also be welded, much like any other architectural metal. Because titanium will corrode steel, aluminum, galvanized steel, and other metals, stainless-steel fasteners must be used when making connections.

Zinc

Zinc is a very dense and corrosion-resistant architectural material. It is non-ferrous, and thus not subject to rusting. In the U.S. market today, zinc is most commonly used as a coating on steel and as an alloy with copper and titanium. It is used much more widely in the European architecture market, frequently as cast hardware, grilles, details, and surface panels.

MANUFACTURING
Refining zinc is much like refining copper. Zinc ore is crushed into particles and then concentrated by flotation, which separates the waste from the minerals. Zinc is cast on a continuously rotating cylinder and then rolled through pressure rolls to a specified thickness. When in a pure state, zinc has a very low tensile strength, but after being pushed through rolls, which develops a directionality to the material, its strength increases considerably. It is usually alloyed with copper and titanium in furnaces for added strength.

APPEARANCE
Pure zinc tarnishes quickly to a light blue-gray color due to the formation of a patina of basic zinc carbonate upon exposure to the atmosphere. Natural zinc has a semi-matte, light gray color that can be pre-weathered to a darker gray, while zinc alloys will tarnish to a darker gray. Zinc can also be lacquered with a polyester lacquer in the furnace to create different colors.

WEATHERING
When zinc is exposed to the atmosphere, the surface film of basic zinc carbonate develops, which protects the underlying metal and checks further corrosion. Zinc's corrosion resistance is due to this protective layer that develops and limits the amount of oxygen contact to the surface. Depending on the atmospheric conditions, a darker gray patina may develop within six months to two years.

In unpolluted areas, this protective film ensures that zinc building components will have a long, maintenance-free life. In industrial environments and areas with high levels of pollution, however, the corrosion rate increases dramatically. Sulfurous and sulfuric acids react with the zinc carbonate film to form zinc sulfate, which is soluble and washes off in rain. When employed in industrial areas, zinc is therefore most often used as vertical cladding or on pitched roofs.

Zinc should not be used in contact with copper or with acidic woods such as cedar and oak. It has good compatibility with other building materials, although mortars and any moist cements can increase its level of corrosion.

JOINING

Because zinc has a low melting point, it makes for easy resistance welding and soldering. When fastening zinc mechanically, galvanized or stainless-steel nails, screws, rivets, and clips are recommended. One should never use copper or brass fasteners or bimetallic corrosion will occur.

Lead

Lead is a dense, soft, toxic metal of low strength. It is one of the most weather-resistant materials, even exceeding stainless steel and zinc in corrosion resistance. It is a dull-gray colored metal that is soft yet dense. Once the main material used in plumbing, and often used as a roofing surface, the use of lead in construction has declined notably since the early 1900s. Use of lead is strictly controlled in water supplies and is no longer used in building interiors, including as pigment in interior paints. Lead for cladding applications is referred to as *desilverized lead*, which is a minimum of 99.85 percent lead and a maximum of 0.002 percent silver. Today's lead is relatively expensive and is usually only used for waste pipes, coatings, and flashing. Lead's toxicity makes many of its other possible uses unsuitable. Lead sheet, used for flashing, for example, is now often made from an alloy containing 6 percent antimony, which increases its stiffness and strength. When lead is used in applications such as roofing, it must always be fully supported by another material beneath. It is not a self-supporting metal due to its weight and low stiffness. Lead can also be used in ceiling or wall panels for sound insulation and vibration absorption. It can be produced in rolled sheets, shot, or bar forms. Its softness makes many metal fabrication processes impossible. Lead is frequently used in non-architectural applications, such as shields from X-rays and radiation and for automobile batteries.

Lead can be easily worked, is corrosion resistant, and is relatively impenetrable to radiation. Although it is a heavy metal, its malleability and durability may make it an appealing cladding material. It is traditionally used in construction for roofing, flashing, sound isolation, acid and radiation resistance, and in some hardware items. Lead dust and vapor are toxic to humans and must be strongly considered when used.

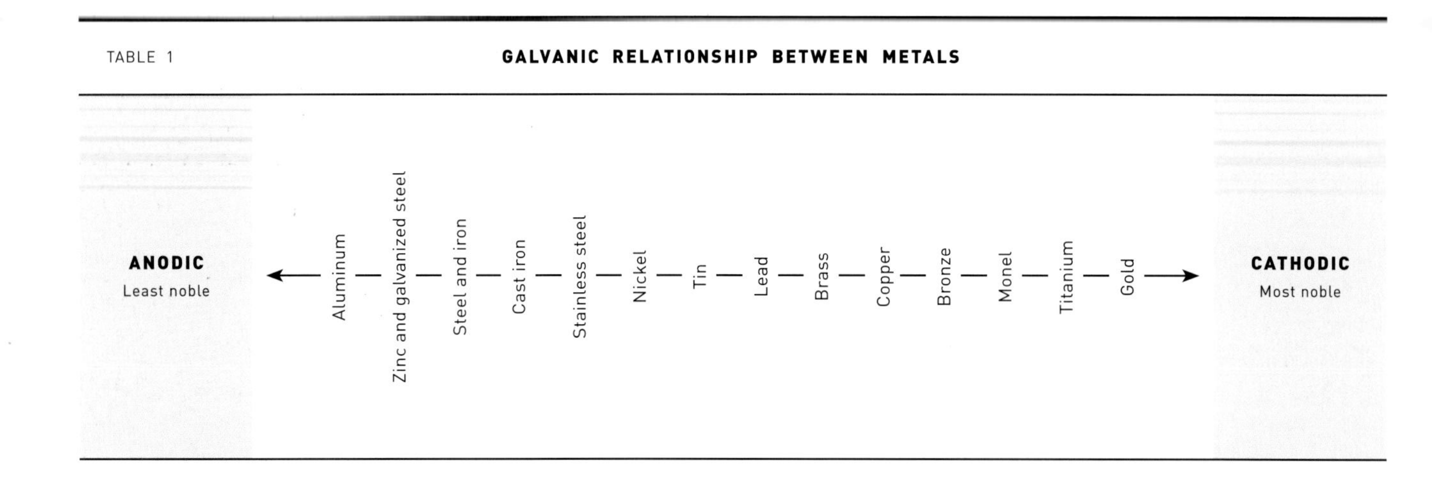

TABLE 2

COMPARISON OF METAL PROPERTIES

METAL	SPECIFIC GRAVITY	MELTING POINT	TENSILE STRENGTH	YIELD STRENGTH	COEFFICIENT OF THERMAL EXPANSION $\times 10^{-6}$ in./in./°F	COEFFICIENT OF THERMAL EXPANSION $\times 10^{-6}$ mm/mm/°C
Aluminum	2.70	1,220°F 660°C	13.0 ksi 90 MPa	5.0 ksi 35 MPa	13.0	24.0
Copper	8.96	1,980°F 1,080°C	29.0 ksi 200 MPa	10.0 ksi 69 MPa	9.3	16.8
Iron and steel	7.90	2,780°F 1,530°C	39.8 – 272.0 ksi 276 – 1,882 MPa	26.9 – 109 ksi 186 – 758 MPa	6.6	11.7
Lead	11.34	621°F 327°C	1.7 ksi 12 MPa	0.72 ksi 5 MPa	16.1	29.0
Stainless steel	7.90	2,640°F 1,450°C	74.4 – 119 ksi 515 – 827 MPa	3.0 – 79.7 ksi 207 – 552 MPa	9.8	17.8
Titanium	4.51	3,049°F 1,675°C	65.0 ksi 450 MPa	75.0 ksi 520 MPa	4.9	9.0
Zinc	7.14	788°F 420°C	4.0 – 12.0 ksi 110 – 200 MPa	14.0 ksi 97 MPa	13.8	24.9

TABLE 3

EFFECTS OF WEATHERING / CORROSION ON METALS

1 = Low / 5 = High

METAL	COLOR WHEN NEW	REFLECTIVITY WHEN NEW	TEN-YEAR AGING RESULT
Aluminum	Medium gray	3	Little change
Aluminum (mill finish)	Gray-white	4	Dull gray
Aluminized steel	Gray-white	4	Light gray, less reflective
Carbon steel	Dark gray-blue	2	Red rust
Commercial bronze	Red-gold	4	Gray-green
Copper	Red-brown	4	Gray-green
Galvalume	Light gray	3	Gray
Galvanized steel	Light gray	3	Gray-white or white rust
Lead	Dark gray	1	Gray-black
Monel	Medium gray	5	Brown
Nickel silver	Gray-yellow	4	Gray-green
Stainless steel #2B	Gray or white	4	No change
Stainless steel #2D	Medium gray	3	No change
Stainless steel #3	Chrome	4	No change
Stainless steel #8	Chrome	5	No change
Terne	Gray	3	Dark gray
Tin	Gray	4	Dark gray
Titanium	Medium gray	3	No change
Zinc (natural)	Gray-blue	4	Dark blue or gray
Zinc (pre-weathered)	Dark gray-blue	2	No change

TABLE 4

RELATIVE COSTS

1 = Low / 6 = High

METAL	COST BY WEIGHT	COST OF FABRICATION	COST OF INSTALLATION
Aluminum	2	1	2
Lead	2	1	3
Copper	3	1	1
Zinc	3	1	3
Tin	4	1	2
Steel	1	1	1
Iron	1	2	1
Stainless steel	2	2	1
Titanium	5	2	2
Bronze	3	5	3
Gold leaf	6	N/A	4

Tampa Museum of Art

Tampa, Florida, USA — Stanley Saitowitz | Natoma Architects
Perforated aluminum

DESIGN INTENTION

This museum was designed to be a contemporary jewel box filled with all types of art. Its interior spaces, on the other hand, are neutral frames for display. Along its waterfront side, the building is cantilevered 40' (12.2 m) above the first floor to provide a generous urban porch. On the second floor, the building mass is bisected into public galleries and support spaces. These volumes are further subsected to form large balconies on two faces, as well as a top-lit atrium.

At night the museum's exterior becomes a metallic canvas for a light show. The museum's cladding strategy is integrated with a computer-controlled LED display, commissioned from artist Leo Villareal. Lights on the facade turn the museum into a landmark even after it is closed for the night.

MATERIALITY

A single type of perforated aluminum panel is used over both glazed and unglazed exterior walls, on soffits, and in between interior spaces. Over the majority of exterior walls, the architects decided to use a double layer of identically perforated aluminum panels, creating a moiré pattern that appears to change with movement around the large volume. At night, when the perforations can be suppressed, a computerized LED lighting system generates either a monochromatic or a polychromatic display. During the day, the museum's double-layer aluminum screens reflect sunlight and shade the glass from excessive amounts of glare and radiant heat while also allowing air to flow between the layers, releasing unwanted heat. In some locations, fresh air is brought in through operable sash windows to aid building operations during the warm seasons.

TECHNICAL

The double-layer screen is constructed of 3,798 aluminum panels, all custom-fabricated with the same perforation pattern. The 0.125"-thick (3 mm) aluminum sheets have 3" (76 mm) diameter holes arranged 4" (102 mm) on center vertically and horizontally (a straight row pattern). Using digital models, the architect created the moiré pattern by intentionally offsetting the holes in the outer layer 1.5" (38 mm) lower than those of the inner layer. The holes match across seams where panels abut or turn corners vertically or horizontally. The exacting specifications required for the cladding had implications for its underlying assemblies, which had tolerances of only 0.125" (3 mm) vertically and horizontally.

Over the opaque walls, 85,000 flattened stainless-steel rods were installed 16" (406 mm) on center horizontally and 20" (508 mm) on center vertically to hold the two layers 5" (127 mm) apart. These clips also hold the inner layer 1" (25 mm) off a black aluminum liner that covers the weather-wrapped sheathing. The clips slope to discharge water toward the exterior. Both the large holes and the large interstitial zone between the layers permit cleaning if needed. A single layer of perforated aluminum is secured over the curtain wall glass to aluminum tubes that themselves align with vertical mullions but are not secured to them, permitting service access to glass panels and curtain wall frames.

In soffit applications, a single layer of perforated aluminum is secured 1" (25 mm) below the opaque substrate, using stainless-steel clips similar to those used in the walls. An extruded aluminum liner panel with a black Kynar finish protects the sheathing and thermal insulation inside, but it also provides a dark backdrop for the LED light displays at night.

The adjoining Hillsborough River has a relatively high salt content, so all aluminum on the exterior was anodized with a clear coating to combat oxidization; this also produced a desirable satin finish. All metals on the exterior are either aluminum or stainless steel to avoid corrosion.

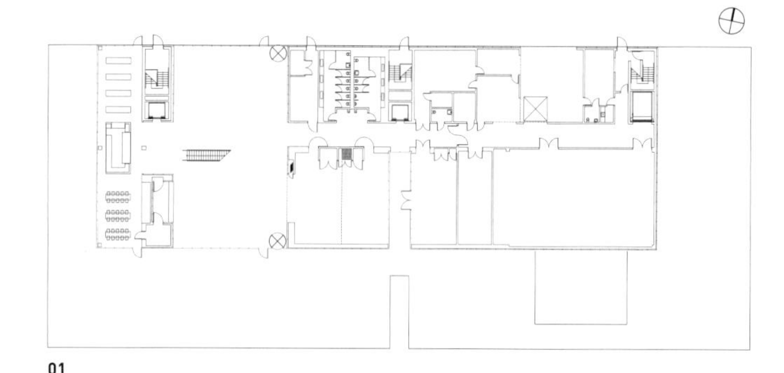

01

02

01 Ground-floor plan

02 Detail view of 3" (76 mm) diameter perforations and stainless-steel supporting rods

03 Computer-controlled LED display on metal screen

04 Double-layer screens over all building surfaces intersect

03

04

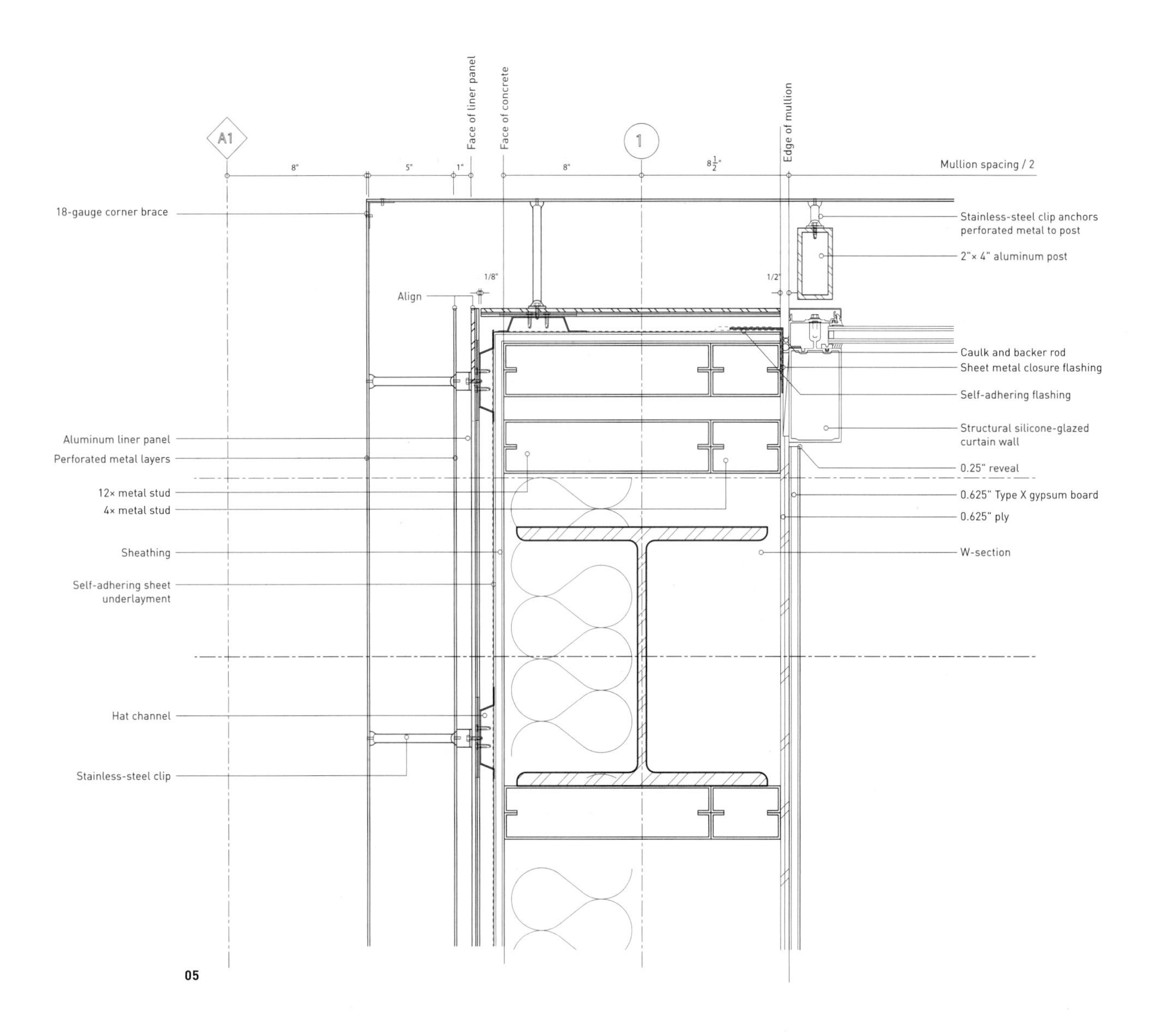

05

06

05 Plan detail of layered screens and curtain wall at corner

06 Exterior view from southeast

07 Section detail at parapet

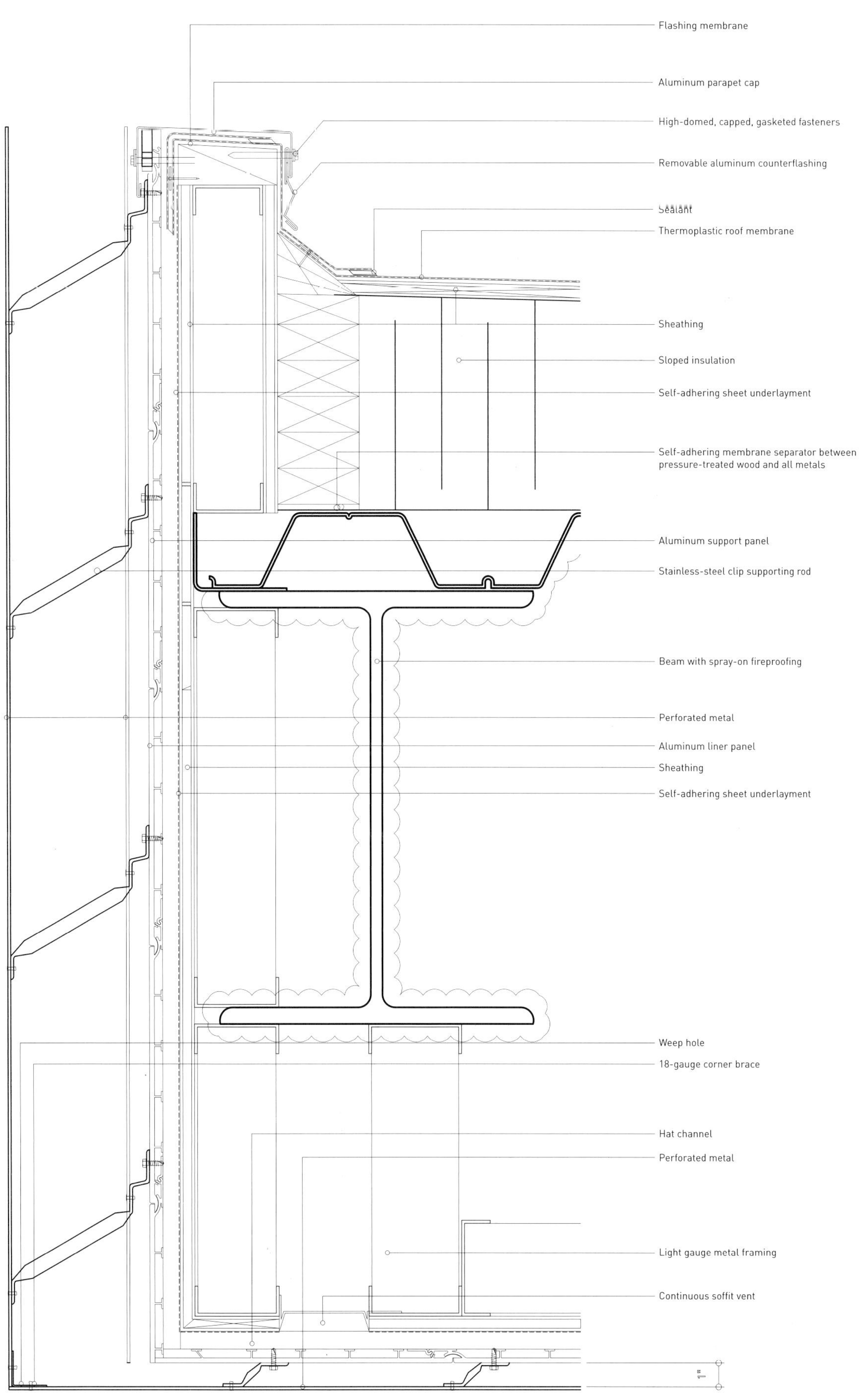

Flashing membrane
Aluminum parapet cap
High-domed, capped, gasketed fasteners
Removable aluminum counterflashing
Sealant
Thermoplastic roof membrane
Sheathing
Sloped insulation
Self-adhering sheet underlayment
Self-adhering membrane separator between pressure-treated wood and all metals
Aluminum support panel
Stainless-steel clip supporting rod
Beam with spray-on fireproofing
Perforated metal
Aluminum liner panel
Sheathing
Self-adhering sheet underlayment
Weep hole
18-gauge corner brace
Hat channel
Perforated metal
Light gauge metal framing
Continuous soffit vent
1"

07

St. Andrews Beach House

Victoria, Australia — Sean Godsell Architects
Oxidized steel

DESIGN INTENTION

Victoria's Mornington Peninsula is one of the few municipalities in Australia that permits construction directly on the foreshore of the Southern Ocean. The site is elevated and exposed to scenic ocean views and, in the winter, to gale-force winds. The three-bedroom beach house is organized in two distinct elements connected by a promenade deck. One element contains an open dining/living space, and the other contains compartmented bedrooms and a study. Only accessible from the deck, movement from room to room necessitates exposure to summer heat and winter chill. The occupants must relinquish their artificial environment (however briefly) and be reminded of their own frailty. The client requested this strategy to use the house each week as a way to decompress after five days stuck in an office.

The architect studied the history of Australian architecture and respects its unique features. Characteristics of the Australian outback homestead are redesigned and abstracted here while still respecting their functional qualities. The sunroom, the breezeway and the sleep-out are reinterpreted while intensifying spatial flow and the ambiguity between inside and outside. The external environment is filtered through a series of layers so that harsh extremes are moderated but not eliminated by the building.

The siting respects the landscape and the local environment, but attempts to rigorously follow an idealized geometric order. The plan is a 1:6 rectangle, supported by columns at the quarter points. Rooms typically are 1:1.5 rectangles in plan, and 1:2 rectangles in section.

MATERIALITY

The primary building materials are recyclable steel and glass. The house has a protective outer layer made from industrial steel floor gratings, which hinge open to form brise-soleil shutters. The shutters reduce glare and radiant heat gain on the home's glass exterior walls. The same grating material covers the roof assembly, and is used as the soffit on the underside of elevated spaces. Inside, it is used on the ceiling to veil the overhead structure and services while permitting ready access. Both the finished flooring and exterior decking are made of recycled wood decking and supported by conventional lumber, a renewable resource.

The structural frame is highly rationalized, to the point that only essential elements are present. The building is raised on columns with parking and storage underneath. Like the gratings over the glassy walls of this house, the building's elevated position creates a more useful condition below, simply by filtering some portion of environmental exposure.

TECHNICAL

In this particular climate, where annual rainfall averages only 25" per year (650 mm), unfinished mild steel can be exposed without being consumed by atmospheric corrosion. Oxidation occurs, but not at such a rate that requires special weathering steel.

The industrial grating has a rectangular grid composed of 0.12" (3 mm) vertical steel fins at intervals of 1.2" (30 mm), with horizontal steel cross rods at 4" (100 mm) intervals. The vertically oriented fins are as wide as their on-center spacing, meaning that views are permitted approximately from 45 degrees up to 90 degrees to the exterior walls. At angles closer to the wall, the grating is opaque. The gratings are used in their uncut widths of 35.3" (900 mm). This module agrees with those of the primary structural grid and glass curtain wall system, and was used to proportion the rooms of the house.

Deep steel trusses cantilever approximately 36' (11 m) to the east and west, from a simple span of 72' (22 m). The trusses are made of 15" × 4" (380 × 100 mm) channels for the top and bottom chords and 4" × 4" (100 × 100 mm) diagonal struts. The channels are secured to the faces of 15.75" × 15.75" × 0.4" (400 × 400 × 10 mm) steel columns.

The hinged steel gratings on the sunny north side are supported by a continuous 2" × 2" × 0.2" (50 x 50 x 10 mm) steel angle at the top, and a continuous folded 0.4" (10 mm) steel plate bracket at the bottom, which also acts to direct precipitation passing through the grating to the exterior.

01 Transverse section

02 Exterior view from southwest

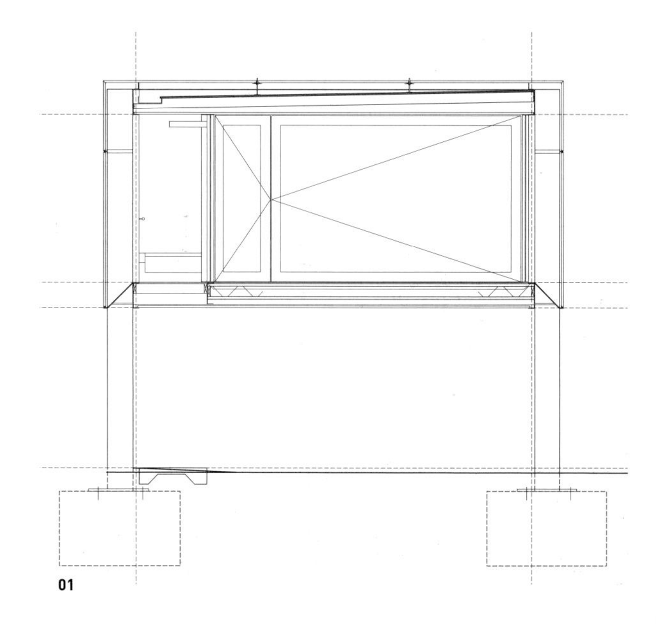

01

02

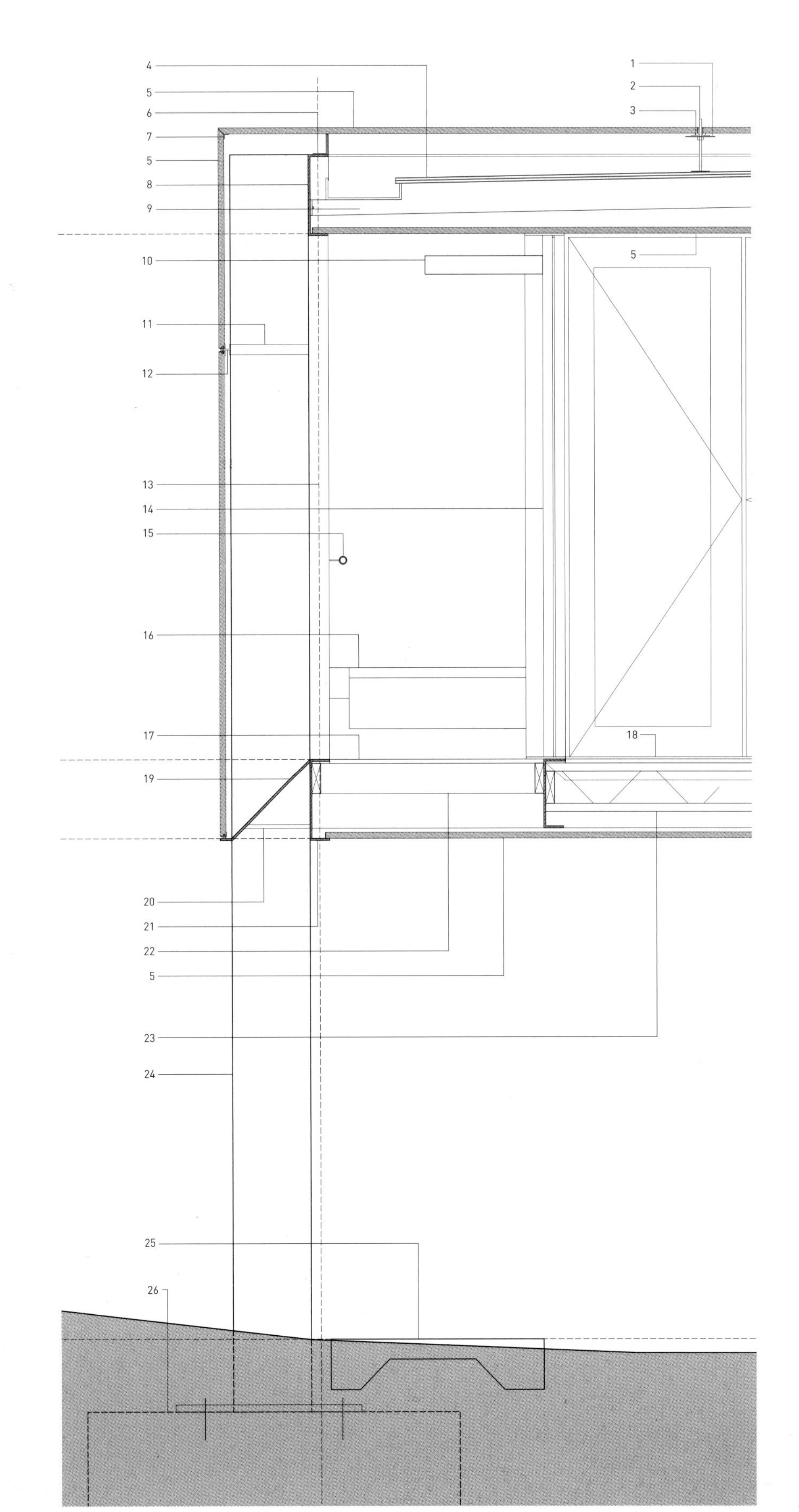

1. 150 mm diameter × 6 mm oxidized mild-steel disc
2. 12 mm diameter threaded galvanized rod
3. 40 × 40 × 5 mm mild-steel angle
4. Double-layer corrugated fiberglass
5. 30 × 3 mm Webforge oxidized mild-steel industrial floor grating
6. 100 × 75 mm oxidized mild-steel angle
7. 25 × 25 x 3 mm oxidized mild-steel angle
8. 390 × 100 mm oxidized mild-steel PFC
9. 150 × 100 mm RHS rafters at maximum 600 centers
10. Folded 1.6 mm mild-steel light fitting
11. 50 × 50 × 1.6 mm oxidized mild-steel RHS
12. 50 × 50 × 5 mm continuous oxidized mild-steel bracket
13. 100 × 100 mm oxidized mild-steel truss
14. 110 × 10 mm oxidized mild-steel window frame
15. 32 mm diameter CHS oxidized mild-steel handrail
16. Seat-folded 2 mm mild-steel plate around 150 × 100 × 4 mm mild-steel RHS
17. 19 mm recycled timber decking
18. 19 mm recycled timber flooring
19. Folded 10 mm mild-steel support bracket
20. 18 mm diameter mild-steel rods at 1,800 centers
21. 390 × 100 mm oxidized mild-steel PFC
22. 150 × 50 mm floor joists
23. 200 mm Posi-Strut trussed floor beam
24. 400 × 400 × 10 mm oxidized mild-steel column
25. 75 mm reinforced concrete path
26. 1,500 × 1,500 × 1,200 mm reinforced concrete pad footing

04

05

03 South wall section

04 View of north passageway

05 Elevation showing assembly of frame and skin

Prefabricated Nature

Cedeira, Spain — MYCC Architects
Perforated COR-TEN steel

DESIGN INTENTION

This vacation home was fabricated in three months, and assembled on the site in three days. The house was erected on a steeply sloped landscape within a eucalyptus forest in a remote location in the northeast corner of the Iberian Peninsula. The surrounding terrain of row crops, pastures, and pitched-roof houses defines the form of the house. Interior spaces are free-flowing and open to the surrounding landscape. Six prefabricated modules were transported to the site on trailers, conforming to dimensional constraints of 9.8' (3 m) wide and 19.7' (6 m) long.

Three of the prefabricated modules were combined into the open living space, while the other three contain bedrooms, a bath and stair, and a kitchen, respectively. A generous attic space situated above the modules opens up to sea views toward the southwest and the forest to the northeast. This space flows into the living volume on the main level, and can be used as extra sleeping space, a children's play area, or an exercise room.

MATERIALITY

The two gabled facades are clad with perforated COR-TEN weathering steel panels. The panels were CNC-machined to represent the silhouettes of surrounding indigenous eucalyptus trees. The weathering steel resembles the hardworking steel hulls of fishing boats in coastal towns such as Cedeira. The steel's oxidation results in a varied patina, without paint or sealants. The interplay of natural and manufactured qualities translates to the interior spaces, where sunlight is filtered through the perforated metal screen, mapping the decorative tree's branches onto interior surfaces. The weathering steel screens also act as shutters, providing protection from storms and intruders.

The roof and side facades are clad with Viroc, a prefabricated panel composed of eucalyptus wood shavings in a cement-based matrix. The cement-bonded wood fiber panels have excellent strength, are light and easy to manipulate, and require little maintenance. The panels are secured to vertical furring strips as a ventilated rainscreen.

The two cladding materials are contextual to the house's landscape and, despite its bright appearance on the slope, its presence is materially appropriate for and integrative to the site. The forest where the house sits is both a literal reference for construction and a graphic representation that is ever present within the house.

TECHNICAL

The project is a hybrid of prefabricated modules for the ground-floor elements, two-dimensional design elements for the upper walls, and conventional construction methods for the assemblies surrounding the modules. The modules were fabricated in the facilities of a construction company near Madrid in the town of Valdemoro. The modules and roof trusses were assembled to verify fit, then were taken apart, packed, and transported the 435 miles (700 km) for the final installation. They were assembled in only three days, with minimal on-site waste or disruption. Quality control for the technical subsystems was best achieved at the factory, and skillful resolution of module connections was achieved in the field.

Beams and galvanized steel columns are the primary frame, with composite steel decking and concrete slabs for floor decks. Concrete was cast in the composite decks at the factory. Perforated COR-TEN screens are secured with stainless-steel screws to vertical steel furring strips. Inside, several plies of waterproofing are laid over interlocking sandwich panels, which are formed using two sheets of aluminum with 3.15" (80 mm) thick polyurethane cores. Interior gypsum finishes are supported by an independent steel stud frame, which contains additional rock wool insulation. The facade walls total 2.2' (660 mm) in thickness, and include a ventilated rainscreen and a total of 4.7" (120 mm) of insulation.

Weathered steel screens on the lower level are 1.9' wide and 8.2' tall (0.59 m wide and 2.5 m tall); on the upper level the panels are the same width, but heights vary due to the pitched roof. Perforated panels in most locations are fixed in place, but they are operable, bi-folding steel-framed shutters over windows and doors. As the COR-TEN steel oxidizes, it produces a water-soluble residue that falls to the ground.

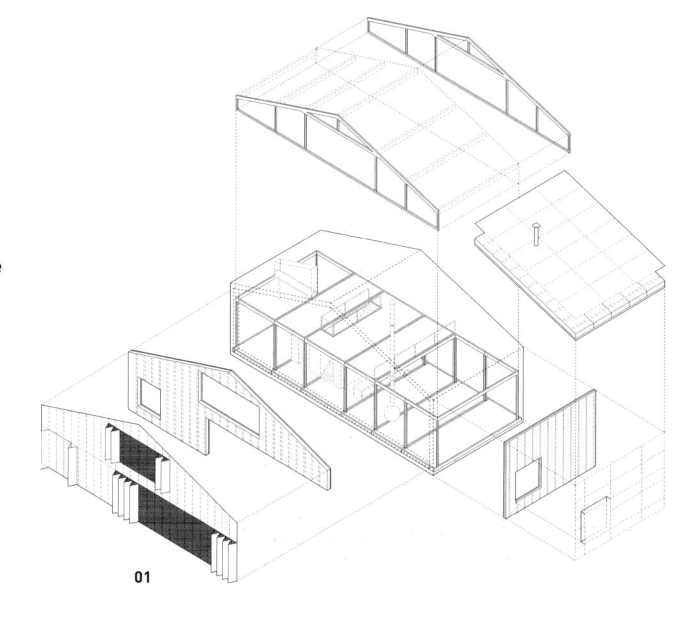

01

01 Exploded axonometric of construction assemblies

02 Exterior wall section

03 Perforated metal shutters opened

04 Perforated metal shutters closed

05 Graphic perforations in operable COR-TEN shutters over glazed doors

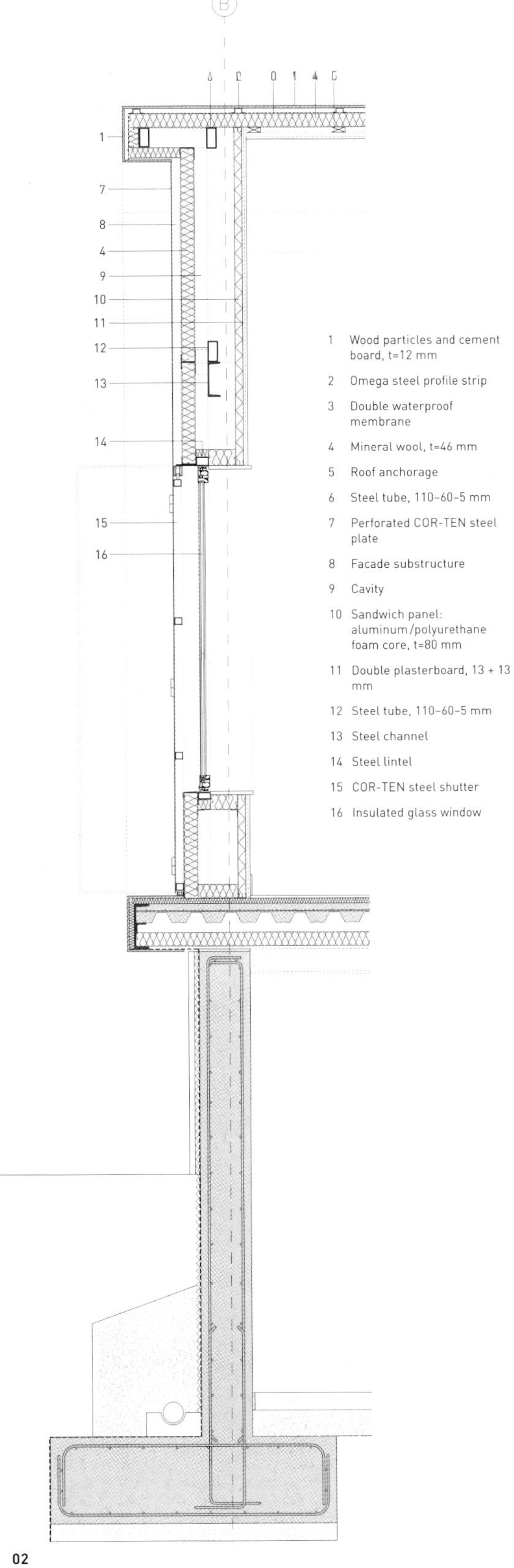

02

1 Wood particles and cement board, t=12 mm
2 Omega steel profile strip
3 Double waterproof membrane
4 Mineral wool, t=46 mm
5 Roof anchorage
6 Steel tube, 110-60-5 mm
7 Perforated COR-TEN steel plate
8 Facade substructure
9 Cavity
10 Sandwich panel: aluminum/polyurethane foam core, t=80 mm
11 Double plasterboard, 13 + 13 mm
12 Steel tube, 110-60-5 mm
13 Steel channel
14 Steel lintel
15 COR-TEN steel shutter
16 Insulated glass window

03

04

05

OMS Stage

Winnipeg, Manitoba, Canada — 5468796 Architecture
Extruded aluminum, flexible connections

DESIGN INTENTION

Through an open competition, the City of Winnipeg called for submissions to design a bandshell for Old Market Square in the historic Exchange District. The winning submission by 5468796 Architecture yielded a structure and community space that was occupied and used all year round and that added a flexible gathering space in addition to the functioning stage. OMS Stage is an adaptable public structure that serves as a stage, pavilion, projection screen, and city beacon. Its presence can be both a visually striking mark in the neighborhood park and a busy hub for citywide festivals.

The four outer faces of the stage are membranes composed of diamond-shaped extrusions strung together to form a flexible curtain that draws back to reveal a stage within. During performances, the skin becomes an undulating ceiling landscape, serving as a visual backdrop for performers and allowing for adjustments to the stage's acoustics. When closed, the angled diamond pieces capture and refract light or images, creating a pixelated display. Programmable lighting shines onto the skin, making it into an interactive canvas. In its closed position, the stage hosts small gatherings and exhibitions inside. The roofscape can transform into a small open-air performance space.

The enclosing screens needed to be configurable, but also strong enough to secure the stage when not in use, so the challenge was to create a unique meshwork that would be both flexible and strong.

MATERIALITY

While the foundation is cast-in-place concrete, the primary structure is a flexible, faceted aluminum skin. The project demonstrates that aluminum is lightweight yet strong, as well as weather resistant. The diamond-shaped aluminum extrusions allow the skin to move and reflect colored light and projected images.

The architect explored many prototypes, varying the depth of the cells, and assessing their ability to flip the projected image and maintain image resolution and integrity. Early prototypes were developed that examined chain-mail armor as a precedent. Once a suitable prototype was selected, the fabricator cut the aluminum extrusions using a self-feeding saw and employed a polishing drum to grind down and finish the edges of the 20,000 individual metal pieces. The process used to develop the screen demonstrates the efficacy of designers working directly with local producers and manufacturers to source customized products. Approximately 30 percent of the total project cost was directed toward the research, manufacturing, and installation of the screens.

TECHNICAL

OMS Stage is essentially a 28' (8.53 m) cube, the facade screen of which is animated by changing daylight and artificial lighting. The surfaces of the cube appear opaque from some angles and transparent from others. Though functionally complex in its final form, the screen is made of simple repetitive elements, joined in a simple repetitive manner; rigid elements are joined using non-rigid connections.

Its aluminum pieces are cut at 45-degree angles from 4" × 4" × 0.19"-thick (102 × 102 × 4.8 mm) aluminum extrusions that are diamond-shaped in section. Unlike normal square-profile extrusions, these profiles have faces that intersect at corners at 30 and 60 degrees. The individual extrusions are linked together by threading aircraft cable through pre-cut holes in each cell. The orientation of each piece then alternates up and down vertically along the line of the cable, with adjacent rows of cells riveted together at every third piece. The faceted membrane gently cascades into a catenary shape while maintaining continuous surface integrity. Pre-strung panels of screen were erected on site before they were riveted together, forming a continuous assembly.

On two of the cube's faces the screens are anchored at the top and bottom, and are not retractable. On the other two faces, the aluminum curtain is drawn by three aircraft cables, each powered by an electric winch. These cables can be disconnected from the curtain when the interior of the space is in use. When the stage is not in use, a locking rail located at the edge of the concrete floor slab can secure the aluminum operable curtains.

On the structure's less public faces, pulling the skin outward and propping it open with a metal arm makes a passage through the screen.

01 West elevation without screen and with screen

02 View from southwest with the flexible aluminum curtain open

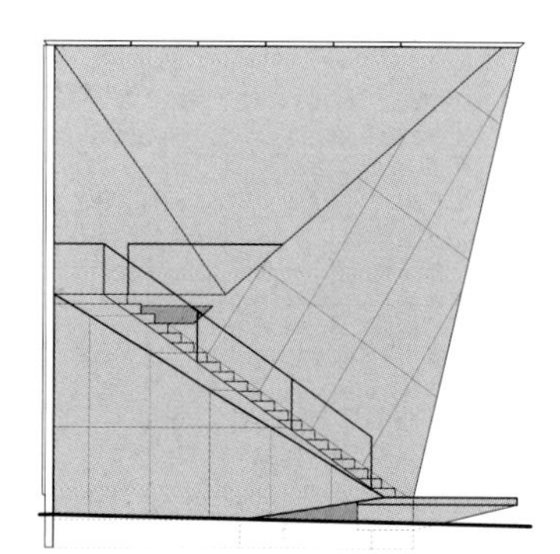

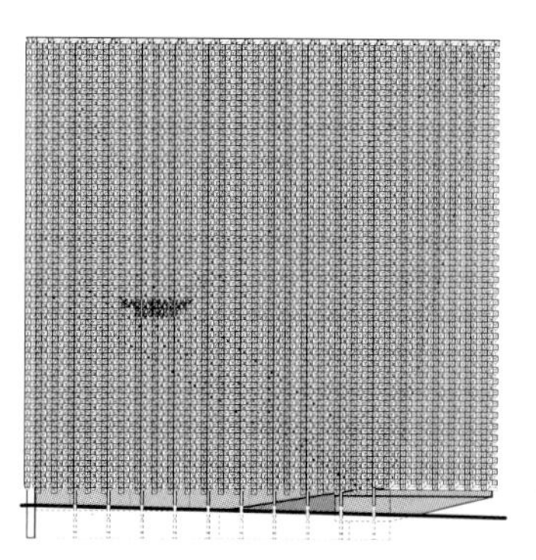

01

02

03 Section and details of aluminum screen connections

04 Luminous cube in Old Market Square

05 Patterns created by the aluminum screen

06 Altering cube appearance with colored lighting

07 Diamond-shaped aluminum extrusions yield the various elements used to make the flexible curtain.

08 Winches retract flexible aluminum curtain to desired shape

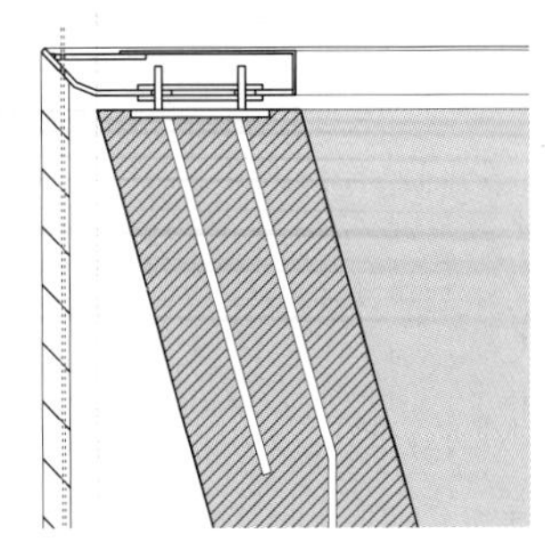

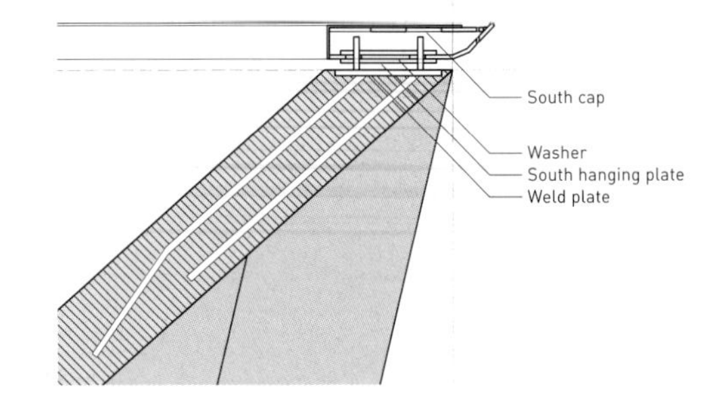

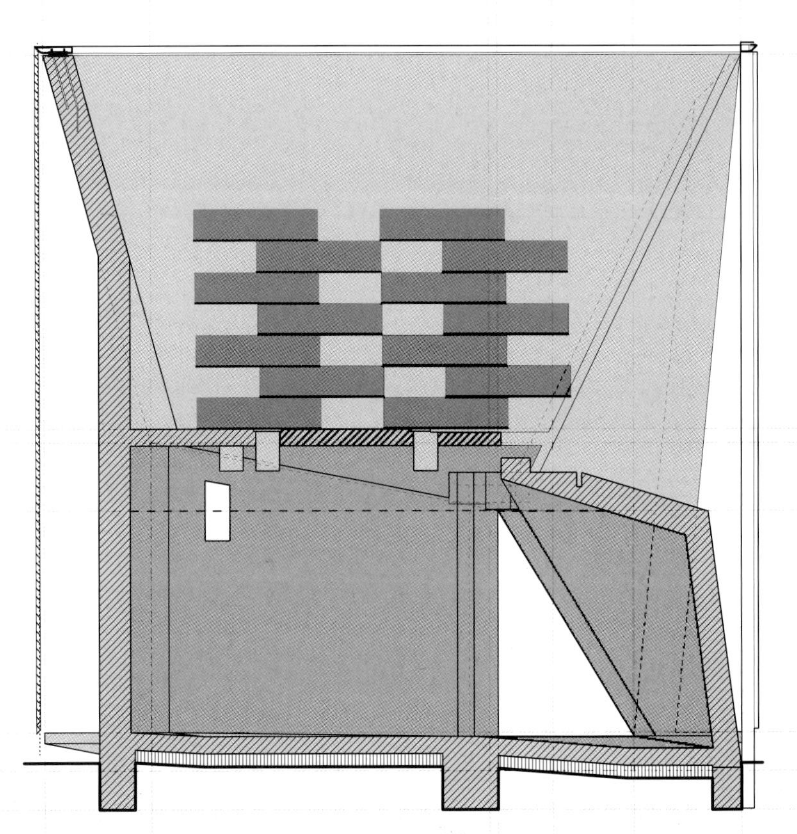

03

04

05

06

07

08

Lady Bird Lake Hiking Trail Restrooms

Austin, Texas, USA — Miró Rivera Architects
COR-TEN steel

DESIGN INTENTION

This restroom structure is the first building in thirty years to be added to the Lady Bird Lake Hike and Bike Trail, a scenic path that runs along ten miles of the Colorado River and provides an escape from nearby Austin. The architects were charged to create a dynamic sculpture that complemented the active trail and the beauty of the surrounding landscape. The design achieves this by creating a unique sculptural landmark from the banal nature of public restrooms. It required several considerations, in particular that the new restrooms require minimal maintenance, and be universally accessible.

MATERIALITY

A single material, COR-TEN weathering steel, was used for the structure as well as the cladding, roof, and one door. Because of COR-TEN's natural weathering process, it will not lose its structural integrity over time or require any coating. For the design's sculptural element, freestanding upright plates of COR-TEN were staggered to form the edge of the entry path and coil around to create the restroom enclosure. Steel plates of varying heights and widths are used to give a naturalistic, varied appearance. Where privacy is required, the plates are arranged to block any views, still allowing light and air to pass between them.

Plumbing fixtures, the structure's only services, were chosen for their durability. The polished stainless-steel toilet and sink create a stunning contrast with the rough steel cladding. The exterior drinking fountain and rinse shower are encased with galvanized steel.

Integration with the context was accomplished through the building's organic form and the natural mineral tones of the materials. Over time the steel will form a speckled pattern as it oxidizes to a reddish-brown hue. Concrete flooring inside and an orange-hued crushed granite exterior will take on the steel's rust-staining runoff that will inevitably flow into the space and over surfaces. The designers selected and utilized the materials' inherent qualities to be harnessed and exploited into the overall design, resulting in a unique and compelling project.

TECHNICAL

The restroom facility takes advantage of the many qualities of alloy steel that allow it to be used in its raw, planar state. Weathering steel—ASTM606-Type 4, in this case—is mild steel with at least 0.2 percent copper, and up to 0.55 percent total alloy metals including copper, chromium, and nickel. This combination makes it stronger than mild structural steel and corrosion resistant because of the dense, semi-protective layer of rust that forms when it is exposed to the elements. And while Type 4 weathering steel can be left bare, the project has very few visible welded COR-TEN connections because the welded joints can often weather unevenly compared to the panel faces.

Because of their high strength, the forty-nine plates were placed as freestanding elements, with support only at their footing. The plates are 0.75" (19 mm) thick and range in widths of 1–2' (305–610 mm) and heights of 2–13' (610–3,960 mm). The roof of the enclosure is formed by a single plate; it is held in place by five brackets welded to the vertical plates, all of the same material and thickness as the plates they join.

The foundation consists of a continuous shallow concrete footing. Steel angles were welded to the bottom of each plate, coated with a cold galvanizing compound, and bolted into the concrete with steel embed anchor bolts. Although the depth of the foundation is less than 2' (610 mm), it supports vertical cantilevers of up to 13' (3,960 mm) high. The footings' continuous winding shape below the discontinuous steel plates is exceptionally stable.

The restroom's stout door was also fabricated from 0.75" (19 mm) thick steel plates, and weighs approximately 650 lbs. (295 kg). A CNC mill was used to carve a commemorative inscription in a COR-TEN panel alongside the path, with no need for superficial finishes to make it long lasting.

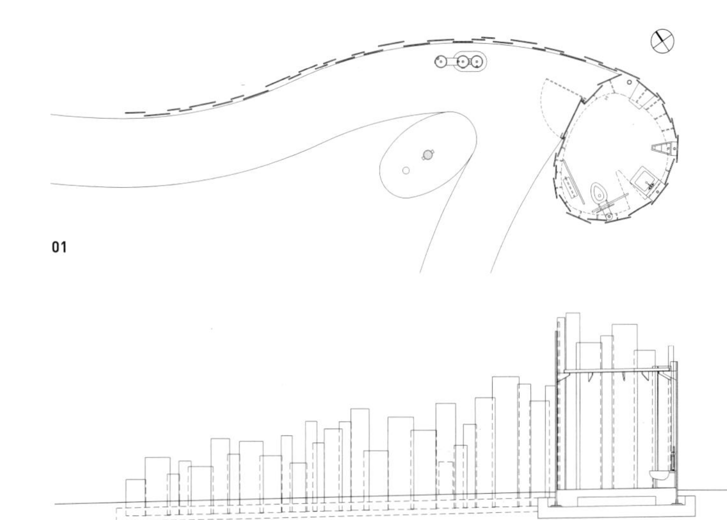

01 Plan

02 Section through restroom with elevation beyond to COR-TEN steel plates

03 COR-TEN steel plates frame path toward restroom from hiking trail

04 Weathering steel wall plates

03

04

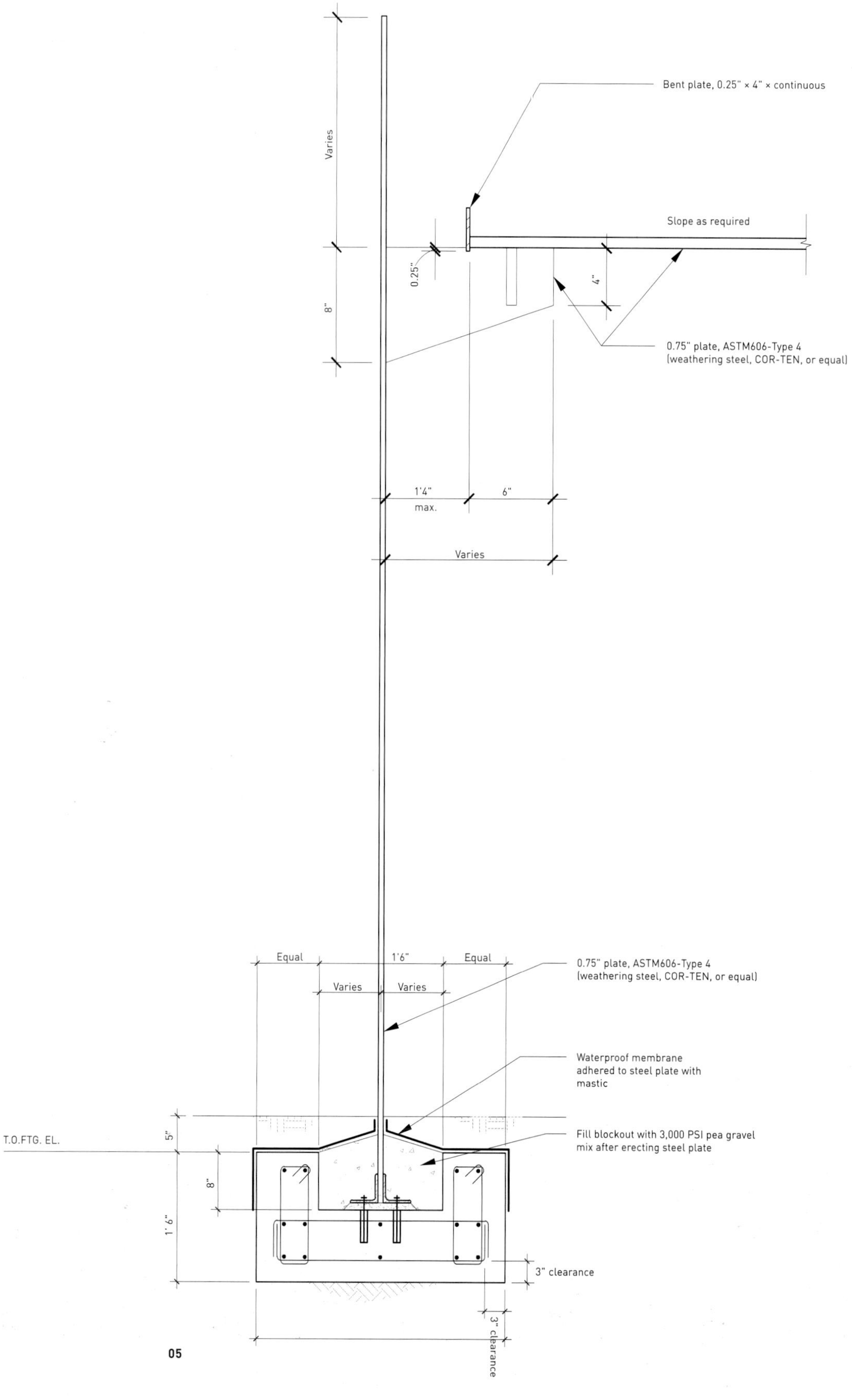

Bent plate, 0.25" × 4" × continuous

Varies

Slope as required

0.25"

4"

8"

0.75" plate, ASTM606-Type 4
(weathering steel, COR-TEN, or equal)

1'4"
max.

6"

Varies

Equal

1'6"

Equal

Varies

Varies

0.75" plate, ASTM606-Type 4
(weathering steel, COR-TEN, or equal)

Waterproof membrane
adhered to steel plate with
mastic

T.O.FTG. EL.

5"

Fill blockout with 3,000 PSI pea gravel
mix after erecting steel plate

8"

1' 6"

3" clearance

3" clearance

05

05 Section details where vertical steel plates connect to foundation and COR TEN roof of restroom

06 Restroom interior

07 Weathering steel plates along the path toward rinse shower, drinking fountain, and restroom

06

07

Kunst-Depot, Henze & Ketterer Art Gallery

Wichtrach, Switzerland — Gigon / Guyer Architekten
Perforated steel

DESIGN INTENTION

The Kunst-Depot is an artwork storage unit that doubles as a showroom for work that is not currently on display in the nearby gallery. It also functions as a gallery in its own right. Two floors above the ground level allow all three types of use.

The floor plan is simple and open. A staircase, the adjoining sanitary block and kitchen, and a central, load-bearing service wall define the open galleries. There are two windows on the ground floor and two on the top, which allow daylight viewing of the works of art and provide views out to the surrounding landscape. To minimize the risk of water damage to the artworks, only forced air is used for heating and humidity control. Wall and roof assemblies are massive and tightly sealed to assure a stable interior climate.

The design optimizes the space inside and outside the building within the limits of its bell-shaped plot of land. The building's shape responds to the local building code, which requires a pitched roof and eaves on all new buildings located in the historic center of the village. The design is not only a sensitive response to the surrounding farmhouses, but also an appropriately modern artistic composition.

MATERIALITY

The building's roof and facades are clad in corrugated steel sheeting, a material more commonly used for warehouses, but its distinctive look is a result of dividing the cladding into two perforated layers. The outer shell is like a curtain wall and functions as a sunscreen. The smooth metal roofing sheets are rectangular, but folded over the edge of the roof at an angle such that they echo the irregular, trapezoidal plan of the building. The architects used the irregular steel sheets as a design tool with which to reinterpret the vernacular forms of contextual farmhouses and make them fit appropriately within the gallery's program.

TECHNICAL

The heavy concrete and masonry structural system is wrapped by 7" (180 mm) of mineral wool insulation covered with a colored fiberglass air and water barrier, under the perforated steel cladding. This creates a ventilated enclosure system to maintain the art collection inside the Depot in a controlled microclimate.

The perforated metal panel on the wall is profiled to a 2.3" (59 mm) deep trapezoidal shape that repeats at 8.9" (225 mm) on center. The profiled shape stiffens the sheet metal, making it possible to maintain strength and stability with less sheet metal thickness. To increase sun shading and further protect the walls from weather, a second layer of perforated steel screens surround the building, supported on aluminum struts that extend from the walls and roof. The perforations in both metal panels are 0.2" (5 mm) in diameter, arranged in a staggered pattern with a pitch of 0.3" (8 mm) on center. The perforations uniformly cover the surface but because of the profile, a vertically striped pattern results. The screens here are similar to those on the wall, but use a deeper trapezoidal profile (6" [153 mm] deep, repeating at 11" [280 mm] on center) that adds strength and minimizes the number of framing elements necessary to support it. The space between the outer screen and the building wall is typically 32.3" (820 mm), but increases near the entry.

The Depot's unperforated profiled metal roofing hovers 1.6" (40 mm) above the insulated concrete roof assembly. Near the edges of the roof, the profiled metal panels are covered with flat sheets of the same type of metal, like giant pieces of flashing. These sheets are impermeable covers for especially challenging details and appear wherever a pitched roof is used on a trapezoidal plan configuration. The flat sheets overlap the seams between roof and wall by a margin sufficient to prevent water intrusion, but that still allows ventilation to occur.

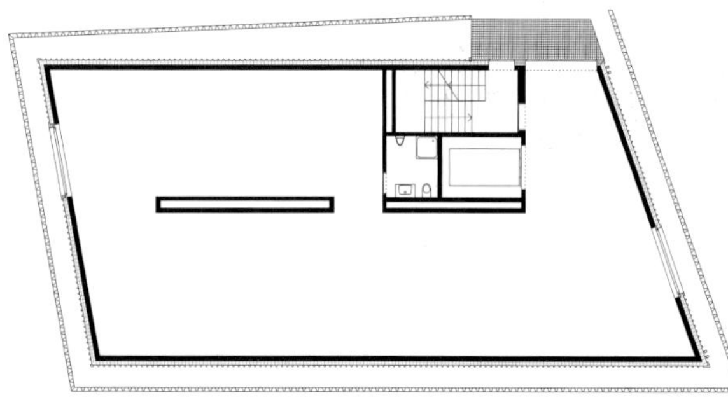

01

01 Ground-floor plan

02 Exterior view from northeast; unperforated metal roof flashing drapes over the perforated screens

03 Space between the rainscreen (left) and sunscreen (right)

04 Section and elevation of light metal sunscreen and rainscreen, which are installed over the insulated structure

02

03

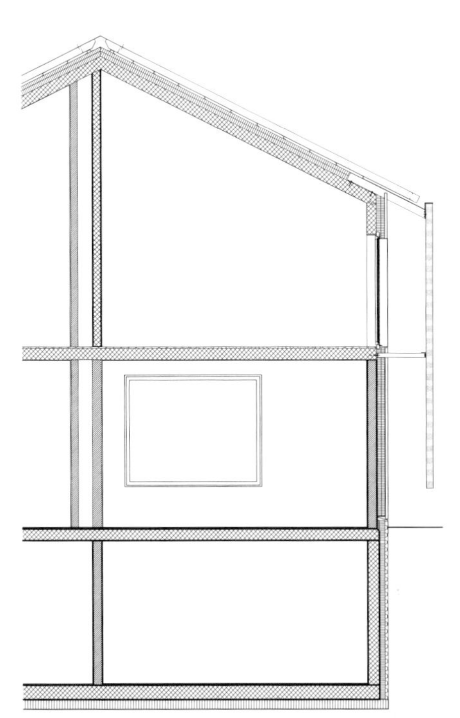

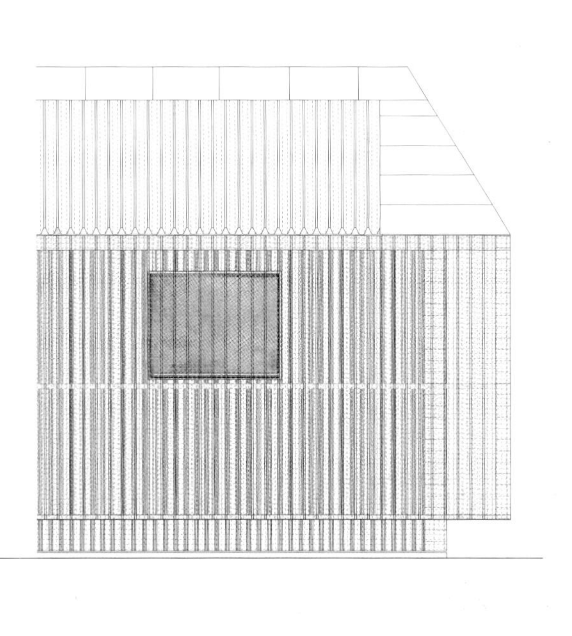

04

05

06

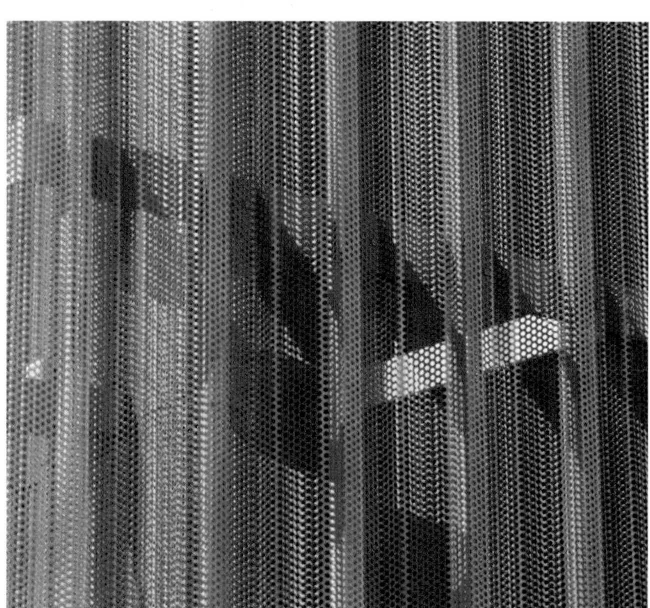

07

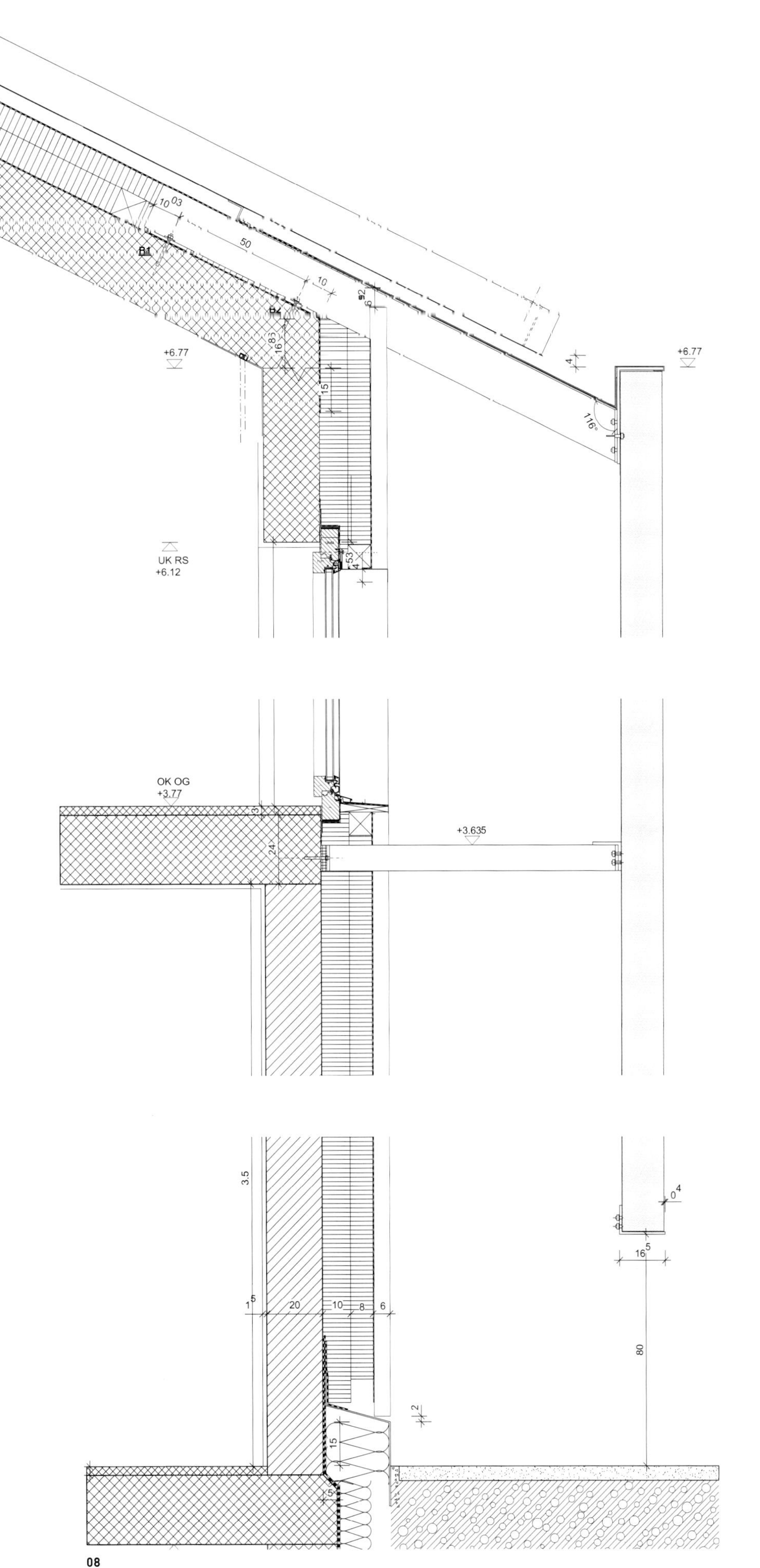

05 Exterior view from southeast toward entry

06 View through profiled perforated steel sunscreen

07 Perforated steel sunscreen, rainscreen, and wall

08 Section detail of exterior wall and roof assemblies

Herstedlund Fælleshus Community Centre

Albertslund, Denmark — Dorte Mandrup Arkitekter
Anodized aluminum, composite panels

DESIGN INTENTION

The Herstedlund Fælleshus Community Centre supports activities for a residential area of approximately six hundred families. The project program and spaces had to adapt to varied uses, be able to accommodate visitors of different ages and interests, and perform multiple independent functions simultaneously. The building provides space for a wide range of functions such as meetings, teaching, dancing, sports, theater, aerobics, barbecues, bridge tournaments, community meals, and weddings.

The building was conceived as a metaphorical tree house within its parkland setting. To maximize the possibility of mixed concurrent use, the building can be entered either through the ground floor or by direct access to the first elevated floor via an outdoor staircase. Common park areas also surround the Community Centre. A skateboard ramp merges with the wall on one elevation and a rock-climbing wall on another. An indoor kitchen is connected directly to an outdoor eating space, giving more programmatic function to the surrounding landscape. Direct access from outside to the washrooms is also provided. A rooftop terrace offers 1,560 sq. ft. (145 sq. m.) under the sun. It has a small semi-enclosed court for outdoor events and athletics.

MATERIALITY

The community center is constructed of concrete columns and a deck of filigree (bubble-deck) slabs. The external cladding uses both solid and perforated anodized aluminum panels. A stair and an elevator shaft stabilize the overall building frame. Its glass panels are made of insulated glass with aluminum-clad wood frames. Aluminum panels give this building a strong identity in the community; they also support the many programmatic functions the building must sustain.

TECHNICAL

In most locations, the aluminum panels are 0.07" (1.8 mm) thick rainscreens, supported by stainless-steel hat channels over a composite panel substrate. The hat channels assure alignment between adjoining panels, which have a 0.4" (10 mm) reveal at each edge. Stainless-steel dome head screws secure the panels to the channels, and the channels to the substrate.

The composite panels below the facings are 9.6" (243 mm) thick interlocking Paroc waterproof panels—two layers of aluminum glued to a core of rigid mineral wool. These panels are both fireproof and high in thermal resistance, with almost no heat train between the two faces. The interior of these composite panels is covered with an additional 3.75" (95 mm) of mineral wool insulation, and two layers of 0.5" (13 mm) gypsum board.

A portion of the building's west facade is a climbing wall where 0.07" (1.8 mm) aluminum facings are adhered to 0.6" (15 mm) waterproof plywood, and then secured to the composite panel substrate. A grid of embeds consisting of T-nuts in the back of the plywood receive the climbing grips and other accessories in many possible course configurations.

Windows with sunny exposures are sometimes covered with perforated panels to moderate glare and radiant energy. In addition to these environmental functions, the perforated metal also softens the transition from the open to the closed parts of the skin. Panels over windows are hinged on a vertical edge to easily swing open for cleaning. The frames for both the windows and doors are made of anodized aluminum, matching the finish of cladding panels.

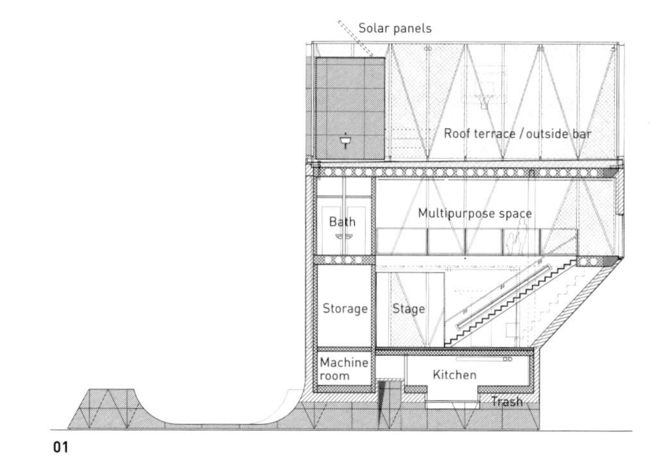

01

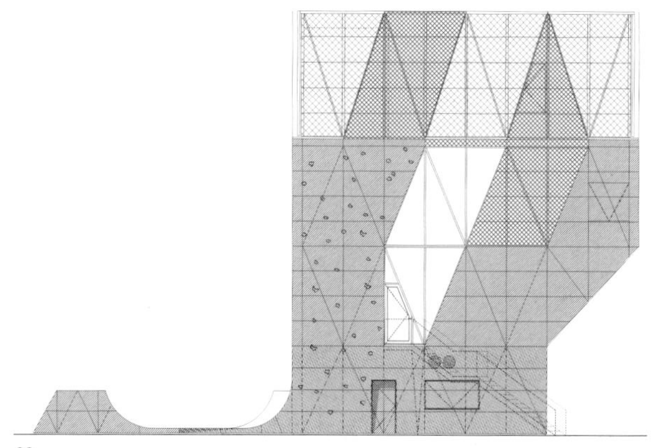

02

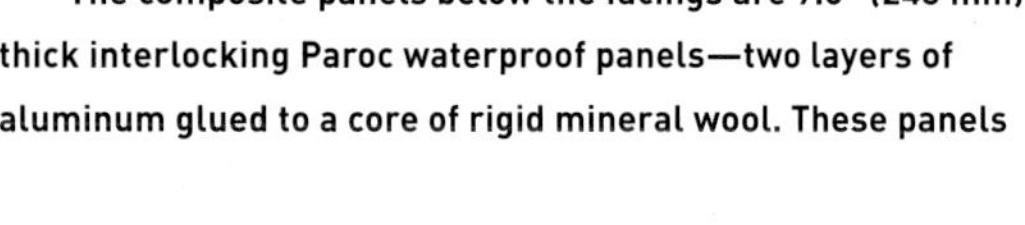

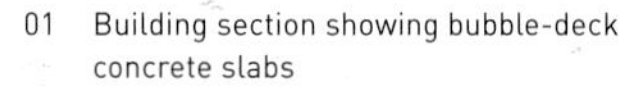

01 Building section showing bubble-deck concrete slabs

02 West elevation with climbing wall on left

03 Exterior view from southwest showing pattern of aluminum rainscreen panels and mesh around rooftop activity court

03

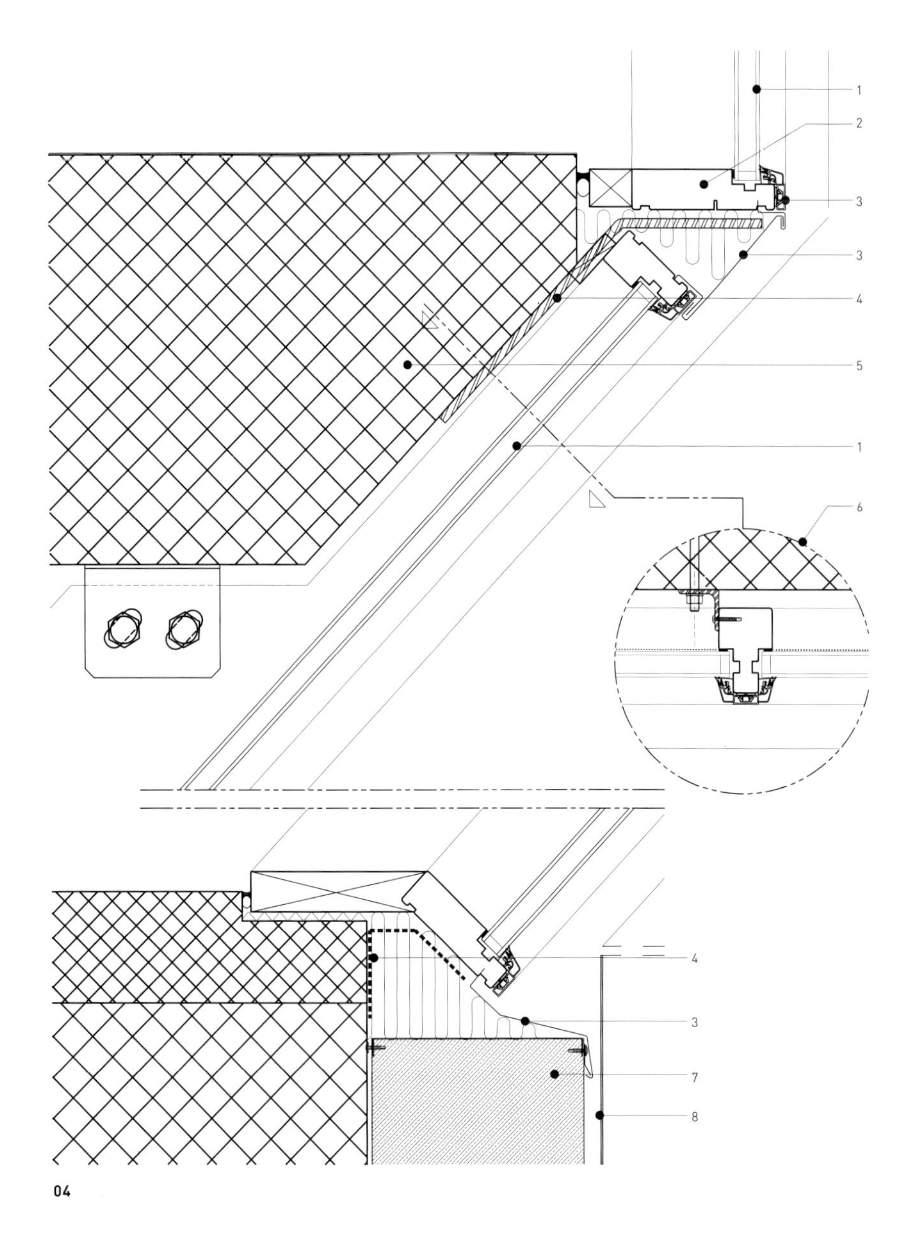

1 Glass facade
2 Wooden mullion
3 Anodized aluminum covering
4 Steel support
5 Concrete
6 Cross section of vertical mullion and steel support
7 Prefabricated insulation element
8 Anodized aluminum facade cladding

04

04 Section detail of anodized aluminum cladding assembly and openings in exterior wall

05 View from west

06 Rooftop activity court

07 Section detail of anodized aluminum cladding assembly at roof deck

08 Anodized aluminum rainscreen secured with stainless-steel screws

09 Anodized aluminum rainscreen installed with 0.39" (10 mm) reveals between panels

05

06

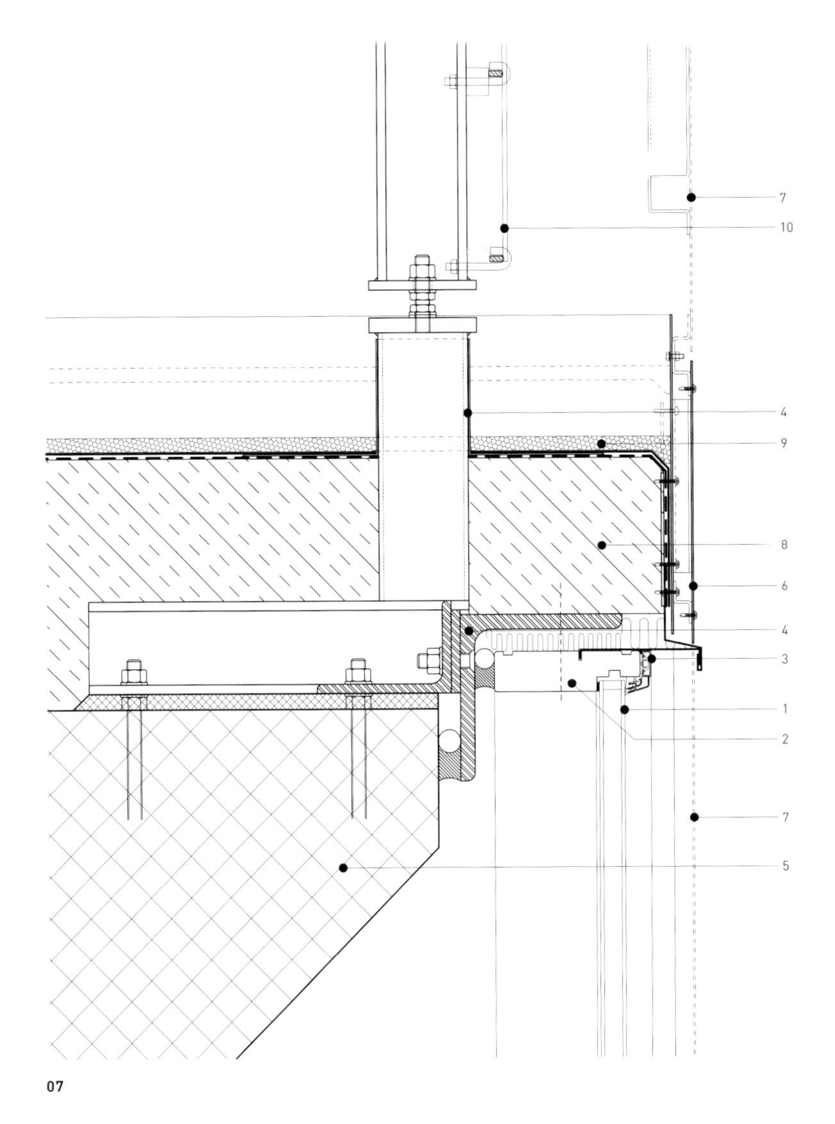

1 Glass facade
2 Wooden mullion
3 Anodized aluminum covering
4 Steel support
5 Concrete
6 Anodized aluminum facade cladding
7 Perforated anodized aluminum facade cladding
8 Roof insulation, foam glass, and asphalt roofing
9 Rubber granulate
10 Steel fence

07

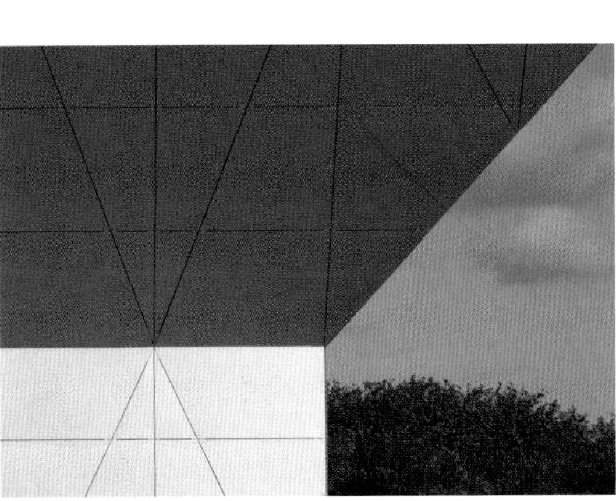

08

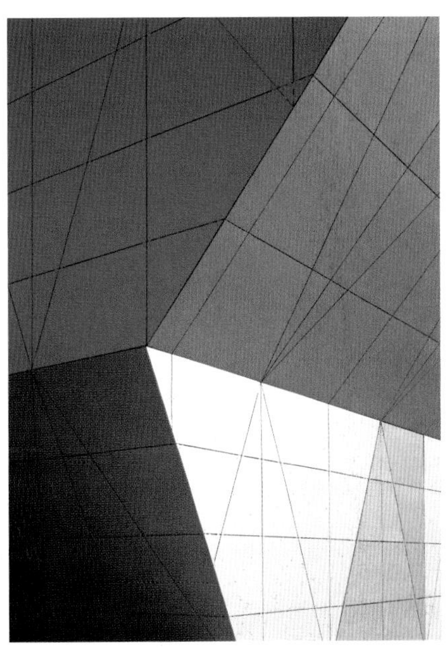

09

Halftecture O

Chūō-ku, Osaka, Japan — Shuhei Endo
COR-TEN steel

DESIGN INTENTION

Osaka's Castle Park has always been a historical gathering place for the people of Osaka. The ancient fort is also one of the few outdoor spaces left in the city center with an abundance of trees. This project is one of a series of three public restrooms planned at the important landmark for use by local residents and tourists.

The architect describes this project as "halftecture" because it is not fully enclosed; rather, it is simultaneously open (for convenience) and closed (for privacy). Entrances are not defined; they appear in the spaces between fixed objects. Closed compartments are grounded but do not touch the roof plane, permitting fresh air to freely pass above them. The sculptural qualities of the design disguise the building's banal purpose while projecting an artful presence in the park. Changing stations and toilet booths, for example, were set into the open space below a curved roof plane. One is never completely inside Halftecture O.

MATERIALITY

The primary structure, roof, and walls of this building are constructed of weathering steel plates, the rusted surface of which blends into the surrounding environment. The steel alloy will oxidize, becoming a passive barrier against further corrosion. Welded connections between the steel plates exploit the material's unique potential to form connections using the very material being connected. The result is a monolithic structural system, with very few fasteners. To add a level of contrasting refinement to the composition, the booths beneath the oxidized steel roof contain glistening porcelain, stone, and metal finishes.

TECHNICAL

The project's defining characteristic is the roof, which is made of 0.6" (16 mm) thick steel plates welded into a single plane using continuous welds. The roof plane is suspended from walls made of 1" (25 mm) thick steel plates, set 65.6' (20 m) apart. The steel roof spans 125 times its thickness.

The catenary curve form of the roof is an instructive illustration of the self-weight of the steel plate, which, because of its shallow cross-section, has a low moment of inertia. In contrast, the steel plates that support the roof are stable triangulated frames with no visible response to gravity.

The supports have upper edges that slope in opposite directions, causing the roof plane to take a warped curve shape.

01 West elevation

02 Entry to open-air washrooms

03 COR-TEN steel plate roof suspended above washroom

04 Details of continuous partial-penetration welded connections where roof meets supports

05 COR-TEN steel plates form triangular supports for curved roof plane

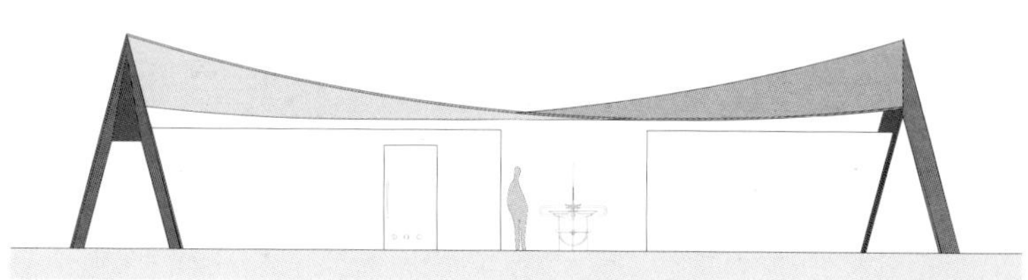

01

02

03

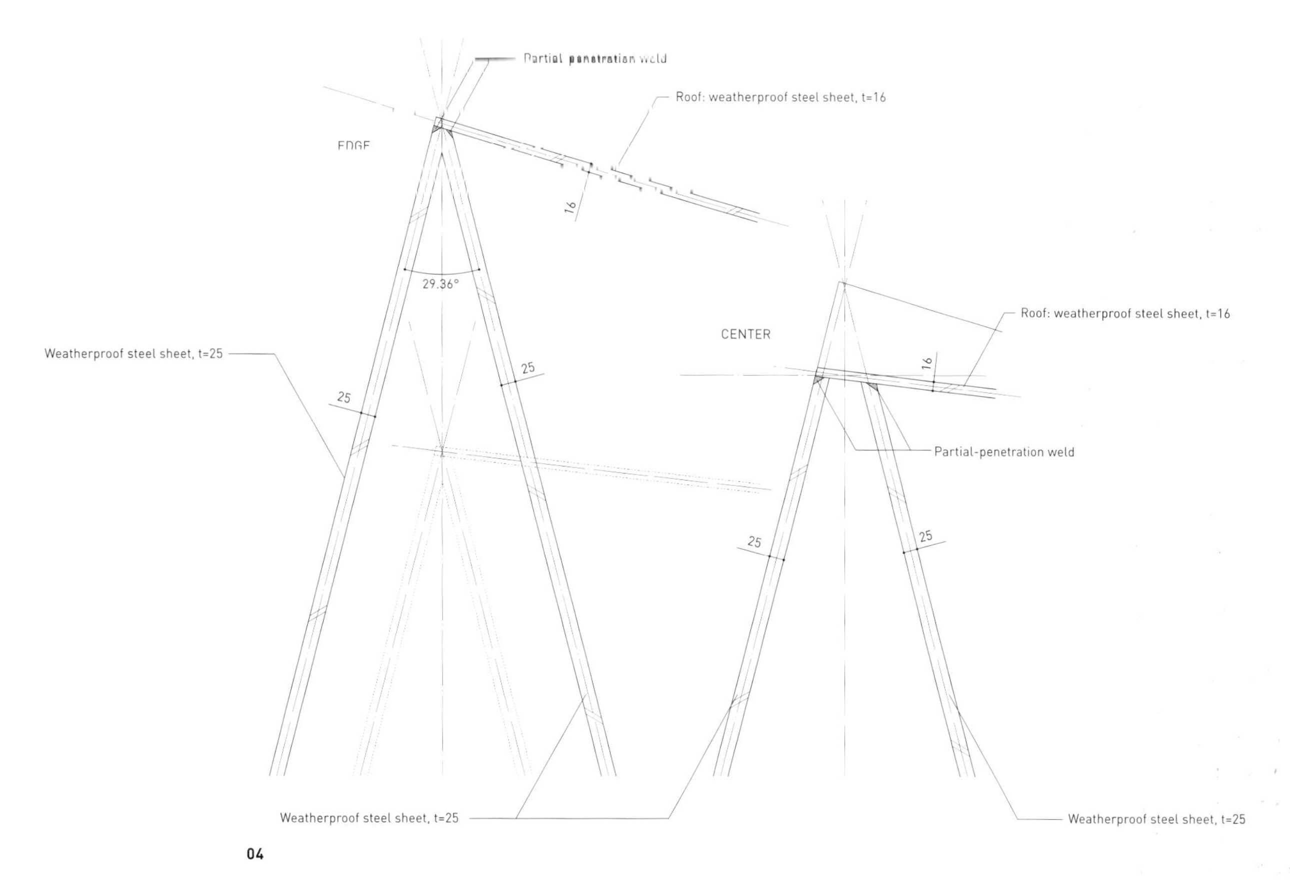
Partial-penetration weld
Roof: weatherproof steel sheet, t=16
EDGE
16
29.36°
Weatherproof steel sheet, t=25
25
25
CENTER
Roof: weatherproof steel sheet, t=16
16
Partial-penetration weld
25
25
Weatherproof steel sheet, t=25
Weatherproof steel sheet, t=25

04

05

Cantonal School Canteen

Wettingen, Switzerland — :mlzd
Stamped aluminum sheets

DESIGN INTENTION

The designers converted a former barn known in the town of Wettingen, Switzerland, as the Löwenscheune, or "lion barn," into the dining hall for the cantonal school of Aargau. The facility is located on campus, midway between a monastery and a spinning mill. As the old barn was extensively renovated, a new addition was built onto its southern end. The design is respectful of the existing barn typology but features a new architectural language that offers an emphatic statement of the Löwenscheune's new function. The addition's simple, abstract mass fits proportionally with its historic neighbors, but the perforated metal skin is a clear departure from the past. A new floor was added to the existing barn, dividing the volume horizontally and creating space for the cafeteria on the ground floor and a dining hall upstairs, connected by a lateral opening with a generous staircase. The addition houses a kitchen and food-serving spaces.

MATERIALITY

The new facade is made of stamped, anodized aluminum sheets that run across the roof and the windows, abstracting the volume. The building's formal reductivist strategy and dark facade surface express restraint.

The use of metal (once a precious resource) and the ornamental flower and leaf stamping refer to the historic monastery and its natural surroundings. The voids in the dark metal permit filtered views outside, and allow precise natural patterns to be projected by sunlight into the shadows of the various interior surfaces. In this way, the building's skin ornamentation extends into its interior spaces.

TECHNICAL

The stamped aluminum sheets are formed from 0.08" (2 mm) sheet metal with a dark bronze anodized finish on both faces. They are cut into rectangular flanged trays with fasteners at two points on each horizontal edge. Each panel is approximately 3' × 8' (0.9 × 2.4 m), with exceptions where this otherwise regular grid is adjusted at vertical corners or the sloping roof edge, which require special screen elements that are continuous from one plane to the other.

The distribution of the screens, which were stamped by a number of different dies, makes it difficult to identify any repetition on the entire surface of the building, mimicking the irregularity of tree canopies in forests. The more thoroughly stamped screens are secured over glazed windows and doors, where views and daylight are desired. Despite their operation, swinging door and window panels do not disrupt the consistency of the screen's grid on the mass. In this project the mass and the ornamented surfaces dominate.

Secured to vertical aluminum frames, the aluminum screens create a 6.3" (160 mm) space over the underlying opaque wall and roof assemblies. Drainage occurs in this space, including concealed gutters and leaders that remove stormwater from the roof. All materials used for the screen assembly were chosen to meet the thermal and moisture challenges of the environment. The screens can be removed from the outside if necessary to service the underlying elements.

The design of the facade is the result of collaboration between the architects, facade planners, building physicists, and a local artist.

01 West elevation with renovated portion in the center and addition to the right

02 The addition at right is informed by the massing of the adjoining existing structures

03 Exterior view of addition from south

04 Sunlight enters circulation space through stamped aluminum screens

05 View through stamped aluminum screen toward exterior

06 Wall section showing stamped aluminum screens installed over glazed openings and over insulated opaque walls

01

02

03

04

05

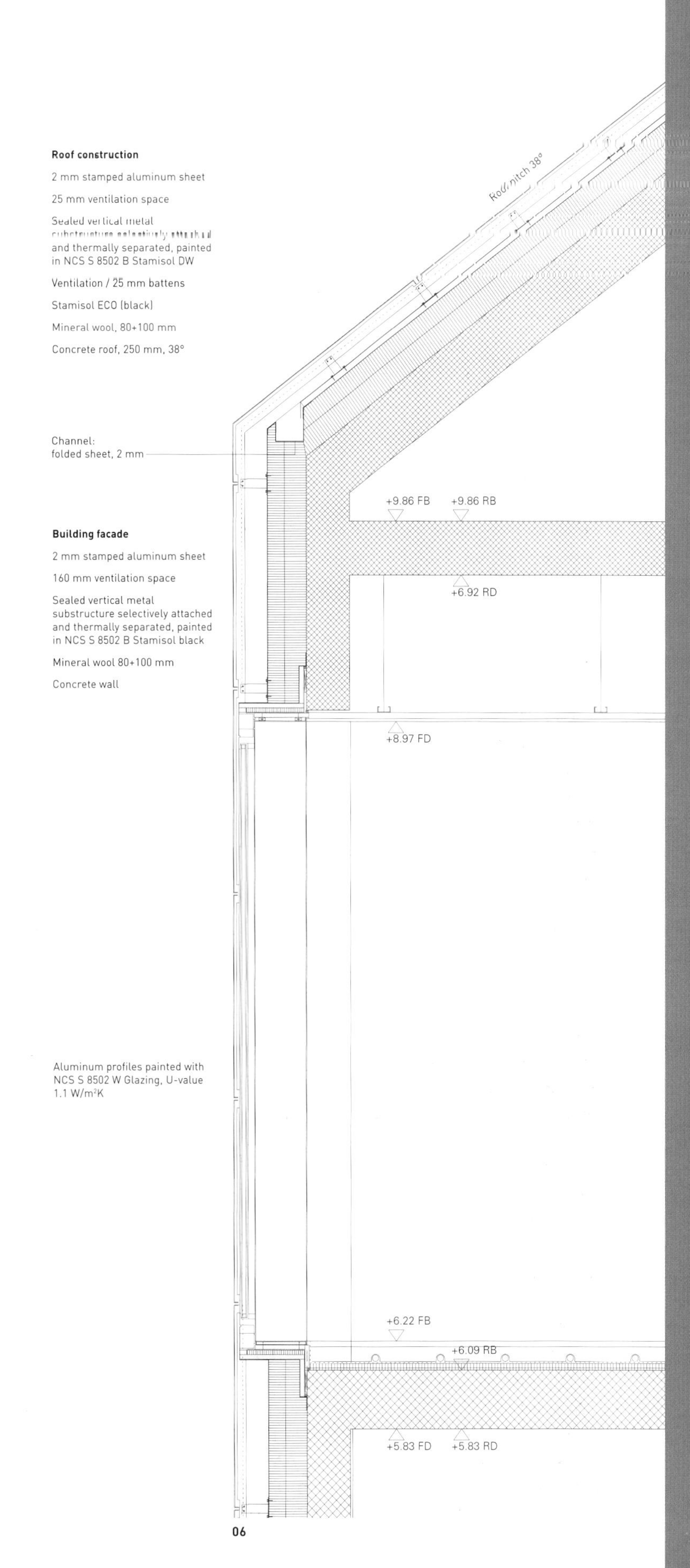

Roof construction
2 mm stamped aluminum sheet
25 mm ventilation space
Sealed vertical metal
and thermally separated, painted in NCS S 8502 B Stamisol DW
Ventilation / 25 mm battens
Stamisol ECO (black)
Mineral wool, 80+100 mm
Concrete roof, 250 mm, 38°
Channel: folded sheet, 2 mm
Building facade
2 mm stamped aluminum sheet
160 mm ventilation space
Sealed vertical metal substructure selectively attached and thermally separated, painted in NCS S 8502 B Stamisol black
Mineral wool 80+100 mm
Concrete wall
Aluminum profiles painted with NCS S 8502 W Glazing, U-value 1.1 W/m²K
+9.86 FB
+9.86 RB
+6.92 RD
+8.97 FD
+6.22 FB
+6.09 RB
+5.83 FD
+5.83 RD

06

Artists' Studios in Aberystwyth

Aberystwyth, Wales, UK — Heatherwick Studio
Stainless steel, crumpled foil

DESIGN INTENTION

The Artists' Studios in Aberystwyth were intended to provide low-cost facilities for sixteen start-up arts organizations for the Aberystwyth Arts Centre, part of the University of Wales, Aberystwyth. In an effort to respect the character of the wooded site, the program was broken down into eight smaller studios and placed among the trees. The shed-like studio buildings have simple timber frames that are conceptually split down the middle and pulled apart to bring light and ventilation to the centerline, and then organized around a common entryway.

MATERIALITY

Heatherwick Studio wanted a cladding material that was thin yet durable and resistant to weather. Stainless steel was an obvious choice, but its high cost was problematic. By keeping the steel sheet's thickness to a minimum, costs were kept within reason, as weight drives metal costs. Typically stainless steel is rolled to thicknesses measuring no less than 0.04" (1 mm), but a rolling mill in Finland was able to achieve 0.005" (0.127 mm) thickness specifically for this project. At this point, the sheet metal is the thickness of a soft drink can—so thin that it dents easily and offers little structural integrity. The designers employed this weakness to their advantage, intentionally crinkling the thin foil prior to installation. To achieve the rigidity needed for durable cladding, a spray foam was applied to the inner face of the foil after it was installed. Due to the reflective qualities of the crinkled steel foil, the colors and patterns of the surrounding forest scintillate upon the facade surface.

This project shows the innovative results the designers were able to accomplish in their desire to use stainless steel in a new and more accessible manner. Even though stainless steel has never been used for a cladding material at this thickness, the designers used the creative program of the studios as the inspiration for their creativity in the material.

TECHNICAL

Each of the eight buildings is elevated off the sloping site by fifteen concrete piers, which bear the steel frame of the floor deck. The superstructure of the studios consists of simple, light wood-frame construction joined with nails. A band of windows was created by omitting one ribbon of the stainless steel along the side elevations and inserting a sash in its place.

The stainless-steel cladding is brightly annealed marine-grade 316L (1.4404), chosen because it optimizes strength and cold-forming capabilities. The thickness is only 5 mil (0.005" or 0.127 mm). The seams of the stainless-steel ribbons were joined to 1.4" × 2" (35 × 50 mm) framing battens at all edges. The fragile edges of the sheet metal would likely have torn at fasteners, so the foil was wrapped around the battens, spreading the load transfer over a large portion of the sheet metal. The cladding was installed like giant pieces of metal siding, starting at the lowest part of the wall, then overlapping each new layer over the upper edge of the preceding layer. This made the seams watertight, and efficiently used the doubled battens to firmly pinch the edges of the metal.

Rigid thermosetting polyurethane foam was sprayed onto the cladding's inner face, which bonds it to the face of the metal as well as insulates. In the thicknesses used here, the walls and roof are minimum values of R-23 (164 m^2K/W), much more in some locations. The reflective, polished metal exterior is also an excellent radiant energy barrier. The studio walls tremendously reduce all forms of heat transmission: conduction, convection, and radiation. The polyurethane expands dramatically in its first few moments, then it hardens. The inner shape of the foam is naturally irregular and hard to control, but in this design a cavity conceals this irregularity behind a vertical plane of interior gypsum and wood studs.

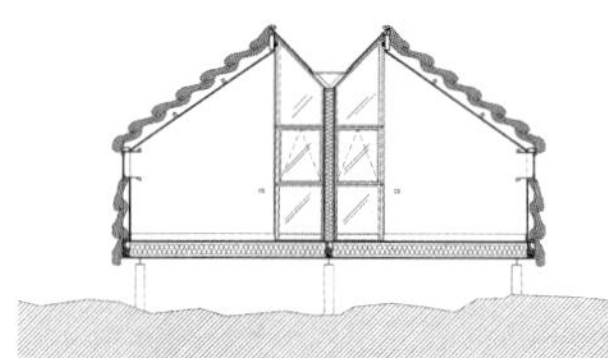

01

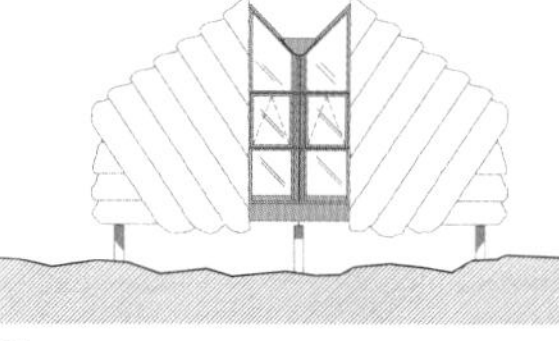

02

03

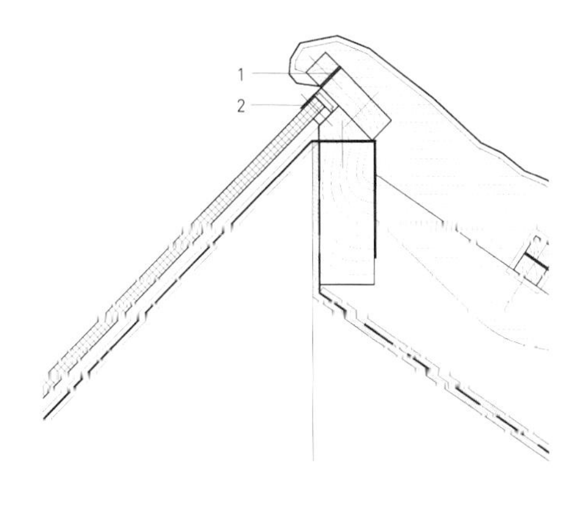

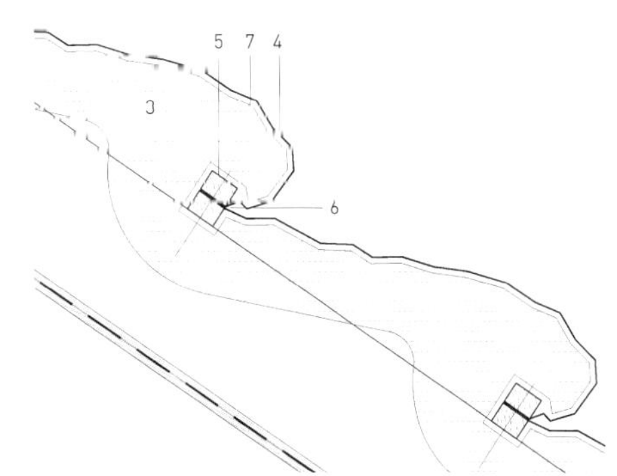

1 Continuous bead of proprietary silicon-based sealant between stainless-steel flashing and cladding

2 Stainless-steel flashing

3 HFC blown polyurethane rigid foam insulation

4 Bright-annealed stainless-steel grade 1.4404 (316L), 0.127 mm thick

5 Battens (35 × 50 mm)

6 Continuous bead of proprietary silicon-based sealant between stainless-steel cladding sheets

7 HFC blown polyurethane hard core foam, 10 mm

01 Transverse section

02 West elevation

03 Apparatus used by the fabricator to crinkle thin stainless-steel sheets

04 Two of the structures on the wooded site

05 Overlapping layers of stainless-steel foil cladding with windows and skylights at seam between studios

06 Section detail through wall and roof assemblies

04

05

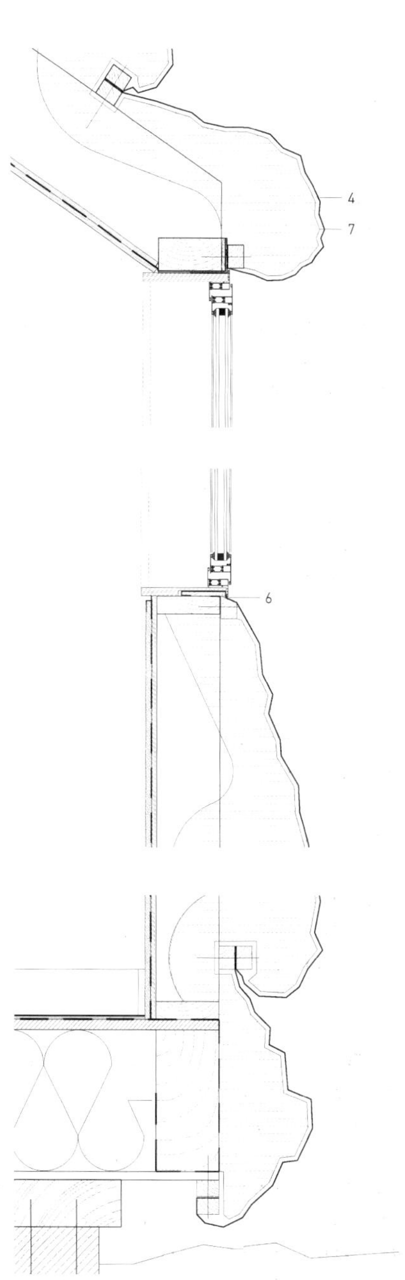

06

Plastics

THE BASICS

Plastics are lightweight, resilient, generally resistant to corrosion and moisture, and can be molded and formed into complex shapes. The material is relatively new to the construction industry, although recently there has been extraordinary growth in their use in building construction. Plastics can be generally defined as chainlike molecular structures that are made by either altering natural products or by transforming petroleum, natural gas, or coal products into an object. Most synthetic plastics, however, are made from distilled crude oil, accounting for approximately 8 percent of the world's application of oil resources. All plastics contain carbon, which has the ability to combine with other atoms to form rings or chains at the chemical level. A long chain of molecules is called a *polymer* and a short chain is called a *monomer*. A polymer is a chain of molecules that can be opaque, transparent, or translucent; it is capable of being molded, extruded, cast, or drawn into filaments.

Plastics are more generally defined by two types, *thermoplastics* and *thermosetting plastics* (see page 177), which indicate the way in which heat is involved in their formation. Thermoplastics will deform under heat or pressure and can be re-formed into new shapes multiple times. Thermosetting plastics, after being set and formed, will not break down under heat to their constituent chemicals for re-formation; however, these plastics can be used in higher temperature situations.

Materialistically, synthetic polymers, or plastics, have a short history, yet have transformed almost every industry since their invention, including medicine, electronics, aeronautics, fashion, engineering, and construction, to name just a few. In building and construction, plastics were first used as ornament, as a superficial finish, or as secondary parts for enclosure systems. Only recently have they begun to gain respect and appreciation as a viable primary material, today offering a wider scope of uses such as interior finishes, glazing, plumbing fixtures, and even structural components. Compared to other construction materials, plastics have a lower fire-rating and their use in applications requiring fire resistance is limited. Some of the advantages plastics can offer is that they are lightweight, lower in cost, resistant to corrosion and moisture, can be relatively strong, and are readily shaped. Their reputation as a short-lived trend, brittle and prone to discoloration, has recently been revised due to enormous advances in plastics technology. The industry, in collaboration with designers, now manufactures an unprecedented variety of new products with improved physical properties, higher-quality materials, and a much broader range of products, particularly for glazing and finishing applications in buildings. Since the material is intrinsically man-made, its characteristics are not limited and will continue to expand. It is highly malleable and changeable, and its depth in color and opacity are equally varied. It has become a design tool of which many architects have taken advantage.

HISTORY

Plastics were first formulated in the nineteenth century, although significant advancements did not occur until well into the twentieth. In 1836 Charles Goodyear processed rubber, which is a natural polymer type of plastic, by treating it chemically with sulfur. The first plastic made from organic material, cellulose, was debuted twenty-eight years later at the Great International Exhibition in London by Alexander Parkes. His remarkable material, aptly named Parkesine, was moldable under heat and hardened when cooled. It could be transparent or opaque and sculpted into any imaginable shape. It was touted as having all the qualities of rubber yet was less expensive; unfortunately, Parkes's investors ceased funding the product, ironically, due to its high production costs.

The first completely man-made synthetic material was discovered in 1907 by a chemist named Leo Baekeland in New York. He created a thermosetting liquid resin, dubbed Bakelite. It was electrically resistant, chemically stable, heat-resistant, shatterproof, and impervious to cracking or fading. Bakelite came to be used in many applications and is still used today as an electrical insulator or is added to wood to make it more durable. The U.S. military began using it to produce lightweight war machinery and weaponry that was superior to steel, and by World War II it was used in many weapons and equipment.

The 1920s was a time of great plastics innovation and invention. Petroleum and natural gas refinement increased, shepherding in a new level of experimentation and discovery of uses for insulation, molded parts, and chemical- and water-resistant products. DuPont was an industry leader, employing chemists who became responsible for the invention of many plastics taken for granted today, such as nylon and Teflon. Waldo Simon, a chemist at B. F. Goodrich, discovered and developed polyvinyl chloride (PVC), or vinyl, which became an immensely versatile product in the building industry, still commonly used today for components such as pipes, flooring, and siding, among others.

In 1933 two organic chemists stumbled upon perhaps the most significant plastic invention. E. W. Fawcett and R. O. Gibson, working for the Imperial Chemical Industries Research Laboratory, accidentally discovered polyethylene, a product that subsequently came to play a key role in World War II for insulating radar and other military applications. Polyethylene was the first plastic in the U.S. to sell over a billion pounds per year, and continues to be the highest selling plastic in the world today. It is most commonly seen in soda bottles, milk jugs, plastic food storage containers, grocery bags, and many other common objects, but it is also widely used in construction in the form of films and sheets.

Another common plastic, nylon, became widely used in the 1940s, in everything from women's stockings to military materiel. In 1957 a Swiss engineer named George de Maestral took nylon hooks and loops and invented Velcro, revolutionizing many common products. The 1950s brought additional plastics to the clothing industry, notably Lycra and polyester. Laminates such as Formica and molded melamine formaldehyde resin were becoming widely used in furniture and dishware. Tupperware, a polyethylene, was first introduced in 1948 and quickly became a household name.

By 1956 polyester and fiberglass were being used for automobile and boat body parts, and in the 1960s, plastics played a critical role in spacecraft parts and computer equipment. The 1970s brought more plastics to the consumer with more selections in housing interiors, clothing, household products, furniture, and electronic products. As computer technology grew, plastics became even more significant, becoming commonplace as the growth of fiber-optic cables and telephone cables were made. Indeed, each decade since the 1950s has brought new and unheralded advances to the plastics industry, making it one of the most ubiquitous materials in the world. Relative to other architectural materials, plastics are still very much in the early stages.

There is plenty of remaining potential for plastic in architectural applications. Customization in molds, forming, and the free range of shapes that can be created open an endless world of potential for designers using plastics. Manufacturers and suppliers are eager to enter new markets and find new applications and materials to satisfy designers and architects. As more products become fire-rated to meet building codes they will continue to be seen more frequently in construction.

But despite their usefulness and growing potential, designers should not disregard the fact that petroleum-based plastic products are in some cases detrimental to the environment. The desirable permanence of plastics is also what makes them not biodegradable. On the other hand, some argue that glass manufacture and transport is more energy-intensive, and others who say lumber-inspired plastic products can lessen demand for trees and reduce future deforestation.

There are clear advantages and disadvantages to using plastic. Meanwhile considerable plastics research continues for new advances in the construction industry as well as for how to produce plastic products with alternative fuels and use more recycled materials. Reducing embodied energy and CO_2 emissions are concerns with any industrially produced products. With plastics we must also be concerned with safety and environmental emissions associated with their manufacture, as well as outgassing during their service life.

DESIGN CONSIDERATIONS

Plastic is a generic term used to describe several chemical compounds. The most common are polyethylene, polyurethane, polystyrene, polycarbonate, polyvinyl, and polypropylene. As a group, these share many characteristics, such as their ability to achieve different levels of transparency and color. Plastics typically have a high coefficient of thermal expansion, so construction details must allow for a substantial amount of expansion and contraction due to temperature changes. Plastics are easily cut, formed, and bent, and some are fire-resistant or classified as slow burning.

The building and construction industry is the second largest consumer of plastics, closely behind the packaging industry. Plastics play an integral role in construction due to their durability, high performance, easy handling, and low cost. They continue to proliferate in the construction of all building types, but most particularly residential buildings. We commonly see plastics in construction today in plumbing fixtures, siding, flooring, insulation, doors, windows, railings, lighting, and glazing, and the list continues to grow. They are also used to modify the properties of other, more traditional construction materials, but recently they have replaced traditional materials altogether in many conditions, largely due to their lower cost, excellent corrosion resistance, and light weight. Additionally, one of the biggest advantages of plastics is their ability to be shaped into limitless forms. Plastics are generally lower density than other building materials, while their strength-to-weight ratio is typically higher. They are usually less affected by water or decay and have a lower thermal and electrical conductivity. Most plastics can be formed and finished to mimic another material, making them popular substitutive options. They can be joined with heat, mechanically with screws or bolts, or by snapping interlocking pieces together with no fasteners. Heat or solvents can be used to soften plastics, allowing two members to harden together and join.

The largest disadvantage to plastics in building applications is that they can be destroyed by fire and may give off toxic gases. Given the wide range of plastics, all perform differently when subjected to fire. Some plastics burn and create a dense toxic smoke, while others produce combustible vapors, and still others melt. Some plastics are slow burning, such as the acrylics, polystyrene, polyethylene, and cellulose plastics, while others such as the silicones have substantial fire resistance. Rigid PVC is *intumescent*, meaning it burns but becomes self-extinguishing, so the fire is not sustained. Fire ratings depend on the type of plastic, its thickness, and its coating. Many plastics have flame retardants or resins applied to their surface to increase fire resistance. Ratings exist for flame spread, smoke development, and toxicity of combustion products, all of which should be checked before installation of any plastic, especially for interior applications.

Other disadvantages to plastics include a high level of deformation, expansion, and contraction due to thermal changes, making control joints, expansion joints, and other measures of controlling volume change critical. Compared to other construction materials, plastics are not stiff, and they deflect under heavy load conditions, especially under prolonged loading. Plastics can also be scratched or become brittle if protective films or layers are not added to their surface. Hazing and discoloration can also occur due to age or environmental exposure such as ultraviolet light. This has increasingly become less prevalent with advances in the protective agents that are placed on or in plastics to prevent changes in color or transparency.

TYPES

Plastics fall into two general categories: *thermoplastic* and *thermosetting plastics*. *Thermoplastics*, which include acrylics, nylons, vinyls, polycarbonates, and polystyrenes, are generally linear molecules and will hold their shape at normal temperatures but can be re-formed or re-molded into new shapes when placed under high temperatures. These plastics are recyclable and regain their original properties after being cooled again. They are used for glazing, pipes, vapor barriers, flooring, lighting fixtures, and foam insulation. *Thermosetting* plastics, which include epoxies, melamines, polyurethanes, and silicones, have a more complex molecular structure that is cross-linked in three dimensions. They can only be formed once and cannot be returned to their basic components through reheating; once they have set or cured, they remain rigid. Thermosetting plastics are generally harder and stronger than thermoplastics. Typical applications of these are for adhesives, laminates, rigid foam insulation, waterproofing membranes, and window frames, among others. Three types of thermoplastics are most often used in building construction:

Polyvinyl chloride

Polyvinyl chloride, generally called PVC or vinyl, is the most commonly used plastic in building construction. It is resistant to water and some chemicals, is low in cost, and is resistant to tearing. *Rigid PVC* is used most often for hot and cold water pipes, rain gutters, ducts, window frames, tiles, and panels. *Flexible PVC* is used for flexible tubing or hoses, flashing, films, sheets, or floor tiles. Although most rigid PVC is self-extinguishing when exposed to fire, and flexible grades will burn slowly, it cannot be used for purposes requiring high temperatures. The highest tolerance in some grades is 212°F (100°C).

Polycarbonate

Polycarbonate is often used as a substitute for glass. Depending on its color and thickness, different desired levels of light can be achieved, ranging from 35–50 percent light transmission for white sheets and up to 88 percent for clear sheets. It is also half the weight of standard architectural glass. It has one of the highest impact resistances of the thermoplastics; its impact strength over glass is excellent and has over fifteen times the impact resistance of even high-impact acrylics. It can maintain transparency up to two inches thick, has good dimensional and thermal stability, and is stain resistant. Polycarbonate is commercially available even in remote locations and can easily be installed by unskilled workers using commonly available tools and fasteners such as nails and screws. Polycarbonate panels are also easily cleaned, making them a good choice for an urban environment.

Polycarbonate has a thermal expansion coefficient that is eight times higher than that of glass. This movement must be compensated for in detailing and sheet size selection. If polycarbonate is not treated with a UV-protective layer on one or both sides, it will discolor. Polycarbonate panels, such as Lexan and Polygal, come in a wide range of thicknesses, shapes, colors, and specific solar and thermal resistance features. They offer the designer choices because of their varied light transmission, from opaque to translucent to virtually transparent. They also provide inexpensive moderate thermal insulation with the use of the multi-walled sheets. They are lightweight, easy to install, and are 100 percent recyclable. However, they are vulnerable to alkalis and aromatic hydrocarbon. Polycarbonate maintains its properties over a wide range of temperatures, from -40 to 280 °F (-40–138 °C).

Acrylic

Acrylic, such as Plexiglas, Acrylite, Lucite, or Perspex, is a thermoplastic most commonly used for skylights, light fixtures, and other glazing applications. Its most valuable characteristic is its transparency, allowing as much as 92 percent overall light transmission with many varying levels of opaqueness and transmission levels below this. An acrylic sheet is eight to ten times stronger than glass of the same thickness, though acrylics can scratch more easily than glass. Acrylic is easily fabricated and machined and when heated can be formed into different shapes. It has good resistance to weather, heat, and chemicals; however it is combustible. Acrylic sheet is lightweight—usually less than half the weight of a piece of glass—and has moderate resistance to shrinkage and dimensional instability.

POLYMETHYL METHACRYLATE (PMMA, or Plexiglas) is an acrylic plastic that can be used in enclosure conditions as a substitute for glass. It is lightweight, transparent, and shatter resistant. Originally sold under the trade name Plexiglas, today "plexiglass" has entered the lexicon to identify this type of plastic. At room temperature, PMMA is solid and glasslike, but at very low temperatures it becomes brittle and is easily shattered. Ultraviolet light-inhibiting coatings can be applied during manufacturing to increase its life span. Its strength can be enhanced by the use of an additive during its formative chemical reaction, yielding a high-impact acrylic. PMMA's unique chemical structure makes its clear visibility and hardness an ideal choice for some architectural applications, such as skylights, windows, or signage.

—

POLYETHYLENE TEREPHTHALATE (PET) is a thermoplastic polymer that can be semi-rigid to rigid depending on the thickness. The material is also very lightweight, inexpensive, mildew resistant, and can be a good gas and moisture barrier. It is naturally colorless but can be colored. Like all polymers, ultraviolet degradation and low fire resistance are two of PET's disadvantages. It can be used as a film, cast, or extruded.

—

POLYURETHANE FOAM (PUR) is a low-density, rigid foam used primarily for thermal insulation. It has a low thermal conductivity, low water absorption, and has a very high strength-to-weight ratio. PUR foam has excellent adhesion properties. It can be manufactured in rigid boards and can be spray-applied in place. However, being a thermosetting plastic, it cannot be recycled.

—

GLASS-FIBER-REINFORCED PLASTIC (GFRP) is a composite plastic reinforced by fine glass fibers. Each fiber is strong in tension and compression and is weak in shear and bending. The glass filaments are embedded in resin to create a composite material that is easily manipulated during fabrication and hardens to become a strong material in tension, compression, and shear. A great variety of fabrication strategies can be used to create composite products. The resin used in GFRP is a thermosetting plastic, and cannot be recycled.

—

UPM PROFI WOOD PLASTIC COMPOSITE material attempts to combine the best properties of wood fibers and plastic. It is manufactured primarily from recycled cellulose fibers and plastics—mainly recycled paper—and can be completely recycled. Polyethylene and polypropylene are the thermoplastics used most often to manufacture wood plastic composites, which is often used in decking and siding. The material does not need finishing. It is not intended for structural use due to its vulnerability to creep under long-term stress.

—

CORIAN ACRYLIC POLYMER is a DuPont material that has been popular for more than forty years for interior applications such as counters, tabletops, and lab environments. It is considered a solid surface material made up of acrylic polymer and alumina trihydrate that is thermoformed in 300°F (150°C). It is not often seen in exterior architectural applications, but when used as exterior wall panels, a uniform and smooth appearance can be achieved. Corian has a high-performance durability, excellent UV and weather resistance, easy maintenance, and a fairly good fire rating. It can be thermoformed or bent to a customized shape or form, and can also be engraved, colored and finished with no sealants or treatments. It is fairly easy to install and join with inconspicuous seams. Corian can be cut and finished easily for an array of different interior or exterior wall applications, and using oven and pressure molds, a wide range of forms can be created.

—

FLUOROPOLYMER FILMS, specifically polytetrafluoroethylene (PTFE) and ethylene tetrafluoroethylene (ETFE) membranes, can be used to create lightweight, air-inflated cushions for wall, roof, or enclosure applications. ETFE, a modified co-polymer, has a tensile strength that is about twice that of PTFE. With approximately 1 percent of the weight of glass, lower costs, and excellent light transmission, both materials offer significant advantages compared to a glass curtain wall. Both can produce a wide range of colors, prints, patterns, translucency, and density, and thus can control the amount of UV light transmitted. ETFE was first developed for space applications and thus has high insulation properties and a low level of embodied energy. These fabrics and films can withstand a wide range of temperature changes and can have a tensile strength of up to 500,000 psi.

—

POLYESTER FABRIC can be used for tensile structures with great flexibility, translucency and elasticity. The fabric permits 50 percent of the available visible light to pass through, but blocks approximately 80 percent of the incident ultraviolet light. Tensile structures can perform under tension or compression but the members cannot resist bending stresses.

—

COATED POLYESTER FABRICS such as polyvinylidene fluoride (PVDF) have a good resistance to UV light, weathering, environmental stresses, and are relatively inexpensive. This type of fabric can be sewn or electrically welded, and is 100 percent recyclable. PVDF fabric is often used to wrap a steel frame for a quick construction. It can come in different fade-resistant colors but is most often used in white for optimum interior daylighting without chromatic distortion.

MODIFIERS AND ADDITIVES

More than any other construction material, plastics are formulated to yield specific physical properties. Modifiers and fillers are added to base plastics to produce optimum properties in the finished product.

PLASTICIZERS are organic compounds that are added to reduce brittleness and provide flexibility and softness.

—

STABILIZERS are organic compounds added to reduce deterioration from the effects of sunlight, weathering, heat, and other volatile conditions.

—

FILLERS are non-reacting materials usually added to reduce costs or to improve hardness or resistance to heat or electrical current. Talc and marble dust are two common fillers.

—

EXTENDERS are waxes or oils added to give bulk and reduce costs.

—

REINFORCING FIBERS—glass, metal, carbon, or any other material fibers—can be added to increase strength, hardness, stiffness, resistance, and other improvements for a given condition.

—

FLAME RETARDERS are chemical additives usually added to plastics used in interior spaces or areas near electrical appliances in buildings.

PROCESSING METHODS

There are many ways to process plastics. Below are five of the main methods:

INJECTION MOLDING allows for a wide range of opportunities in designing and creating any plastic form. Polymer pellets are placed into a hopper and then heated to form a liquid resin, which is then injected into a mold and cooled. *Co-injection* is when two colors or materials are injected into a mold for a two-color or two-finish product. Although initial production expenses can be high, this process results in a high volume of products at a relatively fast rate, yielding low unit costs. Examples of injection-molded products are electrical boxes, exit signs, computer casings, foam plastic, LEGO toys, and plastic cutlery.

—

CASTING begins with a liquid form rather than a granule or pellet. It is not normally used in mass production, but rather to produce a higher-quality plastic product. It is however one of the simplest and most accessible means of producing a custom-designed plastic form. A casting mold is first made from either soft or rigid materials, and then the plastic is placed and set. Typical casting plastics include epoxy, polyester, synthetic resins, and acrylics. If a mold can be created, the casting process allows for an almost endless range of shapes to be produced.

—

EXTRUSION is most often used for the production of thermoplastic pipes, sheets, films, and unusual shapes. Their lengths can vary greatly, but extrusions are consistent in cross section. The extrusion process is fairly simple to visualize. Granulated polymers are placed into a hopper where they are heated and pushed through a shaped die by a rotating screw. The material is then pushed through different temperature zones, where it is cooled by water or air and is condensed, plasticized, and homogenized. A continuous shape is produced and then cut to the desired length. Some examples of extruded plastics include window frames, siding, pipes, and any long shape that has a consistent profile, even if complex. The processing cost is low compared to injection molding, but manufacturers require a minimum order length to justify die fabrication. *Pultrusion* is a variation of the same concept, except the plastic is pulled rather than pushed through the die.

—

BLOW MOLDING is a variation of the extrusion process, in which blowing the plastic through a die against a mold can produce large thermoplastic objects. This process is much like blowing up a balloon made of plastic within a mold, thus creating the shape of the object. Air pressure forces softened vinyl or other plastics into a hollow mold or die to create specific forms, such as plastic bottles.

—

CALENDERING involves taking plastic pellets and feeding them through hot rollers, forming a sheet or film of a desired thickness, and then feeding it through cold rollers. The rolling temperature is a primary factor in the plastic's ability to be molded. Embossing the hot rollers allows for any desired textures or patterns to be imprinted on the plastic. Films of PVC, sheets of polycarbonate, and laminates are created in this manner, for use as flooring, wall covering, and other fabric-like applications.

SelgasCano Architecture Office

Madrid, Spain — SelgasCano Arquitectos
Acrylic, polymethyl methacrylate

DESIGN INTENTION

When SelgasCano Arquitectos decided to move their studio into the woods, they wanted to keep the space as transparent as possible while protecting their workspace from excessive solar gain. Their new office is a long, tubular structure, partially buried in the wooded site to literally integrate it into the landscape and provide favorable thermal mass. SelgasCano's solution explores the use of very thin plastic sheets instead of glass. On the northern side of the studio, they used a single transparent layer, while on the sunny southern side, they designed panels composed of reinforcing steel structure and translucent thermal insulation sandwiched between two plastic sheets.

The innovative design of these panels created the challenge of finding a contractor who was willing to take on such a small, yet complex project. Some of the more intricate plastic pieces had to be ordered from Deutsche Bahn, the German national railway, which uses the same materials in its carriages. The architects had to wait until a larger order was placed, since their material order for this project did not warrant putting the factories into operation.

MATERIALITY

Few materials can simultaneously function as structure, enclosure, and light transmitters on their own. Even fewer can be efficiently manipulated to form a curved shape and enable, for example, a roof to seamlessly become a wall. The outer envelope of the office consists of two such resin products, both of which share all of these qualities.

The northern side is a 0.8" (20 mm) PMMA acrylic skin made up of ten standardized units that are cross-tongued at the abutting edges and sealed with silicone, creating the uniformly transparent result. A translucent 0.4" (10 mm) sheet of Perspex acrylic was used to create the two cable-and-pulley-operated gates at either end of the tube. The southern side is 4" (100 mm) thick, and composed of translucent white polyethylene insulation pressed between two 0.4" (10 mm) fiberglass sheets. The result creates a protective shade for the workspace that lines the southern wall and obscures the structural steel members inside the sandwiched sheets. The translucent skin nonetheless allows for some level of site presence, as the shadows of the tree canopies are visible through translucent plastic layers. The sound of rain on the skin also pleasantly reverberates through the interior.

The subterranean portion of the walls uses cast-in-place concrete formed by horizontal tongue-and-groove boards and protected on the exterior by a waterproofing layer and a geo-textile drainage membrane. The floor is pine boarding laid on top of steel square hollow sections secured to a concrete slab. It is painted yellow and white, but the rhythms of the boards are still apparent, and recognizably similar to the adjoining painted board-formed concrete walls. The operable cable-and-pulley shutters at the ends of the tube allow for varying levels of natural ventilation.

TECHNICAL

While the tubular shape of the plastic sheets gives them some intrinsic structural rigidity, it is primarily the T-profiled steel frame that contributes the most to structurally support the pressed plastic sandwich assemblies. Additional white-painted galvanized steel angles and rectangular tubes detail the assembly of the plastic sheets.

Acrylic is a thermoplastic, so it can be softened and reformed repeatedly using heat. The acrylic panels on the north side were initially produced as flat planes and were then heated and curved into their final shapes. The fiberglass panels on the south side were manufactured using a pultrusion process in which fiberglass mesh was pulled through a bath of polyester, and then formed into the desired curve while the plastic hardened. The fiberglass sandwiched between the panels is composed of a thermosetting polyester resin, itself the result of an irreversible one-time chemical reaction that occurs during production. The biggest concern with the use of these polymers is the eventual degradation caused by exposure to UV rays. A polymer UV-inhibitor was added to the resin during manufacture of the transparent and translucent plastic sheets as a preventative measure.

01 Transverse section with site influences

02 Studio work stations view landscape through curved acrylic windows

03 View into studio from northwest

04 Curved acrylic windows supported by slender steel frames

05 Installation of T-profiled steel frame elements

06 Preparation of polyethylene / fiberglass composite panels

07 Panel installation

01

02

03

04

05

06

07

El B Conference Hall and Auditorium

Cartageña, Spain — SelgasCano Arquitectos
Acrylic, polycarbonate

DESIGN INTENTION

El B Conference Hall and Auditorium occupies one of the most prominent sites in Cartagena: the Paseo Alfonso XII dock, a 3,280' (1 km) length of the harbor front. Buildings must respect a 65.6' (20 m) setback from the pier edge, creating a public promenade where the city meets the Mediterranean. The pier's profoundly straight, long, and horizontal form was a cue for the design of this large facility.

Compartmented portions of the building program were placed on the side of the plan that abuts the city, or in subterranean floors, leaving the interior relatively open on the side facing the water. The generous dimensions of circulation spaces and the many memorable colorful visual episodes make spatial orientation within the building easier for visitors. The substantial building program is, in some locations, deeply embedded into the site.

The building is intended to be compatible with the massing of the site but distinct from its material palette. Rather than being heavy, hard, and solid, the building is translucent, delicate, and light; clear and ephemeral, it is almost aquatic.

MATERIALITY

The glossy wall and partition materials are composed of two plastic products of varying color and transparency made from a single custom extrusion profile.

Acrylic (PMMA) is used for the exterior wall surfaces, and fire-resistant polycarbonate (PC) is used for interior surfaces. The long north and south walls are double-layered assemblies applied over custom steel trusses, with sufficient thickness to contain lighting fixtures and moderate the transmission of sound and heat from outside. Inside the building, an undulating variation of this double-layered assembly separates meeting rooms from the long circulation space. Given the large size and the visual prominence of this building, the lightweight and translucent polycarbonate is an appropriate choice of materials. The architects also carefully broke the building down visually by combining color and colored lighting with the polycarbonate panels to give each space its own identity.

TECHNICAL

The acrylic exterior cladding uses a UV-resistant modifier to increase its service life in this sunny location. Colored dye was also introduced to the polymer as it was manufactured, which contributed colorful accents to the skin while also reducing the penetration of UV light into the body of the plastic sheets.

01 Interior elevation of auditorium wall faced with 967 polymer pieces

02 Longitudinal section through building

03 Auditorium wall cladding

04 Custom acrylic extrusion with integral colored lines

05 Waterfront facade from southwest

01

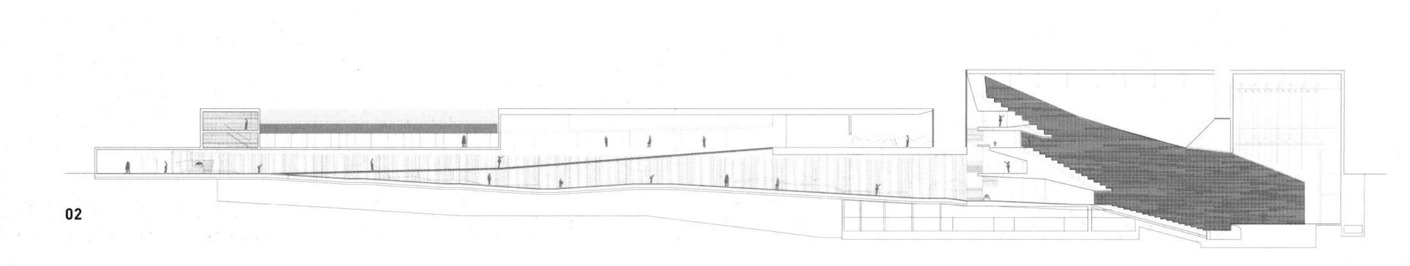

02

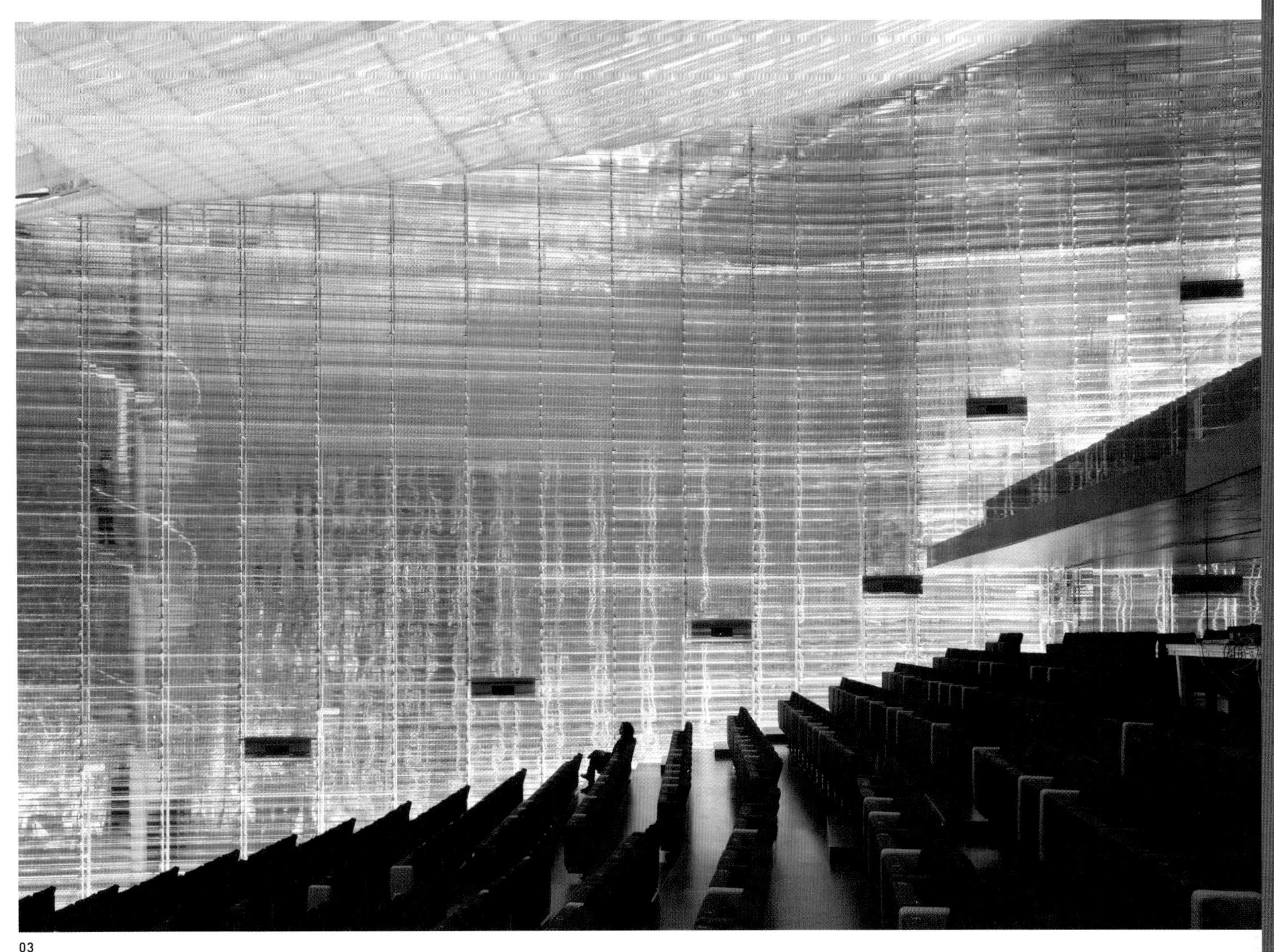

03

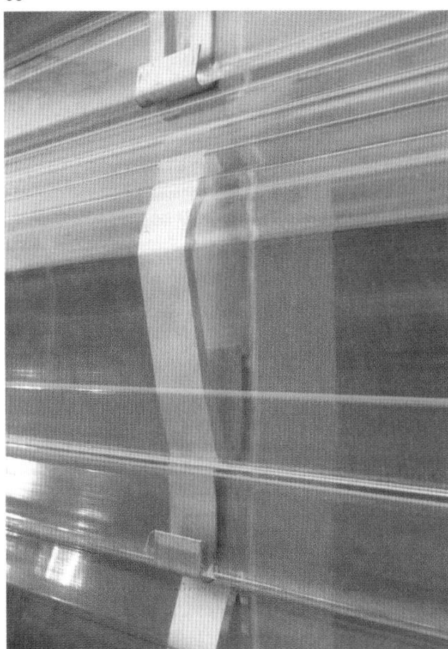

04

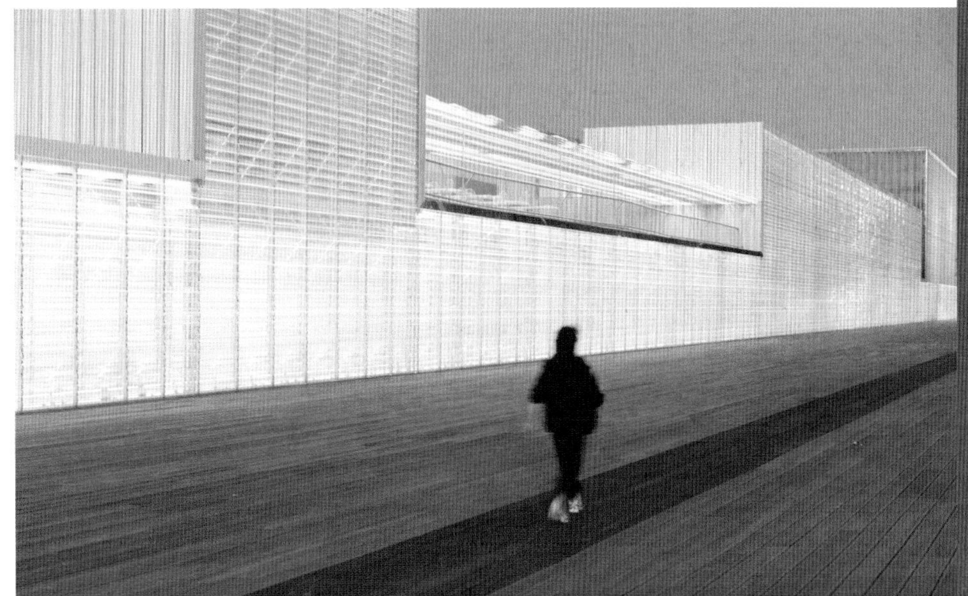

05

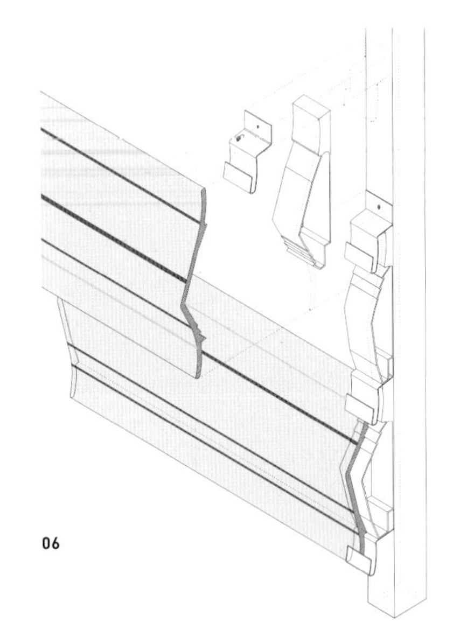

06

07

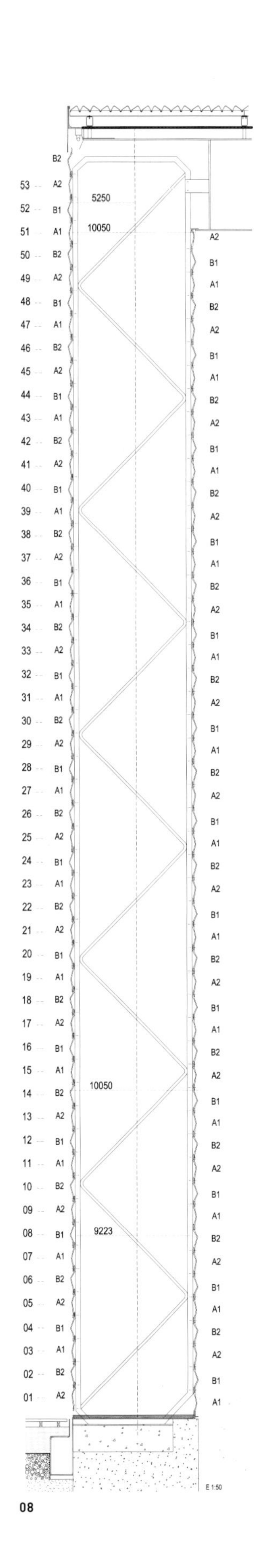
B2
53 A2
52 B1
51 A1
50 B2
49 A2
48 B1
47 A1
46 B2
45 A2
44 B1
43 A1
42 B2
41 A2
40 B1
39 A1
38 B2
37 A2
36 B1
35 A1
34 B2
33 A2
32 B1
31 A1
30 B2
29 A2
28 B1
27 A1
26 B2
25 A2
24 B1
23 A1
22 B2
21 A2
20 B1
19 A1
18 B2
17 A2
16 B1
15 A1
14 B2
13 A2
12 B1
11 A1
10 B2
09 A2
08 B1
07 A1
06 B2
05 A2
04 B1
03 A1
02 B2
01 A2
5250
10050
10050
9223
A2
B1
A1
B2
A2
B1
A1
B2
A2
B1
A1
B2
A2
B1
A1
B2
A2
B1
A1
B2
A2
B1
A1
B2
A2
B1
A1
B2
A2
B1
A1
B2
A2
B1
A1
B2
A2
B1
A1
B2
A2
B1
A1
B2
A2
B1
A1
B2
A2
B1
A1
E 1:50

08

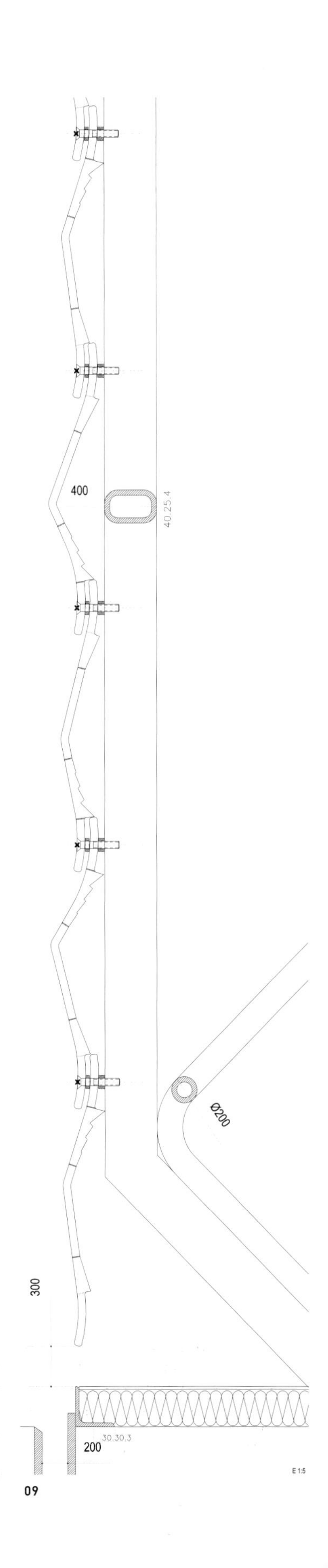
400
40.25.4
Ø200
300
30.30.3
200
E 1:5

09

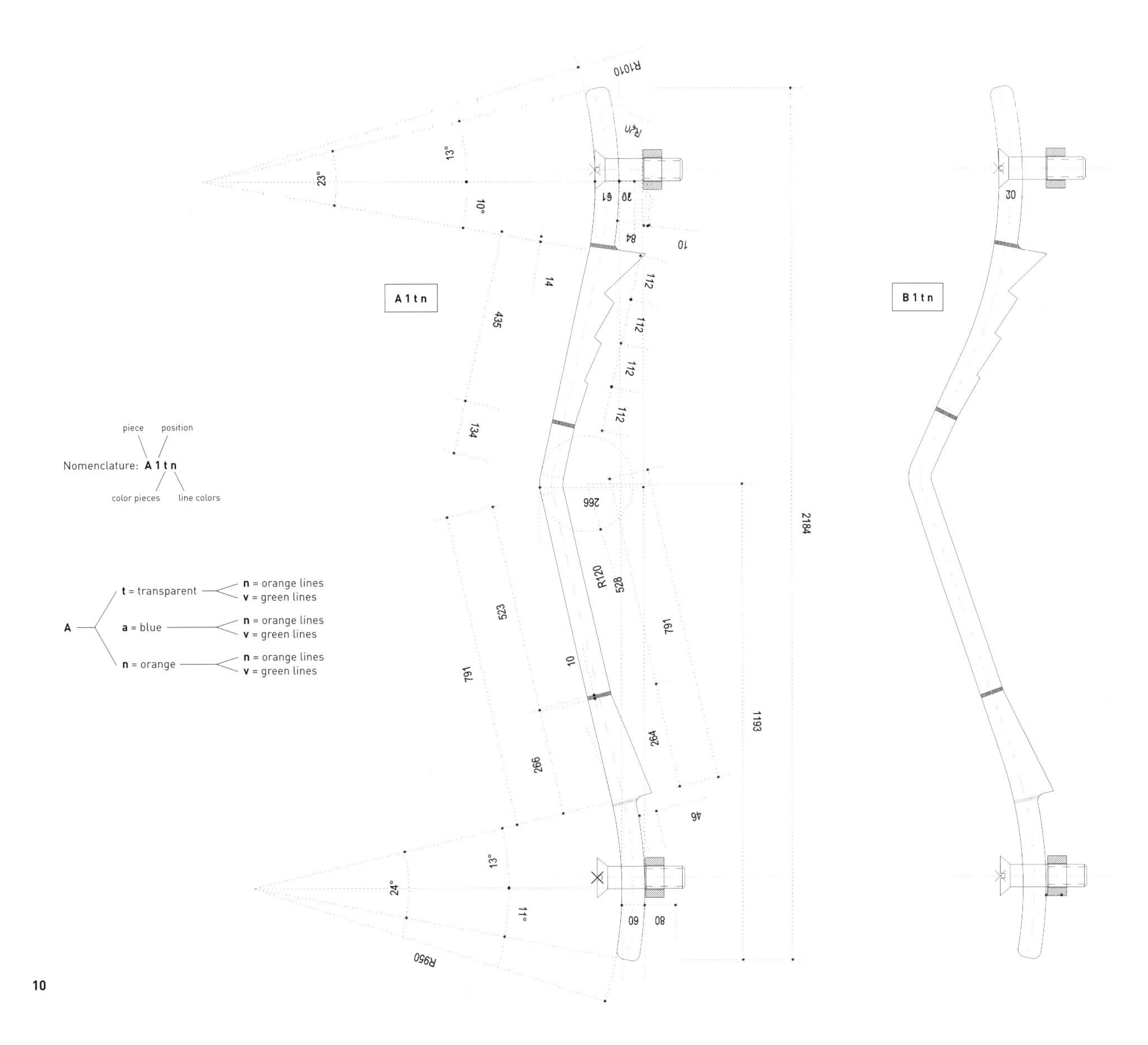

10

06 Axonometric view of aluminum brackets used to secure acrylic and polycarbonate profiles to steel frame

07 Lapped polymer cladding over inner and outer faces of custom steel trusses

08 Section through exterior wall identifying profile and color of each piece of polymer cladding

09 Section detail at base of exterior wall

10 Architect's drawing of polymer profiles with specification of integral colors and locations

Novartis Entrance Pavilion

Basel, Switzerland — Architect Marco Serra
Polyurethane foam, glass-fiber-reinforced plastic

DESIGN INTENTION

The Entrance Pavilion to the Novartis campus makes a dramatic architectural and structural statement while providing functional security and reception areas. The pavilion marks the arrival point for visitors emerging from the parking deck below, as well as for those approaching the campus at ground level. The visually striking form is based upon remarkable yet understated structural concepts for its roof and walls, creatively adapting materials and processes to new expressions.

The roof rests directly on the facade's structural glazing, without the use of any beams or columns, giving the illusion that it floats above the glass cube beneath. At night, recessed lights in the ground plane create the impression that the roof is a floating, glowing volume.

MATERIALITY

In order to keep the floor plan as open as possible, the monolithic roof element had to be fabricated out of a lightweight yet structurally sound material. Polyurethane (PUR) foam and glass-fiber-reinforced plastic (GFRP) offered the solution, not only as the form and the structure, but also as a waterproof and thermally insulating skin. The roof covers an impressive 4,300 sq. ft. (400 sq. m). It spans 38.4' (11.7 m), and cantilevers 16.2' (4.9 m), or 42 percent of the simple span. It is worth noting that cantilevers do not normally exceed 30 percent of the simple span.

The cross-section of the roof tapers from 24.4" (620 mm) in the middle to a slender 2.7" (70 mm) at the edges. The varying thicknesses of the PUR foam correspond to the structural requirements to support the roof. It is deepest where bending stresses are greatest at midspan, then tapers to the edge of the overhangs where stresses are least. To achieve the clean silhouette and slim forms of the project's design goals, this roof material was an ideal match.

TECHNICAL

Individual glass fibers, while strong under tension and compression, are relatively weak when subjected to bending or shear loads. GFRP is a composite of thermosetting plastic resin (most often polyester) reinforced by fine glass fibers. Embedding the fibers in plastic resin creates a composite that is easily manipulated during fabrication, and which quickly hardens into a product that is strong in tension, compression, and shear.

PUR foam is a low-density, rigid foam used primarily for thermal insulation. It has low thermal conductivity, low water absorption, and most importantly, a very high strength-to-weight ratio. The excellent adhesion properties of PUR foam and its chemical compatibility with GFRP allows it to be directly bonded together to form a stressed-skin assembly. For the Novartis Entrance Pavilion most of the structural stress is borne by the fiberglass skin, which is held far from the neutral axis by the PUR foam, and results in a very high moment of inertia.

The roof is constructed of a checkerboard pattern of 460 PUR foam blocks of varying density. Each of these blocks was initially 35.4" × 35.4" (900 × 900 mm) but CATIA modeling and CNC-controlled machines cut them into the desired shape, including all necessary recesses. Upper and lower surfaces of the foam blocks curve to radii that change continuously. The blocks were assembled into four large pieces measuring 18.4' × 60.7' (5.6 × 18.5 m) and hand-wrapped longitudinally with multiple layers of GFRP to bind the individual blocks into a structural unit. These four modules were transported to the construction site and carefully assembled on elevated scaffolding. They were epoxy-bonded on the abutting faces and hand-laminated once more on the faces to create a seamless, monolithic body. A top coat of polyester gel contained modifiers to assure waterproofing and resistance to UV light.

Approximately 100 small-scale tests were done to assist the dimensioning and detailing of the GFRP laminates, including tensile tests on the laminate strips and shear tests on overlapping joints. Four large-scale tests were performed on prototypical beams to verify various aspects of dimensioning, including large-scale tensile strength of face sheets, buckling resistance of face sheets and webs, tensile strength in thickness direction at face sheet deviations, creep behavior, and shear lag in face sheets. During fabrication of the final pieces, quality control of the laminate structure was assured by cutting 1.6" (40 mm) diameter specimens out of the face sheets. The laminate thickness was measured and the configuration of the glass fibers was checked after burning off the polyester matrix.

In addition to being an excellent insulator in this sometimes-cold climate, the roof's extensive overhangs shade the tall glass walls at the south and west from the sun.

The structural glass walls use pairs of laminated glass fins perpendicular to the primary insulated glass facade elements. Vertical steel tension rods anchored to steel embeds within the roof are located between the glass fins to resist potential uplift of the roof assembly.

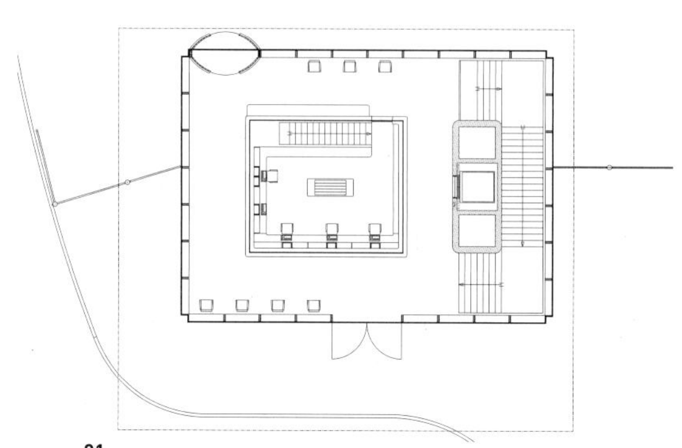

01

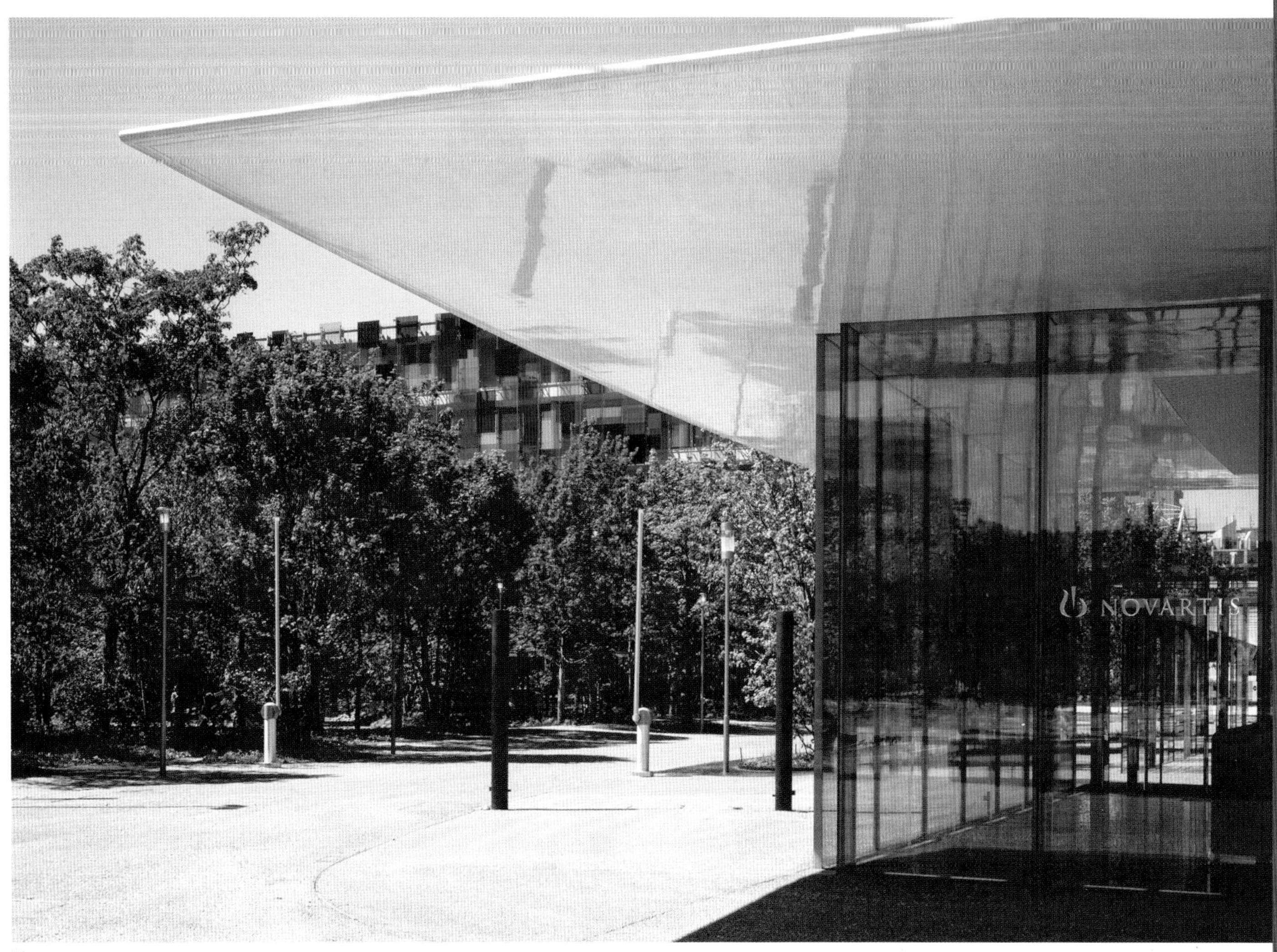

02

03

01 Ground-floor plan

02 Tapered GFRP-laminated roof assembly cantilevers beyond the structural glazing that supports it, providing shade for interior spaces

03 Pavilion at entry to campus from southwest

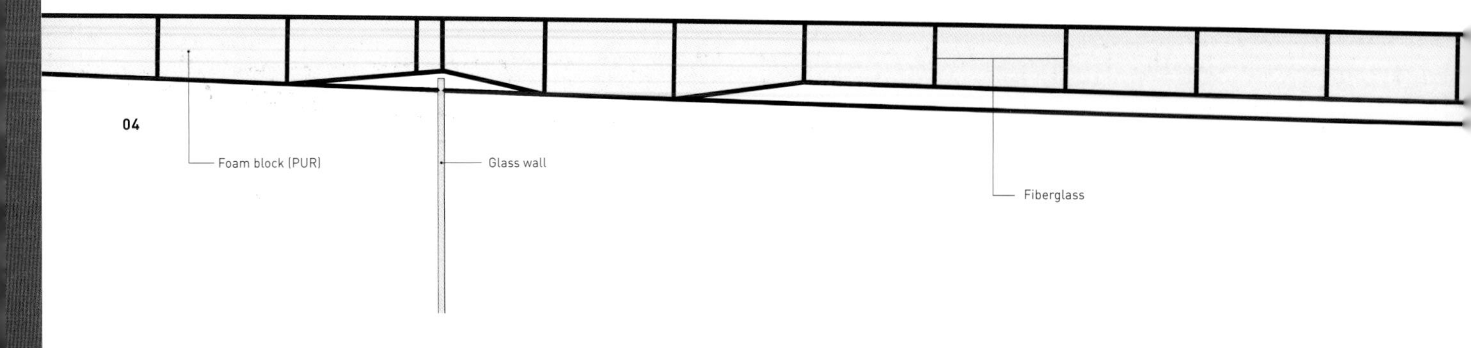

04

05

06

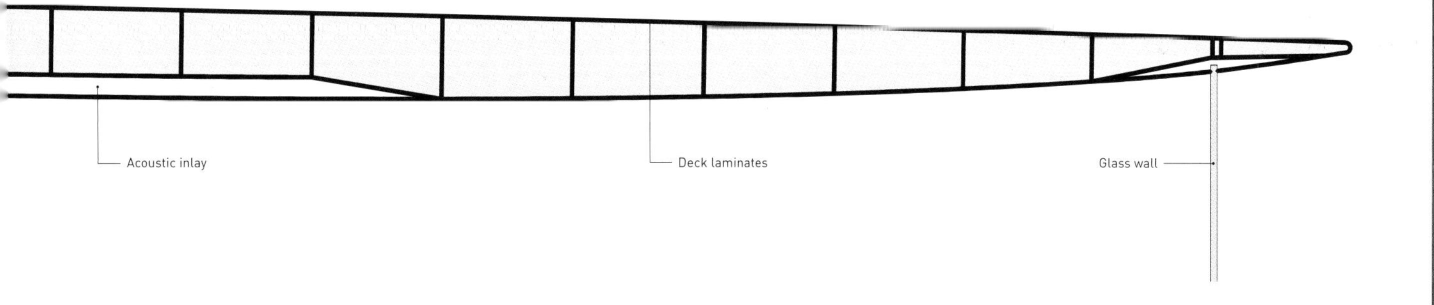

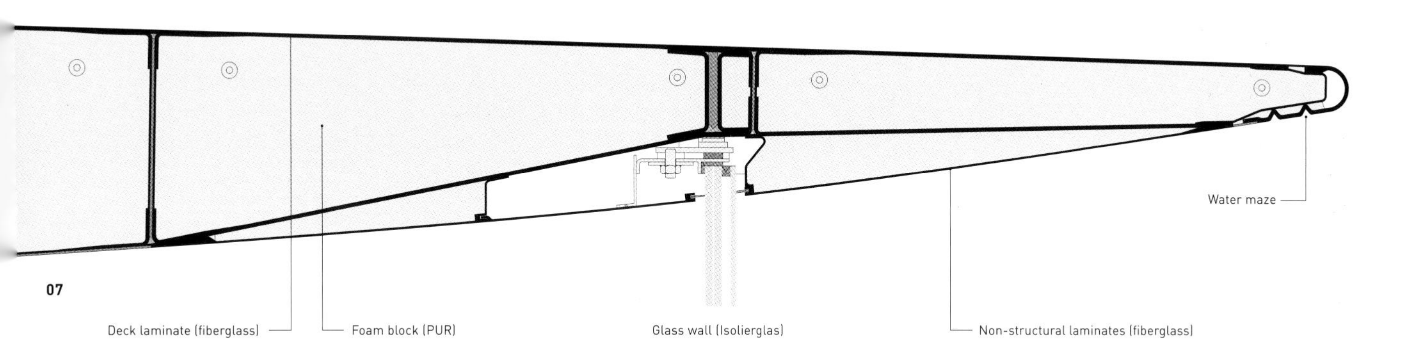

07

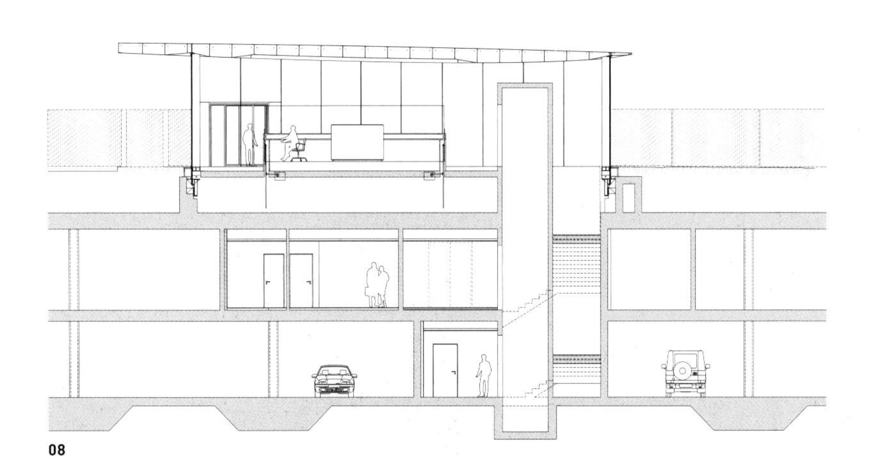

08

04 Section through composite GFRP/PUR foam roof assembly

05 Textile acoustic panel suspended below composite roof assembly

06 Installation of one of four composite roof sections

07 Detail at edge of roof assembly at connection to structural glazing

08 Section through pavilion and subterranean parking

UK Pavilion at World Expo 2010

Shanghai, China — Heatherwick Studio
Cast and extruded acrylic

DESIGN INTENTION

The theme of the 2010 Shanghai World Expo was "Better City, Better Life," which focused on sustainability. Heatherwick Studio won the competition to design the UK's pavilion. Nicknamed the "Seed Cathedral," the pavilion contains over 200,000 seeds, collected from all over the world and encased in over 60,000 acrylic rods that gently sway in the breeze.

The pavilion's architecture is a manifestation of its exhibition contents. It also provided sizable public open space at the Expo, and managed to find a simple idea that was strong enough to stand out amid the many other high-energy pavilions, all competing for attention. Heatherwick intentionally designed an understated, simple building to house a rich idea. Its purity is intended to make it memorable.

MATERIALITY

Over 60,000 slender transparent acrylic rods pierce a CNC-routed steel and wood composite box to create the Seed Cathedral's unique pixelated texture. The seeds, many acquired from Kew Gardens, near London, were incorporated into cast acrylic nodes at the end of each acrylic rod, creating a transparent showcase for each tiny cluster of seeds. The rods draw light into the structure during the day, illuminating the seeds inside. At night, precisely placed LED lighting fixtures direct light into each individual rod, backlighting the seeds and making the pavilion glow. Both extruded and cast acrylic elements were used in this project; each material contributed its own unique properties to the finished product.

TECHNICAL

The little-seen armature that holds the acrylic rods is a large rectangular box, framed with laminated veneer lumber and faced with plywood on the inside and outside surfaces. Holes for the rods were carefully calculated using digital tools, then CNC-routed into the plywood to hold them at the desired position and angle.

The clear acrylic rods average 24.6' (7.5 m) in total length, and extend approximately 16.4' (5 m) outside the wood armature. The rods are 0.8" × 0.8" (20 × 20 mm), and are centered approximately 4" (100 mm) apart. Two-thirds of the rod's length is encased in a 1" × 1" × 0.08" (25 × 25 × 2 mm) wall-thickness extruded aluminum sleeve as it passes through the wood box, simultaneously securing each rod in place. The sleeve leaves only the outermost 5.25' (1.6 m) of the rod exposed without cover. A bright red bead of high-density polyethylene sealant prevents water from entering the sleeve. It also protects the acrylic from scratches where it makes contact with the end of the metal sleeve, which would affect a rod's ability to optimally transmit light along its length. Engineered wood elements were positioned inside the box to not interfere with the passage of the rods.

The acrylic rods were made in two sections: the long extruded portion that extends outside the structure, and the portion that was cast and holds the seeds. The two parts are bonded chemically so that light transmission is not halted at the seam. Larger clusters of seeds were cast in larger cast nodes.

From the exterior, the clear acrylic resembles a glowing halo around the metallic silhouette of the aluminum spikes. While the aluminum prevents the acrylic from drooping or snapping off, the rods may deform over time due to creep (the material's response to a sustained load). The rods are thin enough to sway in a breeze, but the assembly was designed to withstand significant winds.

01 Section of "Seed Cathedral" elevated above other parts of exhibit

02 Exterior view

03 Site plan

04 Seeds in cast acrylic nodes

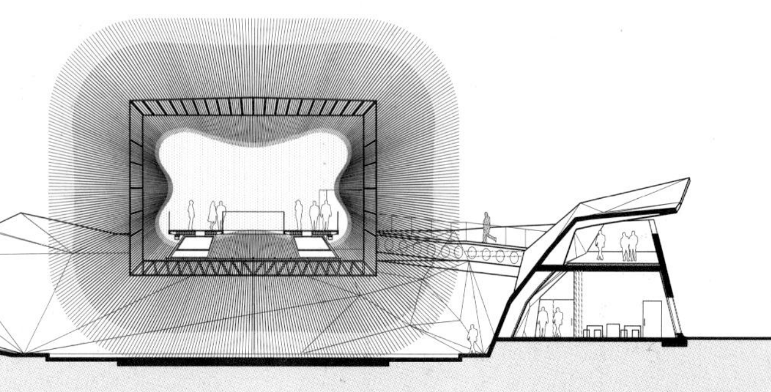

01

02

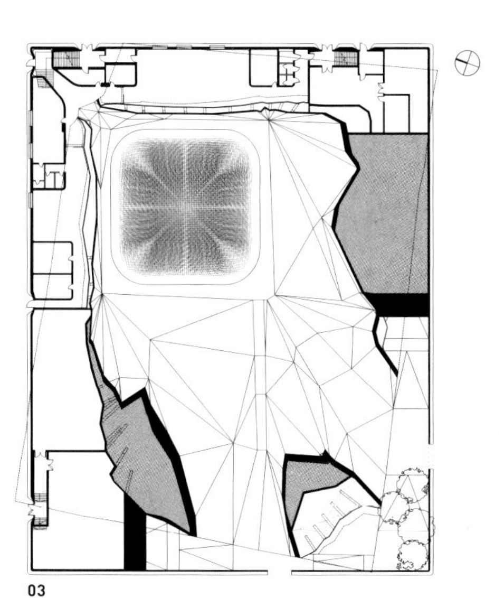

03

04

05 Interior space showing 60,000 glowing seed nodes

06 At dusk the light-transmitting quality of the acrylic rods is apparent from the outside

07 Exterior view

08 Elevation and section of acrylic rod assembly

09 Detail through acrylic rod and aluminum sleeves, at pin that fixes their position in frame

10 Details of LED light-source embedded in each acrylic rod

11 Details of high-density polyethylene cap

12 Section and plan detail

05

06

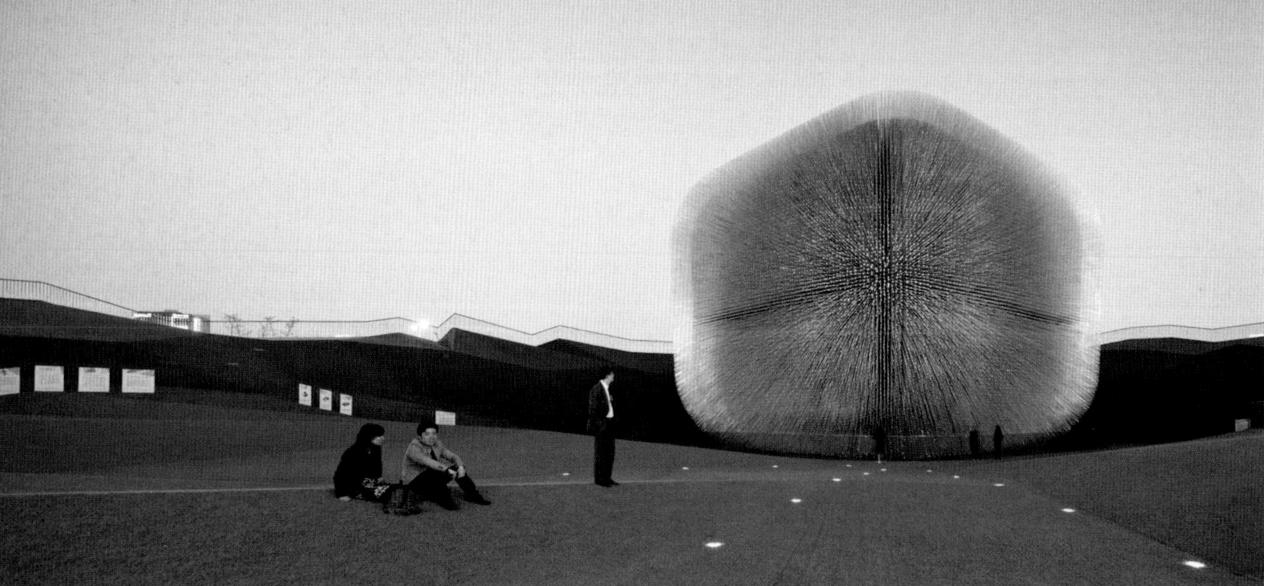

07

INTERIOR END

EXTERIOR END

Elevation

1 20 × 20 mm clear extruded acrylic rod
2 25 × 25 × 2 mm wall, extruded aluminum tube
3 30 × 30 × 2 mm wall, extruded aluminum tube
4 Clear acrylic bulb with seeds cast inside, bonded to extruded acrylic rod

Section

1 20 × 20 mm clear extruded acrylic rod
2 HDPE end cap to provide friction joint and partial waterproof seal
3 25 × 25 × 2 mm wall, extruded aluminum tube
4 2× silicone O seal to provide waterproofing
5 30 × 30 × 2 mm wall, extruded aluminum tube
6 Secondary fixing 3 mm steel pin glued in position
7 Reflective wedge cut off the acrylic rod
8 Light cast by LED reflected toward both ends
9 Aluminum LED housing cover
10 Silicone-sealed LED and cover to provide waterproof seal
11 Silicone O seal to provide waterproofing
12 PMMA bond joint
13 HDPE end cap to provide partial waterproof seal
14 Clear acrylic bulb with seeds cast inside, bonded to extruded acrylic rod
15 Seeds

08

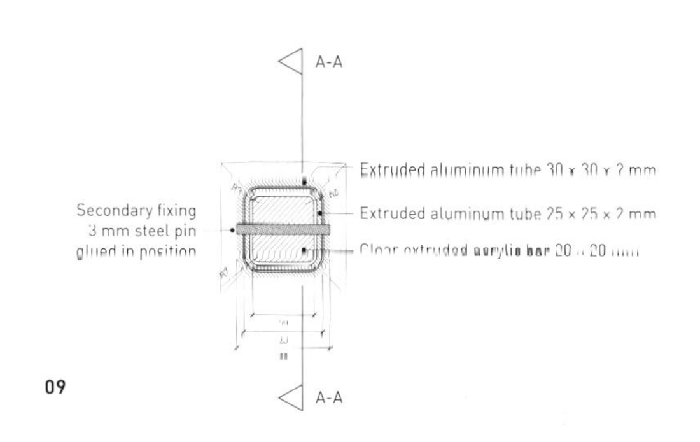

09

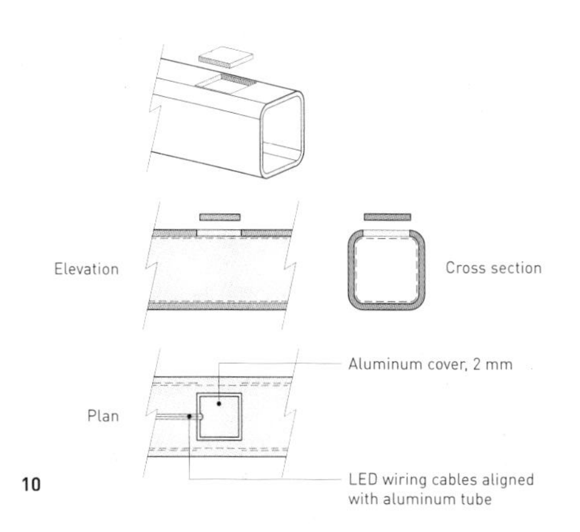

10

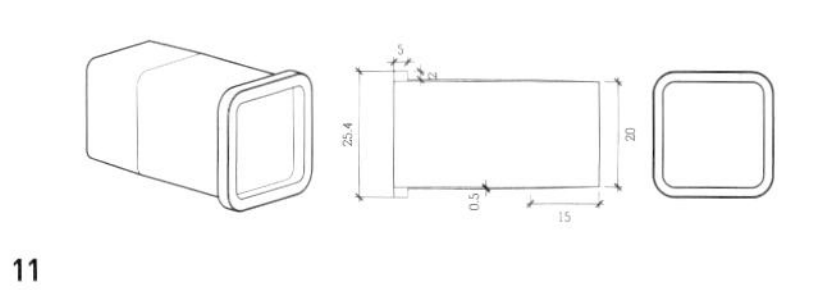

11

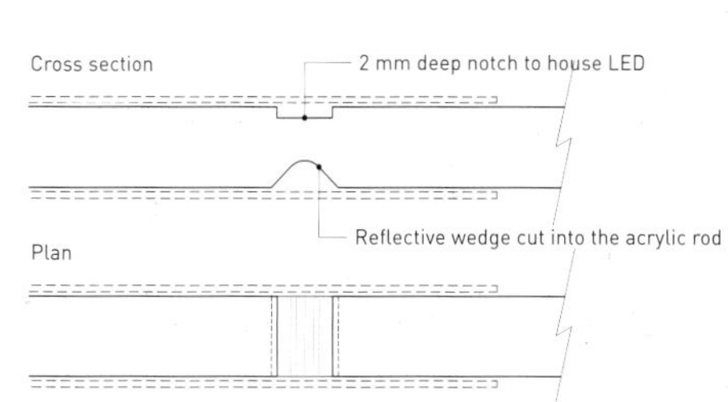

12

Cellophane House

New York, New York, USA — KieranTimberlake Architects
Adapted polyethylene terephthalate film

DESIGN INTENTION

This project was part of the Home Delivery installation, an exhibition on the factory-produced house at the Museum of Modern Art (MoMA) in New York City in 2008. The 1,800 sq. ft. (167 sq. m) residential prototype contained two bedrooms, two bathrooms, and a living/dining space, as well as a carport and a roof terrace. This basic strategy is designed to be mass-customizable, and can be adapted to a range of site conditions including climatic factors, solar orientations, slopes, and adjacencies. The client can also choose materials, colors, and textures. One of the goals was to create a fully recyclable prototype; the other was to maximize each material's functional performance with minimal mass.

This housing prototype demonstrates highly sustainable strategies by using photovoltaic cells that collect energy, an active double-wall system to control temperature, and a customizable skin that provides proper daylighting.

MATERIALITY

The skin of the Cellophane House uses a material called SmartWrap, the second version of a product first developed by these architects in 2003. Developed as an alternative to the thickness and bulk of conventional walls, SmartWrap was developed to be a thin, lightweight composite that integrates various systems (lighting, power, climate control, and information display) into the skin itself. Lighter and thinner than glass, SmartWrap also has lower total embodied energy and minimal volume of material, and is easily manipulated.

SmartWrap is not actually cellophane (which is made out of cellulose); rather, this skin is a PET film. PET is colorless and transparent, inexpensive, quick drying, and mildew resistant, with a low moisture absorption and a relatively high mechanical strength. It is also a major part of an established post-consumer recycling stream, so it was a logical candidate for this experiment. Ink-jet printing and roll-coating onto PET can be done under normal room conditions, eliminating the cost and logistic complexity of clean-rooms, high temperatures, and vacuum manufacturing.

This particular application of PET film exploits many of its virtues, but also reveals some vulnerabilities—it can be abraded or dented by impact (although it will not shatter) and it is vulnerable to fire (but will not support combustion or flame spread). Rather than a robust barrier, this is a wall system that relies on multiple layers of specialized elements to comprise the envelope. It is easily replaced, and has a low environmental impact.

During the three-month demonstration period at the MoMA exhibit, there were no problems with strength, discoloration, or UV degradation of the PET. After the exhibition, the house was unstacked from the top down, disassembled, and placed in storage for re-deployment at a new location. The SmartWrap panels remain intact for possible future use.

TECHNICAL

The structural frame is chiefly made of an off-the-shelf system of aluminum extrusions and connections by Bosch Rexroth. It has many applications, but had never before been used as the primary structural system for a building. The kit of parts can be assembled quickly with bolted connections, ensuring each element could be disassembled, modified, or exchanged with ease. Some standard aluminum structural elements such as channels, angles, and grating were also used. For this urban location, units of construction were assembled in nearby shops and then transported to the site, where they were quickly assembled without special tools or skilled labor. These are all compatible metals, will not rust, and do not need finishing.

Each SmartWrap panel in this project consists of four 0.12" (3 mm) layers of PET film secured to the extruded aluminum frame. This includes an outer transparent weather barrier, a layer coated with thin-film photovoltaic cells, a layer engineered to repel solar heat and UV light, and another interior layer. Air space between the layers acts as a vented cavity to trap heat in the winter and vent it to the exterior in the summer.

To make these SmartWrap products, KieranTimberlake devised a custom fabrication table to stretch the PET film to a variety of frame sizes—a total of seventy-four sheets. Thin-film photovoltaic cells, thin-film batteries, and LED lighting circuitry were then accurately printed onto the film. The PET film layers are attached to the aluminum frames by bolting them between a frame and a custom panel insert. The aluminum frame can also receive conventional glass wall panels in some locations, as well as solid roof and floor cartridges in others.

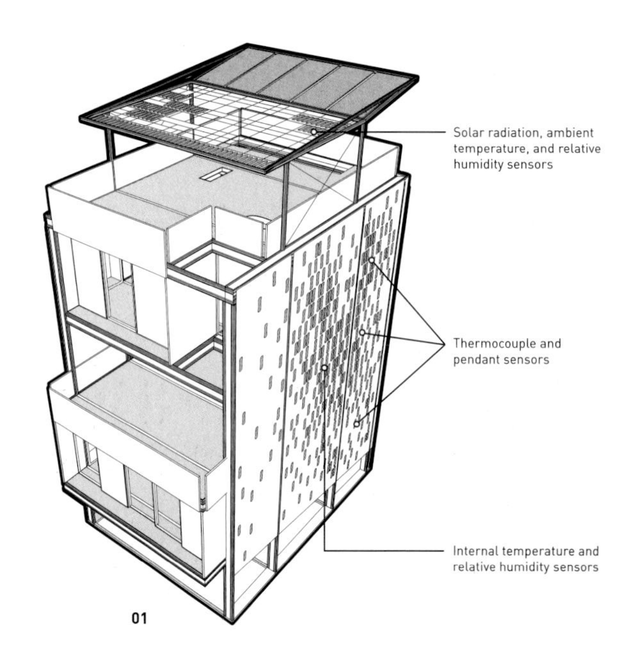

01

01 Locations of light and temperature sensors applied to PET SmartWrap skin on elevation

02 Section through double-skin assembly showing intended performance

03 Interior view of elevated floor

04 Exterior view during MoMA exhibit

05 PET SmartWrap films are secured to metal frame

06 Application of technology to PET film on custom fabrication table

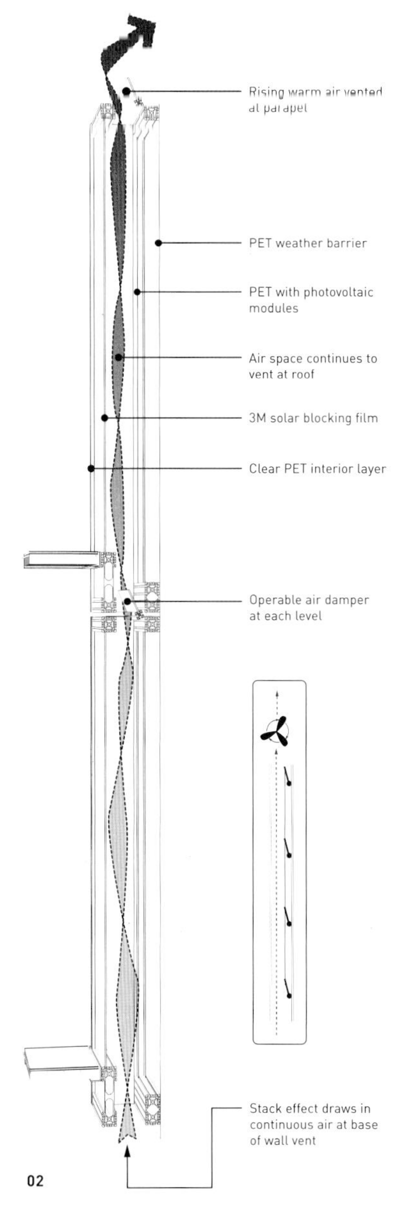

02

04

05

03

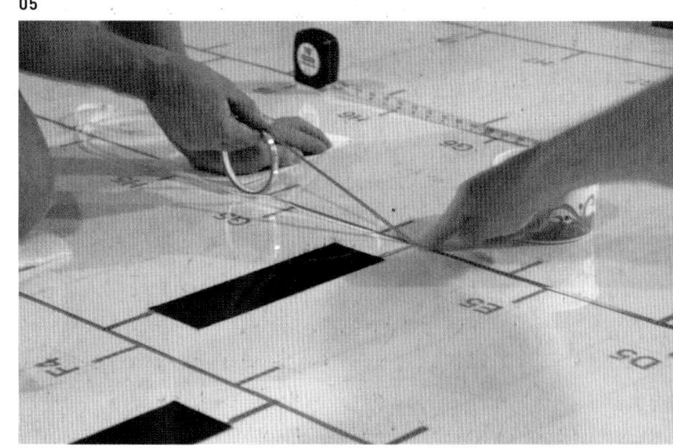

06

Anansi Playground Building

Utrecht, The Netherlands — Mulders vandenBerk Architecten
Corian acrylic polymer

DESIGN INTENTION

This daycare facility complements the surrounding playground and park, providing interior play spaces and related support functions. The 1,600 sq. ft. (150 sq. m) building is a linear scheme composed of three squares. Each interior playroom engages an individual facade, and has a specific orientation to an outdoor space.

The building divides the playground in half with one side used chiefly by teens and the other by younger children. The building's interior features bright colors, simple furniture, and child-appropriate elements like the durable interactive wall treatments (such as blackboard or magnetic shapes) inside each room, which the children use to give each space a particular identity. The design invites children to play, discover, and invent games of their own. The interior's ever-changing graphics contrast with the permanent design of the exterior wall surfaces.

MATERIALITY

Corian was developed by DuPont, and has been used for more than forty years in interior applications, primarily in kitchen, bath, and lab environments, where its impermeability and hardness are highly valued. In the past twenty years it has been adapted for use in windowsills, outdoor furniture, and lighting fixtures. This is only the second application worldwide of Corian on a building exterior, and the first in The Netherlands.

The building's linear form is wrapped with simple, well-proportioned white walls that are decorated with characters found in fairy tales from around the world. A local graphic design studio, Design Arbeid, together with the neighborhood children, selected the various fairy-tale images to be CNC-milled into the Corian facade. The art engages the children with a sense of playfulness. The building surfaces became decorative but also meaningful to the children and community.

TECHNICAL

The opaque portions of the building's walls are made of large white Corian solid surfaces. The Corian panels are 23.6' × 11.5' (7.2 × 3.5 m). They were initially manufactured as eight 2.9' × 11.5' (0.9 × 3.5 m) panels. Each was milled with its unique graphic pattern and then glued together at the site using the manufacturer's proprietary color-matched acrylic epoxy. These seams are nearly invisible because they were sanded and polished after being joined.

The Corian panels in this project are 0.5" (12 mm) thick. Because the product is uniform in color and texture throughout its thickness, the exterior color and weathering resistance of the milled recesses match those of the panel faces.

The panels were secured to the wood-framed wall by matching aluminum elements that are mounted to both the wall's substructure and the back of the Corian panels. The panels were then simply hung onto the fixed substructure. Air circulates naturally behind the panels, maintaining equivalent conditions on both sides to deter distortion.

The facade panels are elevated off the ground plane using a reveal. This isolates the facade panels from any minor settlement of the hard-surface pavers, permits maintenance access, and foremost in the architects' mind, produced a pleasing aesthetic separation between the facade and the hardscape below.

The material homogeneity of this facade treatment is unusual. It is a rare advantage that so few materials look so similar on all surfaces, even when cut. The facade panels in this project march along the face with unnoticed seams, and even turn the corners without major visual interruption of the surface. The material's uniformity of weathering means that the clean, consistent appearance will be long lasting. The architects claim that cleaning has seldom been needed, but if a panel does get dirty it can be cleaned "as easily as washing a window."

01 Plan and primary elevation

02 Exterior view

03 Fairy-tale figures milled into Corian cladding panels

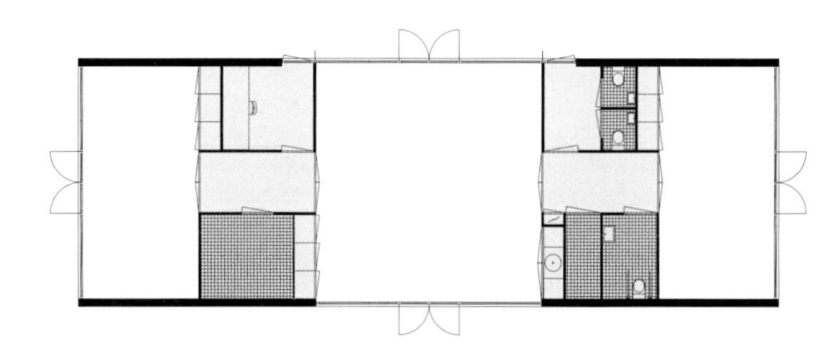

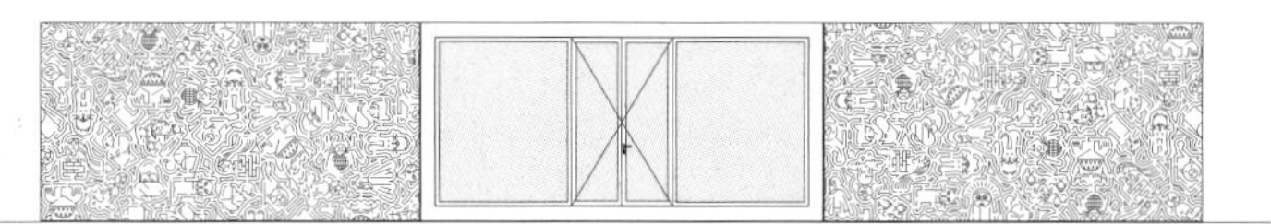

01

02

03

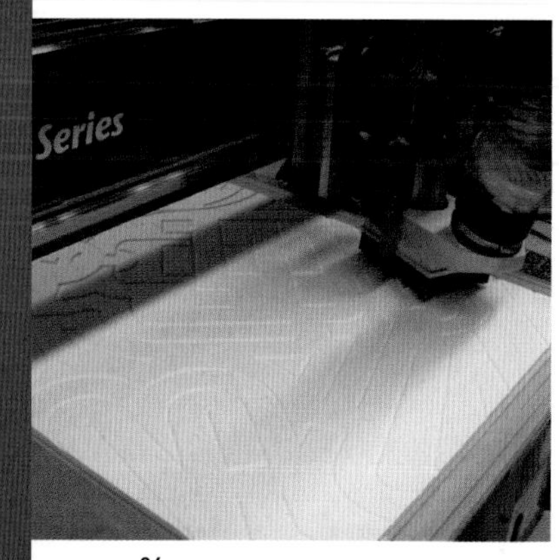

04

05

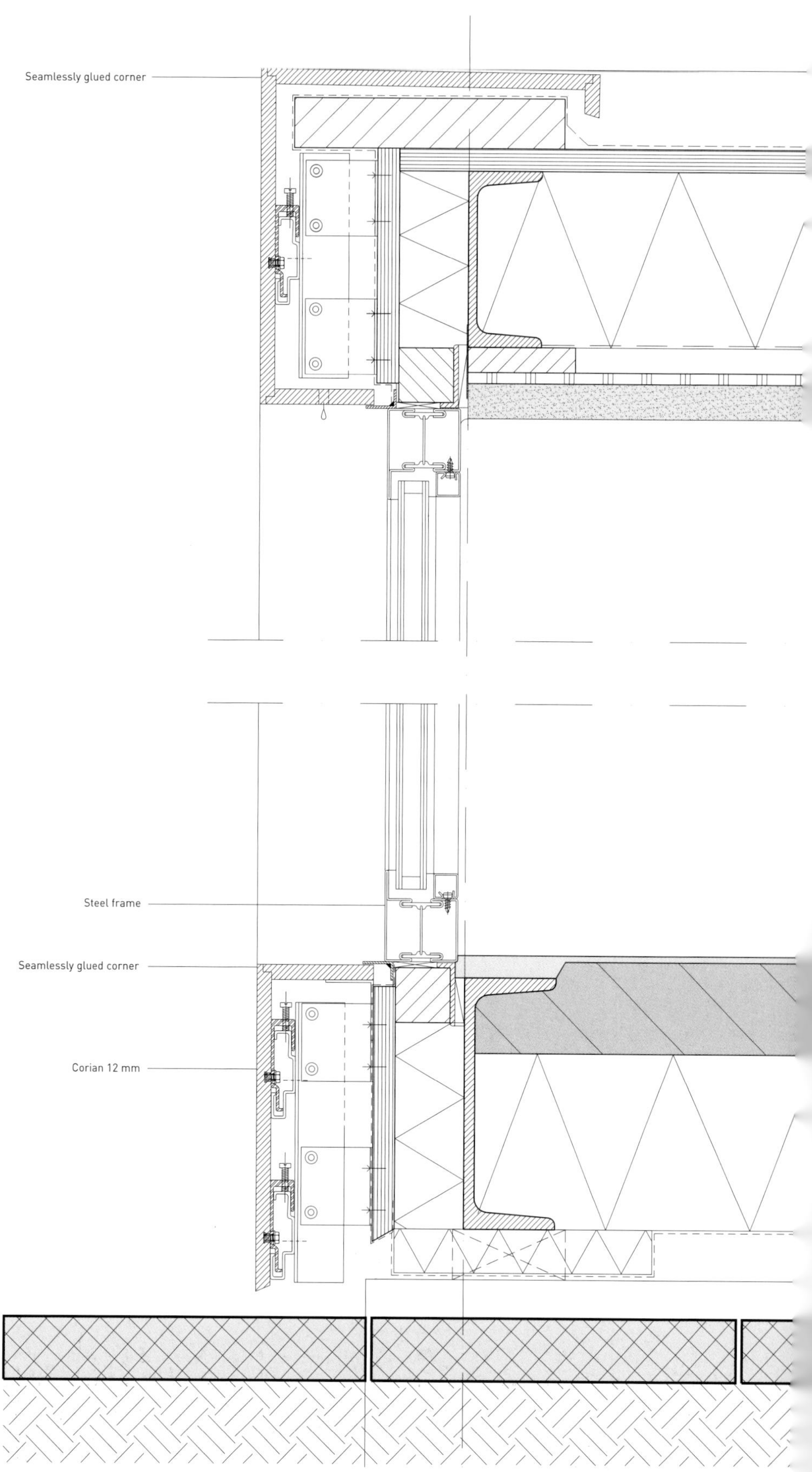

06

04 CNC milling of figures in a panel

05 Detail of graphic showing how Corian panels are uniform in color and texture at any depth

06 Section of rainscreen panels at window

07 Section of rainscreen panels

08 Installation of Corian panel to aluminum frame, secured to weatherproof wall

09 Panel seams are glued and aligned during installation

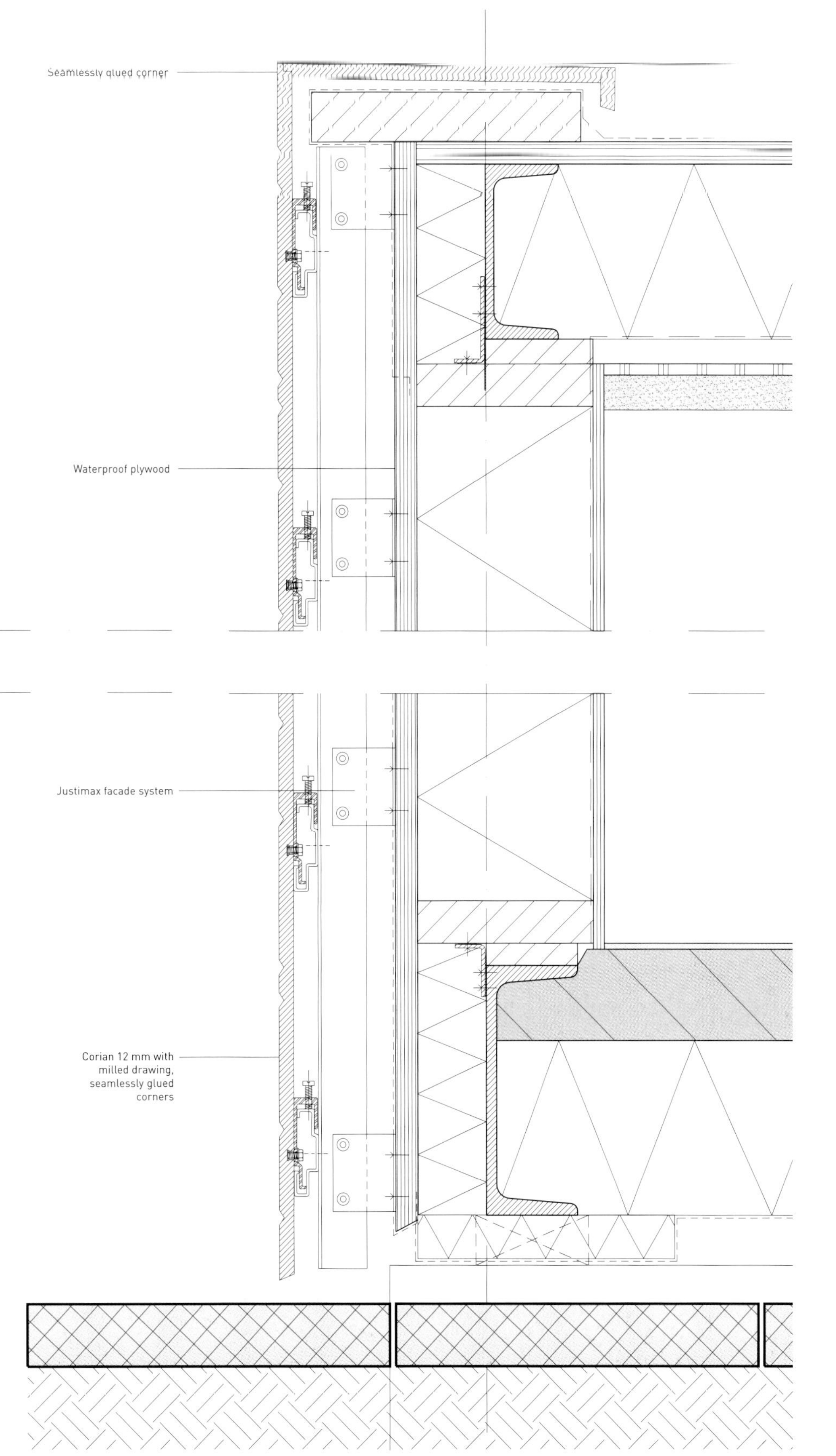
Seamlessly glued corner
Waterproof plywood
Justimax facade system
Corian 12 mm with
milled drawing,
seamlessly glued
corners

07

er 2460

08

09

Miroiterie Retail Building

Lausanne, Switzerland — B+W Architecture
Polytetrafluoroethylene, ehtylene tetrafluoroethylene (ETFE)

DESIGN INTENTION

The architects were asked to place a four-story commercial building above a large belowground parking structure in the city center of Lausanne. This building is glass-walled at the sidewalk level to enable visual exchange between the inside and outside. The three elevated floors are clad in a soft translucent membrane to let in optimum daylight and provide retailers with a neutral display background for their products. The air-inflated cladding system on the elevated floors also reduces dead loads in comparison to standard materials.

The massing of the building is comparable to its neighbors, but its materiality establishes its uniqueness in the city. When illuminated at night, the building becomes an especially memorable beacon in the dense urban fabric.

MATERIALITY

The facades are constructed with translucent, air-inflated cushions. The lightweight character and the light-transfusing qualities of these cushions make this an ideal material for this particular design application.

Major diagonal structural members transfer loads obliquely, and are complemented by minor diagonal wind-bracing elements that organize the faces of the upper floors. The locations of the vertical seams in the fabric membrane are identical to the mullion locations in the curtain wall. The rhythm of the diagonals on the faces of the building agrees with the module of the fabric and mullions.

In this design, the intrinsic vulnerability of fabric envelopes to accidental puncture (or for that matter, intentional intrusion) is addressed by using a conventional glass curtain wall at the public level. Fabric membranes are used only on the elevated wall surfaces.

TECHNICAL

A complex tree of structural members collects the loads from the commercial building floors and delivers them to the load-bearing spine of the parking structure. Each triangular pillow that makes up the building's exterior envelope is actually an assembly composed of four layers of fluoropolymer (otherwise known as Teflon) films. The outermost layer of the membrane is made of polytetrafluoroethylene (PTFE), chosen because it is fireproof and has greater resistance to impact and weather. The inner three layers are ethylene tetrafluoroethylene (ETFE), which is transparent and possesses greater tensile strength, about twice that of PTFE. Both types of films offer significant advantages compared to a glass curtain wall, at only 1 percent of the weight with superior light transmission and much lower installed costs.

Air pressure between each layer is sustained somewhat higher than ambient pressure (between 0.06 and 0.09 psi [400 and 600 Pa]) by a network of small ducts leading to a centralized compressor. Much like layered clothing, the multiple-layer assembly increases the exterior wall's thermal resistance by reducing conduction. It also provides redundancy to insure that the failure of any single element will not extend to the whole assembly.

The membrane sheets are fixed in position at all edges using an anodized aluminum clamping profile that pinches them between two ethylene propylene diene monomer (EPDM) gaskets. The aluminum mullions can be adapted to accept either fabric or glass skins, and are attached to the steel tube framework with stainless-steel hardware.

+3

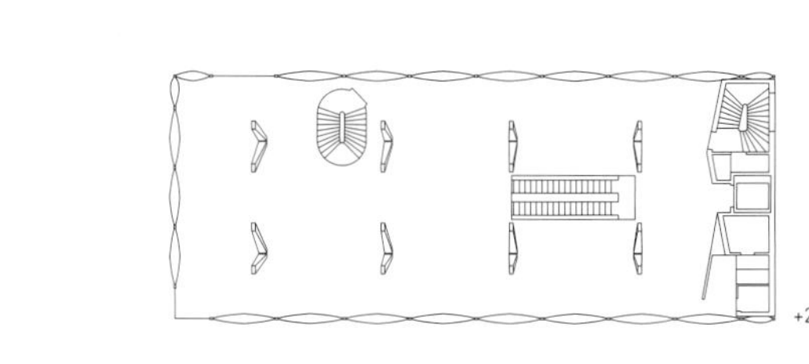

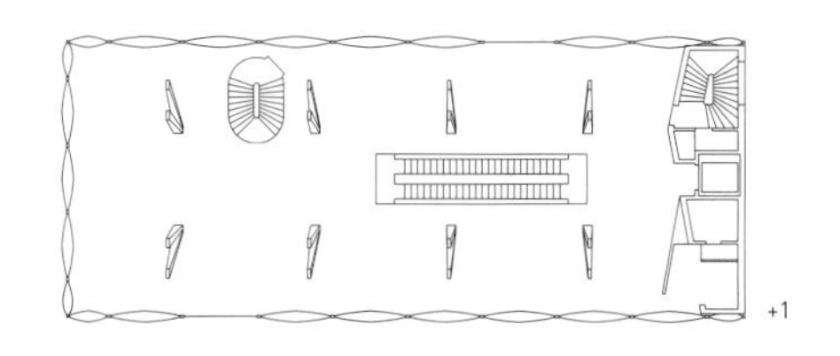

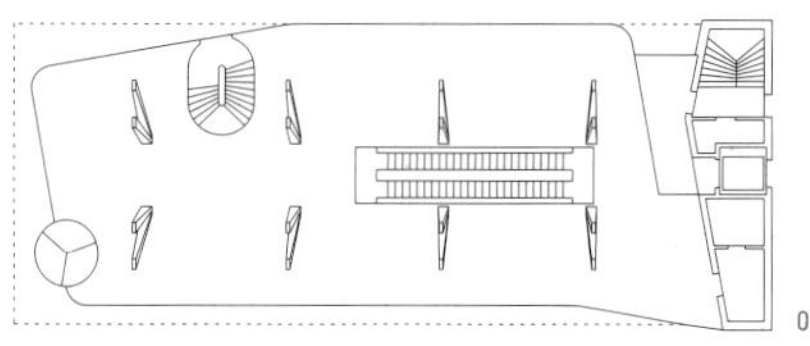

01

01 Ground- and upper-floor plans
02 View from northwest
03 Transverse section
04 Longitudinal section

02

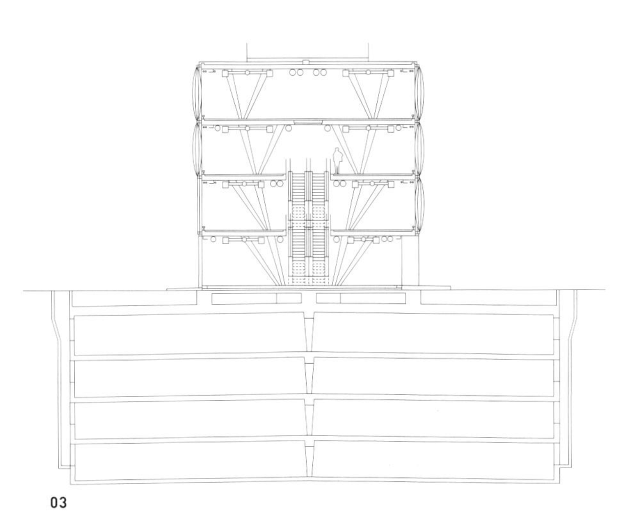

03

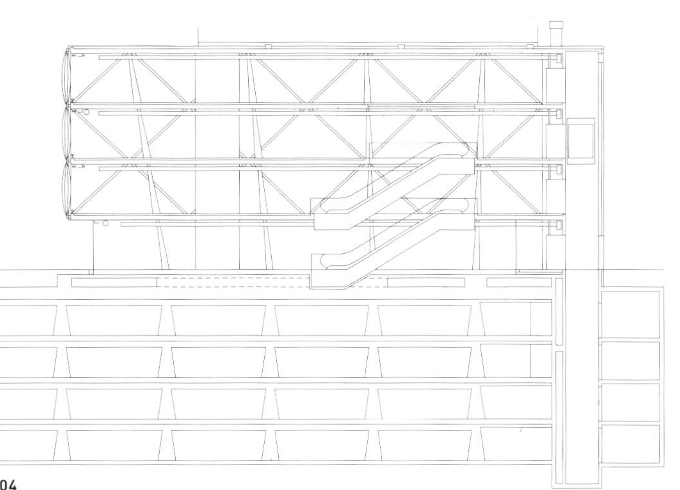

04

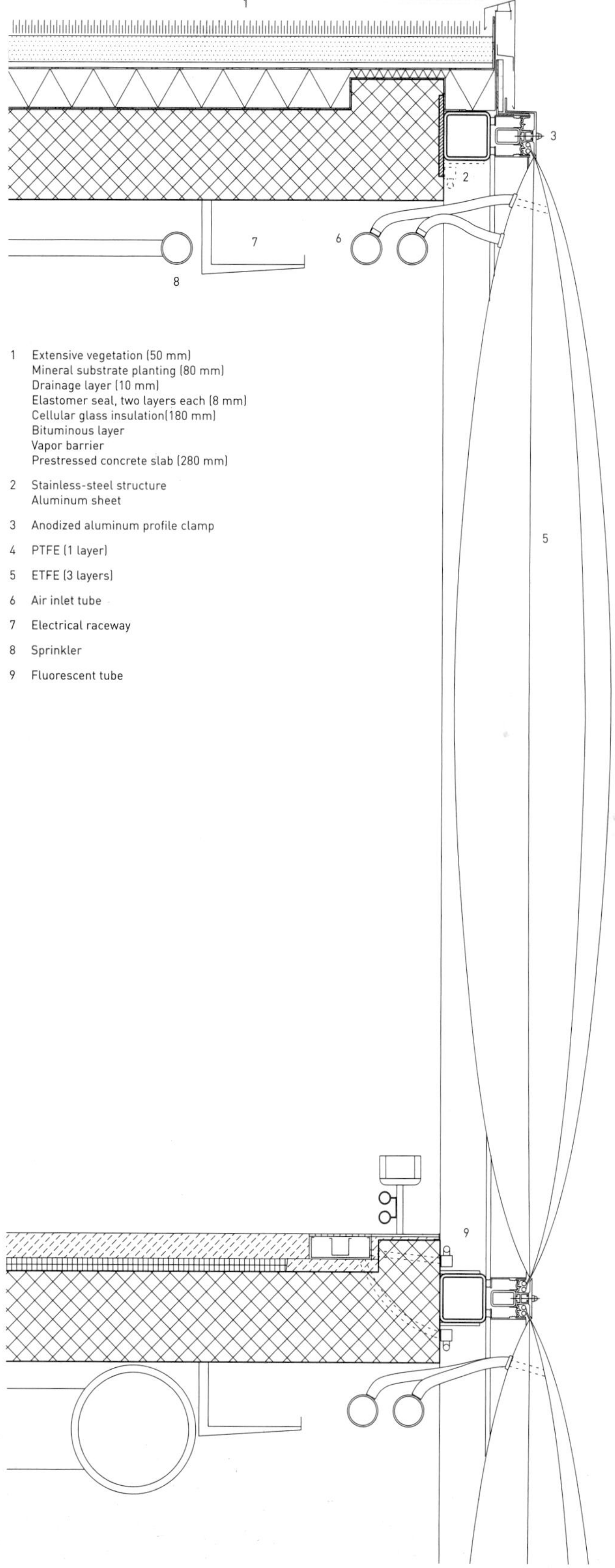

05

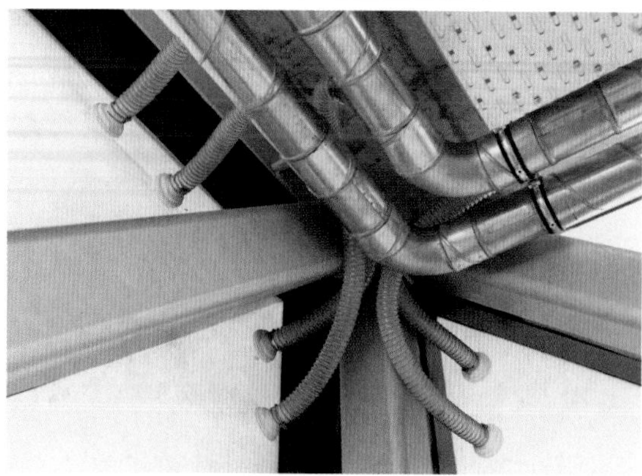

06

05 Wall section at roof and upper floor

06 Air supplies to the fabric envelope

07 Section detail at horizontal mullion with glass and fabric envelope

08 Section detail at typical horizontal mullion

09 Air-inflated PTFE outer layer

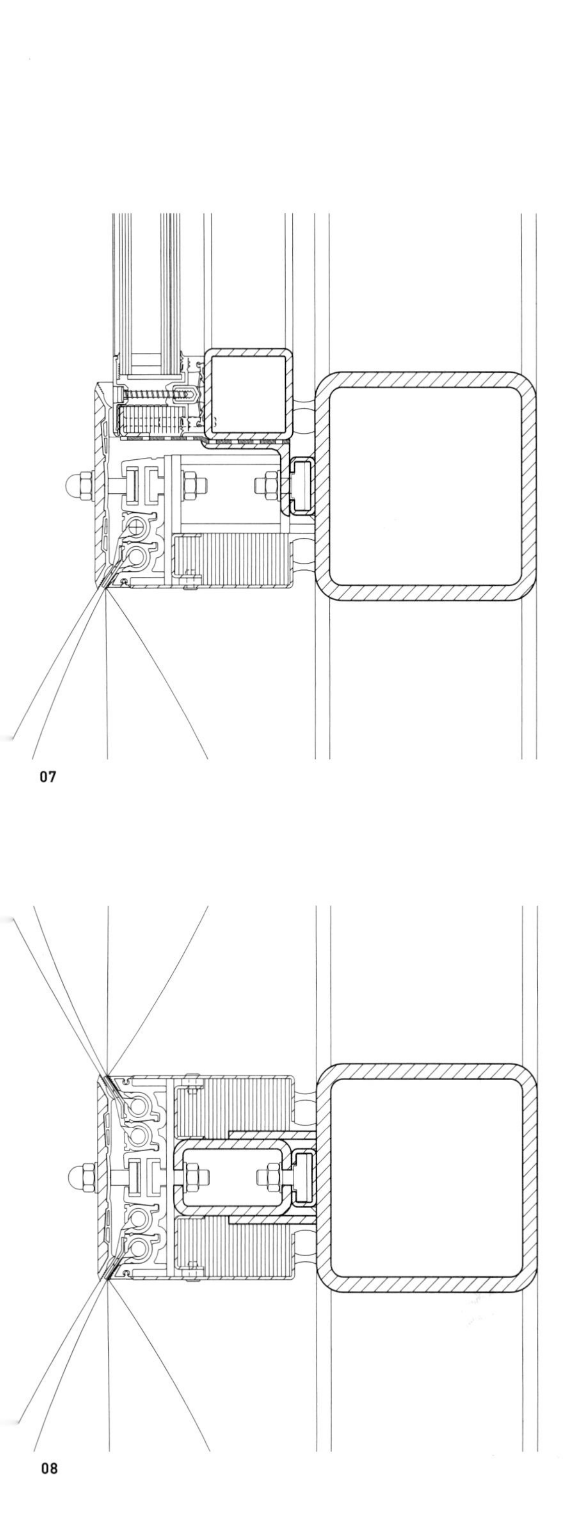

07

08

09

International Committee of the Red Cross Logistics Complex

Geneva, Switzerland — Group8
Coated polyester fabric, polyvinylidene fluoride (PVDF)

DESIGN INTENTION

Symbolic and pragmatic considerations equally influenced the choice of cladding materials for this major depot, from which vital food and medical resources are distributed to the International Committee of the Red Cross (ICRC) delegates around the world.

The building's efficient rectangular plan and section required a watertight, lightweight, inexpensive wrapper, preferably one that would provide natural daylighting. The tent solution met these objectives, while also suggesting the image of a refuge. The white color connotes neutrality, a central theme in ICRC's vocation and in the design of this facility.

The program contains secure warehouse functions, as well as offices and gardens. It also houses the ICRC archives, which contain unique and irreplaceable documents tracing the organization's activities over the years. In order to preserve these documents, the archive rooms were built following strict standards in terms of space, operation, and climate control.

The facility achieves its impressive scale and functional goals through the straightforward use of common construction materials. At the top, the building is a simple white volume, but it becomes articulated by folded surfaces adapted to the program and the undulating ground plane.

MATERIALITY

In reference to the tent concept, this building is a fabric-wrapped frame. The primary structural system is made of steel but other materials are also used based upon their life span, embodied energy, and recycling potential. The steel frame is wrapped with a thickly insulated composite panel system and covered by an outer layer of white synthetic fabric, supported by a secondary structural steel frame. The fabric layer is sometimes snug to the primary frame, and in other locations departs from it to create canopies or shade windows. Though sometimes called canvas, this cladding material is actually a relatively high-performance synthetic material. Canvas is a heavy, coarsely woven natural fiber such as cotton, hemp, or flax, while these synthetic fabrics are refined from petroleum.

TECHNICAL

This particular synthetic fabric, Serge Ferrari's Précontraint 1002, is woven polyester under a polyvinylidene fluoride (PVDF) coating. It can be sewn or electrically welded (as it was here). The high concentration of PVDF finish increases the textile's resistance to UV light, weather, dirt, and pollution, staying cleaner for longer. Since the high-concentration PVDF coating has to be abraded before welding the seams, a lower concentration of PVDF is used on the inner surface, which can be welded without special preparation.

PVDF-coated fabrics are flexible, easily handled, resist cracking, and generally have a life span of fifteen to twenty years depending upon environmental conditions. Précontraint 1002 fabric is 100 percent recyclable. But there are drawbacks: white is the only standard color for PVDF-coated fabrics, so other color choices are limited and must be specially manufactured. PVDF-coated fabrics will maintain their color longer than many other synthetic fabrics.

Fabric structures typically rely on curved surfaces under tension to avoid fluttering of the membrane. In this project, the fabric either continues across the fold in the polygonal shape, or is trimmed and separated from its neighbors by a consistent 2" (50 mm) reveal. In the reveal all hemmed edges of the fabric panels are gripped by a special profile that post-tensions the fabric using threaded hardware to the secondary steel frame. The result is a clean outer elevation, with most fasteners protected from weathering forces.

01 Administrative-floor plan
02 Ground-floor plan
03 North-south section
04 East-west section
05 View from northeast

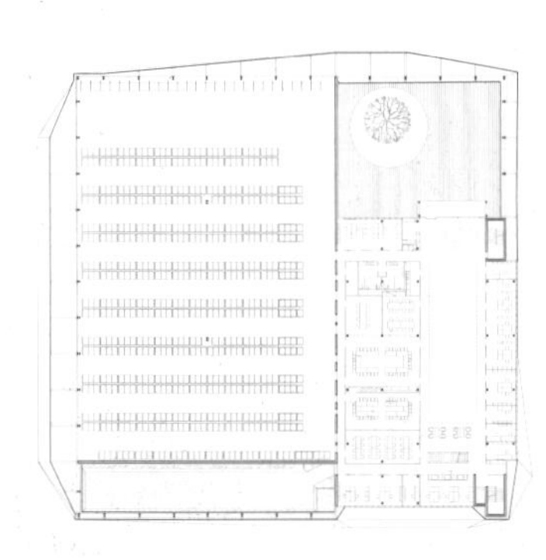

01

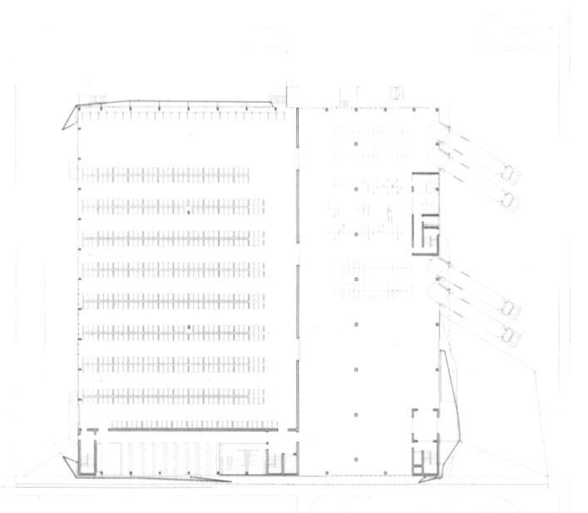

02

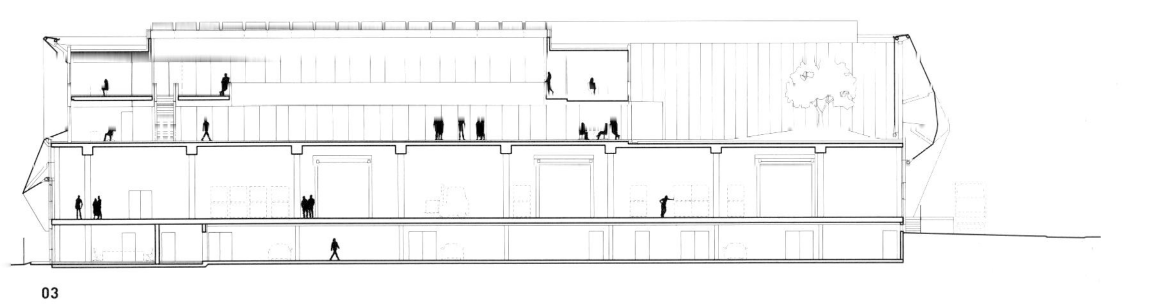

03

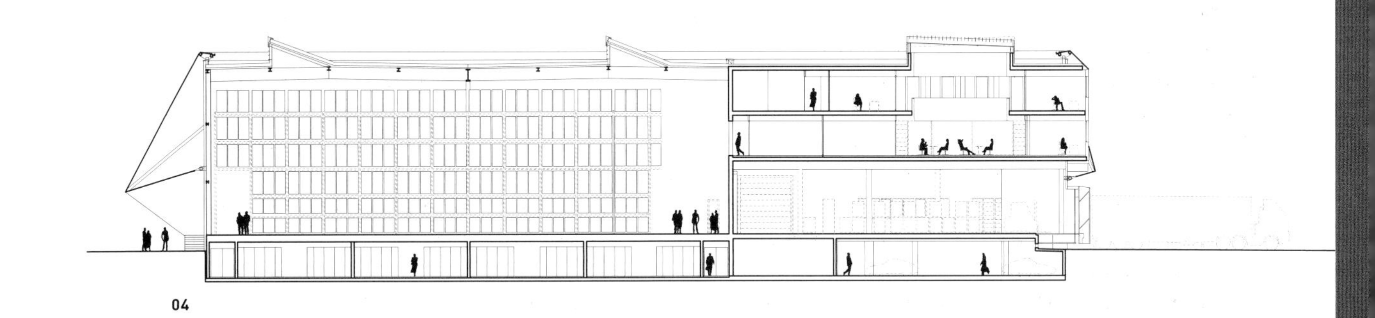

04

05

06

08

07

06 East elevation showing how fabric-wrapped frame shelters entry and defines loading docks

07 Synthetic fabric extends from building wall to keep goods dry

08 Daylit atrium in administrative area

09 Isometric detail of building structure and wall, wrapped by steel frame for fabric envelope

10 Plan detail of fabric facade and frame outside of building wall and structure

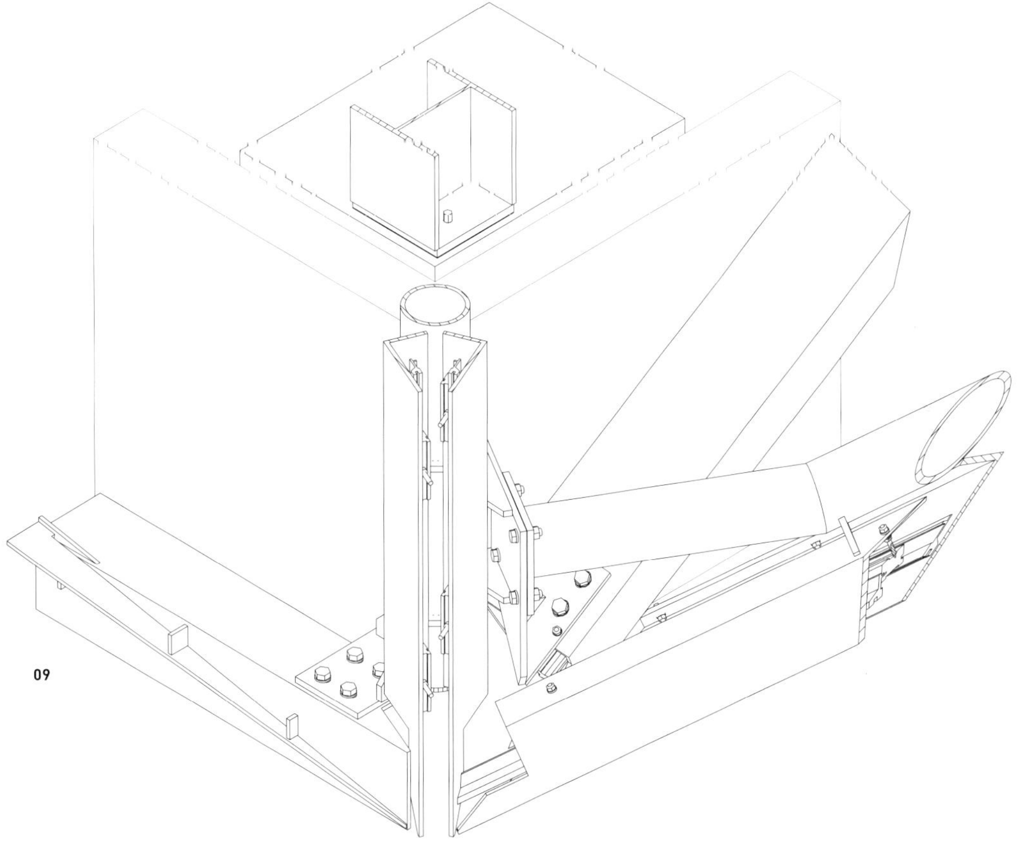

09

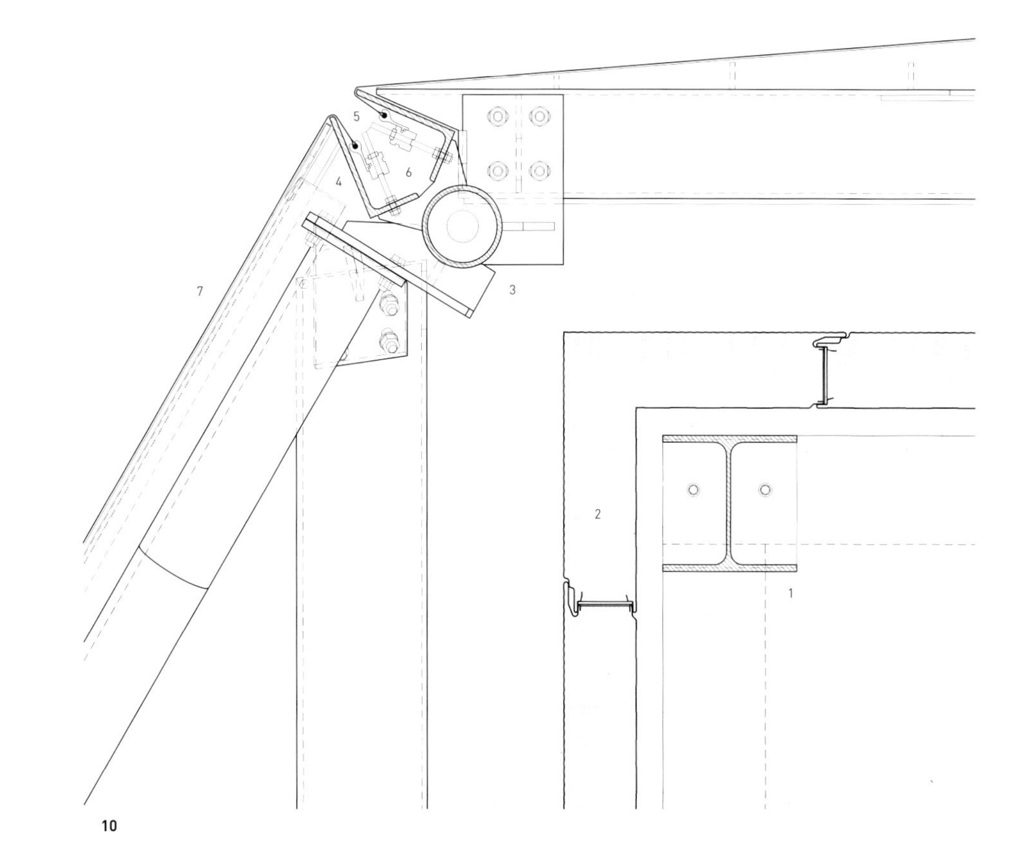

10

1 Steel structure, HEA 260

2 Sandwich panels "Montana MTW LL 140/900" (λ=0.025 W/mK), e=14 cm

3 Vertical structure of the textile sleeve, ROR 152.4 x10

4 Profile corner LNP 200/100/10

5 Profile of canvas attached

6 Canvas clamping profile

7 Textile membrane "Ferrari Précontraint" type 1002 T2 PVDF, white, e=0.1 cm

Plastic House

Gothenburg, Sweden — UNIT Arkitektur
Acrylic, polymethyl methacrylate (PMMA)

DESIGN INTENTION

An existing house was taken down to its foundation and rebuilt to locate daytime spaces on an elevated floor in order to gain better visibility to the surrounding seaside landscape. In the time since the original house was built, this district near Gothenburg has become more densely built, obscuring the sea view that was once available from the ground floor. Swedish building regulations have also changed and now require that at least one kitchen, living room, bathroom, and bedroom be made accessible to disabled persons.

To meet the clients' objectives within the very limited budget, the designers used a simple geometry and a commonly available material palette. The boxlike form keeps the floor plans clean and simple. Any indulgences went to increasing room sizes rather than toward luxurious building materials. In the new configuration, the living spaces and kitchen are on the upper floor and the bedrooms are placed below. The plan will allow a lifting plate to be installed to adjust the house for a disabled person in the future. The upper level is inspired by Craig Ellwood's residences of the 1960s, with spaces interrupted only by sliding doors.

MATERIALITY

The facade's varied materials reflect the different activities that take place inside the house. The ground floor, for instance, is clad with sawn spruce paneling—typical of Swedish vernacular architecture—painted with a mixture of equal parts turpentine, linseed oil, and tar. The upper floor is clad with a homogeneous modern material, white polymethyl methacrylate (PMMA). Large panoramic windows capture the remarkable reclaimed view, while a large steel balcony provides an outdoor space connected to the living room.

TECHNICAL

The PMMA-panel rainscreen was installed on factory-painted steel Z-shaped furring strips and secured to a well-insulated structural wall. Small gaps between the plastic panels serve as vents, while the bottom of the cavity is detailed to discharge any water to the exterior of the wood-clad wall of the ground floor below. The rhythm of the vertical furring strips is faintly visible through the somewhat translucent acrylic.

The acrylic panels are 23.6" wide × 78.7" tall (0.6 × 2 m) and only 0.2" (5 mm) thick. The elevations were designed to require only rectangular shapes of acrylic panels, making fabrication and installation easier. In some locations the acrylic panels are secured to the vertical metal furring strips with a high-strength bonding tape, such as 3M's VHB tape. Here, VHB tape joins the vertical steel furring strips to the back of the PMMA panels approximately 4" (100 mm) inside the vertical edge. By locating the tape joints away from the edges, the architect reduced the amount of thermal expansion at the tape joint. The architect's details indicate the size of the reveals between abutting acrylic panels, as well as the temperature at which that dimension is relevant.

VHB tape has become an increasingly utilized alternative to screws, rivets, welds, and other forms of mechanical fasteners. Unlike screws or rivets that join materials tightly at each fastener, high-strength bonding tape adheres one substrate to another while spreading the stress across the greater length of the joint. The manufacturer claims that materials joined with this tape are held together by a "virtually indestructible weld." The product carries a two-year warranty, but the manufacturer claims a much longer useful service life.

Before its application here, VHB tape had never been applied to PMMA in a non-laboratory setting. Due to manufacturer's specifications, panels using VHB tape could only be installed when the outside temperature was at least 59°F (15°C). Screws were used for connections that were installed below that temperature threshold. The strength of the VHB tape's bond depends on its thickness in relation to thermal expansion. In this case, the tape is 0.04" (1 mm) thick and can accommodate approximately 0.12" (3 mm) of thermal expansion and contraction. Performing within that limit, one can potentially expect a service life of up to fifty years. The experimental use of the two methods to secure the panels will become a test of VHB tape's functionality in such applications. The expectation is that this experiment will validate warranties of much more than two years for future users.

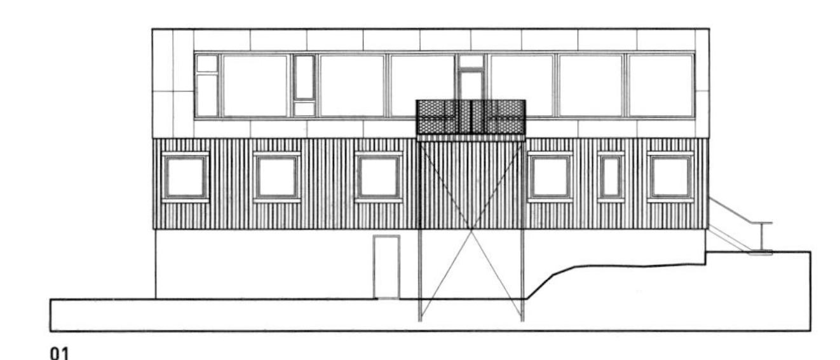

01

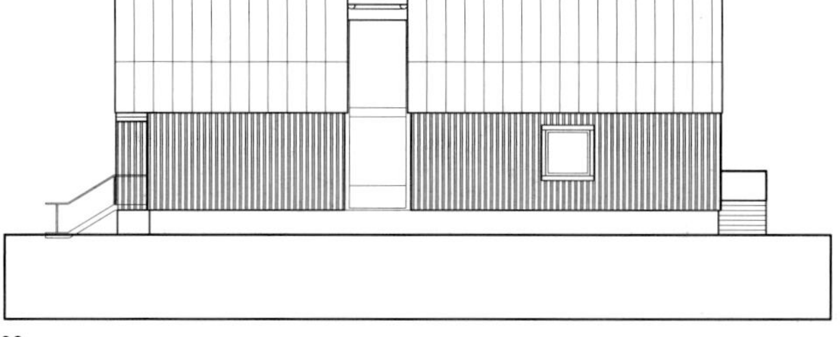

02

03

01 Southwest elevation

02 Northeast elevation

03 View from south

04 VHB-tape-adhered acrylic panels

05 Tests of VHB tape bond strength to acrylic panel

06 Installation of acrylic panels to primed metal vertical furring elements

07 Plan and elevation of acrylic panel installation; note that dimensions of reveal specify relevant temperature to accommodate thermal expansion

08 Section of acrylic rainscreen installation showing cavity drainage and ventilation

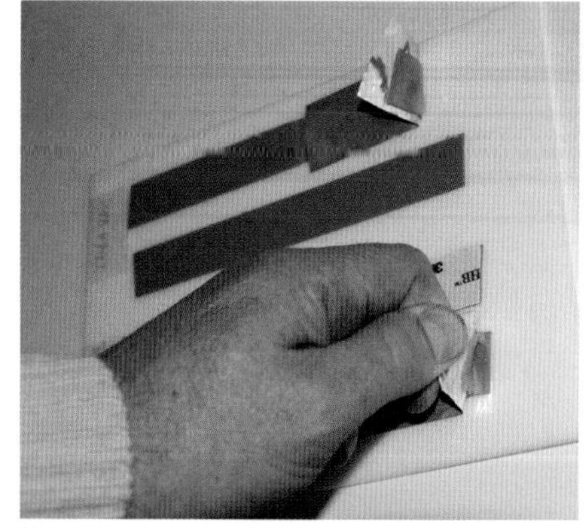

05

06

04

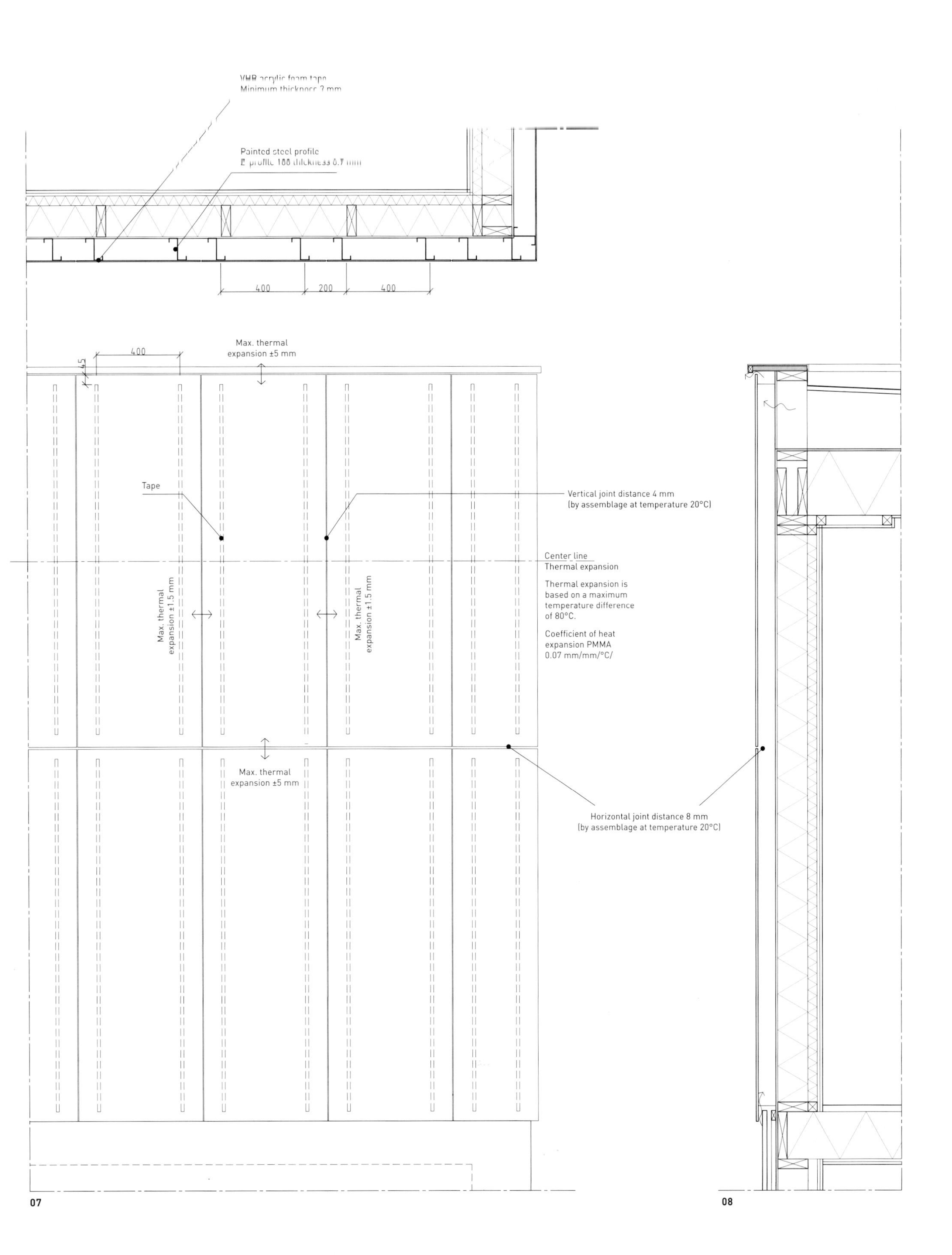
VHB acrylic foam tape
Painted steel profile
400
200
400
400
45
Max. thermal expansion ±5 mm
Tape
Vertical joint distance 4 mm (by assemblage at temperature 20°C)
Center line
Thermal expansion
Thermal expansion is based on a maximum temperature difference of 80°C.
Coefficient of heat expansion PMMA 0.07 mm/mm/°C/
Max. thermal expansion ±1.5 mm
Max. thermal expansion ±1.5 mm
Max. thermal expansion ±5 mm
Horizontal joint distance 8 mm (by assemblage at temperature 20°C)

07

08

MOOM Tensegrity Membrane Structure

Chiba, Japan — Kazuhiro Kojima Lab / Tokyo University of Science
Polyester fabric, tensegrity structure

DESIGN INTENTION

Tensegrity is a term coined by Buckminster Fuller in the 1960s to describe tensional integrity, a structural principle using compression and tension. MOOM was an experimental application of the principles of tensegrity structures in a space-defining membrane. The project was undertaken by the faculty and students at Tokyo University of Science's Kazuhiro Kojima Laboratory, in collaboration with a fabric manufacturer and local structural engineers. MOOM was exhibited on campus for approximately two weeks, where its construction was a festive event that evoked community pride.

The feature that distinguishes this tensegrity structure from its predecessors is that its reliance on the membrane for its tensile capacity; preceding structures used tension cables to make a stable frame, upon which a membrane was placed.

Several objectives guided this experiment: It was intended to be extremely lightweight and to be executed without lifting apparatus, large equipment, or highly skilled labor. Its palette of materials included only the membrane, aluminum compression rods, and ropes to secure it to the ground.

MATERIALITY

The tensile membrane material is a woven polyester fabric developed by Taiyo Kogyo called Shade Azul. This fabric is elastic as well as translucent. The material permits 50 percent of visible light to pass through while blocking approximately 80 percent of incident UV light.

TECHNICAL

Tensegrity structures have two primary characteristics. They only load members in either tension or compression—no members undergo bending stresses—and they employ continuous tension but discontinuous compression elements.

MOOM covered 1,572 sq. ft. (146 sq. m). The clear spans were 85.3' × 24.6' (26 × 7.5 m). It had a maximum height of 13.9' (4.25 m). The single piece of fabric that forms the envelope was only 0.03" (0.7 mm) thick and weighed 7.8 oz/sq. yd. (266 g/m²), in total approximately 220 lb. (100 kg). Exploiting the fabric's elasticity and the capacity to sew twenty-four gathers, the designers were able to create the curvature of the dome-shaped enclosure. Gather locations coincided with sleeve locations, making fabrication more efficient.

A total of 212 aluminum rods were used, of which 131 were compression struts elevated off the ground and had contact only with the membrane. The other 81 rods contacted both the membrane and the ground plane. Varying in length from 2'–9.2' (0.6–2.8 m), the rods were slipped into sleeves or pockets that had been sewn onto the fabric.

01

01 Erection sequence of polyester fabric tensegrity structure

02 Side elevation

03 Plan

04 Illuminated polyester membrane and discontinuous compression members

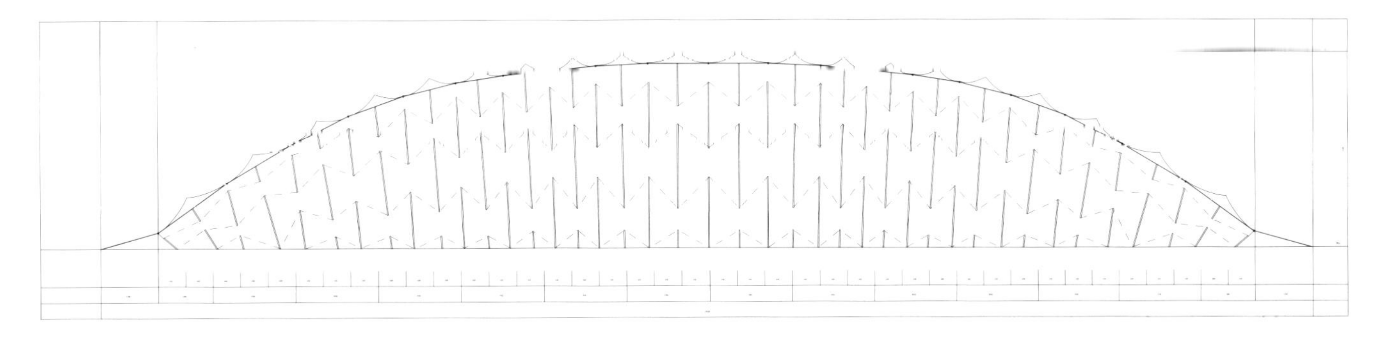

02

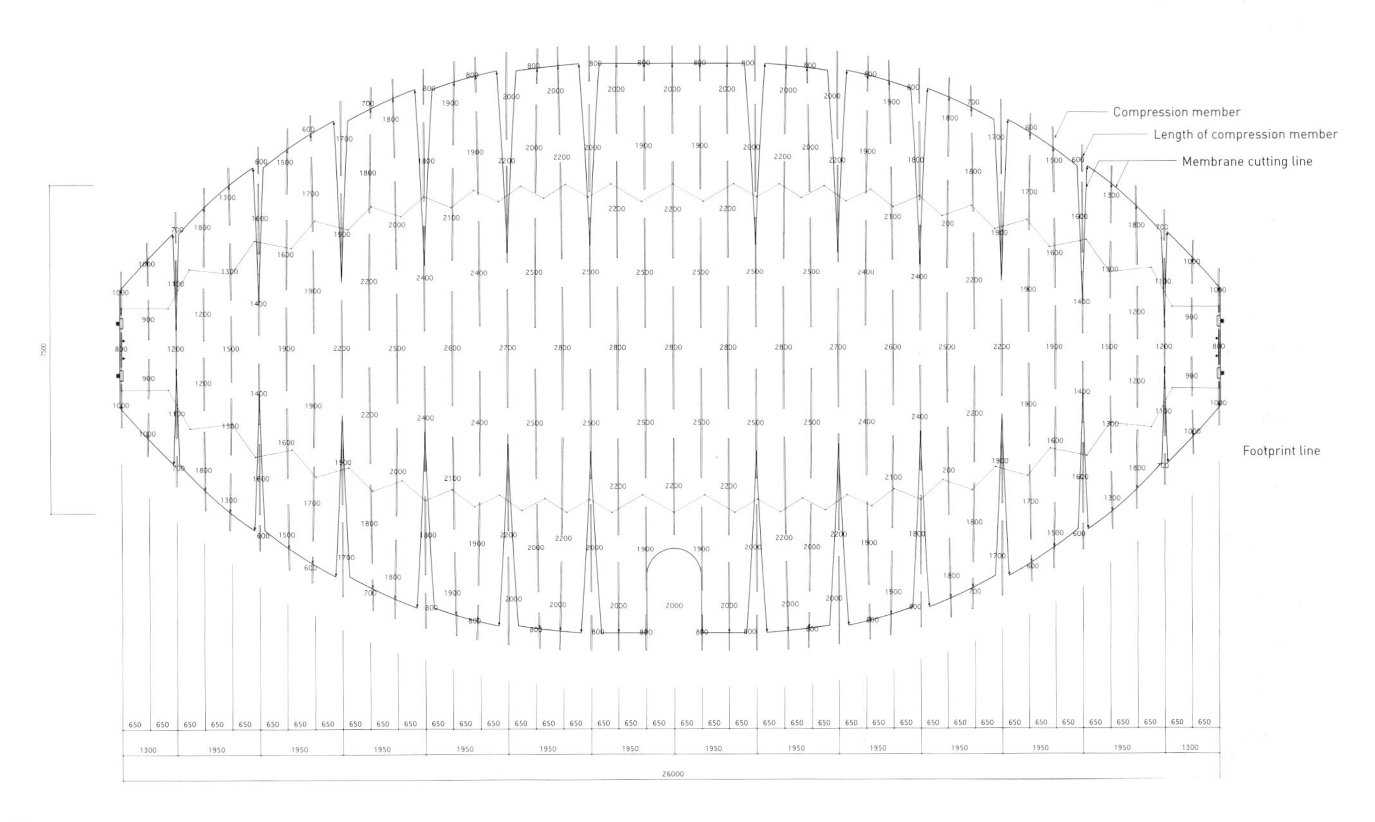
Compression member
Length of compression member
Membrane cutting line
Footprint line

03

04

Masonry

THE BASICS

In some ways masonry is the embodiment of architectural materiality. Masonry is one of the oldest materials and simplest methods of building, enabling early builders to construct as never before seen. It was the first medium to present designers with the endless arrangements possible with a stone or a small unit. The material empowered them for millennia to understand the construction and scale of a building through imagining how a hand-placed stone or brick could be morphed into an architectural masterpiece or a simple utilitarian wall.

Masonry generally refers to the material units of natural stone, concrete, and brick, and is considered a modular construction material. Today masonry most often refers to clay bricks and concrete masonry units (CMUs), but thousands of variants are also viable. Derivative products such as adobe, clay tile, terra-cotta, glass block, cast stone, and autoclaved aerated concrete units are also considered masonry units, because they are relatively small in scale and installed by hand, following the principles of masonry construction. In its broadest definition it covers the use of natural units and manufactured units used for construction. Masonry is best used in a compressive state given its intrinsic physical properties. Since all masonry units are made of minerals that come from the earth, they are reliably durable for use in foundations, pavers, and any functional features implanted in the earth.

Masonry walls, or walls that are built of masonry units, can either be load-bearing or ornamental. There are four types of masonry walls: solid masonry, reinforced, cavity, and veneer. Solid masonry walls were the standard until the beginning of the twentieth century. Solid walls do not contain reinforcing bars, nor do they have continuous cavities within them. It is rare today to see a new building with solid masonry walls due to expense, but they are still valid solutions for some projects.

A reinforced wall allows the wall to be thinner and taller. Reinforced walls typically use steel reinforcing bars and grout or other means to strengthen their load-bearing capacity. The steel rebar cannot be laid in the bed joints, but must be incorporated between *wythes* (a vertical plane of masonry one unit thick) in large core holes (e.g.: concrete block voids) vertically, or in lintel blocks or other special units horizontally. Joint reinforcement and metal anchors can be found in cavity and veneer walls too, but this does not necessarily make them reinforced masonry walls. In areas of high stress, such as surrounding wall openings, steel horizontal joint reinforcements (such as steel lintels or shelf angles) are used. It is also possible to pre-stress or post-tension masonry walls with steel in the hollow voids to give more strength.

Cavity walls are composed of at least two wythes with a continuous vertical cavity separating them. The cavity is an air space (usually 2–4" [50–100 mm] in width) between two wythes and may or may not contain thermal insulation. Masonry hardware or ties connect the wythes, and consideration and precautions for moisture inside the cavity is critical. The main reasons for using a cavity wall is to help resist moisture penetration within the masonry wall; it also improves the wall's thermal properties, sound resistance, and fire resistance.

Veneer walls use a non-structural external layer of masonry, usually brick, backed by an air space. The innermost element of the wall is usually structural, and may consist of wood, metal framing, or another type of masonry such as CMUs. Today veneer walls are the most common type of masonry construction.

Composite walls are cavity walls built of concrete block units that support a stone or brick facing layer. Masonry hardware, anchors, or ties connect the layers together. The multiple materials give it strength as well as a suitable exterior quality.

There are also many types of masonry arches including the Gothic arch, the Roman arch, the segmental arch, the keystone arch, and the crown arch, to name a few notable forms. All types of masonry arches use the compressive strength of the masonry to redirect vertical forces outward and create the open span.

Mortar

While standard sizes in brick can vary, most mortar joints are 0.375" (9.5 mm) to agree with the nominal dimensions of masonry units. Standard tolerances allow mortar joints to be as small as 0.125" (3.17 mm) or as large as 0.75" (19 mm) in size (this also applies to head joints). Mortar (a mix of sand, lime, and cement) needs to have good workability and be durable. More cement in the mix yields greater resistance to frost and varying weather conditions; it also produces greater strength. Lime makes the mortar workable, but also makes it weaker. In structural applications where greater strength is required, a mortar with higher cement content may be specified, but in other applications, a mortar with lower cement content but a bit more lime may be sufficient.

Mortars also come in a wide range of colors to match or contrast the brick. A mortar color close to the brick color produces a more monolithic appearance for the wall. One with a darker color tends to make a wall feel darker and smaller in scale. Masonry wall mock-ups are usually a good idea when using unusual colors of brick and mortar. Mortar joint profiles can be tooled to give different weathering results and different visual effects. Frank Lloyd Wright, for instance, liked to use raked bed joints to emphasize horizontality. Joints can be tooled flush with the masonry for a more monolithic appearance, or can be tooled deep to emphasize the masonry units and give deep shadows between courses.

Mortar is designated in four types: M, high-strength meant for below-grade, frost, or very high compressive loads; S, a medium-strength mortar used for normal compressive loads and weather conditions; N, another medium-strength mortar but generally used always above grade; and O, a medium- to low-strength mortar that is used for non-load-bearing walls and above-grade construction.

HISTORY

Since prehistoric time man has used dried mud as a building material. There were problems with building with dried mud, most apparently its short lifespan and the ultimate deterioration of the material. Cracking and its slow drying time were also problems that were only solved by adding straw or other dry grasses into the mud blocks. Adobe, or sun-dried bricks, have been used for at least 10,000 years, and are still used today in areas where there is insufficient fuel to fire a brick kiln. Parts of the Great Wall in China, which date as far back as 220 BCE, were built with adobe masonry units, and other parts were built with kiln-fired brick.

Kiln-fired brick emerged to meet the need for greater strength and more reliable and durable units. Kilns and brick ovens date back to 2500–2000 BCE. The process of a the kiln-fired brick can be traced back to the Mesopotamians (in what is now Iraq), and was developed simultaneously in the Indus Valley culture (located in what is now India).

Mesopotamians are considered to be not only one of the first cultures to invent the kiln-dried brick but also the most highly skilled, noted for their large-scale brick architecture. Babylon was famous for its impressive ziggurats, stepped towers that stood 50–300' (15.2–91.4 m) tall. What is also striking in these structures is the uniform nature of the bricks in size, color, and shape, demonstrating the consistency of Babylonian brickworks. One can look at these structures and readily understand their construction due to the modularity of the building blocks.

The Greeks used clay masonry in temples around the first century BCE and stone masonry well before this. Roman construction often used fired clay masonry for the load-bearing core of walls, which were then faced with cut stone for a more desirable appearance and durability. The Romans advanced the use of masonry in arches and vaults in palaces, aqueducts, baths, and many large-scale engineering structures. Vitruvius, the Roman architect and author of *The Ten Books of Architecture*, offers a recipe in his second book for a lime mortar. Medieval times brought masonry use to Europe and the Islamic world and gave rise to massive cathedrals, huge fortresses, and walled castle estates. Masonry was essential to the soaring vaults and flying buttresses of Gothic architecture. The use of masonry can be found throughout the historical buildings of Central and South America, as well as in Asia. Significant examples include the Aztec religious complex at Teotihuacan, the famously lost Incan city of Machu Picchu, and Angkor Wat in Cambodia.

In Europe and North America, the Industrial Revolution brought about machines that helped quarry rock and mechanized many masonry production processes. However, as steel began to be emphasized more in construction, stone and clay took a back seat. The nineteenth century saw the mass production of concrete masonry units, which were cheaper to produce than large-format clay tile and required less labor to install than brick. But CMUs also helped bring brick back to the construction palette through the inventions of the cavity and composite walls. CMUs, it was discovered, could be used to back up a thinner brick veneer for less cost and more strength, while steel reinforcement and grout within the CMU added load-bearing capacity. Mortar has also evolved with more consistent properties, and more customizable to match strength and workability criteria. High-strength mortars and different colors now allow for masonry walls in any climate and style.

DESIGN CONSIDERATIONS

Each type of masonry carries different design considerations. Although *masonry* describes a group of naturally occurring, compressive structural material, and many types of masonry walls are similar in construction method, the design considerations are quite varied. Stone, brick, and CMU offer a wide range of colors, textures, sizes, and shapes, and bring many different considerations to the table of today's designer. Despite it being an age-old method of construction, nothing preordains where each hand-placed unit will be located, or how it will function. How the wall becomes load-bearing, whether the masonry is used as a veneer, how it resists weathering forces, and construction details are all critical design opportunities. From the type and color of the mortar, to the size of the mortar joint, to the spacing between stone panels, there are endless explorations in the making of a masonry wall or building.

One consideration unique to masonry construction is *efflorescence*, which affects all types of masonry. It is a white powdery deposit sometimes seen on newly built masonry walls and caused by the crystallization of water-soluble salts on the walls' surface. Its source is seldom from the masonry units themselves; it is more often from the sand or water used to mix the mortar. Salts can also come to the masonry assemblies from adjoining materials including ground sources, and from the atmosphere. Water moving through the assemblies carry water-soluble salts to the surface of the masonry, where the water evaporates and leaves the salts behind. Specifying clean sand and water greatly reduces the chance of efflorescence, as does careful detailing to make sure water does not enter the masonry assemblies.

TYPES

Brick

Brick is the world's oldest manufactured building commodity. Today's bricks are a mix of fine inorganic, non-metallic minerals, mixed with sufficient water to shape the units. The raw materials can vary widely and affect the properties of the final brick product, specifically its forms, sizes, strengths, textures, and colors. How the ingredients are proportioned, mixed, dried, and fired also have significant effect on properties and appearance of the resulting products.

Most commonly "brick" refers to clay brick. In the United States and Europe most bricks are made of clay and fired in similar manners, with unprecedented consistency in properties and appearance for a given product line. Contemporary manufacturing processes and tunnel kilns produce units that routinely meet the highest standards of physical properties.

In the United States, the approximate dimensions of a standard (also called a modular) brick is 4" × 8" × 2.66" (102 × 203 × 67 mm). It fits easily in a hand, making construction flexible and controllable. The nominal brick sizes include the brick's dimension plus one mortar joint, compared to the actual, smaller brick size, which omits the mortar joint. Other brick types vary in height, depth, and width and include Norman, Roman, Engineer Modular, Economy, Utility, and SCR units.

A brick's orientation is also designated with terms shared by designers, masons, and manufacturers. In addition, there are many types of brick bonds. The most commonly used is the running bond, with Flemish, stacked, common, and other bonds designed for specific uses. Architectural historians can date a masonry building based on which bond is used, since certain bonds reflect certain time periods in a given location. The contemporary market for brick shapes and bonding patterns is virtually limitless.

These terms relate to how a brick is oriented within the finished wall:

STRETCHER, a brick laid with its long narrow side exposed.

—

HEADER, a brick laid flat with its width at the face of the wall, or parallel to the face of the wall.

—

SOLDIER, a brick laid vertically with the long narrow side of the brick exposed.

—

SAILOR, a brick laid vertically with the broad face of the brick exposed.

—

ROWLOCK, a brick laid on the long narrow side with the short end of the brick exposed.

—

SHINER, a brick laid on the long narrow side with the broad face of the brick exposed.

CLAY BRICKS

Clay is a mix of very fine inorganic minerals. A clay brick historically was molded into a rectangular block, but today is extruded in a pug mill, usually with a series of holes that facilitate uniform drying and firing. Bricks are fired in a continuous tunnel kiln at a peak temperature of 1,800–2,000 °F (982–1,093 °C) to vitrify the minerals. Physical properties of the brick can be controlled by the firing process; generally manufacturers optimize the process to produce products of high strength and low permeability.

BRICK CHARACTERISTICS

The brick type describes the variations in size, color, and strength of a brick used in construction. There is no standard brick today. Differences vary depending on geographic location but also vary based on the desire of the designer for color, texture, size, and the aesthetic goals. Brick terms will vary from country to country. In the United States, a *common brick* is a term used for a general-use building brick that has no treatment for color or texture. Common is also a term used for a particular brick size: common bricks are a bit taller than modular bricks, with five courses of common brick equaling 16" (406 mm) vertically. They "course out" with every second course of block.

A *face brick* is one that has been manufactured to produce a specific color or texture and is most often used for exterior faces of a building. FBX is a common designation for a face brick where very little variation in size, color, and strength are permissible. FBS is a face brick that allows for a bit more variation in color and size. FBA is a face brick where variations in size, color, and texture of the brick are permissible.

BRICK GRADES

A brick grade designates a clay brick's durability when exposed to weathering. A brick's grade is based on its compressive strength, maximum water absorption, and maximum saturation coefficient. A SW-grade brick is ideal for severe weathering or exposure to water in a subfreezing condition. These bricks have a minimum compressive strength of 2,500 psi (17.2 MPa). MW is a brick grade for moderate exposure to moisture and freezing. It is typically used for above-grade construction and little contact with water. A MW-grade brick has a minimum compressive strength of 2,200 psi (15.2 MPa). A NW-grade brick is a brick for negligible exposure to moisture and freezing. It is typically an internal brick with no exposure to outdoor conditions. Its compressive strength is a minimum 1,250 psi (8.6 MPa). Contemporary brick manufacturers routinely produce SW-grade brick, even in locations where weathering forces are not severe, because it is most readily accomplished and marketable over a broader market. Only custom-made brick, or brick made to match historic products, may not meet the standards for SW-grade brick.

COLOR

The color of a brick is either integral to the brick or on the surface. Bricks are generally grouped into five color classifications: red, red multicolor, buff/yellow, gray/brown, or blue. The color is determined by the amount of iron and other mineral compounds found in the source clay. Red brick has 4–5 percent iron while blue bricks are 7–10 percent iron. Large amounts of iron and magnesium produce a black-colored brick. The amount of heat and firing also has an impact on the color of a brick. The longer the exposure and higher the temperature when firing a brick, the darker the produced color. A brick fired with reducing oxygen or little oxygen produces a black- or blue/black-colored brick. This process causes the iron compounds to form oxides like magnetite or ferrous oxide.

Reducing oxygen and altering temperature conditions in a kiln can produce a multi-colored brick. This process is not precise and causes an unevenly colored brick of a mix of red and blues, which may be desired.

Applying a sand and oxide pigment on the face of the brick before the firing process can produce a superficial or surface color. Some manufacturers will even embed sawdust or other materials on the surface that will combust in the kiln, leaving a colored residue behind. The obvious disadvantage is that if the brick should chip off or deface, a different color will be revealed underneath. Another disadvantage is that customary power washing of the masonry wall to remove mortar stains or other surface blemishes may erode the colored or textured face of the brick.

TEXTURE

The surface of a brick can vary from shiny to a dull and rough surface, and to any quality in between. The texture is determined by the mold used for handmade brick, and by the forming boot on the pug mill that gives the clay its profile when it is being extruded. Extruded bricks, initially, are a continuous linear mass of clay, but are automatically wire-cut soon after extrusion to give them the desired height. The cut faces are not the same texture as those that were against the forming boot, so they are usually on the surfaces that are against the mortar joints, not exposed to view. The texture of a brick also determines how it will age or weather, with a smooth-faced brick weathering better than a rough-faced brick.

Calcium Silicate Bricks

Calcium silicate bricks were invented in Germany at the end of the nineteenth century during experimental attempts to create artifical stone. The raw substance is a mixture of hydrated lime, water, and silica sand (sand lime) or crushed flint (flint lime). The mixture is pressed into its desired shape, hardened in a sealed autoclave, and then pressure-steamed for eight to twelve hours. The curing process increases the bricks' strength and durability. Calcium silicate bricks are usually a dull white color but can be adjusted with pigments to become more pink, gray, yellow, or brown. The bricks can be textured mechanically on the surface if desired; however, they are prone to chipping. The bricks are best avoided around coastal areas as salt and water freezing can quickly deteriorate their structure. They do have advantages, including high thermal resistance and a long lifespan, and are regarded as one of the strongest masonry units. Interestingly, the same product is often used as pipe insulation and as insulation panels.

Concrete Bricks

Concrete bricks are made of concrete with a mix of sand, cement, and an aggregate, or crushed rock. The bricks are molded and chemically cured rather than being vitrified in a kiln like clay brick. Concrete bricks may be most commonly used in areas where the clay products are not locally produced, making them economically uncompetitive. Masonry units made of concrete are more permeable than clay masonry, so designers must accommodate moisture presence, or must specify chemical additives to reduce their permeability. Concrete bricks are commonly available in the same dimensions shown above for clay brick, but they are also easily found in utility sizes of 4" × 4" × 8" (102 × 102 × 203 mm), and 4" × 4" × 12" (102 × 102 × 305 mm).

Slag Bricks

This brick was developed in the nineteenth century by taking slag, the mineral waste produced from smelting iron, and placing it into an iron mold with lime. It was removed from its mold when the exterior surface was hard and the interior was still molten, and then the brick was annealed in ovens to further strengthen its structure. Essentially cast bricks, slag brick was most often used for paving and is no longer in production.

Terra-cotta and Faience

Terra-cotta bricks are similar to their counterparts in tile and pottery. Traditionally, terra-cotta is a mix of fine clays with small amounts of silica and alumina, an alkaline material that gives the surface a vitrification for durability. Unlike building bricks, terra-cotta products are typically molded or extruded to produce units that have more then 25 percent voids, which is the upper limit of "solid" clay brick used in wall construction. The bricks are fired at 1,000 °F (538 °C) to achieve this vitrification. Terra-cotta can be glazed or unglazed, but today is most often unglazed and has a matte surface. Often seen as ornament on buildings, it can also be made into a masonry unit. Terra-cotta blocks can be filled with concrete if needed and anchored with metal fasteners or ties to a building structure.

Faience, like terra-cotta, is found in large, flat slabs or tiles, often with ribbed backs and set on concrete to act as a veneer for a building surface. It has the same physical composition as terra-cotta, and both can come in a wide range of colors from a cream/buff to red. A slip, which is a liquefied suspension of clay particles in water, can be applied to a surface to change the color, most frequently to mimic stone.

Concrete Masonry Units

Concrete masonry units (CMUs) are precast units made of Portland cement, aggregates of various sizes and types, and water. These units are formed in a mold, or (nowadays) quickly extruded vertically onto a conveyor belt in a factory. Unlike clay masonry units, which are vitrified in a kiln, CMUs rely upon a chemical hydration process of the cement to durably bind the aggregates. The curing environment of the CMU is controlled to be warm and humid for the first twenty-four hours, then the CMU is cured further under ambient conditions. Like concrete, the hydration process continues to evolve for weeks or months after being initiated.

CMUs are available in many different shapes and sizes, with the most common having nominal dimensions of 8" × 8" × 16" (203 × 203 × 406 mm), with two or three hollow cores, though they are also available as solid units. Other common sizes are 4", 6", 10", and 12" wide (100, 152, 254, and 305 mm) blocks, with the other two dimensions remaining the same to permit modular coordination. There are many specialized shapes and sizes including units with bull-nose edges, corner blocks, rounded corners, sill blocks, cap blocks, coping blocks, and blocks shaped to look like pilasters or solid structural members. Most hollow load-bearing CMUs have a compressive strength from 600–1,900 psi (4–13 MPa). Fire-resistance ratings for CMUs vary based on the types of aggregate used and the size of the unit.

Like brick, CMUs can be laid up in many different bond patterns. CMU walls are often also used as backup structural walls for stone, stucco, brick, and metal panels. The hollow cavity within the unit can receive grout and reinforcing steel to give it strength.

For exposed applications on building exteriors or interiors, CMUs are produced in many different shapes, textures, and colors. Split-face units have a more stone-like appearance. Fluted or ribbed-faced CMUs give a decorative appearance. Ground-faced units are mechanically abraded to expose the color of aggregate inside a relatively smooth exposed surface. CMUs can be pigmented or glazed from almost white/buff to almost black, with many shades of reds, grays, and creams.

GRADES

A CMU's grade describes its strength and performance around moisture and water. In the United States, Grade N is a load-bearing block with a compressive strength of 1,000–1,800 psi (6.9–12.41 MPa). These blocks can be used either above grade or below grade and be exposed to water and moisture. Grade S is also a load-bearing block but has limited use in exposure to water and moisture, and has lower compressive strengths. It is used above grade and can be used in exterior walls that have a weather-protective coating.

Stone

Stone is a hard, solid, naturally occurring mineral or an aggregate of minerals. An ancient material used in noted architectural works, stone is strongly associated with history and strength. Stone buildings have a long lifespan, in part because of the durability of the materials and laborious details, but also because the projects built of stone were of such civic importance that they were maintained exceedingly well.

Architecturally, stone is usually used in two manners: as a load-bearing wall that is laid in mortar, and as a thin, non-load-bearing veneer, backed up by concrete or another structural substrate. Stone is most often classified by its geological origin into three types: igneous, sedimentary, and metamorphic. Igneous rock is volcanic rock, formed from cooled molten magma. Granite is the most common igneous stone in architectural applications, but others include obsidian, basalt, and malachite. Sedimentary rock is formed over millennia from the deposits of particulate matter (sediment) by glacial movements or by water. In sedimentary rock, the particles are formed under pressure and are bound by natural cement. Examples include limestone, sandstone, and travertine. Metamorphic rock is an igneous, sedimentary, or older metamorphic rock that has been chemically transformed through pressure and heat or by the folding of geological strata. Common metamorphic architectural stones include marble and slate.

Stone naturally occurs in many shapes, colors, and forms since it is not a man-made, manufactured product. Economical stone construction may use field stones, or irregular shapes of quarried stone, but it can also be more refined through the investment of labor or industrial processes. Once quarried and fabricated, cut stone can be laid like typical masonry units with mortar in a patterned course. It is a compressive structural unit, used not only in structural walls, but also in veneer walls, flooring, paving, countertops, and retaining walls. Stone can be laid without mortar or other material between units. The craftsman laboriously carves or chips the stone away to fit the units together snugly like a puzzle. Historic examples are monumental in scale, and include the Egyptian pyramids and the Incan walls at Machu Picchu.

The physical properties of stone vary considerably depending upon the geological classification, and even the species and quarry-specific qualities within those classifications. Generally, stone has great compressive strength, but loses 90 percent of it in shear. Shear is the combined energy of a pair of forces acting in opposite directions along parallel lines of action through the material. Stone is durable and hard, making it a good overall construction material. It can be classified by its color, grain, and texture. Stone is also classified by its density and permeability, which are critical to determining its resistance to freeze/thaw conditions, as well as vulnerability to staining and atmospheric pollution.

There are many considerations in deciding to use stone architecturally. It is always encouraged to use stone that is local or quarried close to a building site to reduce environmental impacts of transport of this massive material. Cost is generally at a premium level. Because it is not found in regular shapes or sizes, quality control by fabricators, designers, and installers regarding specified properties, color and texture must be of the highest order.

We can classify stone into three grades of finish: rubble, ashlar, and trimstone. Rubble is rough, quarry-faced stone, but can have one good face used for wall construction. Ashlar is cut or split stone patterns that we might see in a wall facing or paving. Trimstone is cut stone used for cornices, sills, lintels, and other details of a building. Flagstone is used for flooring or flat surfaces.

CONSTRUCTION

Stone can be used as a load-bearing wall employing the principles of unreinforced solid masonry construction. This is called a double-faced stone wall and is usually not used above a three-story height. Due to high material and labor costs, stone is now most typically used as a veneer, or over a backup wall. The stone facing material is usually between 2–6" thick (50–150 mm) and tied to a load-bearing CMU or concrete wall. In thinstone applications, very narrow prefabricated stone panels may be secured with stainless-steel clips to a metal grid that in turn is supported by the building's primary structure. Alternatively, multiple thinstone panels can be assembled into a unitized cladding panel for quick installation in the field.

Because stone cladding is considered permanent, it is important to use non-corrosive ties, anchors, and flashing so as to not suffer premature corrosion or cause any staining. Copper, brass, bronze, and mild steel should not be used for anchors, while stainless steel is ideal. Tolerances for movement should also be considered regarding hardware selection and in detailing how the stone is secured to its backup wall. Movement and shifting of pieces will occur. The hardware in stone veneer walls is critical because it must accommodate loads, changes in temperature, and manipulation during installation. Stone joints should be regular and consistent in many types of stone walls; in others, irregularity in joints can be considered part of the aesthetic quality of the wall. Shims and moisture barriers should also be considerations when designing a stone veneer wall to ensure its durability.

Stone can be made to look monolithic and solid by using manufactured stone veneer blocks or stone masonry units. Or stone can be used in its natural, irregular state with little shaping. Stone is still considered a green material—it has performed well for centuries and will continue to do so.

Stone carvers and setters were at one time much more common than is the case now. Off-site fabrication of stone elements is now the norm, sometimes using very specialized equipment and computer-controlled tools. Sometimes stone veneer pieces are secured and placed on a concrete panel or steel panel wall unit in a shop, where greater masonry consists of squared blocks of stone that are different heights, thus breaking or interrupting the courses. In addition to hardware, designers must consider the wall's mortar type and how the joints are tooled to ensure regularity, strength, and durability.

Secondary School

Dano, Burkina Faso — Diébédo Francis Kéré
Laterite masonry

DESIGN INTENTION

This L-shaped secondary school is part of a compound of community facilities in a village in Burkina Faso. It exemplifies sustainable design practices with its strategic use of local skills and materials, passive thermal regulation, and long-life / loose-fit approach to design. The building features are uniquely representative of the local cultural, environmental, and economic circumstances.

Three classrooms and an elliptical sheltered amphitheater form the long leg of the L, flanked by a block that contains offices and computer spaces. The school defines the southern edge of the compound, with generous overhangs to shelter the building and to minimize exposure to direct sun. The project utilized the vernacular construction knowledge of local builders, but also reinvigorated the artisanal tradition by training a new generation of workers in these techniques, ensuring that this building method will remain embedded in the community. This project enhanced the economic opportunities for indigenous masonry materials and skills.

MATERIALITY

Economic constraints made it imperative that designers be resourceful with every decision. Local laterite clay was used to construct almost all of the built structure, chosen for its functional value, but also as a pilot project to demonstrate its use in sustainable design. Compressive walls are chiefly made using unfaced laterite clay blocks, which also provide enclosure, security, and passive thermal mass. The rich red color and texture make it an attractive interior and exterior finish.

When at or below the water table, laterite soil is soft enough to be cut with a spade or an axe. Clay is traditionally extracted in roughly rectangular blocks and then trimmed using hand tools. Once exposed to air it begins to dry and become stone-like as the water between the clay particles evaporates and the iron salts in the soil interlock to form a lattice structure of moderate strength. Laterite is unique because when it is thoroughly dry, it becomes solid without needing to be fired in a kiln or bonded with cement additives.

Laterite clays are found in many regions of the world, typically in places where the soil goes through thousands of years of cyclic rainy and dry seasons, like those typically found in equatorial forests or humid subtropical savannahs. During the wet seasons, water-soluble binders leach out of the parent stone or soil, leaving insoluble oxides and sulfates of iron, aluminium, and silica. These minerals then undergo hydrolysis during the hot, dry season. Laterite has been used in building construction for more than 1,000 years, with examples in Southeast Asia and India in addition to North Africa.

TECHNICAL

The laterite blocks were placed in an reinforced running bond pattern, with very thin mortar joints made of cement and sand. The blocks are 12" long (305 mm) and their width varies to facilitate the interlocking of units within the wall. All walls are load-bearing; their height is approximately ten times their thickness. Anticipating the cyclic rainy season, walls are elevated off the ground using an impermeable granite stone bed that varies in height to meet the finish grade.

The roof trusses were custom made by welding 0.55" and 0.63" (14 and 16 mm) diameter steel reinforcing bars into a three-dimensional truss, which supports the unique curved ceiling below and the corrugated metal roofing above. Air naturally convects in the zone between ceiling and roof, moderating interior temperatures. Rainwater from the undulating roof is collected and directed away from the building. Roof trusses rest on a reinforced concrete bond course cast on top of each wall, and by reinforced concrete beams where no wall is below. The reinforced concrete elements accept the concentrated loads from the roof trusses, and then safely distribute them to the masonry walls.

Three suspended ceiling elements hang in each room. Each is made of 9.8' (3 m) broad flat-rolled steel sheet metal, which supports the wood / cement masonry units that provide thermal mass. Openings between the suspended ceiling elements permit hot room air to rise and escape through the roof cavity. Ceilings are painted white to distribute daylight evenly.

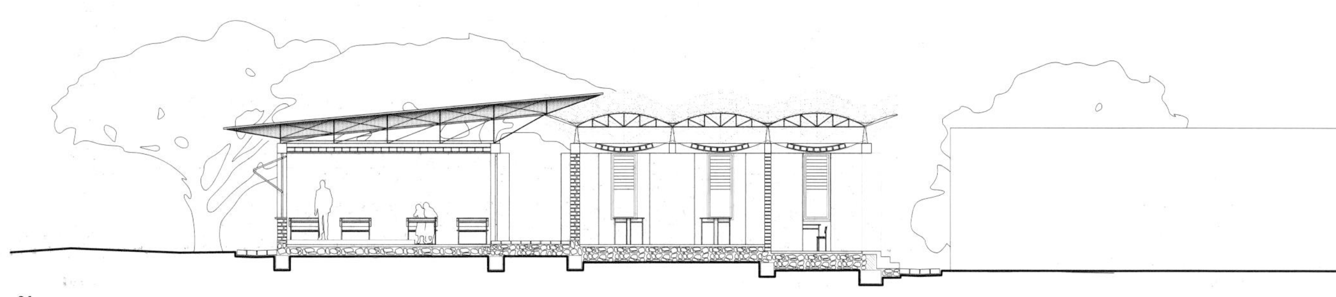

01

02

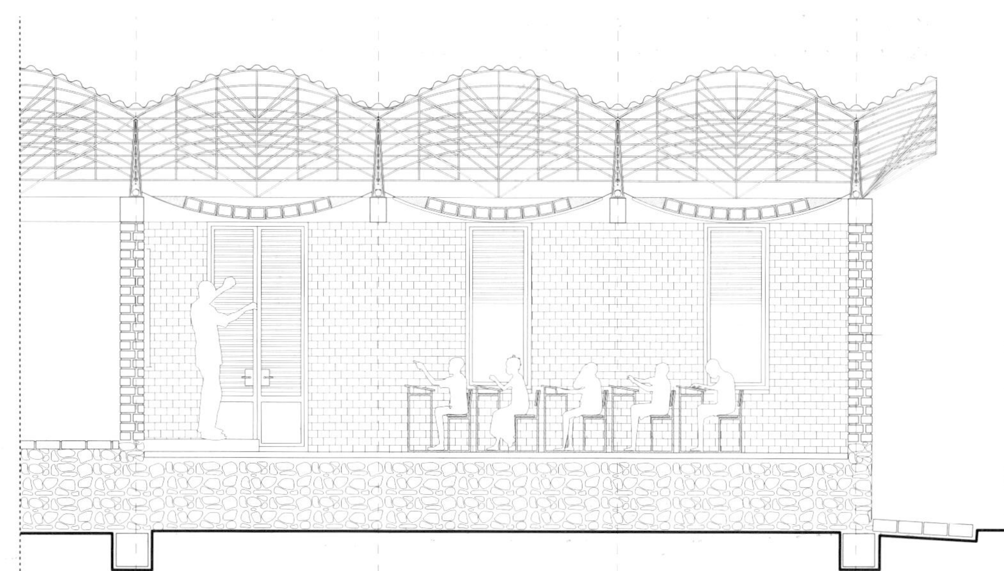

03

01 Section through classroom and offices

02 Laterite masonry units laid in running bond pattern for exterior walls

03 Section through classroom showing masonry use in walls and ceiling

04

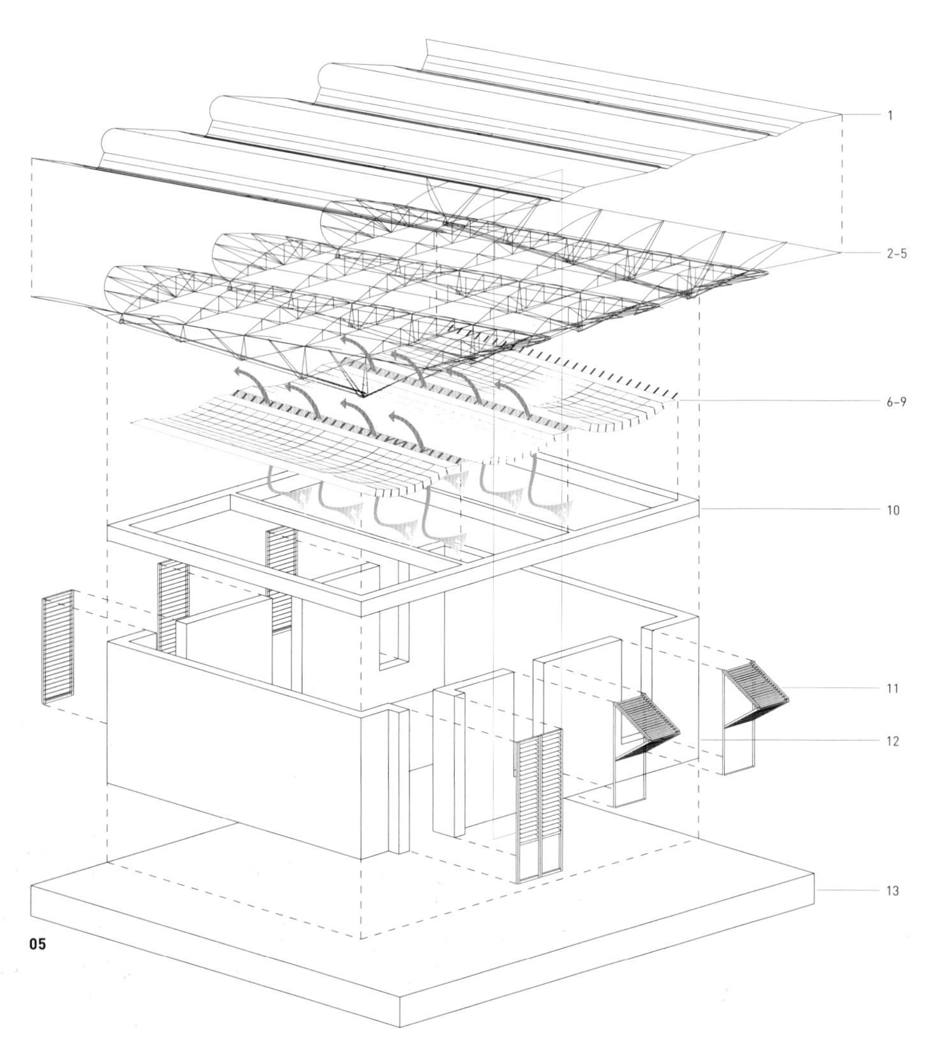

05

04 Laterite solid masonry walls are built upon granite foundations to isolate them from groundwater

05 Exploded isometric of construction assemblies

06 Laterite blocks are extracted from the ground and shaped with hand tools for use in nearby school construction

07 School plan

08 Cut laterite masonry units harden as they dry

09 Classroom interior

Roof covering

1 Corrugated steel

Roof structure

2 Support pillar

3 Bent reinforcing steel O.C.10 mm

4 Welded reinforcing steel O.C. 14 and 16 mm, steel 30 mm

5 Bent reinforcing steel O.C. 20 mm

Suspended ceiling

6 Hollow cement block

7 Mortar

8 Plaster

9 Bearing bar, O.C 80 mm steel tube

Ring beam

10 Reinforced concrete

11 Collapsible and colored wings-shutter for windows and doors with adjustable, collapsible, and colored wings

Walls and columns

12 Laterite stone, 300 mm

13 Granite base

06

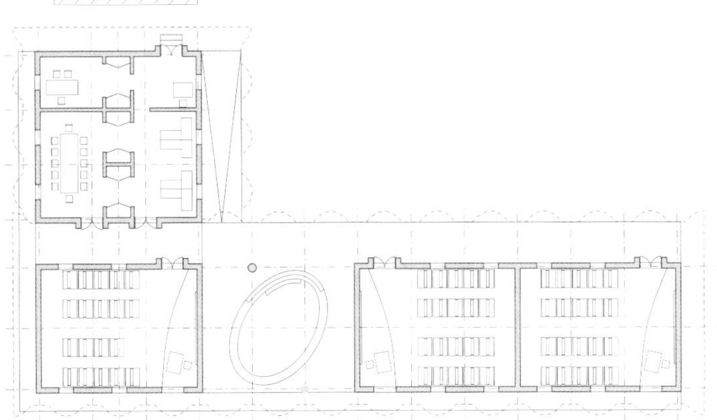
07

08

09

Brandhorst Museum

Munich, Germany — Sauerbruch Hutton
Glazed ceramic rods

DESIGN INTENTION

The Brandhorst Museum occupies an important position in the Museum Quarter, in Munich's neo-classical Maxvorstadt district. Its overall form responds to significant urban influences from this district, as well as to the symbolic vestiges of its predecessors on this site.

The building program is substantial, with some of the volume sitting below ground level. Elements above ground consist of a longitudinal building and a main entrance building connected by a continuous strip window that divides the building visually into two floors. The museum has three floors of exhibit galleries and an adjoining administrative block. Most technical services are subterranean. Also underground is a central patio that is lit directly from above, surrounded by six small galleries for light-sensitive artifacts such as photographs and works on paper.

The simple, white interiors defer to the art, supporting it with ample space and optimal light to create ideal display conditions. However, the exterior is meant to express the museum's presence as a repository of engaging artwork. The facade is composed of several layers of material that create a polychromatic yet ordered finish. These qualities are perceived differently at varied distances.

MATERIALITY

The exterior walls of the galleries are large expanses of opaque reinforced concrete, which are wrapped with insulation and water barriers. A folded two-colored perforated sheet-metal skin covers the solid surfaces and absorbs traffic noise from the adjacent streets. Covering the metal layer are 36,000 separate ceramic rods, each with a permanent glaze from a 23-color palette, organized into three families of colors that are grouped and blended across the facades to make the building mass appear to be three interlocking volumes. The architect's drawings meticulously illustrated where each color occurs on the building elevations.

From a distance the museum is seen as a neutral color with amorphous differing tones, but as one moves closer the three families of colors emerge distinctly. Eventually the individual pixels of each colored rod become dominant. As the visitor moves past the facade, the colored rods create an oscillating optical illusion, which changes according to the viewing angle, engaging the visitor's senses and intellect. The visual play of these ceramic rods establishes the material's presence in the design of the building. It is not only visually engaging as one moves around the exterior, but also representative of the building's function and meaning. A piece of artwork can take on many different views and meanings depending on the vantage point—likewise, so can this building.

TECHNICAL

The ceramic rods are made of terra-cotta, 1.6" square in section and 42" tall (40 mm square and 1.1 m tall), with a wall thickness of 0.35" (9 mm). Called a TERRART Baguette, the museum facade was designed in close collaboration with the rod manufacturer. Colors from nearby buildings influenced those selected for the rods, giving the design a contextual relevance.

The ceramic rods and perforated metal screens form a rainscreen over the substructure. It is ventilated and permits water to drain. The vertically oriented ceramic rods embrace the idea of the rainscreen, with nothing to impede drainage through or behind them. The masonry facade elements were installed mechanically, using technology normally associated with non-masonry assemblies. No mortar or sealants were used.

The visually complex layered assembly is efficiently achieved using a grid of aluminum extrusions that supports both the perforated aluminum acoustic panels and the ceramic rods. Elements making up the aluminum grid have preset points where the metal screens and ceramic rod connections are received. The aluminum grid is anchored to the reinforced concrete wall using brackets that pass through the thick layer of mineral wool insulation.

Each ceramic rod was delivered with two bolts protruding through holes that had been machined at quarter points along its height. Polyamide washers were placed between the metal fasteners and the rods to cushion the connection; the manufacturer also specified low torque connections. The two bolts in each rod were inserted into sleeves that were secured to the aluminum grid using a riveting nut. Transverse set screws secure the rods in the proper vertical position, aligned with rods above and below, but not touching them.

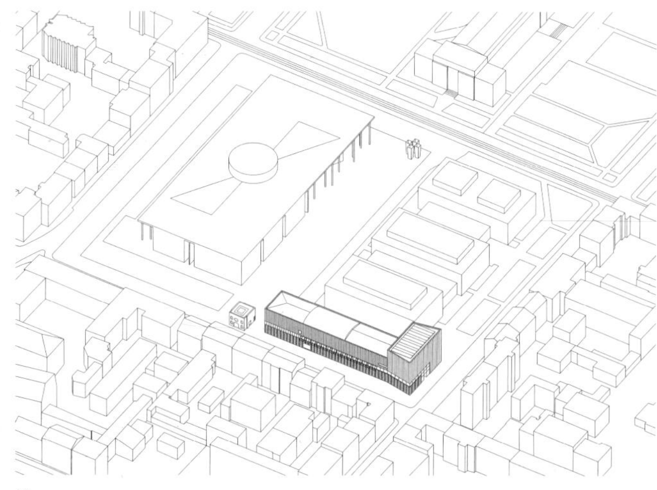

01

01 Site location in the city's Museum Quarter

02 Two threaded rods secure each glazed ceramic rod and the perforated metal backing to the wall

03 Ceramic rods form "families" of colors on the facades

02

03

04 Individual ceramic rods

05 Exterior view from southwest

06 Section of ceramic rod and wall assembly

07 Section detail of fittings that secure ceramic rods and perforated metal backing to building wall

04

05

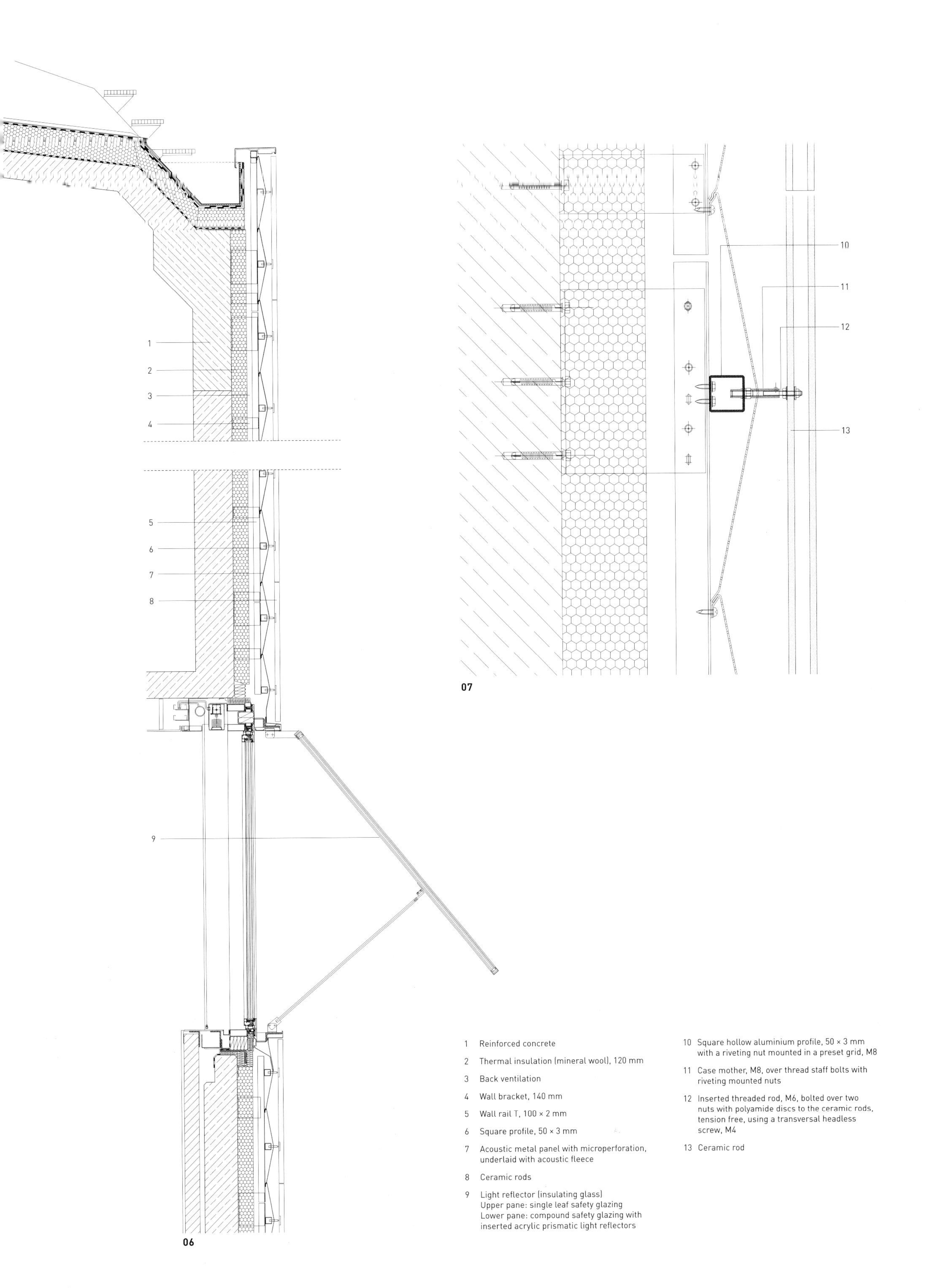

06

07

1 Reinforced concrete
2 Thermal insulation (mineral wool), 120 mm
3 Back ventilation
4 Wall bracket, 140 mm
5 Wall rail T, 100 × 2 mm
6 Square profile, 50 × 3 mm
7 Acoustic metal panel with microperforation, underlaid with acoustic fleece
8 Ceramic rods
9 Light reflector (insulating glass)
Upper pane: single leaf safety glazing
Lower pane: compound safety glazing with inserted acrylic prismatic light reflectors
10 Square hollow aluminium profile, 50 × 3 mm with a riveting nut mounted in a preset grid, M8
11 Case mother, M8, over thread staff bolts with riveting mounted nuts
12 Inserted threaded rod, M6, bolted over two nuts with polyamide discs to the ceramic rods, tension free, using a transversal headless screw, M4
13 Ceramic rod

Padre Pio Pilgrimage Church

Foggia, Italy — Renzo Piano Building Workshop
Post-tensioned masonry, digitally fabricated stone

DESIGN INTENTION

Pio of Pietrelcina, popularly known as Padre Pio, was a Capuchin priest who was canonized in 2002. This church, commissioned by the Capuchin Order, was built on a hill called San Giovanni Rotondo, near the monastery that was Padre Pio's home. Hundreds of thousands of pilgrims travel to the small city each year to pay homage.

Visitors are guided up to the church by a massive wall containing twelve large bells. The sound of the bells and the great size of the wall serve as a landmark even from a distance. In order to accommodate all of the visitors, the interior space has a capacity for 6,500 people. The large triangular piazza greets visitors near the church, and on feast days it becomes a place of worship, with room for 30,000. Secondary spaces, some of which are tucked underground, include a crypt, three conference halls, various reception areas, prayer rooms, confessionals, and offices.

The sanctuary has a semi-circular plan to soften the hierarchy found in traditional sanctuary configurations. A simple glass front makes the interior visible from the square. To further blur the difference between outside and inside, the stone paving of the courtyard extends into the church itself. Bold parabolic stone arches were arranged in a complex radial pattern, seen both inside and outside the glassy envelope, and give the visitor the feeling of a grand space characteristic of cathedrals.

MATERIALITY

The main challenge was using state-of-the-art technology to manipulate local stone to into unprecedented large spans for the primary structural material. Because the location is seismically active, the load-bearing stone structure was reinforced with steel post-tensioning cables through each stone for the entire length of each arch.

The church took thirteen years to build. Its lengthy construction period indicates the careful measures that were taken to ensure flawless execution in the selection and extraction of stone from the quarry, and the transportation and dressing of stone blocks in each stage of its production. Apricena, a local limestone which holds traditional significance and a warm appearance, was chosen. However, specialized cutting and dressing systems were not available locally, so the blocks were sent to more modern facilities in other parts of Italy for fabrication. The selection of this limestone represents the endurance and strength appropriate for a church of this scale and caliber.

Two overlapping concentric rings of post-tensioned stone arches support the roof, supplemented by a three-dimensional stainless-steel structure interposed between the arches and the roof. The steel struts also provide lateral stability to the arches. Walls, pavers, supporting arches, and roof decks are made of the Apricena limestone, expressing unity in the design. Other materials used were natural or long-lasting man-made materials, such as stainless steel for the roof struts, laminated larch timber for the upper beams, and pre-patinated copper for the roof to display affinity with the green patina of existing church roofs in the area.

TECHNICAL

Stone blocks were quarried using chain saws or diamond-wire systems to preserve the material's mechanical attributes. A CNC-milling machine with a large circular blade was used to precisely cut 1,320 finished stones out of raw blocks to tolerances of 0.02" (0.5 mm); such close tolerances required upgrading the electronics in the machinery.

Custom CNC mills were created to bore holes through each stone block for the reinforcement cables to pass through them. Two central holes are 4.7" (120 mm) diameter each and four corner holes are 1.8" (45 mm) each, positioned to receive post-tensioning cables and less tense reinforcement cables. The four corner cables are employed primarily in the event of seismic activity. Each stone subassembly had to receive a certification of conformity to project specifications before being carefully transported from the fabricator to the construction site.

After thoroughly cleaning each stone block, a 0.12" (3 mm) layer of high-performance, fiber-reinforced adhesive and a 0.08" (2 mm) thick stainless-steel band were used to secure each subassembly to the next block. The resin provides cohesion between blocks, but also cushions any irregularities in the adjoining faces.

A reinforced concrete foundation was cast at the bases of each arch. Movable steel scaffolds were mounted below, and a fixed machine known as a tipper gripped each stone subassembly by its side holes and lifted it into place. The arches were assembled from the bases in alternating fashion until they met at the top, where the keystone was inserted. Some of the twenty-two arches span an impressive 164' (50 m) and are 52' high (16 m).

Once all elements of an arch were put in place, reinforced steel cables were inserted into the prepared sheaths and placed in tension. Access to the cable ends was provided in niches formed in the reinforced concrete foundations at the bases of each arch. Scaffolding was taken down to allow the cables to stretch and settle into place. Grout was then injected into the sheaths around the cables to fuse the entire structure together.

In this church, new design and fabrication technologies were used to build a worship space using one of the oldest construction materials. The traditional concept of the arched cathedral has been transformed and modernized into a vaulted space of unprecedented stone curves.

01

02

03

01 Approach toward church across piazza from the east

02 Construction of two rings of masonry stone arches

03 Some of the more than 1,300 stone blocks, each made to tolerances of 0.02" (0.5 mm)

04 Section through church and piazza

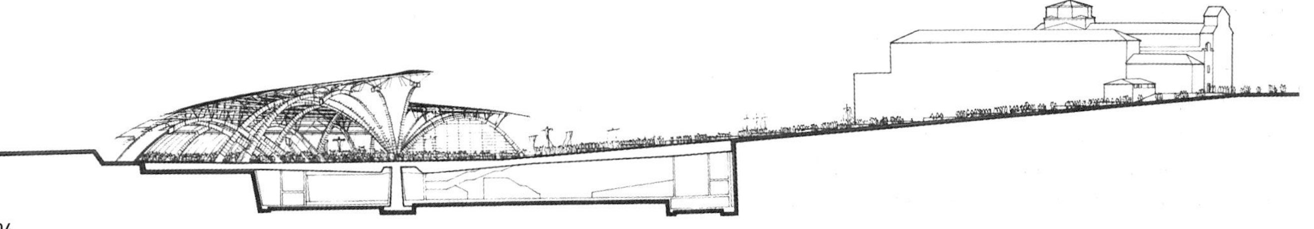

04

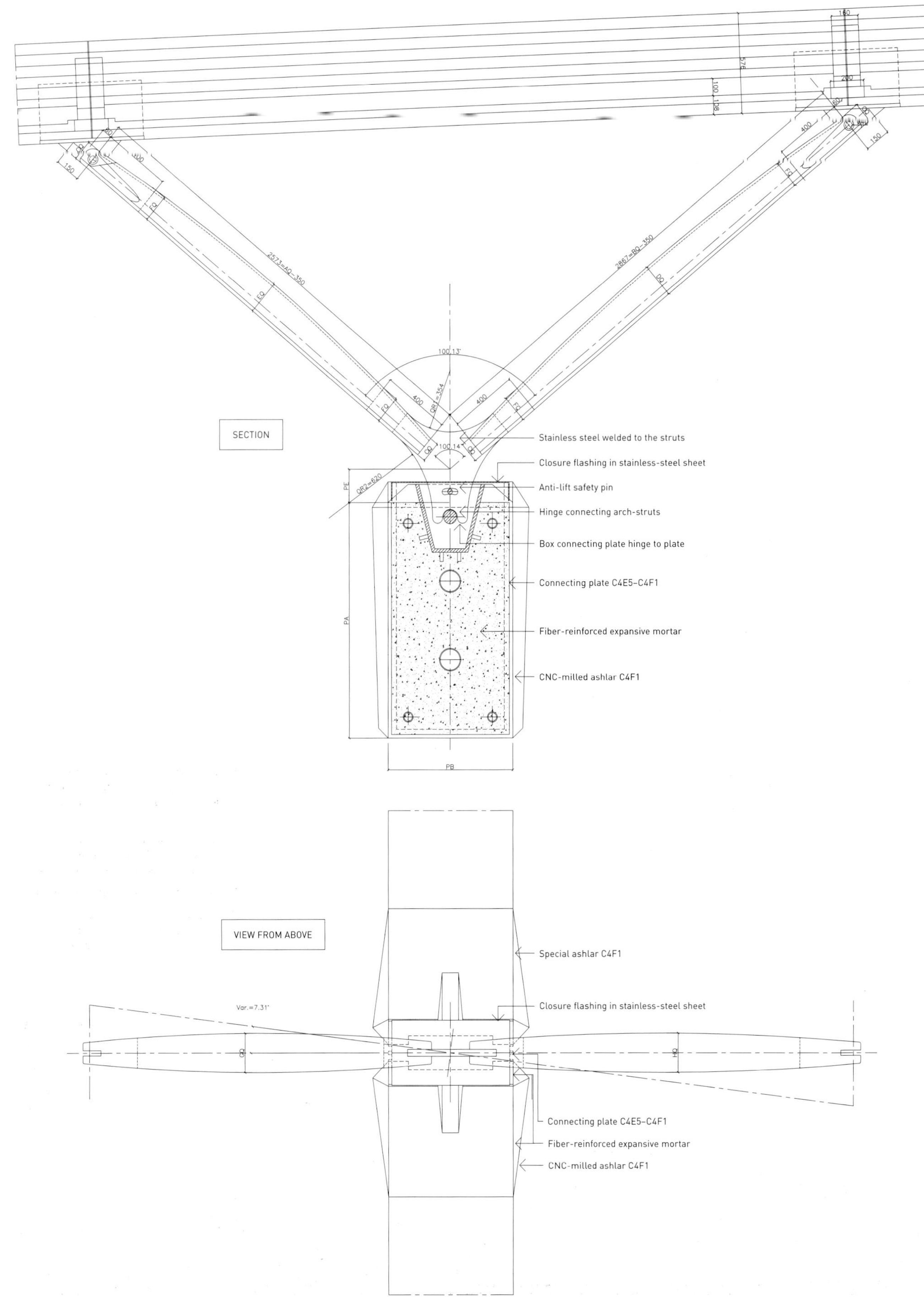
SECTION
Stainless steel welded to the struts
Closure flashing in stainless-steel sheet
Anti-lift safety pin
Hinge connecting arch-struts
Box connecting plate hinge to plate
Connecting plate C4E5–C4F1
Fiber-reinforced expansive mortar
CNC-milled ashlar C4F1
VIEW FROM ABOVE
Special ashlar C4F1
Closure flashing in stainless-steel sheet
Connecting plate C4E5–C4F1
Fiber-reinforced expansive mortar
CNC-milled ashlar C4F1

05

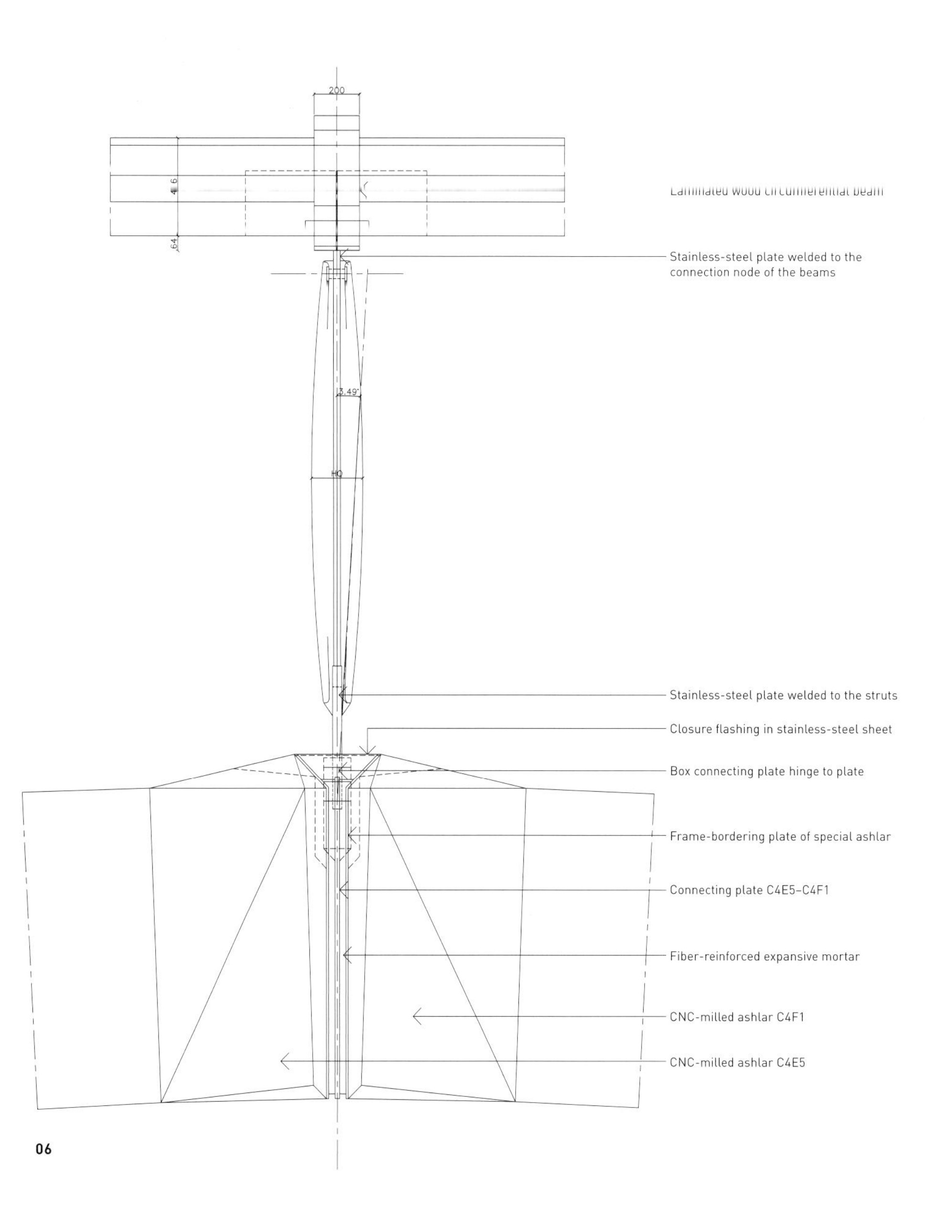

06

05 Section and plan of connection between post-tensioned stone arch and stainless-steel struts supporting the roof assembly

06 Detail of connecting plate joining stainless-steel struts and stone arch, located at seam between stone blocks

07 Section through structural assemblies

08 Construction of reinforced concrete base of arch in foreground; arches under construction in background

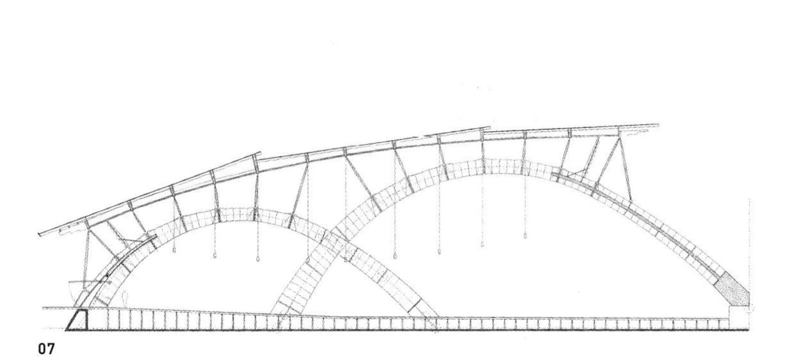

07

08

South Asian Human Rights Documentation Centre

New Delhi, India — Anagram Architects
Bonded masonry, modular coordination

DESIGN INTENTION

The South Asian Human Rights Documentation Centre (SAHRDC) is an administrative office for this non-governmental organization to investigate, document, and disseminate information about human rights. SAHRDC is a small office with limited resources; their facility was designed on a small urban corner site, which emphasizes spatial efficiency and cost-effective construction.

The 538 sq. ft. (50 sq. m) site is located at the intersection of two busy pedestrian streets, so controlling and restricting street-level acoustic and visual disturbance into the work-spaces was a critical priority. The site's longer dimension faces the western sun, which in this climate required strategies to reduce solar thermal gain while permitting ventilation of interior spaces. The outer wall is intended to optimize solidity and privacy while still conversing visually with the urban realm. The street wall is animated to reflect the energy of the city outside, satisfying the need for privacy using a richly engaging masonry surface.

The building is diagrammatically simple, organized with a single, open administrative space on each of its three aboveground floors, which are buffered by a service and stair bar on the western, sun-facing side. The porosity of the stair wall permits natural ventilation horizontally and vertically.

MATERIALITY

To meet the tight budget, walls were constructed of exposed brick. Floors and roof decks are made of gently vaulted brick spans with a concrete topping, eliminating the need for beams and reducing slab thickness. The underside of the brick vaults are exposed, making a hung ceiling unnecessary and reducing floor-to-floor heights to only 10.33' (3.15 m).

A single repeating brick module creates a visually complex pattern in the manner of traditional South Asian brise-soleils. This is achieved with standard solid brick, and without joint reinforcement in the masonry walls. No material other than brick masonry was to be visible in the facade. This innovative bricklaying method uses a common material in an unconventional manner to engage the urban streetfront and stay within the limited budget. The masonry's sense of movement and textural qualities exemplify innovative designers that use common materials creatively and thoughtfully, to the benefit of everyone.

TECHNICAL

Twirling cubic stacks of brick (three shiners in one course and three rowlocks in the other) repeat to form an undulating wall surface. By laying the bricks on their edges, voids created by omitting brick in certain locations enhance ventilation.

The construction of the screen wall was the result of a five-week collaboration between masons and architects, searching for a solution that would be well crafted using structural bonding of the brick courses. The architects used computer modeling to show the masons that a simple rotating module of bricks would create the kind of visual and textural complexity needed to address the design objectives. Architects and masons used full-scale mockups to find a simple and practical bricklaying technique that could be replicated by the various masonry teams without requiring the skills of a master mason. The designers prepared a set of six individual course drawings, setting forth the angle of rotation of each brick. From these, sets of triangular wooden templates were made, which the masons used to accurately place the bricks.

The bricks used were 9" × 4.5" × 3" (230 × 115 × 75 mm), which is the standard size of a brick in India. Like modular bricks worldwide, the longest dimension is exactly two or three times its two smaller dimensions. The bricks were wire cut but are primarily handmade. Both the head joint and bed joints were 0.4" (10 mm). The mortar is a simple cement/sand mortar in a 1:3 ratio.

The masonry wall is load-bearing, so structural performance could not be compromised by the visual pattern making. The centers of the cubic modules in a stack had to perfectly align in a vertical axis, around which the module would rotate. This was difficult to accurately craft during bricklaying due to human error. Conventional mason's strategies such as dropping a vertical plumb line were not feasible because brick faces were not all in the same plane.

The floor vaults and slabs bear on the walls where two sets of cubic modules align to make the wall thickest and strongest. Structural bonding between modules results from the cross-stacking of the bricks in the modules. In the more perforated central portion of the facade, brickwork is reinforced horizontally by laying a thin reinforced concrete beam within the wall thickness in place of the center brick.

01

01 Perspective of brick coursing; plan views of each course shown to right

02 Exterior view of west screen wall

03 Exterior view of west screen wall with interior illumination

04 Exterior view of tall unreinforced masonry wall from northwest

05 Interior view of screen wall adjoining stair

06 Detail of finely crafted twirling cubic forms of bonded masonry

02

03

04

05

06

NUWOG Headquarters and Housing

Neu-Ulm, Germany — Fink + Jocher
Modular coordination, special shapes

DESIGN INTENTION

This new mixed-use building is located near the Neu-Ulm town center, within the federal fortress of Ulm. The form and appearance of the building seek to blend in with the city, which developed along a dense grid pattern during the nineteenth century. Retail space occupies the ground floor, and the three upper floors contain fifteen apartment units of different sizes and layouts. Sandwiched between the retail and residential uses, the building contains three floors of offices for the Wohnungsgesellschaft der Stadt Neu-Ulm (NUWOG municipal housing society). Only the stairwell walls and external walls are structurally fixed, allowing for flexibility in the floor plan. Interior spatial divisions are light non-masonry construction that allows adjustment in the future depending on changes in user requirements or the real estate market.

MATERIALITY

The bricks' shape and the masonry wall designs draw attention to the geometry, color, and texture of the city's dominant masonry grid. The slipping nature of the block balconies and the orthogonal rhythm of the elevation create a sculptural image of the cityscape itself. Masonry here is a strong and precise material representation of the historic town center. All dimensions of walls and openings are derived from the building's brick module. The building's corner site has one edge that is angled, due to the adjoining oblique street. Individual brick faces and concrete window frames are oriented parallel to the major street, but the walls as a whole undulate, derived from the site's minor geometries. The result is a building that is simultaneously part of the fabric of the district, while also distinguished from it.

The thin-format, specially manufactured bricks were fired with peat to produce their distinctive rich red color, which was matched with pigmented mortar. The precast concrete window frames were likewise manufactured using a pigmented concrete to match the hue of the brick, but in a slightly lighter tone.

The project meets the rigorous low-energy house standards with a favorable ratio of volume to surface area. It also minimizes heat loss through external structural components, and it activates the thermal mass capacity of the solid masonry walls.

TECHNICAL

Exterior walls are made of 8.7" (220 mm) load-bearing reinforced concrete, covered with 3.9" (100 mm) of mineral wool insulation, a slender cavity, and lastly a brick veneer in a running bond pattern. The plasticity of freshly mixed concrete is used to make the undulating shape of the structural substrate, which is translated into the disciplined form language of the orthogonal brick veneer.

In this example of modular coordination, the architects designed the building to gracefully incorporate the particular sizes of manufactured brick into the form of the building, making construction efficient with minimal trimming of the brick. The actual dimensions of the standard brick in this building are 9.4" × 4.5" × 2.2" (240 × 115 × 55 mm), set with 0.4" (10 mm) mortar joints, producing nominal dimensions of 10" × 5" × 2.6" (250 × 125 × 65 mm).

Standard bricks were used when they were laid parallel to the wall or only a few degrees off parallel. When the brick faces are not parallel to the wall, then special trapezoidal-shaped bricks were used, producing saw-toothed courses. Three special trapezoid-shaped bricks were made for this project, with one end of the brick being increased from the standard 4.5" (115 mm) to 5.9", 6.9", and 8" (150, 170, and 205 mm). The face of the largest trapezoidal units is at 22 degrees from the typical brick orientation.

The special trapezoidal brick are wire cut on their exposed faces, giving them a slightly coarser texture than the standard brick. This subtle difference in texture adds detail to the angled wall surfaces. The sawtooth-shaped courses are offset to achieve the running bond pattern. The trapezoidal units are corbeled over the unit below them by up to 2" (51 mm); these brick have no exposed core holes. At transitions between the various textures on the walls, the masons artfully stitched the brick elements together in stepped and interlocking patterns, seldom cutting a brick. At the base of each cavity, weeps occur in head joints at 8" (205 mm) on center to permit water to drain from the cavity.

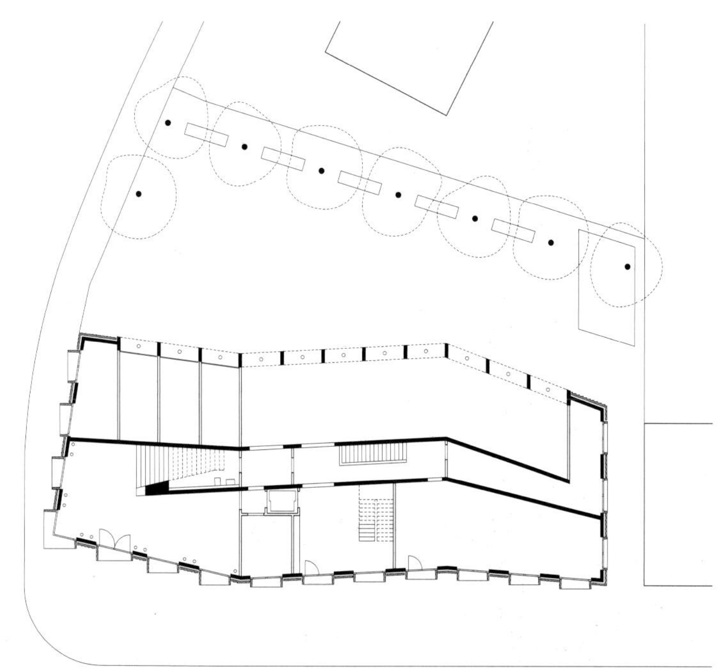

01

01 Ground floor plan

02 Section of exterior load-bearing wall

03 Primary facade from west

04 Detail of wall base with standard bricks in lower portion and special trapezoidal bricks in upper portion

03

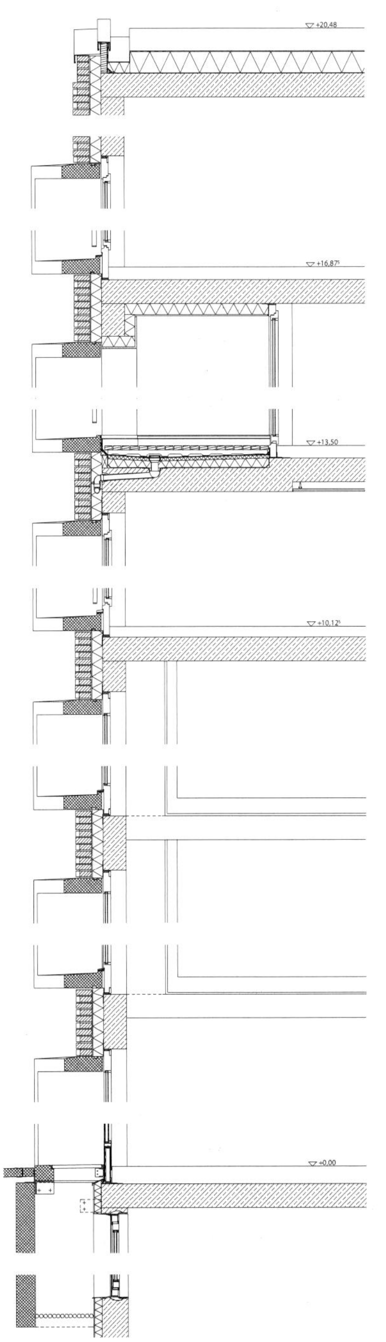

02

04

Pope John Paul II Hall

Rijeka, Croatia — Randić-Turato Architects
Terra-cotta rainscreen

DESIGN INTENTION

This multipurpose hall is part of the complex of the Church of Our Lady of Trsat, a Franciscan monastery in the hills above Rijeka. The monastery is one of the most important pilgrimage sites in Croatia, dating back to the year 1291. The new Great Hall commemorates Pope John Paul II's visit in 2003, and also expresses the renewed stature of the church following the fall of communism in the Balkans. The hall's simple, archetypal form resembles a hip-roofed barn, but upon closer inspection one finds unexpected refinements of the surface and assemblage.

The new project consists of a hall, an L-shaped cloister, and a courtyard for open-air assemblies. The building balances solidity and lightness in simple, subtle ways to achieve a quiet but poetic quality. The building envelope is permeated with openings for light, just as paths for visitors to move through the monastery grounds permeate the cloister. This building is on the eastern edge of the compound, where service buildings were previously located. It creates a new major entrance and is partially recessed, creating a new public walk on the outside.

MATERIALITY

All exterior surfaces of the new hall are clad in a terra-cotta rectangular masonry unit that matches the color of the roofing tiles seen on older buildings in the church complex. The simple form is made visually engaging by creating voids between the terra-cotta units in patterns that were explicitly designed by the architects. The voids begin small at the edge of a pattern, then incrementally grow to a larger size, then become small again as the normal solid pattern resumes. The cladding has been compared to a loosely woven fabric in which the threads are more loosely packed in some locations. This is a relevant analogy, because the supports for the terra-cotta are in fact a rectangular grid of metal supports that adjust their normal tight pattern to create the openings in the cladding.

Remarkably seamless transitions between roof and wall and all other folds in the envelope are possible because the terra-cotta cladding is a rainscreen that is not actually the waterproof barrier of the building, making the normal gutters, overhangs, and flashings unnecessary. Openings in the cladding correspond with translucent glazing in the underlying walls, allowing natural light to softly illuminate the hall interiors. At night artificial light travels in the reverse direction, and the voids become precise luminous pixels on the hall surfaces.

The portico that wraps two edges of the courtyard is supported with a series of concrete walls, creating between them many small spaces for passage to the court, which have also been used as confessionals. Like the voids over the windows, the spaces between the concrete walls are wider near the hall entries, gently informing the pedestrian where the opening beyond is located.

TECHNICAL

The terra-cotta cladding is mounted close to the building walls, but the roof cladding is elevated approximately 13.2" (335 mm) above the actual waterproofed structural deck. Each piece of terra-cotta rests on at least two aluminum frames set at the 45-degree angle of the roof. The rainscreen has no sealant between pieces of terra-cotta, so they were secured using aluminum clips fitted into continuous grooves on their edges, which also provides a gap of consistent size between each piece.

The terra-cotta elements are 19.7" × 5.9" × 2" (500 × 150 × 50 mm), and are extruded with three longitudinal core holes to facilitate manufacturing and reduce dead load. Only a few elements were field-cut to create the intended void patterns and at transitions from face to face.

The aluminum struts that support the terra-cotta were fabricated with fittings to receive the clips that hold the cladding pieces. This meant that the struts largely governed the coursing of the terra-cotta, but that the pieces could slide over the struts to the ideal position before being secured. The position of each strut and terra-cotta element was shown in the architect's drawings, but still depended on attentive craftspeople to carry out the design. This was especially true where the void patterns migrate from one surface to another.

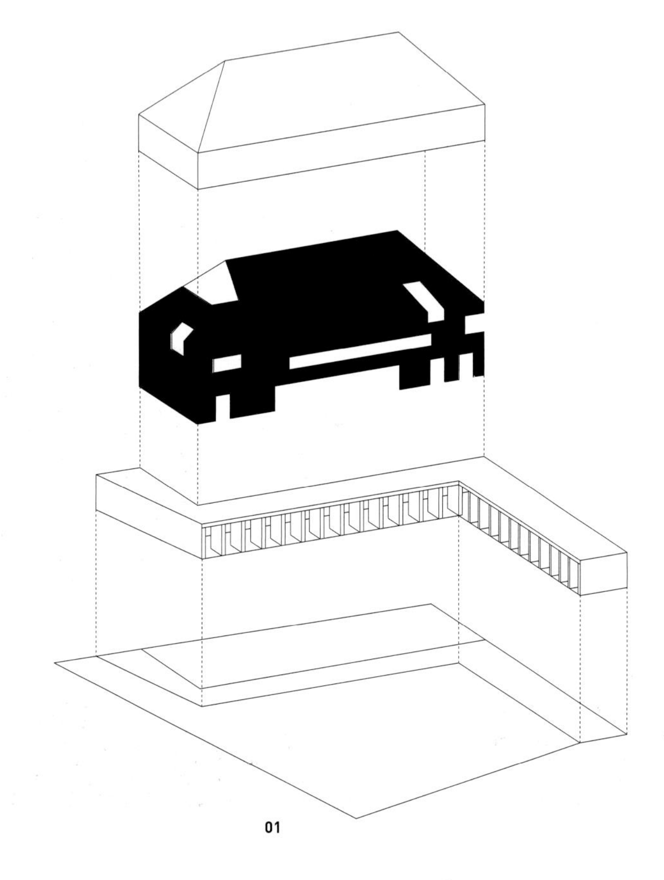

01

02

03

01 Axonometric diagram of scheme

02 View of the hall from the south

03 View toward the hall from the northwest, with interior illumination escaping through voids in masonry cladding

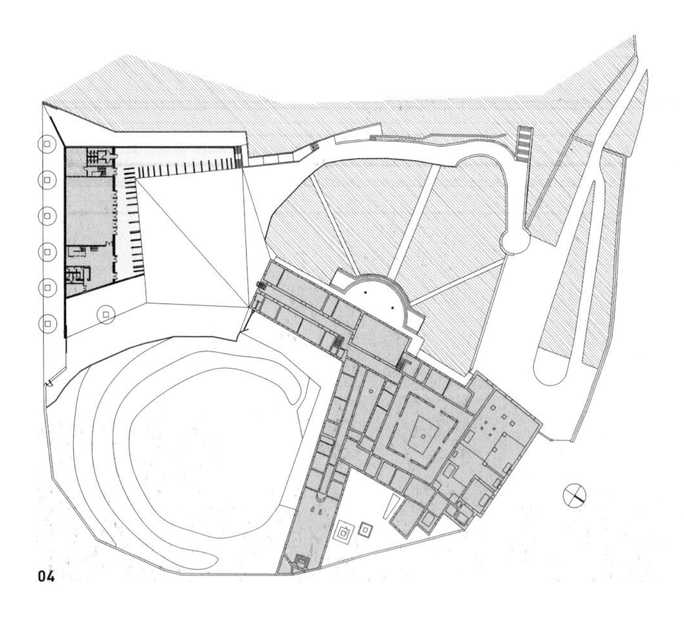
04

04 Site plan, with the hall in upper left

05 Terra-cotta–clad hall is approached from cloistered courtyard

06 Longitudinal section showing rainscreen over building walls and roof

07 Mortarless terra-cotta used at screens and at folds in the planes

08 Daylight passes through masonry screens and translucent glazing to enter the gathering space

05

06

07

08

Chapel of St. Lawrence

Vantaa, Finland — Avanto Architects
Bonded solid masonry

DESIGN INTENTION

Located in the vicinity of the historic Church of St. Lawrence, the new cemetery chapel was designed to be subordinate to the much older stone church on the site. The new chapel ties together different parts of the church landscape and hides the service yard behind it. It actually consists of three gathering spaces of different scales, each accompanied by a distinctive garden. The existing stone walls of the adjoining cemetery are echoed in the orthogonal masonry walls that frame each gathering space. A new bell tower in a corner of the chapel completes the composition.

The cemetery chapel's theme, Path, refers to the mourner's silent route through a series of sacred spaces, each of which prepares the visitor for the next. The whitewashed walls and continuous skylight lead visitors along the path from the low, dimly lit lobby space toward lofty, light spaces. At the chapel the path turns a right angle, with exits through the small garden toward the cemetery beyond. During the proceedings, the passage through the spaces is linear. The routes used by different groups of mourners never cross.

MATERIALITY

The chapel's material palette is derived from other buildings in the context, including rendered brick, natural stone, and patinated copper. Partition walls are white cast-in-place concrete. The lifespan target for the chapel was set at 200 years. An open competition for art installations was carried out before the construction documents were finalized, so that the art could be integrated seamlessly into the architecture. The integration of all of these considerations made solid masonry a thoughtful selection for this project.

The presence of the solid load-bearing walls is unmistakable. They are lightly plastered and whitewashed to become a bright, calm background for the solemn chapel spaces. These massive walls lend consistency to the temperature and humidity of the interior spaces.

Other materials were chosen with attention to their functional and aesthetic qualities, and with a preference for local and handcrafted materials. The copper sheets and mesh were both patinated by hand. The mesh functions as a veil over the windows of the chapel, providing some privacy and reducing heat and glare from the sun. Slate flooring endures the wear of use, and provides a pleasant tactile experience. Stone extracted from the site was used to build the low walls flanking the small gardens and courtyards. A uniform project was achieved by having the interiors, furniture, organ cladding, artifacts, and textiles all designed in the same office as the architecture.

Establishing a 200-year lifespan target for the chapel affected many decisions regarding materials and assemblies. The robust primary structure will certainly last that long, and finish materials were chosen that will age with dignity and require little maintenance. The architects used several models and prototypes to simulate the designs and their lifecycle performance features.

TECHNICAL

Exterior masonry walls are two bricks thick, in this case 21.7" (550 mm) thick, made using traditional bonded solid masonry construction. The masonry walls are fully bonded in all three axes in an English bond pattern, with joint reinforcement installed in every fourth bed joint.

The walls are exposed to view on the inside and outside, and have a light plastering and lime whitewash applied. The wall thickness is sufficient to accept custom light fixtures and urn delivery niches within their depth, as well as embeds for structural members and skylights to bear on them.

In one of the chapels the bricks corbel out of the plane of the wall slightly to form a subtle crucifix shape, made more apparent by sunlight washing the wall. In the large chapel, a sculptor who won the open competition for an art installation designed and prefabricated an abstract cross, which was incorporated gracefully into the solid masonry wall.

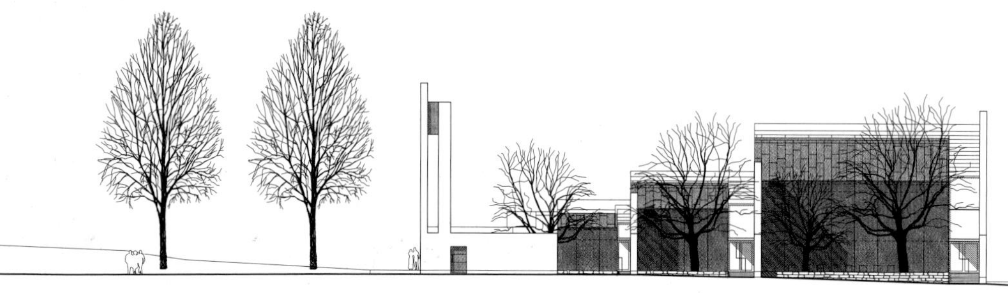

01

02

03

01 South elevation

02 Approach to chapel entries

03 Interior of large chapel

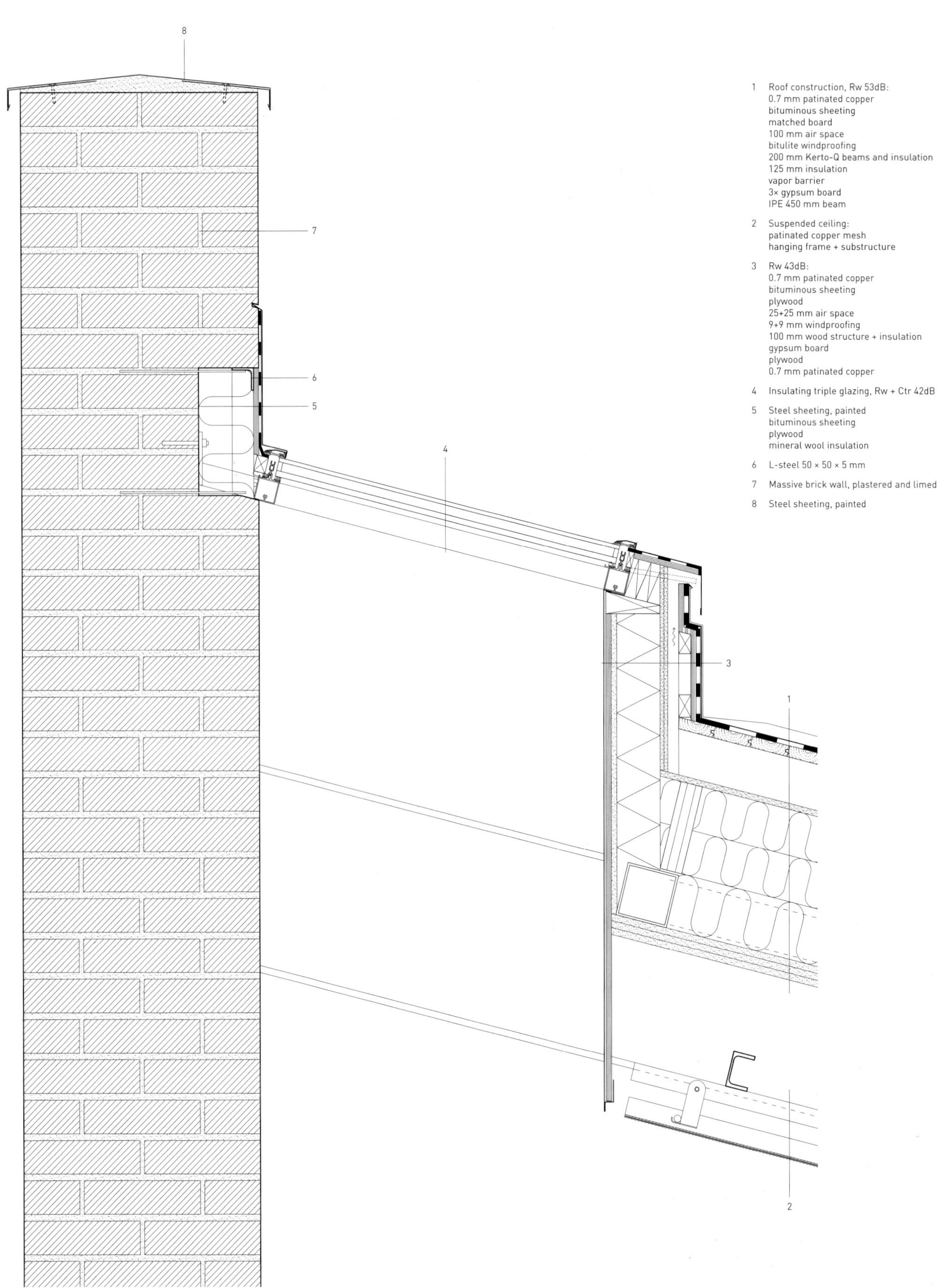
8
7
6
5
4
3
1
2
1 Roof construction, Rw 53dB:
0.7 mm patinated copper
bituminous sheeting
matched board
100 mm air space
bitulite windproofing
200 mm Kerto-Q beams and insulation
125 mm insulation
vapor barrier
3× gypsum board
IPE 450 mm beam
2 Suspended ceiling:
patinated copper mesh
hanging frame + substructure
3 Rw 43dB:
0.7 mm patinated copper
bituminous sheeting
plywood
25+25 mm air space
9+9 mm windproofing
100 mm wood structure + insulation
gypsum board
plywood
0.7 mm patinated copper
4 Insulating triple glazing, Rw + Ctr 42dB
5 Steel sheeting, painted
bituminous sheeting
plywood
mineral wool insulation
6 L-steel 50 × 50 × 5 mm
7 Massive brick wall, plastered and limed
8 Steel sheeting, painted
04

04 Section detail of bonded masonry wall and roof assembly at skylight

05 Commissioned artist sculpting unfired clay masonry units for installation in large chapel

06 Fired masonry units assembled with mortar onto substrate, ready to be incorporated into chapel wall

07 Interior of small chapel; all masonry walls are lightly plastered and whitewashed

08 Interior of intermediate chapel; corbeled brick subtly indicates a crucifix in the wall surface

07

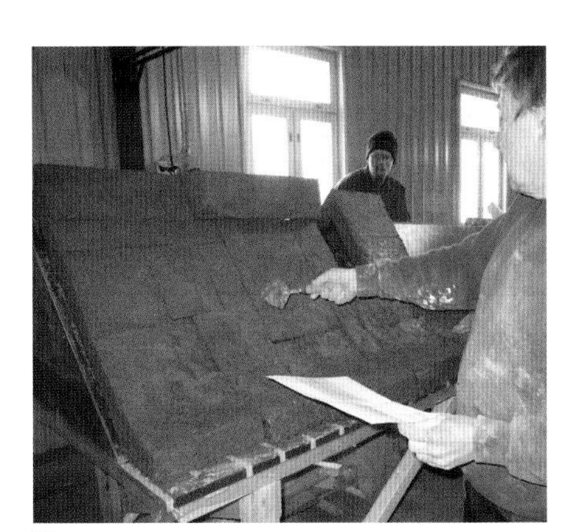

05

08

06

Warehouse 8B Conversion

Madrid, Spain — Arturo Franco Architecture Studio
Recycled masonry

DESIGN INTENTION

In the 1940s a group of utilitarian buildings was built and used as a slaughterhouse by residents of the inner city of Madrid. During the 1980s, the facility's functions were removed to the outskirts of the city and the empty buildings fell into neglect. In 2009 the city council began the process of transforming the deteriorated complex into an avant-garde cultural engine for the surrounding city.

Renovations began by removing the flat clay tile shingles on a few of the buildings, so that new roofing could be installed. A small mountain of usable, intact tile and other rubble started to accumulate on the site, which became an opportunity for material innovation and reuse. The "waste as resource" concept of sustainable design is demonstrated by this project. Warehouse 8B was adapted to serve administrative management, and houses a multipurpose space for talks or presentations, a small work area, and a stockroom.

MATERIALITY

Building elements often expire at different rates. That was the case with the old building, whose wooden roof framing had rotted, leaving clay roof tiles that still had life in them. The tiles were removed with care and the architect repurposed them into partitions and the interior finish, exploiting their texture and color using rhythm and scale. Like the old roof construction, the finished tile partitions also depended on hand labor, but with new challenges and opportunities.

This project represents not only how recycled materials can be used creatively, but also how material itself can set the tone for the final project by telling a story of the past while making it function in the future. The juxtaposition of the worn, tired structure against the new inserts and masonry walls gives a richness of materiality and composition not often seen in architecture.

TECHNICAL

Each of the project's pressed flat clay tiles was manufactured with side ribs that interlock with its neighbor's in a course. These edges were articulated with a small gutter that directs water down and away from the unsealed seam between tiles. The tiles were contoured laterally to channel water more effectively. On the lower edge of each tile, a turned-down headlap matches the profile of the tile it was placed upon, thereby reducing the intrusion of wind-driven rain. On the upper edge these old tiles have downward-facing lugs that catch on wood battens, making it so that the tiles hang on the supporting frame with no nails to secure them. The articulated shapes of the tiles bonded well with mortar as they were being installed, and made it possible to make a loose-fitting arrangement.

Adaptive reuse of the building shell and use of salvaged materials reduced project costs and substantially reduced environmental impact. By reducing the need for newly manufactured materials, physical and human resources were conserved. Embodied energy and carbon impacts were also reduced. In addition, landfill waste associated with disposal of the old building materials was greatly reduced.

01

02

03

01 Section of existing building

02 Condition prior to adaptive reuse

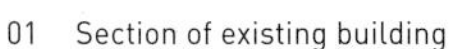

03 Renovated condition

04 Entry to multipurpose space on the left; recycled roofing tiles face walls

04

05 Public facade of renovated facility

06 Careful removal of clay roofing tiles from 70-year-old building

07 Storage of salvaged roofing tiles

08 Experiments with reuse of salvaged roofing tiles

09 Detail of completed installation

10 Process of recycling clay roofing tiles for use as interior wall treatment

11 Interior partition

12 Partition openings of various sizes

13 Ends of partitions show the rich textures and colors of salvaged tiles

05

06

07

08

09

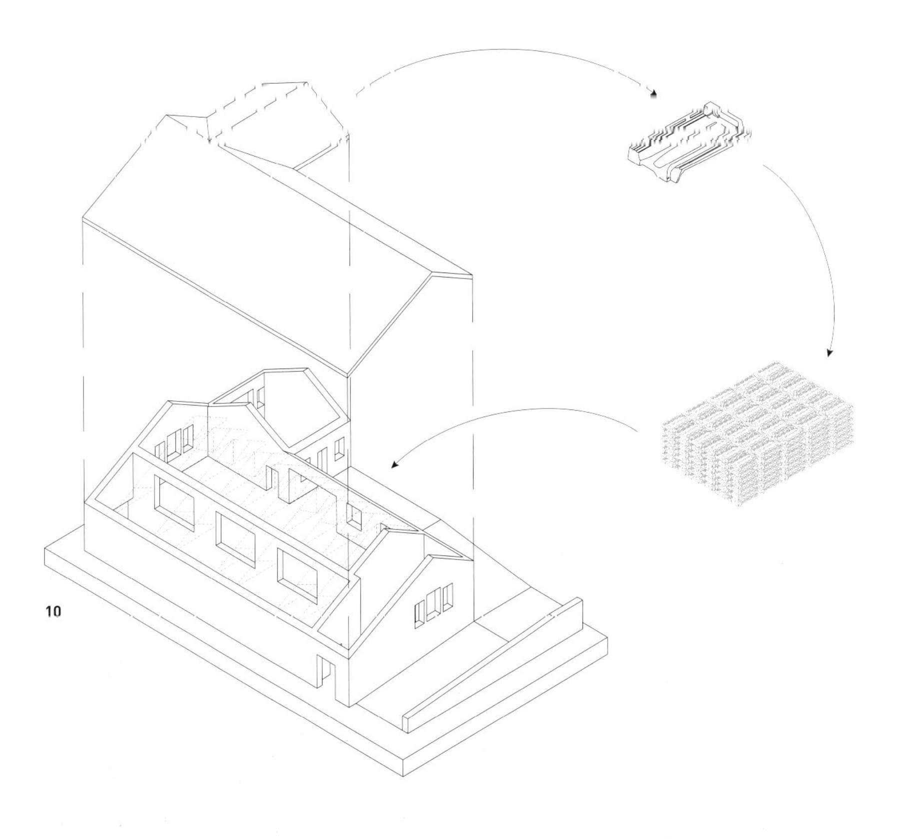

10

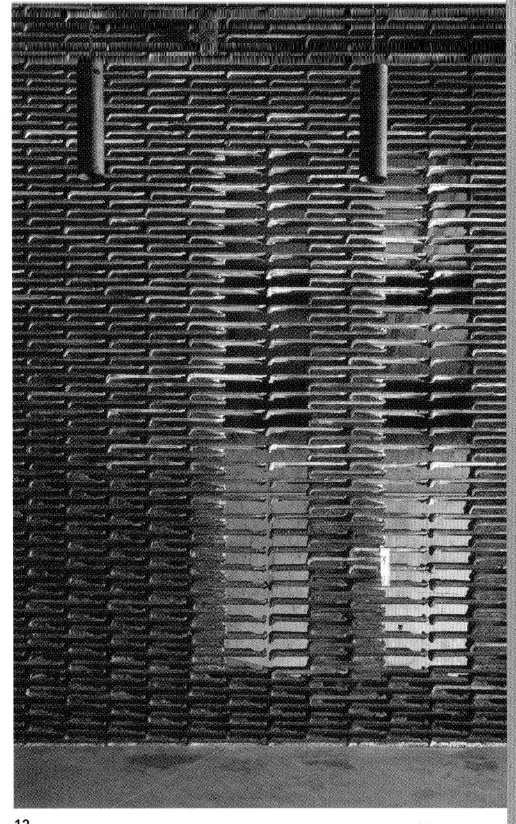

12

11

13

Butaro Doctor's Housing

Burera District, Rwanda — Mass Design Group
Compressed stabilized earth blocks, stone masonry

DESIGN INTENTION

The construction of the Butaro Doctor's Housing accompanied the building of the nearby Butaro Hospital, which together represent a substantial effort to introduce health care to one of the most remote and impoverished regions of Rwanda. Until these facilities were built, the population of 340,000 had no access to doctors or hospitals. The Rwandan Ministry of Health and Partners In Health (a U.S.-based NGO) developed the hospital. Mass Design Group, with support from Brigham and Women's Hospital in Boston, funded, designed, and built the housing to better attract and retain doctors and staff. The project was donated to the Rwandan Ministry of Health upon completion.

In addition to meeting its functional agenda as housing for doctors and nurses, the project also was intended to empower the community through participation in the construction process. The designers provided additional services to the community, educating and training adults to perform the construction and employing 900 residents. The project became a collaborative design-build project, resulting in innovative uses of local materials and a design that was well matched with the physical and cultural context.

MATERIALITY

The local volcanic stone is used as the exterior facing for most of the housing facility. This stone is common in the northern Rwandan landscape, and is reviled by farmers trying to clear their fields. In the past, residents have used it for foundations and garden walls, often covering it with mortar rather than leaving it exposed. In this project, care was taken to install it with minimally exposed mortar joints so that its deep gray color and rich texture can be appreciated. The effect required the craftsmen to carefully trim each piece of stone so that it snugly fit into the irregular patterns of the wall.

The wall's inner layer is made of compressed stabilized earth blocks (CSEBs), which were made at the site using local soils that were excavated to make the foundations. A reinforced concrete frame supports concentrated loads, strengthens intersections of walls, and laterally stabilizes the masonry walls.

Rather than rely on mechanized construction, this project was designed to employ as many workers as possible, with emphasis on hand labor. The size and weight of construction elements were matched to the labor-intensive methods of construction used on the project. Workers quickly acquired new construction skills that were applied to this project; this enhancement of the local labor force had residual economic value for individuals and the community as a whole.

TECHNICAL

The CSEBs used to build the houses have less cement than concrete masonry units, and unlike brick do not require firing in a kiln, reducing CO_2 emissions and avoiding local deforestation. The economic and environmental costs of transportation were also significantly reduced. The designers had to test the local soils to be certain they were suitable, then brought a block press to the site and established a training and production workshop. Ten members of the community formed a full-time block production crew for the three-month duration of the project, producing 29,000 blocks. A stabilizing agent, either cement or lime, was mixed with moistened local soils and constituted no more than 10 percent of the mix. After being formed the blocks were dried in the sun before being placed in the walls.

The typical block has nominal dimensions of 9.8" × 9.8" × 3.9" (250 × 250 × 100 mm). They do not have core holes, but do have two shallow recesses on the top and bottom faces to better bond with mortar. The CSEB press had interchangeable molds, some of which produced units that accepted vertical steel rebar and cement grout into head joints at the midline of the wythe. These vertical steel reinforcements were tied with horizontal steel rebar to the cast-in-place concrete columns, imparting greater tensile and shear strength to the unit masonry planes.

The CSEB surfaces were covered on the outside either with volcanic stone using full collar joints, or on some elevations simply with a cement stucco rendering, painted white. On the interior, the CSEB surfaces were plastered with cement plaster and also painted white. The volcanic stone layer is approximately the same thickness as the CSEB wythe, giving the finished exterior walls an overall thickness of approximately 21.2" (540 mm). None of the walls required the addition of thermal insulation because the density and thickness of the masonry walls create a thermal mass that regulates interior temperatures.

Below finish grade, the stone masonry walls are battered in shape, increasing in thickness with their depth. The outside surfaces of the foundation walls are covered with reinforced concrete, which is integral with reinforced concrete footings below the walls.

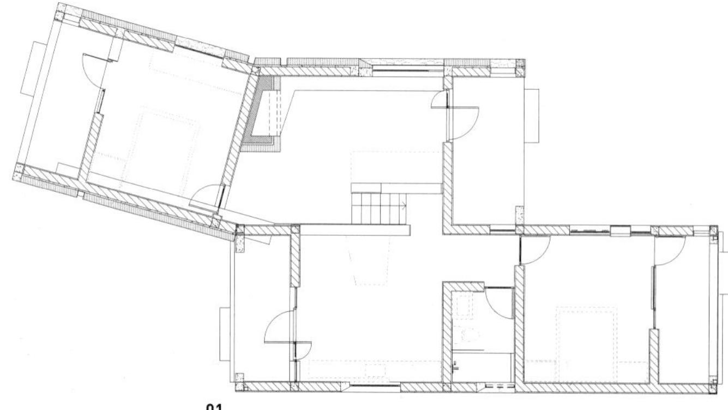

01

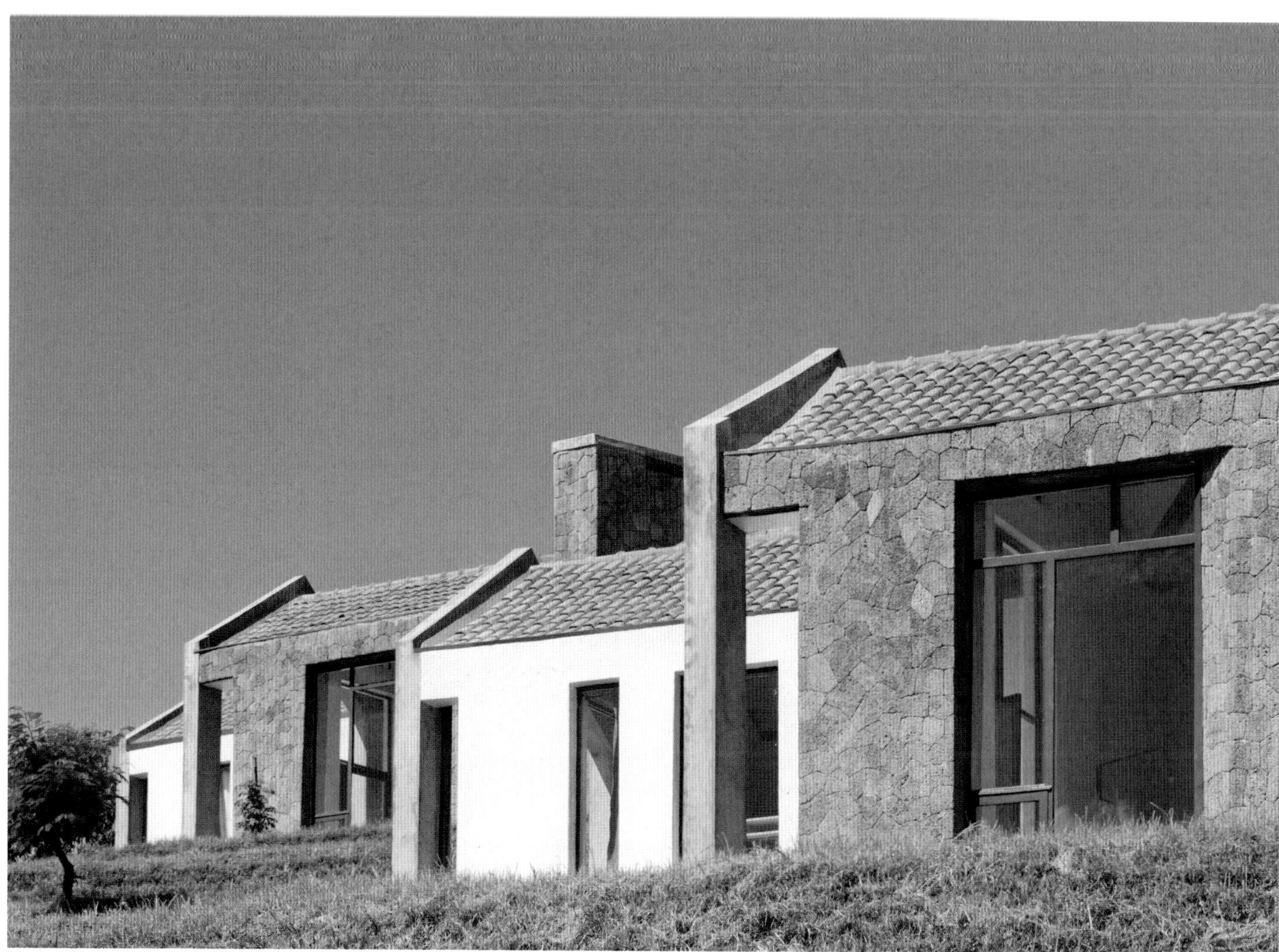
02

03

01 Ground-floor plan

02 Exterior view

03 Emphasis was placed on local sources of construction materials and labor

04

05

06

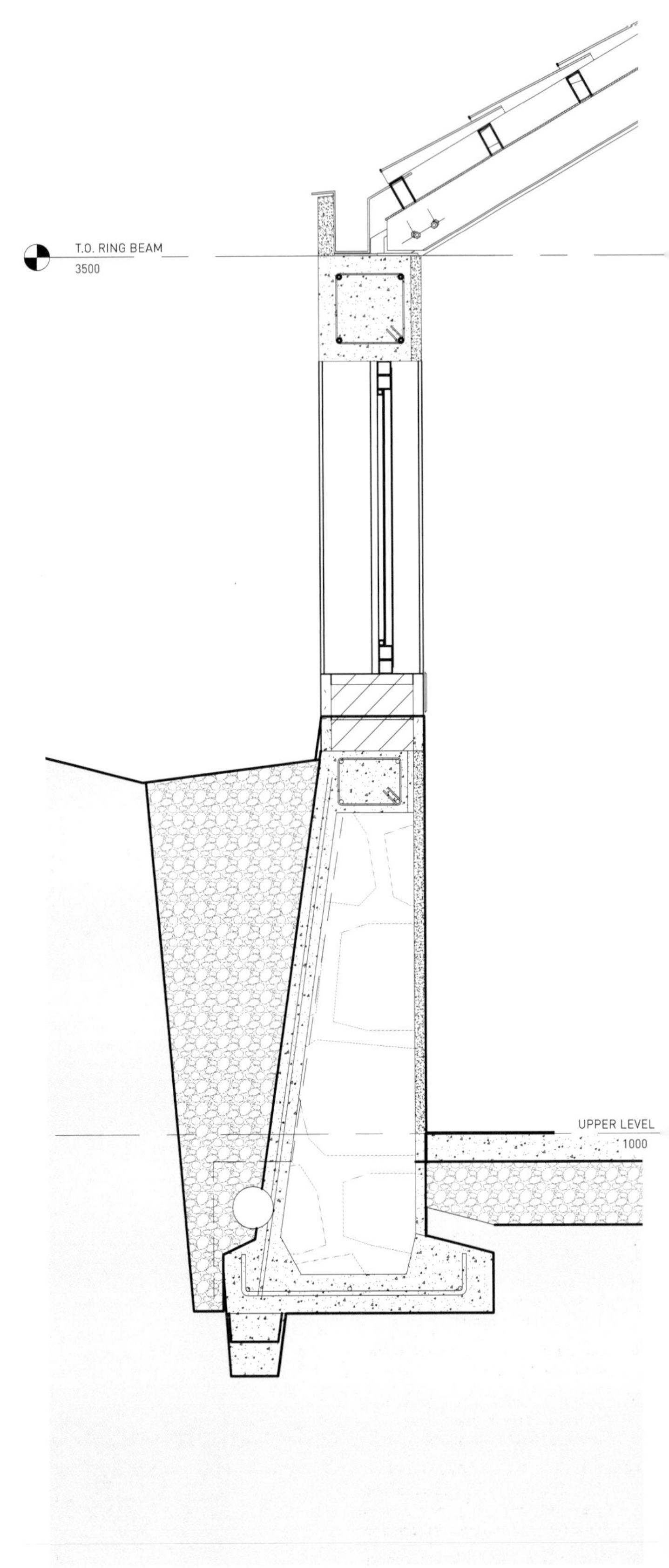

07

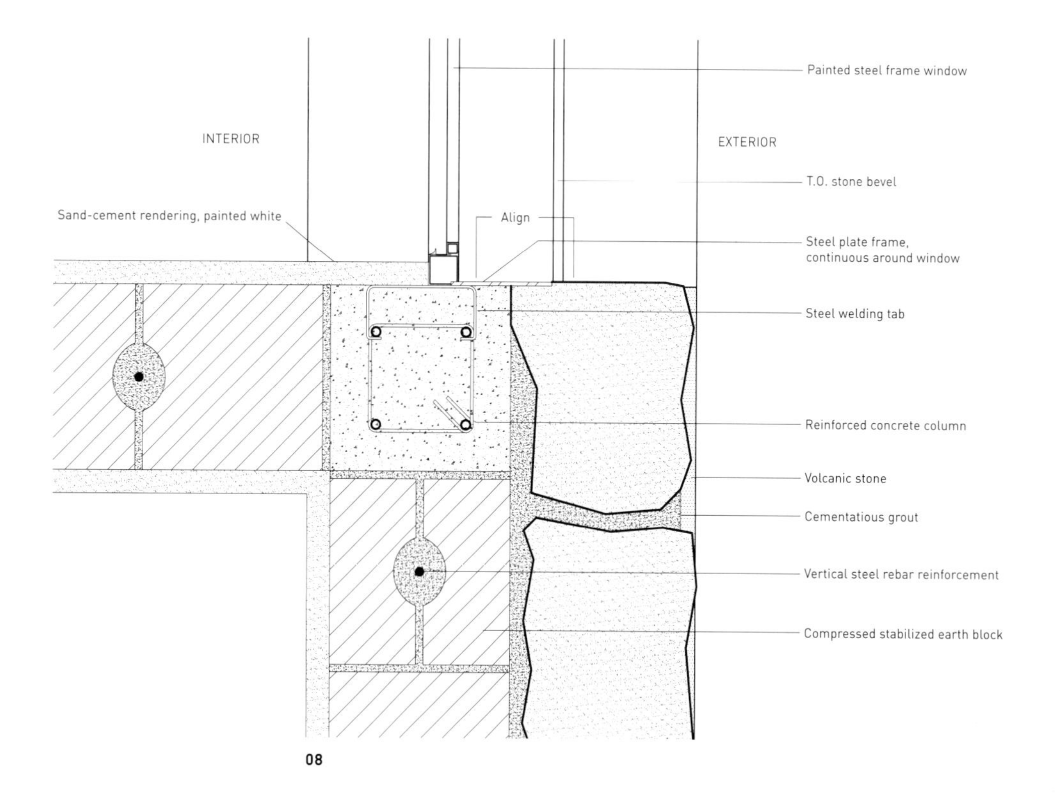

08

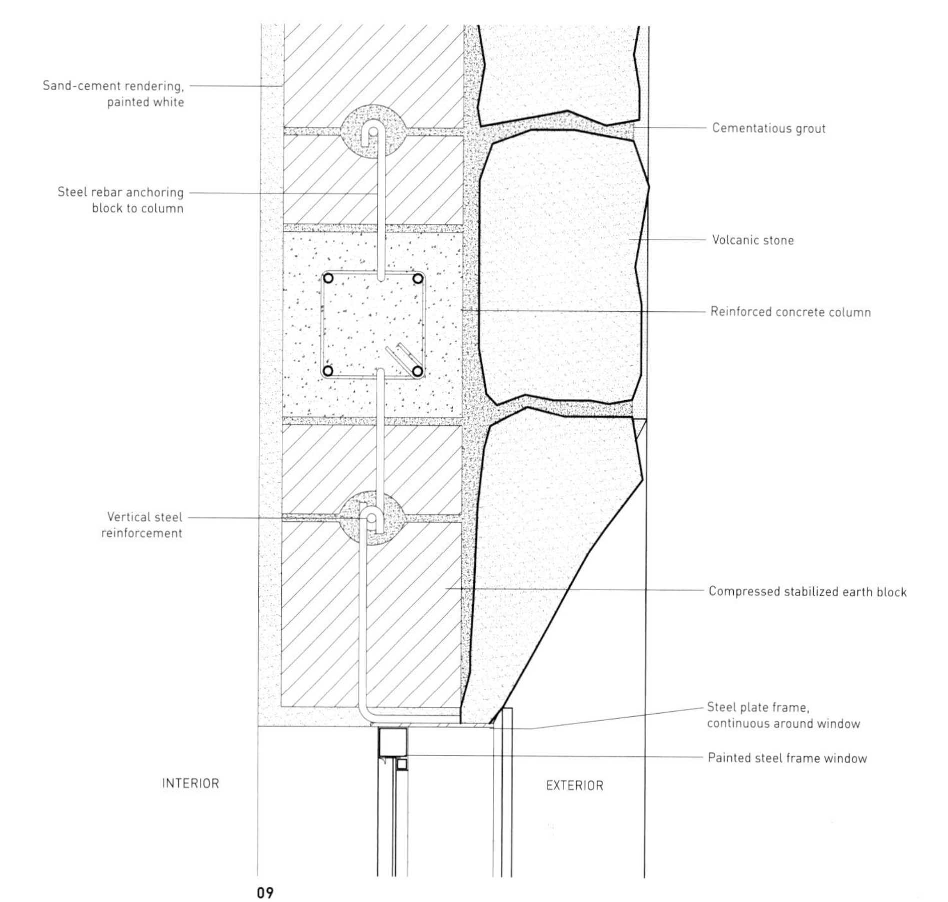

09

04 Workers became skilled at making CSEBs using local soils

05 Soil excavated for the building's foundations were used to make the CSEBs in the new walls

06 Local volcanic stone is applied to the outside of the CSEBs

07 Section through west wall showing hybrid masonry and reinforced concrete structural systems

08 Plan detail at corner of reinforced masonry and reinforced concrete wall structure, faced with volcanic stone on the exterior and plaster on the interior

09 Plan detail of wall at window opening

Silk Wall + J-Office

Shanghai, China — Archi-Union Architects
Concrete masonry screen, parametric design of masonry

DESIGN INTENTION

Archi-Union Architects renovated a neglected silk workshop in a Shanghai industrial park to serve as their own offices. In addition to the normal functions contained in a designer's office, this project contains a large exhibit space and a court-yard framed between two enclosed single-story volumes. The memory of the building's previous use permeates the new construction.

The design intention was to take a common, simple construction element—a cubic hollow concrete block—and bring it to life using a new block-laying method. The designers identified a specific image of silk fabric, which was graphically sampled and its undulating surfaces translated into planes of concrete masonry units. The new screen wall gives uniformity and a contemporary expression to the renovated project, and mediates between the project's internal functions and the surrounding city.

MATERIALITY

The existing building's walls were made using brick coated with painted stucco. They were restored to their original brick and mortar surface, with some residue from the previous finishes allowed to remain. The walls were then wrapped with a freestanding screen wall of concrete masonry units. Blocks were placed at angles to create an interesting texture and to vary the amount of light and breeze that reached the building. Vegetation was planted in the space between the screen and the building wall and at the base; over time the masonry and plants will blend in varied proportions.

Each block's angle of rotation was calculated using a graphic analysis of differing gradients that were visible in a photograph of a length of silk. Parametric processes allowed the designer to recreate the patterning, using each concrete masonry unit as a pixel. The rigid, repetitive expression normally associated with masonry is replaced by a fluid, unpredicted quality.

TECHNICAL

The architects devised a set of guides to be used to position each block. These simple tools allowed the masons to change block angles along the entire length of the masonry screen and produce a complex visual pattern that never repeats.

In the first construction attempt, difficulties with the prototype prompted the development of a simpler system that involved only ten intermediate angles to be set within a 90-degree rotation. The designer taught workers how and where to position the templates to place the blocks in the correct orientation. The accuracy of the bricks' angles depended on the skills of the masons, but any deviations are minor and did not have a major impact on the final effect.

The screen wall is not reinforced vertically or horizontally, but is secured to a cast-in-place concrete frame that stabilizes it structurally. Moisture may be absorbed into the screen wall's concrete masonry units and mortar, but because these materials are detached from the actual building wall, it will not harm other building assemblies or the interior spaces.

01 Translating silk fabric into masonry coursing, then into parametric guide for wall surface

02 Elevation of wall segment

03 Different guides were used by masons to produce each of twenty different block orientations.

04 Completed concrete masonry screen wraps the former silk workshop building

05 Wooden guides allowed masons to accurately position concrete blocks in the wall.

06 Concrete masonry wall appears to undulate

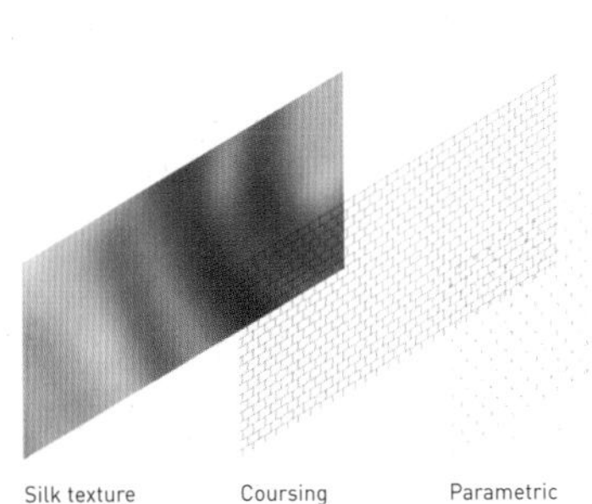

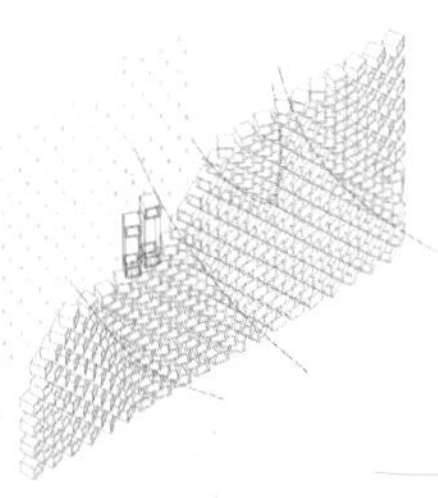

01

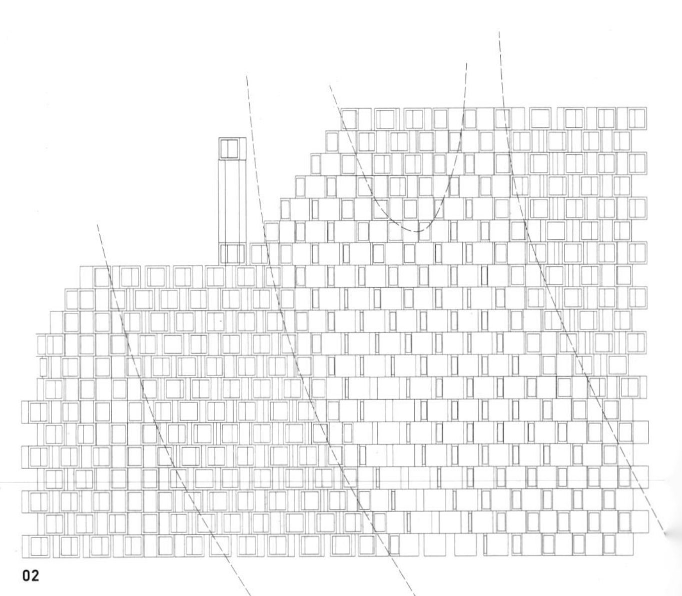

02

Angle guide
Perspective
-10 -9 -8 -7 -6 -5 -4 -3 -2 -1 0 1 2 3 4 5 6 7 8 9 10
Elevation
Plan
-10 -9 -8 -7 -6 -5 -4 -3 -2 -1 0 1 2 3 4 5 6 7 8 9 10

03

04

05

06

Center for Design Research

Lawrence, Kansas — Studio 804 / University of Kansas
Limestone veneer cladding, masonry thermal mass wall

DESIGN INTENTION

The new Center for Design Research is located on the University of Kansas's former dairy farm, alongside its stone house and barn. The Center provides a laboratory for research and design collaborations between multiple schools, led by the School of Architecture, Design, and Planning. The Center emphasizes the education of the University and community regarding sustainable strategies, material innovation, and building efficiency.

This 1,820 sq. ft. (170 sq. m) facility demonstrates exemplary sustainable design strategies, and in fact has earned a LEED Platinum rating and a Passive House Pre-Certification, one of the first commercial buildings in North America to earn that title. The Center generates electricity using a wind turbine and photovoltaic systems, but also has a rigorously designed envelope and site strategy to achieve its environmental goals. These green building technologies and products have set the standard for the University and the surrounding community. The design capitalizes on existing resources, minimizes environmental degradation, and creates a safe and efficient working environment.

Twenty-three architecture students and their professor carried out the design and construction of the Center as an academic design/build project. This is an example of what has become an annual undertaking of the terminal graduate studio at this school.

MATERIALITY

Resourceful use of existing local materials led to the reclaiming of more than one hundred tons of limestone tailings from Kansas quarry operations. Small and oddly shaped tailings were hand cut into thin, stackable pieces to clad interior and exterior walls and become a contemporary version of the existing building's old stone walls. Site waste was reduced by placing all scrap stone from the cladding process along the north side of the building as exposed fill. The clever reclaiming of this limestone not only respects the contextual use of stone historically on the site, but also demonstrates the students' creative use of this material.

The Center's southern facade is a combination of limestone-faced wall and custom-fabricated steel curtain wall. A limestone and CMU Trombe wall is positioned inside the large southern windows to absorb the sun's energy during the day and radiate it at night.

TECHNICAL

The limestone exterior wall cladding was applied as 3.5 in. thick (89 mm) veneers to wood framing above floor level, and to concrete foundation walls below floor level. In both applications metal anchors link the veneer stone to the substrate at 24" intervals horizontally and 16" intervals vertically (610 × 406 mm). The stone pieces vary in width, and were installed with their exposed faces slightly out of alignment, making the small scale of each stone piece visible. The reclaimed cut limestone pieces were split and placed randomly into the wall, along with approximately 25 percent unsplit pieces. The cladding is expected to remain in service many years with little or no maintenance.

The walls and foundations are exceedingly well insulated in order to meet the environmental goals of the project. In the wood framed walls above floor level, the studs used were actually 16" deep wood I-joists at 16" intervals (406 mm); the blown cellulose between studs matches the ample stud width. The insulated wood framing was wrapped with a vapor barrier and an additional 2" (50 mm) layer of rigid polystyrene insulation, with only a slender (approximately 0.5" [13 mm]) cavity behind the stone veneer.

The stone veneer exterior walls take advantage of the limestone's aesthetic qualities and durability. Another wall inside the Center exploits the thermal mass capacity of masonry walls. The Center's large south-facing window permits sunlight to pass through it to thermally charge a stone and masonry Trombe wall that was built 30" (760 mm) inside the glass. This 32' long wall fills the 11.3" tall space (9.75 m long, 3.45 m tall) and has vents at the top, which the building's mechanical systems automatically operate to let heat into the interior spaces. The zone between the curtain wall and the Trombe wall was enclosed on the ends with glass, making it function as a double-envelope assembly for this portion of the Center.

The trombe wall was built with a core of 6" (150 mm) concrete masonry and was faced on both sides with 2" (50 mm) limestone veneers using full collar joints but no joint reinforcement. To make the wall seem less ponderous in the space, a portion of the wall was built using 0.5" (13 mm) plate-glass layers between each concrete masonry course. The slender glass layers contribute to the thermal mass of the wall, but also transmit light through the massive wall in a crisp geometric pattern.

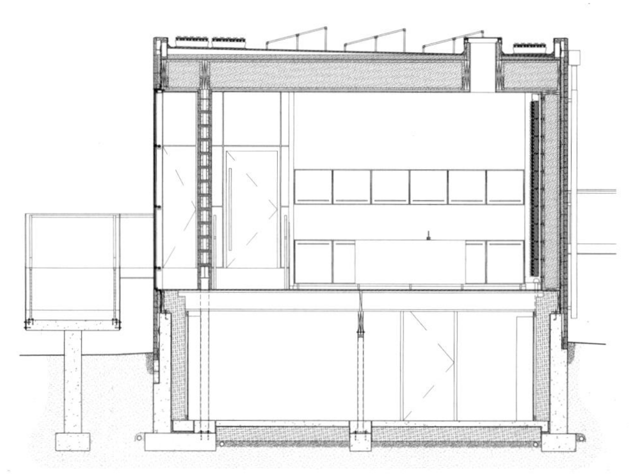

01

02

03

01 Transverse section

02 Exterior view

03 View into space between south-facing glazing and limestone-faced thermal mass wall

04 Section through south-facing wall at thermal mass

05 Detail at top of limestone-faced wall and roof

06 Interior of meeting room showing masonry thermal mass wall on left with horizontal glass laminations between courses

07 Interior view toward entry

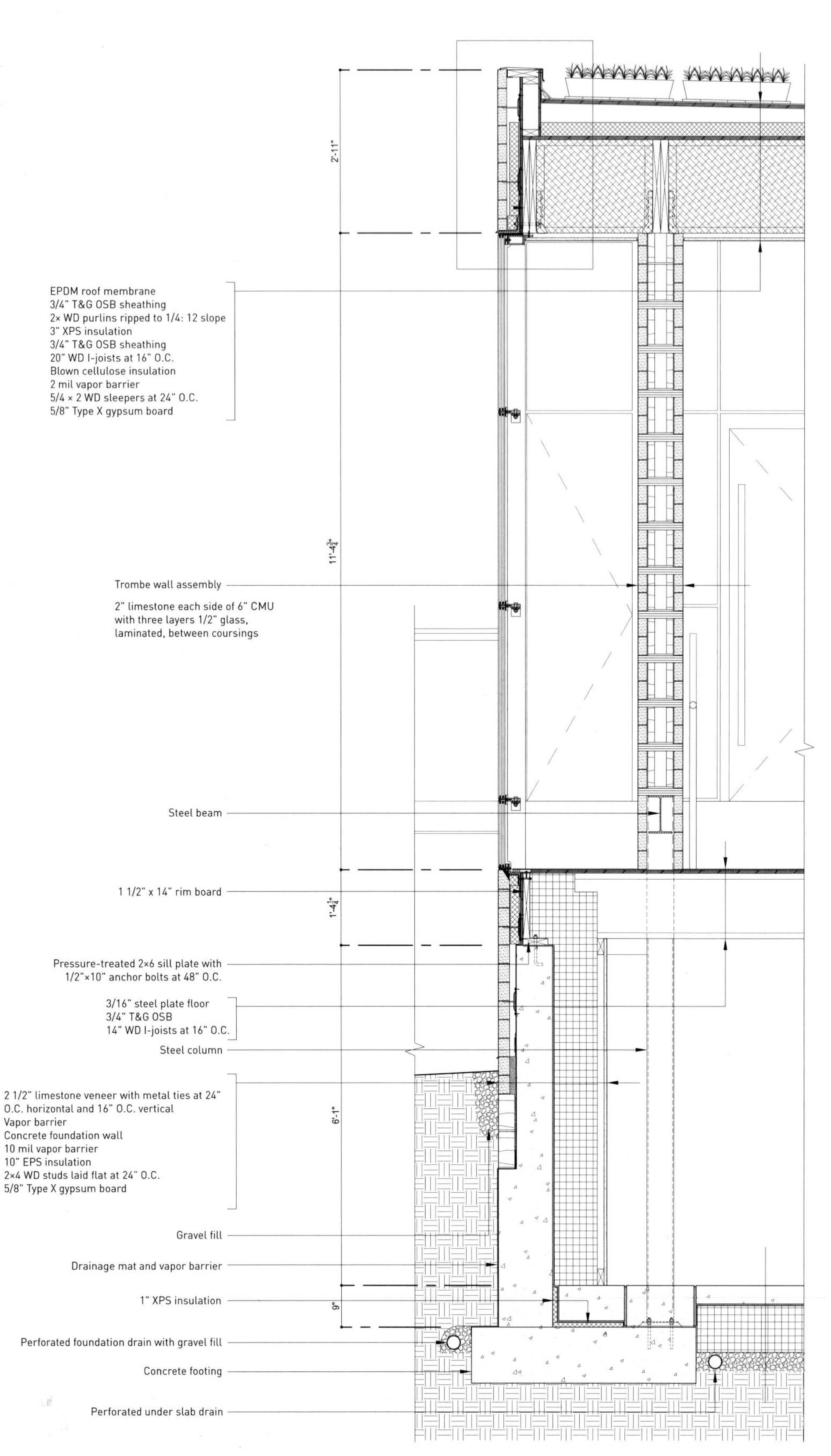

04

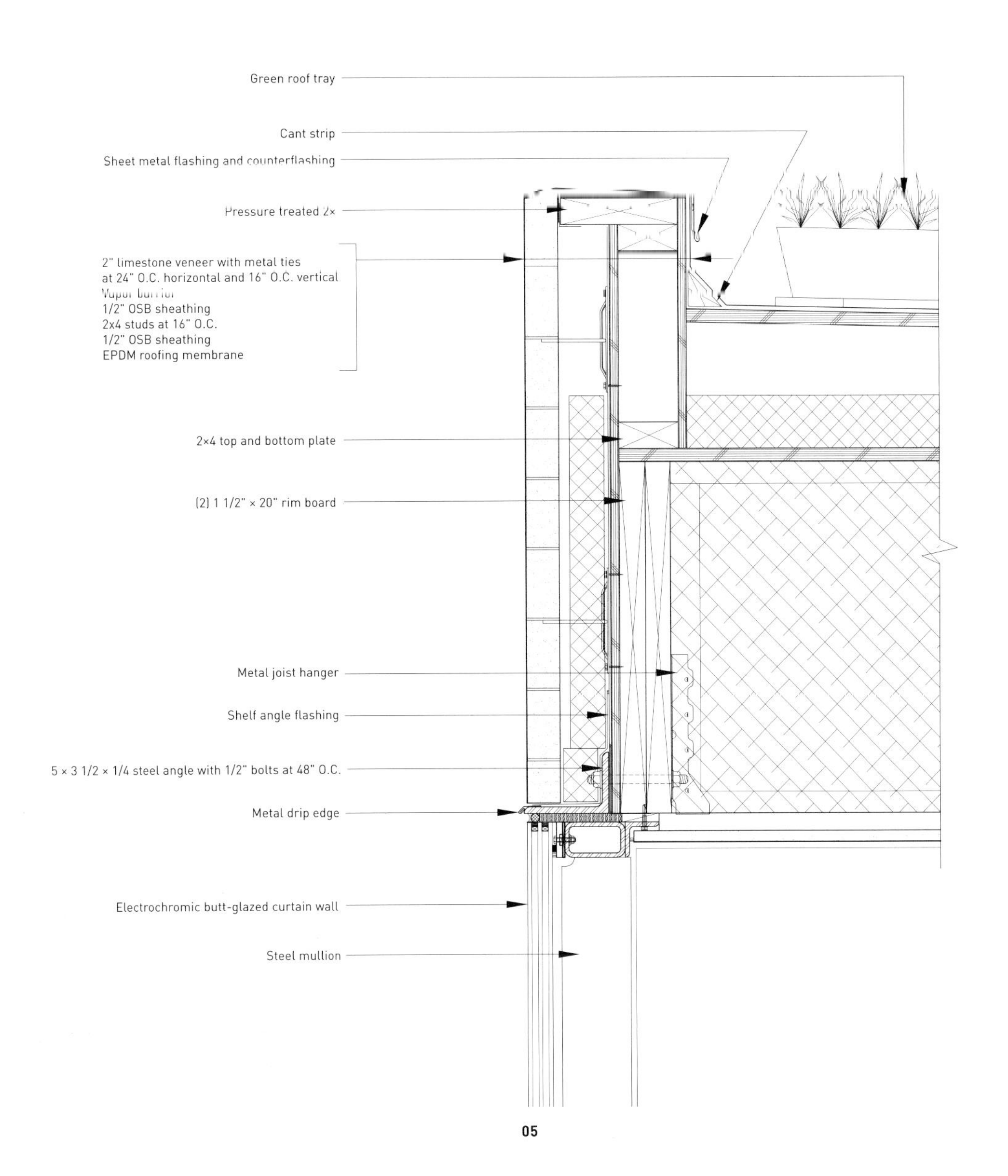
Green roof tray
Cant strip
Sheet metal flashing and counterflashing
Pressure treated 2×
2" limestone veneer with metal ties
at 24" O.C. horizontal and 16" O.C. vertical
Vapor barrier
1/2" OSB sheathing
2x4 studs at 16" O.C.
1/2" OSB sheathing
EPDM roofing membrane
2×4 top and bottom plate
(2) 1 1/2" × 20" rim board
Metal joist hanger
Shelf angle flashing
5 × 3 1/2 × 1/4 steel angle with 1/2" bolts at 48" O.C.
Metal drip edge
Electrochromic butt-glazed curtain wall
Steel mullion

05

06

07

La Pallissa

Catalonia, Spain — Cubus
Renovated stone masonry

DESIGN INTENTION

Family members renovated a seventeenth-century rural home in Catalonia to create several apartments for use during summer visits. The focus here is on the renovation of the former stable and hayloft annex, a secondary building adjoining the main house.

The renovation did not alter the overall form of the annex, but stabilized the existing stone construction and introduced new features to address contemporary expectations regarding the thermal envelope and building services. The annex renovations were restrained, accepting this small building's lower hierarchal position compared to the main house yet respecting its historic qualities.

MATERIALITY

The project began with an empty stone rectangular volume, topped with a shed roof, and a hayloft floor over part of the space. The character of the existing old stone walls was considered the main architectural asset, so the design left them exposed inside and outside. The richness and historic quality of the stone walls give this simple renovated space a complexity and story it would normally not have. Here materiality speaks in a simple but strong voice.

A new window opening through the stone wall was introduced, providing a view to the landscape. This opening used concealed steel elements for its lintel, making it possible for it to have a broad horizontal proportion.

A small two-story core of services was designed to be freestanding in the volume, leaving the stone walls fully exposed. New interior elements were finished in energetic white or red, distinguishing them from the historic stone and timber structural elements.

TECHNICAL

The existing unreinforced stone walls are approximately ten times as tall as they are thick (1.64' × 18.7' [500 × 5,700 mm]). For centuries they have performed well, demonstrating the durability of modest bonded rubble masonry. To sustain the stone walls further, they were reinforced where critical structural concentrations occur. For instance, new reinforced concrete footings were placed below the inner half of the stone walls, where no footings existed previously. The new footings support the walls and bear the loads of the new concrete floor slab and finishes. Higher in the walls, new reinforced concrete bond beams were cast into pockets within the wall thickness to bear the concentrated loads of loft floor beams and the roof rafters.

The renovated annex is protected from moisture intrusion by adding a clear water-repellent treatment to the exposed outer wall surfaces, waterproofing to the subgrade surfaces, and perimeter drain lines to take ground water away. The new floor slab is supported on a ventilated cavity to isolate it from moisture in the soil below.

The loft floor construction employed ceramic tile set into inverted T-shaped steel joists, topped with reinforced concrete and locally made ceramic tile. The freestanding kitchen and bath partitions were built using large-format clay tile units, faced with either plaster or ceramic tile. The ceiling is made of recycled clay tile between wood purlins, and the roof is finished with locally produced clay tile.

The old and the new construction of this project exhibit a great variety of masonry materials and construction techniques. The level of craft in these traditional "trowel trades" persists at a high level.

01 Schematic illustration of new elements within existing stone walls

02 Exterior view of former stable from north, with main building to the left

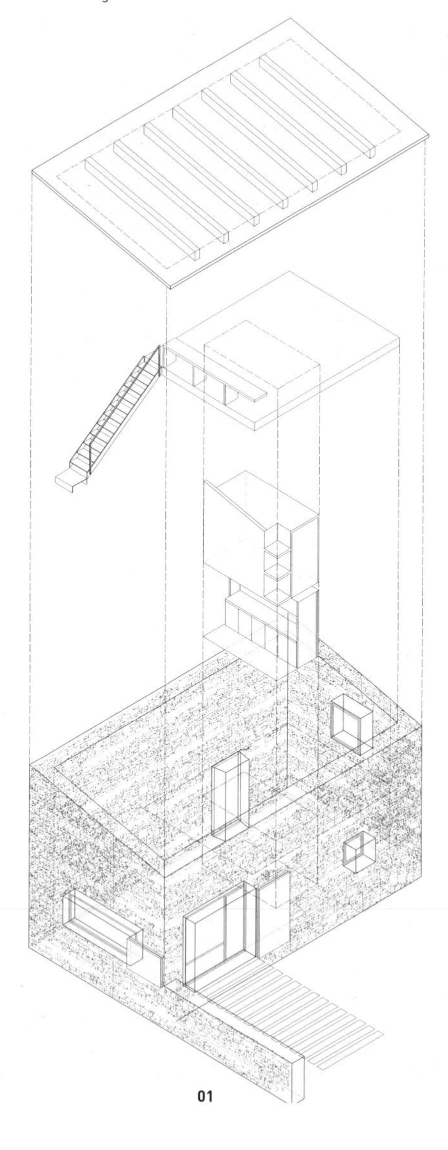

01

02

03

03 New elements are intended to be freestanding from the stone walls and much different in appearance

04 Section showing remedial work to stabilize existing stone exterior wall, and new floor and partitions using clay tile

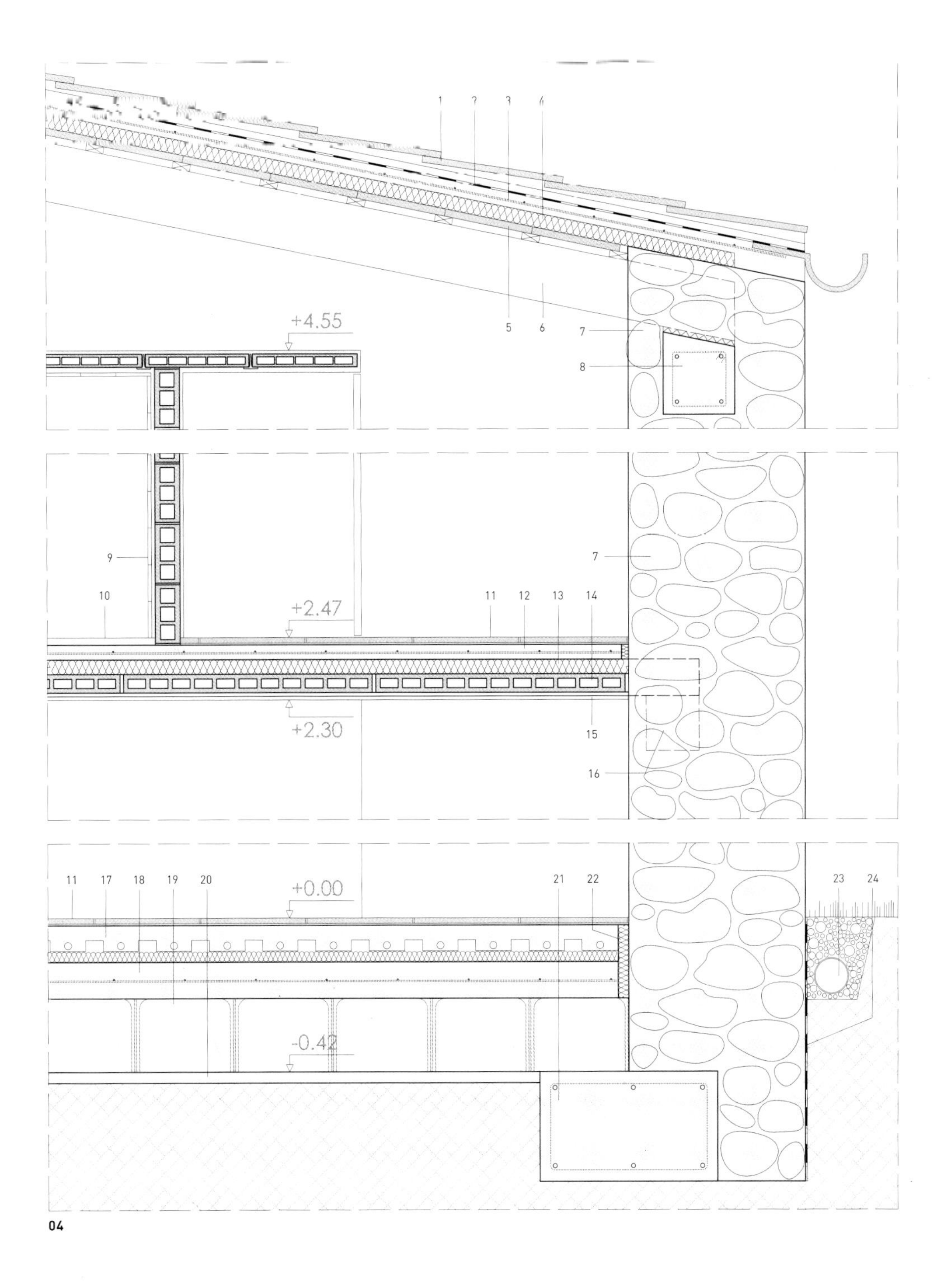

04

1 Ventilated local ceramic tile, rainwater collection

2 Waterproof sheet

3 Reinforced concrete

4 Thermal insulation (40 mm) with vapor barrier

5 Recycled local ceramic tile

6 Wooden beam

7 Existing stone masonry wall with water-repellent treatment

8 Reinforced concrete perimetral band

9 Bath: wall and roof tiling

10 Polished concrete pavement

11 Local ceramic floor

12 Reinforced concrete

13 Acoustic insulation

14 Ceramic vise between HEB-100 beams

15 Plastering ceiling

16 HEB-100 concrete cube support

17 Underfloor heating

18 Reinforced concrete (100 mm)

19 Plastic cavities (200 mm), ventilated air space

20 Concrete base for cavities

21 Phased reinforcement concrete foundation

22 Perimetral expanded polystyrene

23 Perimetral drainage with gravel

24 Waterproof drain

Index

:mlzd, 170–71
3M, 210
5468796 Architecture, 152–55
96 percent silica glass, 13

Aalto, Alvar, 8
Aberystwyth Arts Centre, 172
Aberystwyth, Wales, United Kingdom, 172–73
absorbency (A), 12
acrylic, 178–79, 182–83, 184–87, 188–91, 192–95, 196–97, 198–201, 202–5, 206–9, 210–13, 214–15
coated polyester fabric, 179, 206–9
Corian acrylic polymer, 178–79, 198–201
fluoropolymer films, 179
glass-fiber-reinforced plastic (GFRP), 178, 188–91
polyester fabric, 179, 214–15
polyethylene terephthalate (PET), 178, 196–97
polymethyl methacrylate (PMMA), 178, 182–83
polyurethane foam (PUR), 178, 188–91
UPM ProFi wood plastic composite, 178
Acrylite, 178
adhesives, 92, 122
admixtures, 49, 50, 52, 53, 54–55, 58, 72, 80
accelerating, 54
air-entraining, 54
corrosion-inhibiting, 55
fibrous, 55
fly ash, 55
freeze-protection, 55
pigmenting, 55, 56, 58
chemical stain, 55
dry method, 55
integral method, 55
pozzolans, 55
retarding, 54
shrinkage-reducing (SRAs), 55
superplasticizers, 54
water-reducing, 54–55
adobe, 218
aggregates, 4, 50, 54, 56, 58, 72, 80. *See also* admixtures
Agrippa, Marcus, 129
Albertslund, Denmark, 164–67
alloy steel, 132, 133, 156, 168
alloys, 129, 134–35, 136, 137, 139, 168
alumina, 49
aluminosilicate glass, 13
aluminum, 26, 30, 38, 42, 56, 90, 108, 129, 130, 132, 133, 134–36, 142–45, 170–71, 192, 196, 198, 202, 214, 228, 240
alloys, 134–35, 136, 137, 139, 168
casting alloys, 135
heat-treatable, 135
non-heat-treatable, 134
anodized, 164–67
appearance, 135–36
chemical finishes, 135
clear-coat anodizing, 135
coatings, 135–36
construction use, 134, 135
corrosion, 134, 142
costs, 134
customization, 152
environmental conditions, 152, 164, 170
extruded, 152–55
finishes, 135–36, 142
H-sections, 42
joining, 136
manufacturing, 134–35
mechanical finishes, 135
perforated, 142–45
plastic coatings, 135–36
recycling, 134
stamped sheets, 170–71
strength, 134, 135, 152
temper, 135
weathering, 136, 142, 152, 164
Aluminum Association, 135
American Society for Testing and Materials (ASTM), 52, 132
Anagram Architects, 236–37
Anansi Playground Building, 9, 198–201
Andes Mountains, 58
Angkor Wat, Cambodia, 218
Anmahian Winton Architects, 9, 108–11
annealing, 11, 133
anode, 131
anodized aluminum, 164–67
Apple Flagship Store, 9, 46–47
Apple, Inc., 9, 46–47
Archi-Union Architects, 256–57
Architectura, De, 86
Arizona, 137
Artists' Studios in Aberystwyth, 9, 172–73
Arturo Franco Architecture Studio, 248–51
ashlar, 222
Aspdin, Joseph, 49
Asplund, Erik Gunnar, 8
ASTM. *See* American Society for Testing and Materials (ASTM)
Atelier Deshaus, 30–33
Austin, Texas, 156–59
Australia, 137, 146–49
autoclave, 52
Avanto Architects, 244–47

B. F. Goodrich, 175
B+W Architecture, 202–5
Baekeland, Leo, 175
Bakelite, 175
balloon framing, 86, 87, 88
bamboo, 91, 104–7
Barnard College, 26
Barragán, David, 58–59
Basel, Switzerland, 42–45, 188–91
basic oxygen process, 133
Basque Health Department Headquarters, 16–19
bauxite, 130
BCHO Architects, 9, 64–67
Belgium, 14, 49
bendable plywood, 126–27
Benedictus, Edouard, 12
Berrel Berrel Kräutler Architekten, 42–45
Bessemer, Henry, 130
Bethlehem Steel, 130
Bibliothèque Sainte-Geneviève, 8
Bilbao, Spain, 16–19
bimetallic corrosion. *See* weathering
blister copper, 137
boards, 89
Bohlin Cywinski Jackson, 9, 46–47
bolts, 91–92, 134, 156, 228
high strength, 134
lag, 92
nuts, 91
washers, 92
bonded masonry, 236–37, 244–47
borosilicate glass, 13
Bosch Rexroth, 196
Boston, Massachusetts, 9, 108–11, 252
brace frame, 86
Brandhorst Museum, 228–31
brass, 130, 136
Brazil, 68–69, 137
brazing, 129
bricks, 8, 26, 217, 218, 219–22, 224–27, 228–31, 236, 238–39, 240–43, 256–57
calcium silicate, 220–21
characteristics, 220
clay, 219
color, 220
common, 220
concrete, 221
concrete masonry units (CMU), 221–22
face, 220
faïence, 221
grades, 220, 222
orientation, 219
stag, 221
terra cotta, 221, 240–43
texture, 220
Brigham and Women's Hospital, 252
bronze, 129, 136, 137
building codes, 87–88
building styles
exposed, 42
prefabrication, 42
skeleton, 42
bull-eye glass, 14
bullion glass. *See* bull-eye glass
Burera District, Rwanda, 252–55
Burma, Myanmar, 104
Butaro Doctor's Housing, 252–55

calcium silicate bricks, 220–21
Canada, 76–79, 126–27, 137, 152–55
Cantonal School Canteen, 170–71
Cape Town, South Africa, 60–63
Capuchins, 232
carbon, 132
carbon steel, 132
Carnegie, Andrew, 130
Cartageña, Spain, 184–87
Casa Pentimento, 58–59
CAST (Center for Architectural Structures and Technology), 64–67
cast glass, 14
cast iron, 129, 130, 132
decorative use, 132
cast-in-place concrete, 51, 52, 70–71, 182, 256
casting alloys, 135
Catalonia, Spain, 262–65
cathode, 131
Catholic Church, 11
CATIA modeling, 188
Cedeira, Spain, 150–51
Cellophane House, 196–97
cellulose, 175
cellulose insulation, 112
cement, 54, 72, 217, 252
aggregate, 49
curing, 49
cement-based stucco, 60–63, 68–69
Center for Design Research, 258–61
ceramic frit, 26–29
channel glass, 15, 24–25
Chapel of St. Lawrence, 244–47
Chareau, Pierre, 8
Charles River, 108
chemical finishes, 135
Chiba, Japan, 214–15
Chicago, Illinois, 12, 86, 116–17
Chile, 137
China, 9, 30–33, 46–47, 72–75, 86, 91, 130, 192–95, 218, 256–57
chromium, 133
Chungbuk, South Korea, 64–67
Chūō-ku, Osaka, Japan, 168–69
Church of Our Lady of Trsat, 240
Cité du Design, 38–41
Clavel Arquitectos, 24–25
clay, 49, 86
clear-coat anodizing, 135
CNC fabrication, 96–99, 116, 126, 150, 156, 188, 192, 198, 232
coated polyester fabric, 179, 206–9
coatings, 135–36
coefficients of thermal expansion, 131
Coignet, François, 49
cold hardening, 133
cold joints, 55
Cold War, 137
cold-dipped galvanizing, 133
cold-rolled steel, 133
Coll-Barreu Arquitectos, 16–19
common bricks, 220
composite panels, 89, 90, 108–11, 164–67
resin-core, 108–11
composite resin-core wood panels, 108–11
compressed stabilized earth blocks (CSEBs), 252–255
compressive forces, 13
concrete, 8, 9, 26, 30, 38, 48–83, 87, 94, 96, 150, 156, 160, 164, 172, 182, 228–31, 232, 238, 240, 244, 252, 256–57, 262
admixtures, 49, 50, 52, 53, 54–55, 58, 72, 80
aggregates, 4, 50, 54, 56, 58, 72, 80
architectural use, 48–83, 129
autoclaved aerated (AAC), 52–53
autoclaved cellular (ACC), 52
cast-in-place, 51, 52, 56, 58, 68, 70–71, 182, 256
casting, 49
cement-based stucco, 60–63, 68–69
cladding, 49
clay, 49, 86
coatings, 50
cold joints, 55
compression, 49
concrete masonry units (CMU), 52, 217, 218, 221–22
corrosion, 51, 55
costs, 49, 51, 53, 58, 60, 76
creep, 54
curing, 49, 54, 56, 64
design considerations, 50
disadvantages, 50
energy efficiency, 53, 56, 58
environmental conditions, 50, 51, 52, 53, 54, 55, 58, 68, 70–71, 72, 76, 80
fabric-formed, 54, 64–67
failure, 50
fiber cement, 53
fire resistance, 49
flexibility, 54, 55
form ties, 51
formulation, 49
formwork, 51, 52, 53, 54, 64, 76, 80
foundations, 50
graphic, 53–54, 56–57
high-performance, 50
i.Light, 72
imperfection, 50
insulation, 52, 54, 60, 76
invention, 72
and light, 53
light-transmitting, 72
malleability, 49
masonry, 256–57
as mimic, 50
movement joints, 55
new technology, 50, 53–54, 60, 76, 80
paving, 49
permeability, 55
photocatalytic, 72–75
pigmentation, 55, 56, 58, 80
pigments, 50
Portland cement, 49, 53, 76, 221
post-tensioned, 51
pre-tensioning, 51
precast, 51–52, 56–57, 58–59, 64, 72–75, 80, 238
prestressed, 50, 51
quality, 49
rammed earth, 53, 76–79
recycling, 64–67
reinforced, 49, 50–51, 55, 60, 64, 68, 70, 72, 76, 129, 232, 252, 262
sandblasting, 50
sculptural qualities, 50, 51, 52
and seismic activity, 58
self-consolidating, 50, 54, 80
shrinkage, 55
steel reinforcement, 49, 50–51
strength, 49, 50, 53, 54, 55, 60, 64, 76, 80
stress, 54, 55
surface texture, 50
sustainability, 53
tilt-up, 52, 64
transparent, 50, 53, 72
transportation, 52
types, 50–54
ultra high performance concrete (UHPC), 53, 80–83
uniformity, 50
and utilities, 53
water/cement ratio, 49
workability, 54, 55, 58, 68, 80
concrete masonry screen, 256–57
concrete masonry units (CMU), 52, 217, 218, 221–22
connectors
adhesives, 92, 122
bolts, 91–92, 156, 228
metal plate fasteners, 92
nails, 91
screws, 91
timber, 92
toothed plates, 92
Copenhagen, Denmark, 34–37
copper, 129, 131, 132, 133, 134, 136–37, 232, 244
appearance, 137
architectural use, 136
blister, 137
color options, 137
corrosion, 136, 137
costs, 136
electrolysis refining, 137
environmental conditions, 136, 137
flash smelting, 137
joining, 137
in lighting, 136
malleability, 137
manufacturing, 137
matte, 137
recycling, 137
strength, 136
weathering, 137
in wire circuitry, 136
COR-TEN, 24, 132, 150–51, 156–59, 168–69
environmental conditions, 150, 156
oxidation, 150, 156, 168
perforated, 150–51
prefabricated modules, 150
strength, 156
weathering, 150, 156, 168
Corbusier, Le, 8, 11, 50
Corian acrylic polymer, 178–79, 198–201
architectural use, 198–201
creep, 54
creosote preservatives, 88
crown glass, 14
cruck frame, 86
crumpled foil, 172–73
Crystal Palace, 8, 14, 130
Crystal, The, 34–37
Cubus, 262–65
curing, 49, 54, 56, 64
curved tempered insulated glass, 30–33
curved tempered laminated glass, 46–47

Dairy House Annex, 118–21
Dano, Burkina Faso, 224–27
Denmark, 34–37, 164–67
Design Arbeid, 198
Design Indaba, 60
Design Indaba 10 × 10 Housing Project, 60–63
Design Space Africa Architects (formerly MMA Architects), 60–63
desilverized lead, 139
Despang Architekten, 112–15
Detroit, Michigan, 12

Deutsche Bahn, 182
DIALOG, 76–79
Diana Center at Barnard College, 26–29
digital design, 16, 19, 42, 80, 87, 122, 142, 232–35, 236, 256
digital fabrication, 16–19, 232–35
digitally fabricated stone, 232–35
dimensional lumber, 89
Dorte Mandrup Arkitekter, 164–67
double glazing, 42
drawing, 129
dry method pigmenting, 55
Dulles Airport Terminal, 50
DuPont, 8, 175, 178, 198
Dvůr Semtín, Olbramovice, Czech Republic, 94–95

ECDM, 80–83
EcoBeam, 60
École Supérieure d'Art et Design de Saint-Étienne, 38
economies of scale, 58
EcoWoodBox Kindergarten, 112–15
Edna, Ole Jørgen, 104
efflorescence, 219
Egypt, 11, 14, 222
El B Conference Hall and Auditorium, 184–87
electric arc furness process, 133
electro-galvanizing. *See* cold-dipped galvanizing
electrolysis refining, 137
Ellwood, Craig, 210
embossed glass, 15, 42–45
Endo, Shuhei, 168–69
engineering, 9
England, 49, 86, 118, 192
Ernst Koller Pavilion, 42–45
ETFE. *See* fluoropolymer films
ethylene propylene diene monomer (EPDM), 202
ethylene tetrafluoroethylene, 202–5
Europe, 52, 86, 130, 218
exposed building styles, 42
extruded aluminum, 152–55
extruding, 129

fabric-formed concrete, 54, 64–67
face bricks, 220
Factory Extension, 24–25
faïence bricks, 221
Falconnier, Gustave, 11
Fallingwater, 8
Fawcett, E. W., 176
polyethylene, 176
ferrous metals, 8, 26–29, 30, 38, 46, 49, 50–51, 53, 54, 55, 56, 58, 64, 70, 72, 80, 87, 91, 94, 100, 116, 122, 126, 129, 130, 132, 136, 146–49, 150–51, 156–59, 160–63, 168–69, 202, 206–9, 217, 218, 224, 232
cast iron, 129, 130, 132
steel, 8, 26–29, 30, 38, 46, 49, 50–51, 53, 54, 55, 56, 58, 64, 70, 72, 80, 87, 91, 94, 100, 116, 122, 126, 129, 130, 132, 146–49, 150–51, 156–59, 160–63, 168–69, 202, 206–9, 217, 218, 224, 232
wrought iron, 129, 130, 132
fiber cement, 53
fiberglass, 176, 182
Fink + Jocher, 238–39
Finland, 56–57, 100–3, 122, 172, 244–47
Finnish Forest Council of Certification, 122
flagstone, 222
flash smelting, 137
flat glass, 14. *See also* float glass; plate glass; sheet glass
flexible connections, 152–55
float glass, 12, 14, 118
fluoropolymer films, 179, 202–5
Foggia, Italy, 232–35
forests, 86, 87
forging, 129
form ties, 51
Formica, 176
framing, 86, 87, 88, 146, 170, 172, 198, 258
France, 8, 14, 38–41, 49, 50, 80–83
Freyssinet, Eugene, 50
Fuller, Buckminster, 214
fused silica glass, 13

galvanizing, 131, 133
cold dipped, 133
hot dipped, 133
gas metal arc welding (GMAW). *See* metal inert gas welding (MIG)
gas tungsten arc welding (GTAW). *See* tungsten inert gas welding (TIG)
Gehry, Frank, 9
General Motors Technical Center, 12
Geneva, Switzerland, 206–9
Germany, 112–15, 122, 130–31, 137, 228–31, 238–39
Gibson, R. O., 176
Gigon/Guyer, 160–63
glass, 9, 10–47, 80, 96, 112, 118, 142, 146, 164, 178, 202, 258
96 percent silica, 13
absorbency (A), 12
aluminosilicate, 13
annealing, 11, 14
architectural use, 10–47
blocks, 12, 14, 15
borosilicate, 13
bull-eye, 14
cast, 14, 15
channel, 15, 24–25
chemical coating, 13
common consumer items, 13
composition, 11
compressive forces, 13
crown, 14
curved tempered insulated, 30–33
curved tempered laminated, 46–47
design considerations, 12–13
distortions, 14
domestic uses, 20–23
double glazing, 42
electrical applications, 13
embossed, 15, 42–45
energy conservation, 16
fire protection, 13, 15, 16
flat, 14
float, 12, 14, 118
formation, 11
formwork, 11
fused silica, 13
glassblowing, 11
heat resistance, 13
history, 11–12
insulated, 30–33, 38, 42–45, 164
insulating, 15, 26, 30–33, 34
laminated, 14–15, 42, 46–47, 70, 118
laminating, 12, 13
lead, 13
light, 12–13, 15, 20–23, 24, 26–29, 34, 38–41, 118
load-bearing capacity, 11–12
manufacturing process, 11
mass production, 11
as metaphor, 11
plate, 14, 258
prestressing, 13
properties, 11, 12
recycling, 11
reflectance (R), 12
reflective, 16–19
safety glass, 12, 42
security, 15
shadow box, 26–29
shear forces, 13
sheet, 14
soda-lime, 13
sound insulation, 15, 16, 38
spandrel, 15
spiritual environments, 11
stained glass, 11, 14
strength, 13, 42, 118
stress, 11, 12, 13
symbolism, 11
tempered, 12, 14, 30–33, 46–47
tensile forces, 13
thermal conductivity, 12, 20, 46
thermal insulation, 15, 16, 20–23, 26, 34, 38
translucency, 12–13, 20–23, 24–25, 26–29
translucent, 20–23
transmittance (T), 12
transparency, 12–13, 24, 34, 46–47
Triplex, 12
types, 13–15
windows, 11, 12, 14, 26, 38–41, 42, 96, 112, 164, 170, 210, 240, 258, 262
wire, 15
glass blocks, 12, 14, 15
Glass Townhouses, 20–23
glass-fiber-reinforced plastic (GFRP), 178, 188–91
glassblowing, 11
glazed ceramic rods, 228–31
glue laminates, 86, 100
glue-laminate arches, 94–95
glue-laminated wood, 89, 94
glulam. *See* glue-laminated wood
GMAW. *See* metal inert gas welding (MIG)
gold, 129
Goodyear, Charles, 175
Gothenberg, Sweden, 210–13
Gramazio & Kohler, 96–99
graphic concrete, 53–54, 56–57
Great Basin Desert, 76
Great Britain, 8, 14, 49, 86, 130, 175
Great International Exhibition, [illegible]
Great Wall, 218
Greece, 86
green materials, 9, 60, 76. *See also* sustainability
green technologies, 60, 68. *See also* sustainability
Gregor, William, 130
Group8, 206–9
GTAW. *See* tungsten inert gas welding (TIG)
Guggenheim Museum, Bilbao, 16

H-sections, 42
Hadrian, 129
Hadrian's Villa, 49
Hadspen Estate, Somerset, England, 118–19
Halftecture O, 168–69
Hämeenlinna, Finland, 56–57
Hämeenlinna Provincial Archive, 56–57
Hanil Visitors Center and Guesthouse, 9, 64–67
Hanover, Germany, 112–15
hardwoods, 88, 89
Harmonia 57, 68–69
Harry Parker Community Boathouse, 9, 108–11
heat of hydration. *See* curing
heat-treatable alloys, 135
Heatherwick Studio, 9, 172–73, 192–95
Heikkinen-Komonen Architects, 56–57
Helsinki, Finland, 56–57, 100–3
Hennebique, Françoise, 49
Herstedlund Fælleshus Community Centre, 164–67
high-performance concrete, 50
high-strength bolts, 134
high-strength, low-alloy steel (HSLA), 132. *See also* COR-TEN
Hiroshi Senju Museum, 70–71
Home Delivery (MoMA), 196
Hoston Bakker Boniface Haden. *See* DIALOG
hot-dipped galvanizing, 133
hot-rolled steel, 133
Hyatt, Thaddeus, 49

i.Light, 72
Illinois, 8, 12, 50, 116–17
Illinois Institute of Technology, 12
Imperial Chemical Industries Research Laboratory, 176
India, 9, 86, 91, 218, 236–37
Industrial Revolution, 130, 218
insulated glass panels, 42–45
insulating glass, 15, 26, 30–33, 34
integral method pigmenting, 55
integrated design and fabrication, 126–27
International Committee of the Red Cross Logistics Complex, 206–9
International Design Biennial, 38
Iodice Architetti, 72–75
Iraq, 218
iron, 8, 49, 129, 130, 131, 132, 136, 137
cast, 129, 130, 132
wrought, [illegible]
Italcementi, 72
Italian Pavilion at World Expo 2010, 72–75
Italy, 49, 72, 232–35

J. Mayer H. Architects, 122–25
Japan, 70–71, 86, 168–69, 214–15
Jefferson, Thomas, 8
JFK Airport, 50
JKMM Architects, 100–3
Joachim, 11
John Paul II, Pope, 240
joist hanger, 92

Karen, 104
Karuizawa, Nagano, Japan, 70–71
Kazuhiro Kojima Lab / Tokyo University of Science, 214–15
Keppler, Friedrich, 11–12
Kéré, Diébédo Francis, 224–27
Kew Gardens, 192
KieranTimberlake Architects, 196–97
kilns, 14, 86, 91, 122, 218, 219, 220, 221, 252
Klaproth, Martin, 130–31
knotholes, 85
knots, 85
Koller, Ernst, 42
Kroll, Dr. William, 131
Kunst Depot, Henze & Ketterer Art Gallery, 160–63
Kynar, 26, 142

La Pallissa, 262–65
Labrouste, Henri, 8
Lady Bird Lake Hike and Bike Trail, 156
Lady Bird Lake Hiking Trail Restrooms, 156–59
Lafarge, 80
lag bolts, 92
Lambot, J. L., 49
laminated glass, 14–15, 42, 46–47
laminated veneer lumber (LVL), 116, 122–25
MetsäWood Kerto-Q, 122
laminated wood, 89, 116–17, 192
glue-laminated, 89
laminates
glass, 14–15, 42, 46–47
glue, 86, 100
glue-laminate arches, 94–95
glue-laminated wood, 89, 94
laminated veneer lumber (LVL), 116, 122–25
wood, 89, 116–17
laterite masonry, 224–27
lattice, 116–17
Lausanne, Switzerland, 202–5
Lawrence, Kansas, 258–61
lead, 129, 139
construction use, 139
corrosion, 139
costs, 139
desilverized, 139
durability, 139
non-architectural applications, 139
pigmentation, 139
strength, 139
toxicity, 137
lead glass, 13
[illegible]
LEED certification, 26, 258
Lehman Lawn, 26
lehr. *See* kilns
Lever House, 12
Lexan, 178
light-transmitting precast concrete, 72–75
lime, 49
limestone veneer cladding, 258–61
LIN Architects, 38–41
Lincoln Park Zoo, 116–117
load-bearing construction, 52, 222
log construction, 87, 118
London, England, 8, 14, 130, 175, 192
Lucite, 178
lumber, 85, 89, 146, 192
dimensional, 89
nominal dimensions, 89
plainsawn, 85
quartersawn, 85
Lycra, 176

Machu Picchu, 218, 222
Madrid, Spain, 182–83, 248–51
Maestral, George de, 176
Maison de Verre, 8
manganese, 133, 134
manufactured wood components, 90
box beams, 90
customization, 90
panel and box components, 90
plywood I-beams, 90
trusses, 90
masonry, 9, 26, 68, 160, 216–65
adobe, 218
arches, 217
architectural use, 217, 218–19, 222, 223
bonded, 236–37, 244–47
brick, 8, 26, 217, 218, 219–22, 224–27, 228–31, 236, 238–39, 240–43, 256–57
compressed stabilized earth blocks (CSEBs), 252–55
concrete, 256–57
concrete masonry units (CMU), 217
costs, 218, 222, 224, 236, 252
derivative products, 217
design considerations, 222
disadvantages, 220
durability, 217, 222, 223, 258, 262
efflorescence, 219
environmental conditions, 219, 220, 221, 222, 223, 224, 232, 244, 248, 258
erosion, 220
fire resistance, 217, 221
glazed ceramic rods, 228–31
history, 218
insulation, 228, 238, 252, 258
joining, 217–18, 219, 223, 228, 232, 236, 240, 244, 248, 252, 256, 258
laterite, 224–27
light, 224, 240, 244, 258
load-bearing, 217, 222, 244, 252, 262

moisture, 217, 221, 223, 240, 248, 256, 262
mortar, 217–18, 236, 248, 252, 256
ornamental, 217, 221
parametric design, 256–57
pigmentation, 218, 219, 220, 228, 238, 240, 252
post-tensioned, 232–35
recycled, 248–51
rubble, 222, 262–65
seismic activity, 232
special shapes, 238–39
stone, 222–23, 224, 232–35, 244, 252–55, 258, 262–65
strength, 218, 219, 220, 221, 222, 223, 224, 232, 236, 240, 244, 252, 256, 262
stress, 217
sustainability, 223, 224, 238, 252, 258, 262
thermal mass wall, 258–61
thermal properties, 217
Trombe wall, 258
veneer, 222, 258–61
ventilation, 236
walls, 217
weathering, 219
wythe, 217, 252
masonry thermal mass wall, 258–61
masonry walls, 217
cavity, 217
reinforced, 217
solid, 217
veneer, 217
Mass Design Group, 252–55
materiality, 8–9
matte, 137
mechanical finishes, 135
MEP systems, 26
Mesopotamia, 11, 14, 218
metal inert gas (MIG), 134
metal inert gas welding, 136
metal plate fasteners, 92
joist hanger, 92
metals, 9, 128–73, 258
alloys, 129, 134–35, 136, 137, 139, 168
aluminum, 26, 30, 38, 42, 56, 90, 108, 129, 130, 132, 133, 134–36, 142–45, 152–55, 164–67, 170–71, 192, 196, 198, 202, 214, 228, 240
American Society for Testing and Materials (ASTM), 132
anode, 131
brass, 130, 136
brazing, 129
bronze, 129, 136, 137
cast iron, 129, 130, 132
casting, 129
cathode, 131
chemical finishes, 135
coatings, 135–36
coefficients of thermal expansion, 131
cold hardening, 133
copper, 129, 131, 132, 133, 134, 136–37, 232, 244
COR-TEN, 24, 132, 150–51, 156–59, 168–69
corrosion, 129, 131, 132, 134, 135, 136, 137, 138
costs, 129, 132, 133, 134, 136, 138, 172
crumpled foil, 172–73
definition, 129
design considerations, 131
drawing, 129
environmental conditions, 129, 131, 132, 134, 136, 146, 150, 164, 172
extruding, 129
ferrous, 8, 26–29, 30, 38, 46, 49, 50–51, 53, 54, 55, 56, 58, 64, 70, 72, 80, 87, 91, 94, 100, 116, 122, 126, 129, 130, 132–34, 136, 146–49, 156–59, 160–63, 168, 172–73, 202, 206–9, 217, 218, 223, 224, 232
finishes, 135–36
forging, 129
galvanizing, 131, 133
gold, 129
high-strength bolts, 134
history, 129–31
iron, 8, 49, 129, 130, 131, 132, 136, 137
joining, 134, 136, 137
lead, 129, 139
manufacturing, 131–32
nickel, 133
nonferrous, 26, 30, 38, 42, 56, 90, 108, 129, 130, 131, 132, 133, 134–36, 137, 138–39, 142–45, 152–55, 164–67, 170–71, 192, 196, 198, 202, 214, 228, 232, 240, 244
oil canning, 131
ores, 129, 130, 133, 134, 137, 138
ornamentation, 129
oxidization, 129
patinas, 131
processing, 129
properties, 129
recycling, 134, 137, 146
reflectivity, 131
research, 131–32
rolling, 129
silver, 129
smelting, 129, 130, 137
soldering, 129, 134, 136, 139
stainless steel, 132–33, 142, 156, 172–73, 223, 232
steel, 8, 26–29, 30, 38, 46, 49, 50–51, 53, 54, 55, 56, 58, 64, 70, 72, 80, 87, 91, 94, 100, 116, 122, 126, 129, 130, 132–34, 146–49, 156–59, 160–63, 168, 172–73, 202, 206–9, 217, 218, 223, 224, 232
strength, 129, 131, 132, 135, 136, 156, 172
structural use, 129, 130, 131, 132, 134
titanium, 46, 129, 130–31, 137–38
for tools, 129, 130
weathering, 131, 168
welding, 134, 136, 139, 168
wrought iron, 129, 130, 132
zinc, 129, 130, 133, 134, 136, 137, 138–39
Metropol Parasol, 122–25
MetsäWood Kerto-Q, 122
Mexico, 218
Michigan, 12, 137
Middle Ages, 11, 14, 86, 130
Mies van der Rohe, Ludwig, 8, 12
mild steel, 132
Mill Run, Pennsylvania, 8
milling, 85
minimalism, 8, 42, 70–71
Miró Rivera Architects, 156–59
Miroiterie Retail Building, 9, 202–5
modernism, 8
modular coordination, 236–37, 238–39
modularity, 38–41
molybdenum, 133
Monier, Joseph, 49
monomers, 175, 202
ethylene propylene diene monomer (EPDM), 202
Montana, 137
monumentality, 8
MOOM Tensegrity Membrane Structure, 214–15
mortar, 217–18, 236, 248, 252, 256
movement joints, 55
construction, 55
control, 55
expansion, 55
isolation, 55
Mt. Sobaek National Park, 64
Mulders vandenBerk Architecten, 198–201
Munich, Germany, 228–31
Murcia, Spain, 24–25
Museum of Modern Art (MoMA), 196
MYCC Architects, 150–51

nails, 91, 100
common, 91
finish, 91
galvanized, 91
pennies, 91
Nature Boardwalk at Lincoln Park Zoo, 116–17
Netherlands, The, 9, 198–201
Neu-Ulm, Germany, 238–39
New Delhi, India, 236–37
New Guinea, 137
New York, New York, 12, 26–29, 49, 50, 175, 196–97
Newcastle, England, 49
nickel, 133
Nishizawa, Ryue, 70–71
Nk'Mip Desert Cultural Centre, 76–79
Noh Bo, Thailand, 104–7
nominal dimensions, 89
non-heat-treatable alloys, 134
non-veneer panels, 89, 90
oriented strand board (OSB), 90
particleboard, 90
waferboard, 90
nonferrous metals
aluminum, 26, 30, 38, 42, 56, 90, 108, 129, 130, 132, 133, 142–45, 152–55, 164–67, 170–71, 192, 196, 198, 202, 214, 228, 240
copper, 129, 131, 132, 133, 134, 136–37, 232, 244
lead, 129
zinc, 129, 130, 133, 134, 136, 137, 138–39
Novartis Entrance Pavilion, 188–91
nuts, 91
NUWOG Headquarters and Housing, 238–39
Nykredit Bank, 34–37
nylon, 175, 176

Oak Park, Illinois, 8, 50
oak screen, 94–95
oak timber, 118–121
oil canning, 131
oil-based preservatives, 88
OMS Stage, 152–55
ores, 129, 130, 133, 134, 137, 138
smelting, 129, 130, 137
oriented strand board (OSB), 90
Orly Airport, 50
Osoyoos Indian Band, 76–79
Osoyoos, British Columbia, Canada, 76–79
Owens Illinois Glass Corporation, 12
oxidization, 129
oxidized steel, 146–49

Padre Pio Pilgrimage Church, 232–35
panel products, 89–90, 112, 126–27, 150, 210
composite panels, 89, 90
grades, 90
non-veneer panels, 89, 90
plywood, 89, 90, 126–27
span rating, 90
panelized construction industry, 88
Pantheon, 129
parametric design, 256–57
Paris, France, 8, 49, 50, 80–83
Parkes, Alexander, 175
Parkesine, 175
particleboard, 87, 90
Partners in Health, 252
Passive House designation, 112, 258
Patkau Architects, 126–27
Paxton, Joseph, 8, 14, 130
pennies, 91
Pennsylvania, 8
perforated aluminum, 142–45
perforated COR-TEN, 150–51
perforated steel, 160–63
permanence, 8
Perret, Auguste, 8, 11
Perspex, 178
photocatalytic concrete, 72–75
photosynthesis modules, 38
photovoltaic panels, 38
pig iron. *See* iron
pigmentation, 55, 218, 219, 220, 228, 238, 240, 252
integral method, 55
Pilkington, Alastair, 12
pine slats, 96–99
Pio of Pietrelcina, 232
plastic coatings, 135–36
Plastic House, 210–13
plastics, 8–9, 174–15, 176–77
3M, 210
acrylic, 178–79, 182–83, 184–87, 192–95, 196–97, 198–201, 202–5, 206–9, 210–13, 214–15
Acrylite, 178
Bakelite, 175
blow molding, 180
calendering, 180
carbon, 175
casting, 179, 192–95
cellulose, 112, 175
coatings, 135–36
corrosion, 175, 177
costs, 175, 177, 196
customization, 176, 196
density, 177
disadvantages, 177
environmental concerns, 176
environmental conditions, 177, 182, 184, 188, 192, 196, 198, 202, 206, 210
extenders, 179
extrusion, 180, 192–95
fiberglass, 176, 182
fiberoptics, 176
fillers, 179
fire resistance, 175, 177, 184, 196, 202
flame retarders, 179
Formica, 176
glass-fiber-reinforced plastic (GFRP), 178, 188–91
injection molding, 179
innovation, 175–76
insulation, 188
joining, 177, 210
laminates, 176
Lexan, 178
Lucite, 178
Lycra, 176
malleability, 175, 182, 188
military use, 175, 176
modifiers and additives, 179
monomers, 175, 202
nylon, 175, 176
Parkesine, 175
Perspex, 178
plasticizers, 179
Plexiglas, 178
polycarbonate, 177–78, 184–87
polyester, 176
polyethylene, 176
Polygal, 178
polymers, 175
polyvinyl chloride (PVC), 175–176, 177
processing methods, 179–180
recycling, 177, 178, 196, 206
reinforcing fibers, 179
rubber, 175
SmartWrap, 196–97
stabilizers, 179
strength, 175, 177, 184, 188, 192, 202
stress, 188, 214
sustainability, 196, 206
synthetic, 175
Teflon, 175, 202
thermoplastics, 175, 177–79
thermosetting, 175, 177
toxicity, 177
translucency, 178, 182, 192, 202, 210, 214
transparency, 182, 184, 196, 202
Tupperware, 176
Velcro, 176
wood-simulating, 87
plate glass, 14, 258
platform framing, 87, 88
Plexiglas, 178. *See also* polymethyl methacrylate (PMMA)
plywood, 86, 87, 89, 90, 126–27, 164, 192
bendable, 126–27
polycarbonate, 177–78, 184–87
polyester, 176
polyester fabric, 179, 214–15
polyethylene, 176
polyethylene terephthalate (PET), 178, 196–97
Polygal, 178
polymers, 46, 175
polymethyl methacrylate (PMMA), 178, 182–83, 184, 210–13
polytetrafluoroethylene, 202–5
polyurethane foam (PUR), 178, 188–91
polyvinyl chloride (PVC), 175–76, 177
polyvinylidene fluoride (PVDF), 206–9
Pope John Paul II Hall, 240–43
Port Chester, New York, 49
Portland cement, 49, 53, 76, 221
post-tensioned concrete, 51
post-tensioned masonry, 232–35
postmodernism, 8
poured-in-place concrete. *See* cast-in-place concrete
pre-tensioning, 51
precast concrete, 51–52, 56–57, 58–59, 64, 72–75, 80, 238
Précontraint 1002, 206
Prefabricated Nature, 150–51
prefabrication, 42, 100–3
preservatives, 88
creosote, 88
oil-based, 88
water-based, 88
prestressed concrete, 50, 51
Private Residence in Riedikon, 96–99
PTFE. *See* fluoropolymer films
PUR. *See* polyurethane foam (PUR)
PVC. *See* polyvinyl chloride (PVC)
PVDF. *See* polyvinylidene fluoride

quenching, 133
Quito, Ecuador, 58–59

rammed earth, 53, 76–79
Randić-Turato Architects, 240–43
RATP Bus Center, 80–83
reactive powder concrete. *See* ultra high performance concrete (UHPC)
recycled masonry, 248–51
recycling, 134, 137, 146, 248–51
reduction. *See* electrolysis refining
reflectance (*R*), 12
reflective glass, 16–19
reinforced concrete, 49, 50–51, 55, 60, 64, 68, 70, 72, 76, 129, 232, 252, 262
Renaissance, 129
Renault, 8
renovated stone masonry, 262–65
Renzo Piano Building Workshop, 232–35
Richardson, Henry Hobson, 8
Rijeka, Croatia, 240–43
rolling, 129
Roman Empire, 49
Romans, 11, 49
Rome, Italy, 49
Ronchamp Chapel, 50
rubber, 175

rubble, 222, 262–65
Russia, 137
[illegible]
Rwandan Ministry of Health, 232

Saarinen, Eero, 8, 12, 50
Saez, José María, 58–59
safety glass, 12, 42
Saint-Étienne, France, 38–41
Sander Architects, 20–23
São Paulo, Brazil, 68–69
Sauerbrach Hutton, 228–31
Schmidt Hammer Lassen Architects, 34–37
screws, 91, 108, 150, 210, 228
Seagram Building, 12
Sean Godsell Architects, 146–49
seasoning, 85–86
Secondary School, 224–27
Seed Cathedral. *See* UK Pavilion at World Expo 2010
self-consolidating concrete, 50, 54, 80
SelgasCano Architecture Office, 182–83
SelgasCano Arquitectos, 182–83, 184–87
Senju, Hiroshi, 70
Serge Ferrari, 206
Serra, Marco, 188–91
Seville, Spain, 122–25
SGL Projekt, 94–95
Shade Azul, 214
shadow box glass, 26–29
shale, 49
Shanghai, China, 9, 30–33, 46–47, 72–75, 192–95, 256–57
shear forces, 13
sheet glass, 14
silica, 49
Silk Wall + J-Office, 256–57
silver, 129
Simon, Waldo, 175
SIREWALL, 76
site-cast concrete. *See* cast-in-place concrete
Skating Shelters, 126–27
skeleton building styles, 42
Skene Catling de la Peña, 118–21
Skidmore, Owings & Merrill, 12
SmartWrap, 196–97
Smeaton, John, 49
smelting, 129, 130
Society of American Foresters, 86
soda-lime glass, 13
Soe Ker Tie House, 104–7
softwoods, 85, 88–89
soldering, 129, 134, 136, 139
South Africa, 60–63, 137
South Asian Human Rights Documentation Centre, 9, 236–37
South Korea, 9, 64–67
South Okanaga, British Columbia, Canada, 76
Spain, 16–19, 24–25, 122–25, 150–51, 182–83, 184–87, 248–51, 262–65
span rating, 90
spandrel glass, 15
special shapes, 238–39
Spiral Gallery, 30–33
split ring connector, 92
SRAs. *See* admixtures
St. Andrews Beach House, [illegible]
stag bricks, 221
stained glass, 11, 1[illegible]
stainless steel, 132–33, 142, 156, 172–73, 223, 232
costs, 134
finishing, 134
strength, 133
stamped aluminum sheets, 170–71
Stanley Saitowitz | Natoma Architects, 142–45
Statue of Liberty, 129
steel, 8, 24, 26–29, 30, 38, 46, 49, 50–51, 53, 54, 55, 56, 58, 64, 70, 72, 80, 87, 91, 94, 100, 116, 122, 126, 129, 130, 132–34, 142, 146–49, 150–51, 156–59, 160–63, 168–69, 172–73, 182, 184, 202, 206–9, 217, 218, 223, 224, 232
alloy, 132, 133, 156, 168
alloys, 134–35, 136, 137, 139, 168
annealing, 133
appearance, 133–134
carbon, 132
cladding, 172
cold-dipped galvanizing, 133
cold-hardening, 133
cold-rolled, 133
COR-TEN, 24, 132, 150–51, 156–59, 168–69
corrosion, 134, 168
costs, 134, 172
environmental conditions, 146, 150, 160, 172
finishing, 134
fireproofing, 134
framing, 160, 206–9
high-strength, low-alloy (HSLA), 132
hot-dipped galvanizing, 133
hot-rolled, 133
joining, 134
manufacturing, 133
basic oxygen process, 133
electric arc furnace process, 133
mild, 132
oxidized, 146–49
perforated, 160–63
quenching, 133
raw materials, 133
recycling, 146
shaping, 133
stainless, 132–33, 142, 156, 172–73, 223, 232
standard, 132
strength, 132, 156, 160, 172
strength-grade, 132
tempering, 133
weathering, 156, 168
yield point, 132
Stockholm Library, 8
stone, 8, 86, 222–23, 224, 232–35, 244, 252–55, 258–61, 262–65
ashlar, 222
construction, 223
design considerations, 222
digitally fabricated, 232–35
flagstone, 222
limestone, 258–61
masonry, 222–23, 224, 232–35, 244, 252–55, 258, [illegible]
rubble, 222, 262–65
sustainability, 223
trimstone, 222
Stork Nest Farm, 94–95
structural insulated panels (SIPs), 88
structural solid wood, 89
stucco, 60–63, 68–69
cement based, 60–63, 68–69
stud framing. *See* platform framing
Studio 804 / University of Kansas, 258–61
Studio Gang Architects, 116–17
superplasticizers, 54
sustainability, 26, 34, 53, 76–79, 87, 104, 108, 112, 122, 137, 196, 223, 248–51, 252, 258, 262
Sweden, 210–13
Swiss School for Metal and Building Technology, 42
Switzerland, 9, 42–45, 96–99, 160–63, 170–71, 188–91, 202–5, 206–9

Taiyo Kogyo, 214
Tampa Museum of Art, 142–45
Tampa, Florida, 142–45
Teflon, 175, 202
temper, 135
tempered glass, 12, 14, 30–33, 46–47
tempering, 133
Ten Books of Architecture, The, 218
tensegrity, 214
tensegrity structure, 214–15
tensile forces, 13
Teotihuacan, 218
Terra Firma, 76
terra-cotta bricks, 221, 228, 240–43
TERRART Baguette, 228
Théâtre des Champs-Élysées, 8
thermal conductivity, 12, 46
thermally modified wood, 91, 112–15
thermoplastics, 72, 175, 177–79
acrylic, 178
Acrylite, 178
Lexan, 178
Lucite, 178
Perspex, 178
Plexiglas, 178
polycarbonate, 177–78
Polygal, 178
polyvinyl chloride (PVC), 177
thermosetting plastics, 175, 177
Thompson, Edgar, 130
tilt-up concrete, 52, 64
timber, 89, 118–21, 122, 232
timber connectors, 92
split ring connector, 92
timber framing. *See* framing
timber-frame construction, 87–88
titanium, 46, 129, 130–31, 137–38
appearance, 138
architectural use, 137–38
corrosion, 138
costs, 138
joining, 138
manufacturing, 138
pigmentation, 138
rutile, 137, 138
[illegible] 100
Tokyo University of Science, 214
toothed plates, 92
torrefied wood. *See* thermally modified wood
translucent glass, 20–23
transmittance (*T*), 12
transparency, 46–47
transparent concrete, 50, 53
trees, 85–86
trimstone, 222
Triplex, 12
Triptyque, 68–69
Trombe wall, 258
Trus-Joist TJI wood trusses, 112
tungsten, 133
tungsten inert gas (TIG), 134
tungsten inert gas welding, 136
Tupperware, 176
TWA Terminal, 50
TYIN Tegnestue Architects, 104–7

U.S. Steel, 130
UK Pavilion at World Expo 2010, 192–95
ultra high performance concrete (UHPC), 53, 80–83
UNIT Arkitektur, 210–13
United Kingdom, 172–73
United States, 8, 9, 12, 20–23, 26, 49, 50, 64–67, 76, 86, 108–11, 116–17, 129, 130, 142–45, 156–59, 175, 196, 219, 220, 252, 258–61
Unity Temple (Wright), 8, 50
University of Kansas, 258
University of Manitoba, 64
University of Wales, 172
UPM ProFi wood plastic composite, 178
Uster, Switzerland, 96–99
Utah, 137
Utrecht, Netherlands, 9, 198–201

Vantaa, Finland, 244–47
Velcro, 176
veneer, 8, 9, 89, 90, 100, 108, 122–25, 192, 222, 258–61
Venice, California, 20–23
ventilated double-envelope glass system, 34–37
vermiculite, 68
VHB tape, 210
Victoria, Australia, 146–49
Vigaceros, 24
Viikki Church, 100–3
Villareal, Leo, 142
vinyl. *See* polyvinyl chloride (PVC)
Virginia, 8, 50
Viroc, 150
Vitruvius, 86, 218

waferboard, 90
Wales, 9, 172–73
Ward, W. E., 49
Warehouse 8B Conversion, 248–51
washers, 92
water-based preservatives, 88
waterproofing, 100
weathering, 131, 168
weathering steel, 156
Weiss/Manfredi Architecture/ Landscape/Urbanism, [illegible]
welding, [illegible]
metal inert gas, 134, 136
tungsten inert gas, 134, 136
Wettingen, Switzerland, 170–71
Weyerhauser, 8
white heat state, 132
whole-metal facades, 42
Wichtrach, Switzerland, 160–63
Wilkinson, William, 49
windows, 11, 12, 14, 26, 38–41, 42, 96, 112, 164, 170, 210, 240, 258, 262
Winnipeg, Manitoba, Canada, 126–27, 152–55
wire glass, 15
wood, 8, 9, 20, 42, 50, 53, 60, 76, 84–27, 146, 150, 164, 172, 182, 198, 210, 248, 262
alternatives, 87
architectural use, 84–27
balloon framing, 86, 87, 88
bamboo, 91, 104–7
boards, 89
box beams, 90
bracing, 104
building codes, 87–88
cellular structure, 100
CNC fabrication, 96–99, 116, 126, 150, 156, 188, 192, 198, 232
composite panels, 89, 90, 108–11, 164–67
compression, 85
coniferous, 88–89
connectors, 91–92, 94, 108, 116, 126
construction methods, 87–88
costs, 85, 87, 90, 122
decay, 86
deciduous, 89
density, 85, 91
design considerations, 87
disadvantages, 88, 90
durability, 89
as energy source, 86
engineering, 86, 122
environmental conditions, 86, 88, 108, 112, 116, 126–27
finish work, 85
fire retardants, 88
flaws, 85–86
forests, 86, 87
framing, 86, 87, 88, 90, 91, 112, 146, 164, 170, 172, 198, 248, 258
glue laminates, 86, 94–95, 100
grading, 85, 90
grain, 85
hardwoods, 85, 88, 89
harvesting, 87
history, 86–87
joining, 86, 100, 122, 126
knotholes, 85
knots, 85
laminated, 89, 116–17, 192
laminated veneer lumber (LVL), 116, 122–25
lattice, 116–17
log construction, 87, 118
lumber, 85, 89, 146, 192
manufactured components, 90
milling, 85, 90, 96, 118
moisture, 86, 104, 108, 118
nonveneer panels, 89, 90
[illegible]
panel and box components, 90
panel products, 89–90, 112, 126–27, 150, 210
panelized construction industry, 88
particleboard, 87
pine slats, 96–99
plainsawn lumber, 85
platform framing, 87, 88
pliability, 116
plywood, 86, 87, 89, 90, 126–27, 164, 192
plywood I-beams, 90
prefabrication, 100–3, 112, 116
preservatives, 88
pressure treatment, 88
quartersawn lumber, 85
recycling, 87
seasoning, 85–86
shakes, 100–3
shear, 85
shrinkage, 92, 118
softwoods, 85, 88–89
strength, 85, 86, 89, 90, 91, 100, 116, 122
stress, 91, 118, 122, 126
structural framing, 85
structural insulated panels (SIPs), 88
structural integrity, 85–86
structural solid, 89
sustainability, 87, 104, 108, 122
synthetics, 86, 87
tension, 85
thermal insulation, 100
thermally modified, 91, 112–15
timber, 89, 118–21, 122, 232
timber-frame construction, 87–88
tolerance, 89
trusses, 90, 112
types, 88–89
veneer, 8, 9, 89, 90, 100, 108, 122–25, 192, 258–61
ventilation, 108
waferboard, 90
waterproofing, 100
wood shakes, 100–3
wood-plastic composite, 20
World Expo 2010, 72, 192
World War II, 129, 131, 175, 176
Wright, Frank Lloyd, 8, 50, 218
wrought iron, 129, 130, 132
white heat state, 132
wythe, 217, 252

yield point, 132

zinc, 129, 130, 133, 134, 136, 137, 138–39
appearance, 138
architectural use, 138–39
corrosion, 138
environmental conditions, 138
joining, 139
manufacturing, 138
pigmentation, 138
strength, 138
weathering, 138

Bibliography

Allen, Edward. *Fundamentals of Building Construction: Materials and Methods*. New York: John Wiley & Sons, 2008.

American Institute of Architects. *Architectural Graphic Standards*. New York: John Wiley & Sons, 2007.

Beall, Christine. Masonry Design and Detailing. New York: McGraw-Hill, 2012.

Brock, Linda. *Designing the Exterior Wall: An Architectural Guide to the Vertical Envelope*. New York: John Wiley & Sons, 2005.

Campbell, James W. P., and William Pryce. *Brick: A World History*. London: Thames & Hudson, 2003.

Cerver, Francisco. *The Architecture of Glass: Shaping Light*. New York: Hearts Books, 1997.

———. *House Details*. New York Whitney Library of Design, 1998.

Ching, Francis D. K., and Cassandra Adams. *Building Construction Illustrated*. New York: John Wiley & Sons, 2001.

Compagno, Andrea. *Intelligent Glass Facades: Material, Practice, Design*. Basel: Birkhauser, 1999.

Cowan, Henry J., and Peter R. Smith. *The Science and Technology of Building Materials*. New York: Van Nostrand Reinhold Company, 1988.

Donzel, Catherine. *New Museums*. Paris: Telleri, 1998.

Ford, Edward. *The Details of Modern Architecture* vols. 1 and 2. Cambridge, Mass.: MIT Press, 1990 (vol. 1) and 1996 (vol. 2).

Frisch, David, and Susan Frisch. *Metal: Design and Fabrication*. New York: Whitney Library of Design, 1998.

Hegger, Manfred, et al. *Construction Materials Manual*. Basel: Birkhauser, 2006.

Heikkinen, Mikko, and Markku Komonen, "Light Cutting Green Grid," *The Finnish Architectural Review*. 2/2002; p. 36

Hornbostel, Caleb. *Construction Materials: Types, Uses and Applications*, 2nd ed. New York: John Wiley & Sons, 1991.

Hugues, Theodor, Ludwig Steiger, and Johann Weber. *Timber Construction, Details, Products, Case Studies*. Basel: Birkhauser, 2004.

Juracek, Judy A. *Surfaces*. New York: W.W. Norton, 1996.

Kaltenbach, Frank, ed. *Translucent Materials*. Basel: Birkhauser, 2004.

Knapp, Stephen. *The Art of Glass*. Gloucester, Mass.: Rockport Publishers, 1998.

Krewinkel, Heinz W. *Glass Buildings*. Basel: Birkhauser, 1998.

The Material Connexion Resource Library, New York, N.Y.

McMorrough, Julia. *Materials, Structures, and Standards*. Minneapolis, Minn.: Rockport Publishers, 2006.

Niesewand, Nonie. *Contemporary Details*. New York: Simon & Schuster, 1992.

Plumridge, Andrew, and Wim Meulenkamp. *Brickwork: Architecture and Design*. New York: Sterling Publishing, 2000.

Rosen, Harold J., and Tom Heineman. *Architectural Materials for Construction*. New York: McGraw-Hill, 1996.

Ruske, Wolfgang. *Timber Construction for Trade, Industry, Administration*. Basel: Birkhauser, 2004.

Schittich, Christian, et al. *Glass Construction Manual*. Birkhauser, 1999.

Stungo, Naomi. *Wood: New Directions in Design and Architecture*. San Francisco: Chronicle Books, 1998.

Wiggington, Michael. *Glass in Architecture*. London: Phaidon, 1996.

Zahner, L. William. *Architectural Metals: A Guide to Selection, Specification, and Performance*. New York: John Wiley & Sons, 1995.

Illustration Credits

Page 10 Albert Vecerka
Page 48 Yongkwan Kim
Page 84 Jaroslav Malý
Page 128 Adam Mørk
Page 174 Thomas Jantscher
Page 216 Asim Waqif

GLASS

Basque Health Department Headquarters
01, 04 Aleix Bagué; 02, 03, 06, 07 Coll-Barreu Arquitectos

Glass Townhouses
01, 03, 04, 07 Sander Architects; 02, 05, 06, 08 Sharon Riesdorph

Factory Extension
01, 03 David Frutos Ruiz; 02, 04, 05 Clavel Arquitectos

Diana Center at Barnard College
05 Albert Vecerka; 01–04, 06–08 Weiss/Manfredi

Spiral Gallery
01, 02, 05, 06 Atelier Deshaus; 03 Zhang Siye; 07, 08 Yao Li

The Crystal (Nykredit Bank)
01, 02, 06–08 Schmidt Hammer Lassen Architects; 03, 04, 09 Adam Mørk; 05, 10 Patrick Rand

Cité du Design
01, 02, 04, 05, 08, 09 LIN Architects; 03, 06 Christian Richters; 07 Jan-Oliver Kunze

Ernst Koller Pavilion
01–07, 09 Berrel Berrel Kräutler Architekten; 08 Eik Frenzel

Apple Flagship Store
01 Bohlin Cywinski Jackson; 02 from DuPont SentryGlas; 03, 04 Nic Lehoux; 05 Roy Zipstein

CONCRETE

Hämeenlinna Provincial Archive
01, 03 Jussi Tiainen; 02 Heikkinen-Komonen Architects

Casa Pentimento
01–05 Jose Maria Sáez + David Barragán

Design Indaba 10 × 10 Housing Project
01, 02, 08 Wieland Gleich; 03–07 Design Space Africa Architects (formerly MMA Architects)

Hanil Visitors Center and Guesthouse
01, 04–08, 10 BCHO Architects; 02, 03, 09 Yongkwan Kim

Harmonia 57
01 Triptyque; 02, 03 Nelson Kon

Hiroshi Senju Museum
01, 04, 05 Office of Ryue Nishizawa; 02, 03 Daici Ano ©Hiroshi Senju Museum Karuizawa

Italian Pavilion at World Expo 2010
01–09 Iodice Architetti

Nk'Mip Desert Cultural Centre
01, 03, 05–07 DIALOG; 02, 04, 08 Nic Lehoux

RATP Bus Center
01, 04, 05 ECDM; 02, 06–08 Benoît Fougeirol; 03 Philippe Ruault

WOOD

Stork Nest Farm
01, 02 SGL Projekt; 03–06 Jaroslav Malý

Private Residence in Riedikon
01, 03, 05 Gramazio & Kohler; 02, 04, 06 Roman Keller

Vikki Church
01, 02, 04–06, 09 JKMM Architects; 03, 07, 08 Arno de la Chapelle

Söe Ker Tie House
01, 05 TYIN Tegnestue Architects; 02–04, 06–08 Pasi Aalto

Harry Parker Community Boathouse
01–09 Anmahian Winton Architects

EcoWoodBox Kindergarten
01–09 Despang Architekten

Nature Boardwalk at Lincoln Park Zoo
01–03 Studio Gang Architects; 04, 05 Steve Hall © Hedrich Blessing

Dairy House Annex
01, 05, 07 Skene Catling de la Peña; 02–04, 06 James Morris

Metropol Parasol in Seville
01, 04, 06–08 J. Mayer H. Architects; 02, 05 Nikkol Roth for Holcim; 03 David Franck

Skating Shelters
01–04 Patkau Architects

METALS

Tampa Museum of Art
01, 05, 07 Stanley Saitowitz | Natoma Architects; 02–04, 06 Richard Barnes

St. Andrews Beach House
01, 03 Sean Godsell Architects; 02, 04, 05 Earl Carter

Prefabricated Nature
01, 02 MYCC Architects; 03–05 Fernando Gerra / FG+SG

OMS Stage
01, 03–08 5468796 Architecture; 02 James Brittain

Lady Bird Lake Hiking Trail Restrooms
01, 02, 05 Miró Rivera Architects; 03, 04, 06, 07 Paul Finkel

Kunst-Depot, Henze & Ketterer Art Gallery
01, 04, 08 Gigon/Guyer Architekten; 02, 03, 05–07 Heinrich Helfenstein

Herstedlund Fælleshus Community Centre
01, 02, 04, 07 Dorte Mandrup Arkitekter; 03, 05, 06, 08, 09 Adam Mørk

Halftecture O
01, 04 Shuhei Endo; 02, 03, 05 Yoshiharu Matsumura

Cantonal School Canteen
01, 06 :mlzd; 02–05 Dominique Marc Wehrli

Artists' Studios in Aberystwyth
01–03, 06 Heatherwick Studio; 04, 05 Edmund Sumner

PLASTICS

SelgasCano Architecture Office
01, 05–07 SelgasCano Arquitectos; 02–04 Iwan Baan

El B Conference Hall and Auditorium
01, 02, 04, 06, 08–10 SelgasCano Arquitectos; 03, 05 Iwan Baan; 07 Roland Halbe

Novartis Entrance Pavilion
01, 04, 07, 08 Marco Serra; 02, 03 Lukas Roth; 05 Christoph Haas

UK Pavilion at World Expo 2010
01, 03, 08–11 Heatherwick Studio; 02, 04–07 Iwan Baan

Cellophane House
01, 02, 06 KieranTimberlake Architects; 03–05 OTTO Archive

Anansi Playground Building
01, 04, 06–08 Mulders VandenBerk Architecten, 02, 03 Roel Backaert; 05, 09 Wouter van der Sar

Miroiterie Retail Building
01, 03–05, 07, 08 B+W Architecture; 02, 09 Thomas Jantscher, 06 Jean-Philippe Daulte

International Committee of the Red Cross Logistics Complex
01–04, 09, 10 Group8, 05–08 Régis Golay, FEDERAL studio, Geneva

Plastic House
01, 02, 05–08 Unit Arkitektur; 03, 04 Krister Engstrom

MOOM Tensegrity Membrane Structure
01, 04 Sadao Hotta; 02, 03 Kazuhiro Kojima Laboratory / Tokyo University of Science

MASONRY

Secondary School
01, 03, 05–08 Diébédo Francis Kéré; 02, 04, 09 Erik-Jan Ouwerkerk

Brandhorst Museum
01, 06, 07 Sauerbruch Hutton; 02 Andreas Lechtape; 03–05 NBK Keramik GmbH

Padre Pio Pilgrimage Church
01 Michel Denancé; 02, 04–07 Renzo Piano Building Workshop; 03, 08 Berengo Gardin Gianni

South Asian Human Rights Documentation Centre
01 Anagram Architects; 02–06 Asim Waqif

NUWOG Headquarters and Housing
01, 02 Fink + Jocher; 03, 04 Michael Heinrich

Pope John Paul II Hall
01–08 Randić-Turato Architects

Chapel of St. Lawrence
01, 04–06 Avanto Architects; 02 Kuvatoimisto Kuvio Oy; 03, 07, 08 Tuomas Uusheimo

Warehouse 8B Conversion
01, 02, 06–08, 10 Arturo Franco Architecture Studio; 03–05, 09, 11–13 Carlos Fernández Piñar

Butaro Doctor's Housing
01, 04, 05 Iwan Baan; 02, 03, 06–09 Mass Design Group

Silk Wall + J-Office
01–06 Archi-Union Architects

Center for Design Research
01–07 Studio 804 / University of Kansas

La Pallissa
01, 04 Cubus; 02, 03 Nani Pujol